Crossing Borders

THE MIDDLE AGES SERIES

Ruth Mazo Karras, Series Editor
Edward Peters, Founding Editor

A complete list of books in the series is available from
the publisher.

Crossing Borders

Love Between Women
in Medieval French and Arabic Literatures

Sahar Amer

UNIVERSITY OF PENNSYLVANIA PRESS

PHILADELPHIA

Published by
University of Pennsylvania Press
Philadelphia, Pennsylvania 19104–4112

Printed in the United States of America on acid-free paper
10   9   8   7   6   5   4   3   2   1

Library of Congress Cataloging-in-Publication Data

Amer, Sahar.
   Crossing borders : love between women in medieval French and Arabic literatures / Sahar Amer.
       p. cm. — (The Middle Ages series)
    Includes bibliographical references and index.
    ISBN-13: 978-0-8122-4087-0 (hardcover : alk. paper)
   1. French literature—To 1500—History and criticism. 2. Arabic literature—History and criticism. 3. Lesbians in literature. I. Title.
   PQ155.L47A44 2008
   840.9'3526643—dc22

                                                        2008000401

CONTENTS

NOTE ON TRANSLITERATION   vii

PREFACE   ix

CHAPTER ONE

Crossing Disciplinary Boundaries: A Cross-Cultural Approach to Same-Sex Love Between Women   1

CHAPTER TWO

Crossing Linguistic Borders: Etienne de Fougères's *Livre des Manières* and Arabic Erotic Treatises   29

CHAPTER THREE

Crossing Sartorial Lines: Female Same-Sex Marriage in *Yde et Olive* and *The Story of Qamar al-Zaman and Princess Boudour* from the *One Thousand and One Nights*   50

CHAPTER FOUR

Crossing the Lines of Friendship: Jean Renart's *Escoufle*, Saracen Silk, and Intercultural Encounters   88

CHAPTER FIVE

Crossing Social and Cultural Borders: Jean Renart's *Escoufle* and the Traditions of *Zarf, Jawari*s, and *Qayna*s in the Islamicate World   121

CONCLUSION

Beyond Orientalist Presuppositions   161

NOTES   167
BIBLIOGRAPHY   217
INDEX   239
ACKNOWLEDGMENTS   251

NOTE ON TRANSLITERATION

For the convenience of the nonspecialist, I have omitted Arabic diacritic marks except for the *hamza* (') and the *ayn* ('). These are indicated in the transliteration of less familiar words, but not in that of well-known terms such as Abbasid or Iraq, for instance. It is my hope that this simplified system of Arabic transliteration will ease the reading and facilitate border crossings between French and Arabic.

I have kept citations in the original Arabic script to the minimum (for editorial necessity) and limited them to those sections when the Arabic text is essential to the analysis. I hope that this inclusion of Arabic within this manuscript will contribute both hermeneutically and visually to the border crossings between French and Arabic that this book invites the reader to undertake.

Crossing Borders is a study of cross-cultural representations of gender and female same-sex sexual practices in the medieval French and Arabic traditions from 1000 to 1500. My goals in writing this book are fourfold: to bring together two literatures and cultural traditions that are too often discussed in isolation from each other: medieval Arabic and French literatures; to shed light on a significant medieval Arabic erotic tradition that is today completely neglected or censored; to uncover the determining role that the medieval Arabic tradition on eroticism played in French literary writings on gender and sexuality; and to affirm the centrality of a cross-cultural approach both to medieval studies and to theoretical discussions of gender and sexualities. The main conceptual paradigm underlying this project is the notion of "borders" (cultural, linguistic, historical, and geographic), not as elements of separation and division, but rather as fluid spaces of cultural exchange, adaptation, and collaboration.

Crossing Borders complements the recent line of productive studies on gender and homoerotic relations in non-Western and at times non-Christian literatures that have begun to enrich scholarly investigations of medieval Western European writings. Ruth Vanita's publications on same-sex love in India, Daniel Boyarin's queer rereading of rabbinic culture, Tova Rosen's scholarship on gender in medieval Hebrew literature, and Kathryn Ringrose's work on eunuchs as a third sex in Byzantium, among others, are already complicating our views of medieval Western gender and sexualities.[1] They have demonstrated the extent to which gender trouble was already a non-Western phenomenon before it became a Western one. At the same time, these critical works have unveiled an important body of medieval primary texts that have broadened our understanding of medieval homosexuality; they have provided a much needed historical and comparative vantage point from which to view a broader range of alternative sexual practices.

Building upon these groundbreaking studies, *Crossing Borders* investigates the heretofore unrecognized role that Arabic eroticism has played in the construction of alternative sexualities in Old French literary texts. My research reveals that it was often through the detour of Arabic textuality, through the recourse to thematic motifs and the evocation of Middle Eastern sociocultural traditions, that French narrators named and depicted what remained unspeakable throughout the European Middle Ages. The key Arabic role in French writings is not to be interpreted as the influence of one tradition over the other. For, as we will see, Arabic erotic material is rarely found mimetically reproduced in the French tradition. Rather than exact repetitions from one literary text to the other ("influence"), we find instead various instances of hybridization, cross-fertilization, and at times censorship ("resonances"). Throughout the following chapters, as I identify expressions of lesbian desire in medieval French writings, I focus on their hybridity and on the cross-cultural dialogue they entertain with some of the most prominent Arabic literary productions on same-sex desire. We will see that the strategies of gender representation deployed in the medieval Arabic erotic tradition (Ibn Nasr's tenth-century *Encyclopedia of Pleasure*, al-Jurjani's eleventh-century *Anthology of Metonymic Devices Used by the Literati and Allusions in Eloquent Speech*, and al-Tifashi's thirteenth-century *The Delight of Hearts* in particular), as well as in a multitude of Arabic tales (from the *One Thousand and One Nights* especially) offered some medieval French writers a linguistic and thematic corpus to imitate, contest, subvert, and at times even to censor. By confronting medieval French texts with their Arabic intertexts, I propose to recover meanings that have been lost, obscured, or distorted (perhaps censored) in the process of crossing the borders between French and Arabic. Such a double reading (queer and cross-cultural) will usefully call into question long-cherished paradigms of heterosexuality and Westernness which, until recently, were still thought to characterize the Middle Ages.

From Intertextuality to Interculturality

As I cross the borders between medieval Arabic and French literatures, I focus on the dialogic exchanges between the two cultures, on moments of interaction and collaboration but also of contestation and subversion in each society's articulation of gender difference and sexual practices. Each of the French texts under investigation will be interpreted both horizontally and vertically[2]—horizontally because each word, every sentence and scene in Old French writings holds a specific meaning to its Western audience, and vertically because these same elements hint also at a literary corpus, a cultural tradition that precedes or is contemporary to the moment of French textual production. Old French literature on female homoeroticism may thus be considered an intersection of textual surfaces, a dialogue between different contexts; it is plural by definition, as it absorbs, blends, and transforms Western generic conventions with an Arabic intertext. The medieval French discourse on alternative female sexuality may usefully be thought about as a process of "écriture-lecture" (writing-reading),[3] in which each statement is meaningful only in relation and in opposition to another discourse. It is precisely this intertextuality, the dialogue that French writings engage between Western generic and rhetorical conventions on the one hand and Arabic literary texts and contexts on the other that we will seek to unveil throughout the following chapters.

We will redefine the very notion of "intertextuality" in the process. This poststructuralist notion—introduced by Julia Kristeva, based on her reading of Bakhtin's analysis of Dostoevsky's poetics, medieval farces, and carnival—rejected the view of structuralist semiotic theorists (since Saussure) who viewed texts as discrete structures with their own internal logical codes. Rather than investigating sources and influences and instead of interpreting intertextuality solely in linguistic terms, Bakhtin and Kristeva argued for the importance of also taking into consideration the three-pronged dialogues between author and audience, author and characters, and author-audience and historical context. The expansion of the notion of intertextuality invites henceforth a consideration not only of the linguistic and textual context (the intertextual), but also the sociohistorical and cultural codes inscribed within each text (the intercultural).

Crossing Borders builds upon this reevaluation of the intertextual and shows its operation in specific medieval texts. As it calls into question the boundaries between the medieval Arab Islamicate and the Christian European worlds, it also questions the very notion of textual boundaries. The following chapters will demonstrate that medieval French writings on female homoeroticism are permeable and challenge conventional dichotomies of inside and outside, text and context. Rather than follow a historical chronological order, therefore, the chapters are organized in a manner that shows that intertextuality means both interlinguistic, intertextual echoes (Chapters 2 and 3), as well as intercultural ones (Chapters 4 and 5). They are thus ordered in such a fashion as to follow literary and cultural intermixing from its most explicit to its most *im*plicit manifestations. While I consider at first the most explicit resonances between the French literary representations of lesbianism and the medieval Arabic erotic tradition (linguistic borrowings in Etienne de Fougères, Chapter 2), I proceed in Chapter 3 to examine some less explicit echoes between both traditions, such as the thematic parallels between three versions of the *Yde and Olive* stories and the tale of Qamar al-Zaman and the Princess Boudour from the *One Thousand and One Nights*. I end with even less explicit resonances when I focus on the role that Arab material culture and key sociocultural traditions are rewritten in the *Escoufle* (Chapters 4 and 5). Informed by the critical perspectives of gender, queer, and postcolonial studies, *Crossing Borders* proposes to explore the textual, sexual, and cultural interconnections between medieval France and the Arab Islamicate world.

CHAPTER ONE

Crossing Disciplinary Boundaries

A Cross-Cultural Approach to Same-Sex Love Between Women

The silence of the silenced is filled by the speech of those who have it and the fact of the silence is forgotten.
—Catharine MacKinnon

SAME-SEX SEXUAL PRACTICES between women in the medieval West were perceived to be a sin "against nature, that is, against the order of nature, which created women's genitals for the use of men, and conversely, and not so women could cohabit with women."[1] If this is how Peter Abelard (d. 1142) glossed Saint Paul's epistle to the Romans (Rom. 1:26), he was only reiterating what church fathers had been claiming and echoing the difficulties they had in imagining the very possibility of lesbian sexuality. In fact, Anastasius (d. 518), bishop of Antioch, is said to have asserted: "Clearly [the women] do not mount each other but, rather, offer themselves to the men."[2] Despite repeated attempts to negate their possibility and existence, same-sex practices between women must have persisted since, centuries later, medieval manuals of penance address the question of how to deal with such "vile affections."[3] Jean Gerson, the fifteenth-century rector of the University of Paris, describes this lustful act as one in which "women have each other by detestable and horrible means which *should not be named or written*."[4] This silencing strategy which dictated that female lesbian practices be neither named nor committed to writing seems to have enjoyed especial appeal among jurists in the follow-ing centuries. Indeed, one hundred years later, in his gloss of Spain's law code, the *Siete Partidas* (1256), Gregory Lopez alludes to the sin "against nature" as "*the silent sin*" (*peccatum mutum*).[5] Similarly, a sixteenth-century jurist, Ger-main Colladon, recommended that descriptions of such crimes, requiring the death penalty, should not be read aloud publicly, lest they incite other women to imitate them: "A crime so horrible and against nature is so detestable and because of the horror of it, *it cannot be named.*"[6] This denied, unnamed, un-namable, and silenced sin that must have been common enough in the Euro-pean Middle Ages to warrant such pronouncements from theologians and legal scholars alike and that at times merited the death penalty has led until very recently to a general neglect of medieval female homosexuality among contemporary critics.[7]

The disavowal of female same-sex activity by medieval (male) legal au-thorities goes hand in hand with the prevailing negative attitudes toward women in the Middle Ages, the contradictory notions regarding their sexual-ity in general, including heterosexuality. After all, "natural sex" was limited to a narrow range of acceptable behaviors, as Karma Lochrie reminds us: "sex in the proper vessels with the proper instruments in the proper positions with the appropriate procreative intentions in orderly ways and during times that are not otherwise excluded."[8] These views, based on Aristotle's male-centered model which considered a woman to be an "accidental deviation," a failed male fetus, were recuperated by the Christian church fathers (Augustine, Jerome, Tertulian, and others), who emphasized celibacy and persistently as-sociated sexuality with the Fall, and woman with sin. In this worldview, male and female homosexuality was nothing but a "human distortion of divine order."[9]

Ironically, the invention of the category "sodomy" in the middle of the twelfth century only served to exclude female homosexuality from public dis-course and thus to silence it even further.[10] Even though sodomy was defined as both a male *and* a female sin, few theologians actually concerned them-selves with female homosexuality.[11] Theological discourses regularly focused on men more than they did on women because their primary goal was the control of clerics and their sexual misconduct: Peter Damian's virulent pam-phlet against sodomy contained in his *Book of Gomorrah* (ca. 1048–54), which does not discuss women, is a case in point.

Similarly, medieval medicine and medieval science both paid relatively little attention to homosexuality (male or female) in the Middle Ages. After all, according to the dominant clerical teachings of the period, same-sex relations between women could only be perceived as trivial because women were passive "by nature," played a secondary role in sexuality and reproduction, and were thus at some level not fully sexual. In addition, such relations were overlooked because of the prevailing Western phallocentric view of human sexuality, because "no sperm were spilled," and because sexuality between women did not pose a threat to lineage through the production of illegitimate heirs.[12] Contemporary scholarship seems to have followed Peter Damian's footsteps or medieval theological and scientific perspectives and maintained the primacy of male homosexuality over female alternative sexual practices.[13]

The scholarly neglect of medieval lesbianism has been so profound that in her biography of a sixteenth-century Italian nun, Judith Brown observed: "In light of the knowledge that Europeans had about the possibility of lesbian sexuality, their neglect of the subject in law, theology, and literature suggests an almost active willingness to *dis*believe."[14] Her view has been echoed more recently by Jacqueline Murray in a 1996 essay tellingly entitled "Twice Marginal and Twice Invisible." In this article, Murray describes the status of the medieval (Western) lesbian in contemporary scholarship, observing that "of all groups within medieval society lesbians are the most marginalized and least visible."[15] Almost ten years after the publication of this landmark study, scholarship on the medieval lesbian and on same-sex desire among women in the Middle Ages (in stark contrast to that on medieval male homosexuality) remains scarce. A literary history of medieval lesbianism has yet to be written. While *Crossing Borders* does not purport to write such a history nor to discuss systematically all literary instances of lesbian practices in the premodern period, it aims nevertheless to unearth a medieval French *literary* discourse on same-sex desire and sexual practices between women that has thus far remained unnoticed. In so doing, it will unveil the unsuspected role that medieval Arabic sexological literature and culture has played on the literary constructions of same-sex desire and alternative sexual practices between women in Old French texts.[16] Throughout this study, medieval Arabic writings on sexuality will serve as a crucial basis for reading eroticism in a wide range of Old French texts.

By juxtaposing medieval Arabic texts and medieval French works, *Crossing Borders* will shed light on the literary existence of female homosexuality prior to the nineteenth century in both the East and the West, give voice to a subaltern group that has usually been overlooked, and salvage from oblivion key medieval Arabic and French writings on alternative sexual practices. The comparative cross-cultural strategy adopted here will allow us to grasp nuances in each literary tradition that remain hidden whenever one text is examined singly or is read in isolation from its multicultural context of production. Furthermore, it will permit us to recognize the mixed, hybrid identities that emerge necessarily from contacts between cultures. The medieval French lesbian, as we will see, is an example of such a mixed identity, a product of the "contact zone" that took place between the French and the Arabs during the Middle Ages.[17]

The scarcity of scholarly investigations into medieval female homosexuality is partly attributed to some postmodern (and unfortunately hasty) readings of Foucault's unfinished *History of Sexuality*. Because Foucault focused on homosexuality as a modern (Western) phenomenon, a result of nineteenth-century advances in the fields of medicine and sexology, and because he did not address the medieval period or female homosexuality, some critics have hurriedly concluded that homosexuality did not exist in the Middle Ages, and that there were no lesbians to speak of before the dawn of the twentieth century.[18]

Happily, others have contested the oversimplification of notions of alternative sexual identities derived from readings of Foucault and have taken the latter (and his readers) to task for leaving premodern homosexuality out of history.[19] Despite his usually constructionist stance, David Halperin has even recently observed that Foucault himself would have been the first to be "astonished" at the limitations placed today around his history of sexuality:

> It is a matter of considerable irony that Foucault's influential
> distinction between the discursive construction of the sodomite
> and the discursive construction of the homosexual, which had
> originally been intended to open up a domain of historical inquiry,
> has now become a major obstacle blocking further research into the
> rudiments of sexual identity-formation in pre-modern and early
> modern European societies. Foucault himself would surely have
> been astonished. Not only was he too good a historian ever to have
> authorized the incautious and implausible claim that no one had
> ever had a sexual subjectivity, a sexual morphology, or a sexual
> identity of any kind before the nineteenth century (even if he
> painstakingly demonstrated that the conditions necessary for
> having a sexuality, a psychosexual orientation in the modern sense,

did not in fact obtain until then). His approach to what he called "the history of the present" was also too searching, too experimental, and too open-ended to tolerate converting a heuristic analytic distinction into an ill-founded historical dogma, as his more forgetful epigones have not hesitated to do.[20]

Similarly, feminist medievalists have called into question the validity and legitimacy of keeping medieval lesbians inside the closet of theories of sexuality and outside of scholarship. Karma Lochrie, for instance, has decried Foucault's view of the Christian Middle Ages, which "functions as the historical 'other' in [his] history of sexuality, as that time when discourse about sexuality was 'markedly unitary.'"[21] More recently, Anna Klosowska has asked: "Why need we be so prompt to examine our right to queer readings and precisely what entitles us to take for granted the legitimacy of heteronormative readings?"[22]

But Foucault cannot be made solely responsible for the scholarly neglect of the medieval lesbian. The study of female homosexuality in the Middle Ages has been further hampered by anachronistic views of what constitutes lesbianism. Given the definitional fluidity of this category today (Who exactly counts as a lesbian?), critics have been at a loss as to where to search for medieval literary lesbians. Because the distinction between desire and acts still remains a powerful organizing principle in queer studies, scholars have been struggling with important methodological issues: Should the medievalist search for expressions of female homosexuality in literary depictions of same-sex acts or in the portrayal of homoerotic desires? Can one speak of homosexuality even in the absence of specific (homo)sexual acts? What conclusions should be drawn from texts that insert a brief sexually alternative interlude only to end on a heteronormative note? Where is the line between intimate female friendships and female same-sex attachments? What distinguishes the lives of medieval literary single women, prostitutes, and lesbians? These questions, coupled with the fact that medieval lesbians for the most part did not leave traces of their relations and that the majority of surviving literary texts are composed by men, have all contributed to the further silencing of the medieval literary lesbian in contemporary scholarship.

Perhaps the most persistent methodological (and theoretical) issue facing medievalists is the question of naming: How should the absence of a specific label denoting lesbianism in medieval Western literary texts be interpreted (and this will be the case of all Old French texts that we will be examining)?[23]

Critics continue to struggle over what to call expressions of same-sex desire in the Middle Ages. They have been especially reticent to apply the label "lesbianism" to manifestations of same-sex attraction, sentiments, eroticism, and even behaviors because the notion of sexual identity continues to be viewed as a modern phenomenon. The fact that no specific label to denote lesbianism was used until the sixteenth century has been taken to mean that medieval culture was silent on the question of lesbianism. And yet, as Sautman and Sheingorn remind us, it is "highly problematic to assume that sexuality begins to exist only when discourse says it does, either by explicitly naming it (as in the modern period) or by speaking authoritatively about it (as in the medieval period)."[24] It is equally problematic to assume that the absence of a name necessarily means absence of power, for again, as Sautman and Sheigorm observed, such lack may paradoxically also signify "power reclaimed through resistance to externally imposed categories with their implicit negative assessments and marginalizations."[25]

Recent scholarship has revealed that female same-sex desire and practices, if not a specific identity, then at least an actual consciousness, existed in the West well before the nineteenth century.[26] In fact, classical archaeology has uncovered that the first figurations of female couples (in clay, bronze, and stone) predate any other figuration of human couples including not only that of Adam and Eve, but also Homeric couples such as Achilles and Patrocles. The statues of these female couples, discovered in the Gonnersdof caves in the Rhine Valley and dated to 12,500 B.C.E., are not unique. Some have also been discovered along the Danube River, in Romania, while others were painted on Anatolian vases. In fact, 90 percent of all human couples dating from the twelfth to the sixth century B.C.E. are of female couples, according to Gabriele Meixner.[27] Furthermore, the existence of female homosexuality is attested in Plato's *Symposium* where Zeus's slicing of humans resulted in three types of couplings: male homosexuals, female homosexuals, and androgynous heterosexual couples. Female homosexuals are clearly identified in Plato's text: "All the women who are sections of the woman have no great fancy for men: they are inclined rather to women, and of this stock are the she-minions."[28] The Greek term for female homosexuality that Plato uses here is *hetaïristriai*, but other words circulated as well, including *tribades, dihetairistria*, and *lesbiai*. In Latin, words for female homosexuals were also in use, such as *tribas, fricatrix*, and *virago*;[29] and in the medieval Arabic tradition, the category "lesbianism" existed as is evident in the use of the term *sahq*, as we will see in detail below. Finally, the term "lesbian" (*lesbiai*, plural of *lesbian*)—used to mean same-sex relations between women—is not entirely absent in the Christian Middle Ages since it occurs in a tenth-century Byzantine commentary on Clement of Alexandria, by Arethas (d. 914).[30] After its tenth-century usage, the term seems to have disappeared (it has perhaps been purposefully erased); it did not come into use in French until the sixteenth century and then seemingly only once.[31]

Even though medieval French narrators did not use a specific term to denote lesbianism, we are certainly permitted to read descriptions of female characters whose primary emotional attachments are to other women or those who engage in sexually intimate relations with other women as evidence of lesbian practices in medieval textuality. The absence of a name, rather than meaning the absence of lesbianism, might indicate that lesbianism was constructed publicly as silent and nameless (this is precisely what the medieval jurists' vocal insistence on the *silent sin* described earlier teaches us). It might further reveal that we have read the construction of alternative sexualities in medieval texts with inadequate theoretical and methodological tools. After all, instead of one term that denotes lesbianism and lesbian sexual practices, the premodern period often deployed a wide range of vocabulary and verbal strategies, as Judith Brown has observed: "A large array of words and circumlocutions came to be used to describe what women allegedly did: mutual masturbation, pollution, fornication, sodomy, buggery, mutual corruption, coitus, copulation, mutual vice, the defilement or impurity of women by one another. And those who did these terrible things, if called anything at all, were called fricatrices, that is women who rubbed each other, or Tribades, the Greek equivalent for the same action."[32]

The absence of one specific label to denote lesbians in the European Middle Ages thus reveals the presence of another terminology, another semiotic system. It is precisely the goal of *Crossing Borders* to identify and decode the sign system of alternative sexualities in medieval French literary writings. My reading will thus scrutinize anew the vocabulary of sexual desire and sexual practice in Old French texts in order to better understand the textual strategies at play in the construction of female homoeroticism. Lesbianism in medieval French literature, I submit, was denoted by a wider affective language, a broader range of behaviors, and a more expansive configuration of gender trouble than has traditionally been thought. In the process, the semiotic system characteristic of same-sex desire between women in medieval French texts will be shown to be heavily indebted to Arabic literary and cultural traditions. My goal will hence be to recover the multiple Arabic intertextual resonances that regularly lie beneath the surface of medieval French textuality and its literary depiction of lesbian love and desire.

My reading has benefited from Judith Bennett's concept of "lesbian-like," which has proved to be especially helpful in expanding the scholarly search for "real life" lesbians in the Midde Ages.[33] Because Bennett's goal is to document the sexual practices of "ordinary [Western] women" who represented "more than ninety percent of medieval women" (2)—as opposed to literary lesbians (whose story *Crossing Borders* will begin to tell)—she bids us to broaden our investigation into medieval sources and to include "women whose lives might have particularly offered opportunities for same-sex love; women who resisted norms of feminine behavior based on heterosexual marriage; women who lived in circumstances that allowed them to nurture and support other women" (10). If these are the women that Bennett dubs "lesbian-like," this is how she describes the "range of practices" that such women might engage in:

> If women's primary emotions were directed toward other women, regardless of their own sexual practices, perhaps their affection was lesbian-like. If women lived in single-sex communities, their life circumstances might be usefully conceptualized as lesbian-like. If women resisted marriage or, indeed, just did not marry, whatever the reason, their singleness can be seen as lesbian-like. If women dressed as men, whether in response to saintly voices, in order to study, in pursuit of certain careers, or just to travel with male lovers, their cross-dressing was arguably lesbian-like. And if women worked as prostitutes or otherwise flouted norms of sexual propriety, we might see their deviance as lesbian-like. (15)

Bennett's category "lesbian-like" has many advantages, not least that of being more specific than Adrienne Rich's "lesbian continuum," which includes all woman-identified experiences.[34] It also possesses undeniable value for the study of literary lesbians in the Middle Ages, for, as will become evident in the following chapters, the range of practices that Bennett describes permeates much of medieval French writings. We will see indeed that diverse as the literary medieval French lesbians may be, they all display primary emotional attachments; many live in female quarters, resist marriage, cross-dress, and at times even prostitute themselves. What also unites the different medieval lesbian characters that we will be discussing is their resistance to the heterosexist politics of domination and to normative sexual and social expectations of their period.[35] While the literary depiction of such characters in Old French literature is not labeled lesbian, it can certainly be considered "lesbian-like."

Throughout this study, and while recognizing the historicity of the notions of sexual identity and gender politics, I have opted for the use of the term "lesbian" for several reasons. First, for reasons of convenience and variety: speaking each time of "same-sex desire among women," "same-sex sexual practices," "lesbian" in quotation marks, or even "lesbian-like," while having the merit of being perhaps more theoretically specific, becomes a bit tedious and cumbersome stylistically. More important, such phrases end up maintaining medieval lesbians in othered categories of time and culture. *Crossing Borders* demonstrates however that same-sex desire and same-sex sexuality among women were more prevalent that heretofore recognized. It thus argues in favor of a continuity rather than a rupture between medieval and modern conceptions of alternative sexualities. The use of the term "lesbian" is hence an acknowledgment of this continuum. The third reason for opting for the word "lesbian" in this study is the hope of integrating same-sex desire in the Middle Ages into contemporary discourses and investigations of alternative sexual practices. Without neglecting the historical specificity of medieval same-sex desire and of modern lesbianism, I believe that using a different language when speaking of a strikingly parallel phenomenon ends up obscuring the important dialogue that can (and should) take place between past and present.[36] Finally, using the term "lesbian" invites us to move beyond the debates of essentialism and constructionism, beyond discussions about the concept of "sexual identity" and about the distinctions so many still uphold between acts and identities that have divided the field and have now reached a point of stagnation. I propose instead to focus on other important yet neglected aspects of same-sex desire, namely, those of a (cross-)cultural import.

Same-Sex Desire Among Women in Medieval France

Over the past fifteen years or so, a series of insightful publications has begun to investigate women's alternative sexualities as depicted in literary texts that otherwise maintain a strict heterosexuality (epic, romance, poetry, and religious writings). Medieval literary scholars have come to recognize the fact that if theological discourses had silenced female eroticism, literature offered a privileged space for the expression of female same-sex sexuality. Developments in queer theory invited new readings of medieval literature that focused on the unpredictability and variety of expressions of female attachments. Queering medieval texts permitted scholars to move beyond a description of the sexual in its purely genital connotation to the role of the homosocial and homoerotic in medieval literary productions. By queering medieval literature, critics have thus succeeded in detecting fluid gender positions that challenge the conventional binary sexual ideology, and hence in uncovering unsuspected alternative sexual meanings in medieval texts. They have begun to demonstrate that "nonconforming female subcultures, like other subaltern groups, developed alternative, carefully coded types of discourse and social practices to express both homoerotic desire and resistance to heterosexist politics of domination."[37]

The scholarly production on medieval lesbian practices has focused primarily on three categories of texts:[38]

- The majority of this scholarship has explored same-sex desire in the writings of female mystics (Hildegarde of Bingen, Hadewijch of Brabant, Margery Kempe, Mechtild of Magdeburg, Marguerite Porete) and examined expressions of alternative love in devotional texts to the Virgin Mary or in the *vitas* of Beguines (life of Ida Louvain). Much has been written about the "feminizing of Christ's body" and the "genitalizing of his wound,"[39] about the analogy between wound and vulva, about the metaphorical interpretation of kissing Christ's wound, about devotional "sobs and sighs," and about the "bodily rapture" expressed by some nuns in same-sex contexts.[40]
- A second category of texts that has proved to be especially rich in uncovering the endless possibilities of gender bending and gender trouble in medieval literature includes writings that stage cross-dressed heroines: romances, plays (the fourteenth-century Parisian *Miracles de Notre Dame*), and chronicles of historical heroines (Joan of Arc).[41] The homoerotic resistance that cross-dressed characters inscribe in such texts has demonstrated the extent to which medieval gender categories are elastic and permeable.
- A much smaller group of scholars has focused on medieval love poetry and correspondence purportedly produced by women.[42] The coded poetry of *trobairitz* Bieris de Romans (ca. 1200–1220) has perhaps naturally been the primary focus of these investigations as it remains the sole surviving instance of a text that may have been produced by a "real" medieval lesbian poet. Her only poem has thus generated a heated debate between critics who consider it to be a valuable document on

medieval lesbian expression and those who vehemently deny such a reading.[43] While we will probably never know who Bieris truly was and what her sexual orientation might have been, the debate over her poetry reveals the extent to which female expressions of subversive homoerotic desires continue to be considered anachronistic and hence occulted.

Crossing Borders builds upon these valuable investigations into the multiple fluid gendered positions deployed in medieval French literature, while adding a new dimension: a cross-cultural reading of Old French texts. In the following chapters, I will continue to explore how medieval French literary writings challenge our notions of gendered binaries and resist a heterosexual reading. My reading of the Old French texts selected will be at once queer and cross-cultural. Queer because I will focus on the multiple ways in which literary representations of female desire, even as they appear to confirm and support heterosexual expectations, may be read in fact as unsuspected spaces for the expression of alternative attachments. My reading is cross-cultural because, as I will show, expressions of same-sex love in Old French texts are in constant dialogue with writings about lesbian desire from the Islamicate tradition.

As a matter of fact, my thesis in *Crossing Borders* is that Old French critical discourses on lesbianism have been limited because they have been made without historical contextualization. I have thus sought to understand medieval French lesbianism by anchoring it in its historicity. This historicity points us necessarily to the intertwined histories of the Arab Islamicate world and Western Europe,[44] beginning with the Arab invasion of Spain (711). Cultural interaction continued through the founding of the Latin Kingdoms of the East during the Crusades (1099–1291) and well beyond the fall of Granada in 1492 and the Muslims' expulsion from Spain. If medieval French lesbians as a category of analysis or as evidence of a certain textual (and perhaps even social) reality have often been occulted or thought to be nonexistent, it is undoubtedly because much of medieval French literary writings continues to be read in isolation from the context of cultural interaction, seduction, and anxiety between the Arab Islamicate world and Western Christian Europe.

Cross-Cultural Encounters in the Middle Ages

A considerable amount of research has been conducted by medieval historians documenting the repeated interactions and exchanges (economic, political,

and scientific especially) between the West and the Islamicate world in the
Middle Ages. These investigations have focused primarily on three key historical moments and cross-cultural geographical centers: The Crusades with the
founding of the Latin Kingdoms of the East; the establishment of the Islamic
caliphate in Spain (al-Andalus); and Norman Sicily with Roger II's (1130–54)
international center of learning and Frederick II's (1215–50) relaxed policies toward Muslims.[45] Although until recently the Crusades had been viewed primarily in terms of political and religious conflict and heralded as a paradigmatic
illustration of a "clash of civilizations,"[46] they are now recognized as a privileged moment of cultural and intellectual interaction as well as of material exchanges. Recent studies have indeed unearthed the role of trade and commerce
in furthering the cultural relations between medieval Europe and the Islamicate world, even during the period of the Crusades. Antioch, for instance—
which was occupied by the Franks as early as 1136 when Raymond of Poitiers
married Constance, daughter of Bohemond II—is known to have been a powerful commercial center of international trade and boasted important cross-
cultural *funduks*.[47]

Historians have also shown the decisive role that Arabic medicine, mathematics, and astronomy have played on the development of the European sciences.[48] As early as the late eleventh century and until circa 1250, medieval
Toledo (Spain) and soon Palermo (Sicily) became important centers of translation and key sites for the transmission of Arabic sciences to the West. Well-
known European scholars and translators, including Adelard of Bath, Robert
of Ketton, Herman the Dalmatian, Daniel of Morley, Alfred the Englishman,
and Michael Scot, among others, studied either at Toledo or Palermo. After a
period of time spent seeking Arabic knowledge (*arabum studia*), these European scholars went back to England, France, or Italy to teach and share with
their fellow European intellectuals knowledge acquired among Muslims and
Jews abroad. In addition to being a chief location for the transmission of Arabic sciences to the West, al-Andalus also played a key role in international
trade and in the transfer of desirable luxuries and material goods from the Far
and Middle East to Northern Europe (precious metals, textiles, spices, paper).
As a gateway between Christian Europe and the Islamicate world, the Iberian
peninsula became a habitual passageway to scholars, diplomats, soldiers, travelers, and merchants and a transfer point for letters and commodities "even in
times of political discord."[49]

If the historical role that crusaders, pilgrims, political envoys, scholars,
merchants, and travelers have played in the transmission of *scientific and ma-*

terial goods from the East to the West is amply documented, the diffusion of Arabic *cultural and literary traditions* to Western Europe remains a highly controversial subject area. For while the dissemination of knowledge from the Islamicate world to Europe can be substantiated in some disciplines (medicine, mathematics, astronomy) with a great deal of historical details concerning translators and geographical sites of encounters, it is difficult to document cases of literary and cultural transmission with a similar precision. Two literary topics only have been investigated (and hotly contested) thus far: troubadour poetry and European courtly love and their indebtedness to the Arabic *muwasshahat* and *zajal* traditions;[50] and the fable tradition and the role that *Kalila wa Dimna* has played on Marie de France's *Esope*.[51]

Yet, despite the scholarly resistance to the role that less tangible Arabic cultural categories, such as literature, has played on the West, it is evident from the current state of research that medieval Europe had ample opportunities to learn about Arabic literature and culture. I would submit that Western familiarity with Arabic literature and social customs took place through the same channels that insured the transfer of scientific knowledge and commercial goods from the Islamicate world to Europe in the Middle Ages. European knowledge of Arabic literature and traditions was gained either directly in the West's political or economic dealings with the East or indirectly by hearsay from returning crusaders, pilgrims, travelers, and merchants. Westerners who came to live, trade, or conduct any sort of business in the Orient witnessed firsthand modes of living, cultural traditions, and customs different from their own; they heard stories told, poetry recited, and songs sung all the while engaging in whatever commercial or political transactions they had come to accomplish. Upon their return, along with the material goods that they hauled in their carts, next to the silk cloth and precious stones they transported in their bags, they also carried ideas, stories, poems, tales, and varied new customs which they transmitted to their people.

Literary scholarship, particularly French scholarship, seems to have been especially resistant to the idea that Old French literature may have also been marked by the cross-cultural exchanges of the period. Despite the multiple references to Oriental material culture in medieval French texts, there is a persistent assumption that French literature (in contrast to other disciplines) has escaped the stamp of medieval exchanges.[52] Still today, medieval French and medieval Arabic literatures continue to be read, taught, and studied in different academic departments, by different scholars, and within entirely different (at times opposite) theoretical frameworks. *Crossing Borders* demonstrates that literature, like science, bears traces of its associations with its Eastern neighbors. As it builds upon the important contributions of noted scholars of medieval cross-cultural encounters, this project demonstrates that the medieval Arabic erotic tradition has played a determining role in French *literary* writings on gender and sexuality in the Middle Ages.

Medieval Western Polemics of Homosexuality and Islam

Focusing on cross-cultural (Franco-Arabic) representations of same-sex relations does not mean promoting the view perpetrated by medieval Western polemical writers and some theologians that homosexuality is an importation from the Orient or that Islam sanctions licentiousness and sexual perversity. For, after all, such was one of the most prevalent rhetorical metaphors used in the Christian Middle Ages (and later throughout Western colonization of the Middle East) to justify crusading efforts, the Spanish reconquest, and the unrelenting aspiration to destroy Islam.[53] Ever since the writings of Paul Alvarus (ca. 850) and San Eulogio, medieval Christian discourses associated homosexuality with the Muslim enemy and the Prophet Muhammad with sodomitic practices.[54] The image of the aggressive, predatory homosexual Muslim is perhaps best known through Hrostvit of Gandersheim's tenth-century Latin play depicting the adolescent Christian martyr Pelagius imprisoned and seduced by the Muslim caliph, a man described as "corrupted by sodomic vices."[55] Moreover, medieval Christian writers pointed to Muhammad's multiple wives, the Oriental practice of polygamy, Muslims' ratification of divorce, and Qur'anic descriptions of a material, sensual paradise as proofs of the immorality of Islamic teachings.[56] More than a threat of unbelief, Islam was a threat of (male) sodomy.

In fact, William Adam, a fourteenth-century French bishop, is reported to have proclaimed that: "According to the religion of the Saracens, any sexual act whatever is not only allowed but approved and encouraged, so that in addition to innumerable prostitutes, they have effeminate men in great number who shave their beards, paint their faces, put on women's clothing, wear bracelets on their arms and legs and gold necklaces around their necks as women do, and adorn their chests with jewels. Thus selling themselves into sin, they degrade and expose their bodies. . . . The Saracens, oblivious of human dignity, freely resort to these effeminates or live with them as among us men and women live together openly."[57]

The association between Saracens, Muslims, and homosexuality was perceived to be especially threatening because of the seductive power that homosexuality could exert over Christians. Like others before him (including Orderic Vitalis), William Adam was vocal in calling attention to the contagious nature of Muslim homosexual desire and the danger it posed to Christians who entertained commercial relations with them.[58] Such polemical views persisted throughout the early modern period until the eighteenth century[59] and became especially common in nineteenth-century Orientalism with the popularization of the image of the Orient as an exotic, erotic space where all forms of sexual deviance were permitted and exalted and where a homosexual encounter was always a latent possibility. It is in that spirit that Sir Richard Burton, in his "Terminal Essay" (1886), which concludes his ten-volume translation of the *One Thousand and One Nights*, promulgated his theory of a "Sotadic Zone," a geographic space that extends from the Mediterranean to Japan in which "the Vice [pederasty] is popular and endemic, held to be at the worst a mere peccadillo."[60]

The association of Islam with homosexuality in the Western Christian imaginary focused for the most part on male-male rather than female-female sexual practices. The threat of lesbianism, while not always explicitly described, remained nevertheless at the level of consciousness, as the frequent recourse in Old French romances to the harem as a stereotypically Oriental space replete with lesbian practices indicates. The mid-twelfth-century romance of *Floire et Blancheflor*, for instance, plays on Floire's resemblance to Blancheflor and especially his feminine features in order to depict an intimate scene in the harem. Floire is mistaken for a girl because "k'a face n'a menton n'avoit / barbe, ne grenons n'i parait" ("he had neither on the face nor on the chin / a beard or facial hair").[61] While the scene is really a heterosexual depiction of the reunited couple, the lesbian overtones are not absent, since the chamberlain himself, who sees the sleeping couple, mistakes them for Blancheflor cuddled in the intimacy of Gloris, the daughter of the King of Germany and a fellow concubine in the harem:

Ainc mais si grans amors ne fu Com a Blanceflor, vers Gloris	There has never been as great a love As the one that Blancheflor has for Gloris

Et ele a li, ce m'est avis.	And she for her, it seems to me.
Ensanle dormant doucement,	They sleep together softly,
Acolé s'ont estroitement,	Tightly hugging (or embracing),
Et bouce a bouce et face	Mouth against mouth and face
a face	to face
S'ont acolé, et brace	They are holding each other
a brace.	arms entertwined.
(vv. 2594–2600)	

What is interesting in these lines is the fact that the chamberlain does not appear in the least surprised by the scene he witnesses. He is not shocked to find two girls sleeping tightly together, "hugging, / mouth against mouth and face to face" (vv. 2598–99). In fact, he depicts the love he sees with some degree of admiration, if not tenderness. If he is not surprised, it is likely because in the Western imaginary, such a scene of alternative sexual practices "makes sense" in the context of an Eastern harem. It is precisely the cultural otherness of the harem, moreso than the depiction of any racial otherness in the text, which generates in the text a discourse of sexual alterity. We will see that the recourse to such Middle Eastern sociocultural practices functions as textual/sexual strategies to express same-sex love between women in medieval French literature.

Rather than demonstrating that Islam sanctions lascivious practices, my reading of such homoerotic interludes highlights the interweaving of alternative sexualities with Oriental themes and motifs in medieval French literary writings. At a time when lesbianism was neither named nor spoken in medieval Europe, Middle Eastern motifs, luxury goods, Arab social customs, thematic echoes between Arabic tales and Old French texts, and at times even Arabic vocabulary permitted Old French writers to articulate alternative modes of sexual expression. They may be considered, as we will see, a textual strategy, a cross-cultural literary technique of speaking and of naming that which remained too dangerous to depict openly in medieval Europe.

Same-Sex Desire Among Women in the Medieval Arab Islamicate World

If the absence of a specific terminology to denote lesbianism in medieval Europe seems to have compromised the production of scholarship about same-sex desire among women, the existence of the label *sahq* and *sahiqa* (Arabic words for lesbianism and lesbian respectively) in medieval Arabic writings did not result in a richer critical production.[62] This state of scholarship into alternative sexual practices in the Arab Islamicate world is especially astonishing considering the survival of a noteworthy body of primary texts dealing precisely with this topic. Furthermore, if one broadens the category of Arab lesbian to that of Arab "lesbian-like," as Bennett has suggested in our construction of the history of Western female homosexuality, we uncover even more expressions of Arab lesbian presence. As we will see, the cultural and social life of some women in certain medieval Arab courts, including their work and lifestyle, may well unveil unsuspected spaces in which same-sex activities might have occurred. If it is not always clear that these practices could indeed be dubbed lesbian, they certainly may be considered "lesbian-like."

One might argue that the Arabic terms for "lesbianism," *sahq, sihaq, musahaqat al-nisa'*, and *sihaqa*, refer primarily to a behavior, an act, rather than an emotional attachment or an identity. The root of these words (*s/h/q*) means to pound, to rub, and lesbians (*sahiqat, sahhaqat, musahiqat*), like the Greek *tribades*, are literally those who engage in rubbing (or pounding) behavior, or who make love by pounding or rubbing. In fact, some medieval medical views of lesbianism, reported in the Arabic sexological tradition, point to rubbing as an essential characteristic of the practice. Galen, the second-century Greek physician whose own daughter was reportedly a lesbian, is supposed to have examined her labia and surrounding veins and to have concluded that her lesbianism was due to "an itch between the major and minor labia" that could be soothed only by rubbing one's labia against another woman's labia.[63] In the ninth century, Arab and Muslim philosopher al-Kindi echoes Galen's observation of labial itching and recommends the same treatment, namely, rubbing.[64]

Other Arab physicians thought of lesbianism as an inborn state, caused by the mother's consumption of certain foods that, when passed through the milk during nursing, led to labial itching and lifelong lesbianism. Hence, according to the famous ninth-century Nestorian Christian physician Yuhanna Ibn Masawayh, also known as John Mesué (d. 857): "Lesbianism results when a nursing woman eats celery, rocket, melilot leaves and the flowers of a bitter orange tree. When she eats these plants and suckles her child, they will affect the labia of her suckling and generate an itch which the suckling will carry through her future life."[65] Rubbing is again prescribed and recognized as capable only of relieving, not of curing, the woman; female homosexuality is thus clearly depicted as both innate and lifelong. Foreshadowing the medicalization of homosexuality in the nineteenth century, lesbianism in the medieval Islamicate literary tradition seems to have already been regarded as a medical (though not deviant) category requiring specific treatment, namely, rubbing. Such views were standard and were repeated from one century to the next, from one literary treatise on sexualities to the other.[66]

If etymologically and medically, *sahq* denotes a behavior, *culturally* speaking and in the context of medieval Arabic *literary* writings, *sahiqat* (lesbians) were associated rather with love and devotion and at times they were even known to form an exclusive and supportive subculture. As a matter of fact, the origin of lesbianism according to popular anecdotes in the Arabic literary tradition is regularly traced back forty years before the emergence of male homosexuality (*liwat*) to an intercultural, interfaith love affair between an Arab woman and a Christian woman in pre-Islamic Iraq. The earliest extant erotic treatise in Arabic, *Jawami` al-ladhdha* (*Encyclopedia of Pleasure*), written at the end of the tenth century by a certain Ali Ibn Nasr al-Katib,[67] tells us the story of the first lesbian couple, the enduring love between Christian princess Hind Bint al-Nu`man (daughter of the last Lakhmid king of the Iraqi town of Hira in the late sixth century) and Hind Bint al Khuss al-Iyadiyyah from Yamama (located in present-day Saudi Arabia), known as al-Zarqa' and reportedly the first lesbian in Arab history: "She [Hind Bint al-Nu`man] was so loyal to al-Zarqa' that when the latter died, she cropped her hair, wore black clothes, rejected worldly pleasures, vowed to God that she would lead an ascetic life until she passed away and, as a result, she built a monastery which was named after her, on the outskirts of Kufa. When she died, she was buried at the monastery gate. Her loyalty was then an example for poets to write about. There are also other women who continued to shed tears on their beloved ones' graves until they passed away."[68]

Even though it is impossible to ascertain the veracity of this account, the fact that it continued to circulate throughout the literary Islamicate world is sufficient to demonstrate that lesbianism was thought to be far more than a behavior or sexual practice. In the *Encyclopedia of Pleasure*, this lesbian love story is praised and presented as evidence of the greater loyalty and devotion that women have for their female partners, compared to men's attachment to women. Ibn Nasr cites the following verses written by an unnamed (presumably male) poet about the love of Hind for al-Zarqa':

O Hind, you are truer to your word than men.
Oh, the difference between your loyalty and theirs![69]

If the relationship between Hind and al-Zarqa' is the one most often cited in the Arabic sexological tradition, it is not the only lesbian relation to exist in Arabic literary history. In fact, in his *Fihrist* (The Catalogue), al-Nadim (d. ca. 990–98) lists the names of twelve lesbian couples who were known until the tenth century, but about whom nothing else has been preserved.[70]

Medieval Arab lesbians are said to have formed groups, to have held meetings, and to have led schools in which they taught other lesbians how best to achieve pleasure.[71] Tunisian physician, philosopher, and poet Ahmad al-Tifashi, in his thirteenth-century *Nuzhat al-albab fima la yujad fi kitab* or *The Delight of Hearts Or, What One Cannot Find in Any Book*,[72] for instance, provides several examples of the teachings of famous medieval lesbians, notably on the most successful sounds that ought to accompany lesbian sexual practices (which he calls massage) (252). He also gives information about a lesbian association and the same-sex teachings of Rose, the head lesbian within it (257).[73] Similar associations of lesbians are evoked by Leo Africanus, the fifteenth-century traveler from Granada, in his account of female diviners of Fez: "Female diviners of Fez who, claiming to be possessed by djinns or demons, foretold the future or served as healers, were in fact *suhaqiyat* (*sahacat*, as he transliterated into Italian the current Arabic word for 'tribades,' lesbians), women who had the 'evil custom' of 'rubbing' (*fregare*) each other in sexual delight."[74]

Needless to say, stories such as these are significant not only for the history of lesbianism, but also because they have no equivalent in the medieval French (or Western) literary tradition. Arab lesbians were both named and visible in Classical Arabic literature. Theirs was not a "silent sin"; in fact, lesbianism was a topic deemed worthy of discussion and a fashion worthy of emulation. I do not wish to imply here that medieval Arabic literature on sexuality was prolesbian or protofeminist. Far from it. The Arabic writings that have survived focus on men much more than on women; they remain for the most part phallocentric and ultimately reflect a male perspective. Whenever mentioned, lesbians occupy only one chapter. Even the *Encyclopedia of Pleasure*, which is the first extant erotic treatise in Arabic dating from the late tenth century, speaks more loudly about men and male homosexuality. Nevertheless, the material on lesbianism in the Arabic Middle Ages, while undoubtedly a smaller proportion in the overall economy of medieval Arabic sexological literature, and while at times contradictory, is significant and merits investigation.

From the existence of the category lesbianism in medieval Arabic writings and from the information gathered about Arabic (literary) lesbian subcultures, we must not rush to equate the medieval Arabic Islamicate notions of female-female sexuality with contemporary Western notions of lesbianism and sexual identity. The categories of heterosexuality and homosexuality, like those of "natural" or "unnatural" sexualities, it must be stressed, are Western concepts and do not have parallels in the medieval Arabic tradition. To begin with, if indeed medieval Arabic sexological writings are obsessed with identifying and defining every variety of sexual practice and thus regularly use the terms *sahq* (lesbianism), *sahiqa* (lesbian), *mutazarrifat* (elegant ladies-lovers); *haba'ib* (beloveds), *liwat* (active male homosexuality), *luti* (active male homosexual), *hulaq* (passive anal intercourse, term used until the ninth century), *ubnah* (passive male homosexuality), *ma'bun* (passive male homosexual), *qatim* (passive male homosexual in Andalusian dialect), *mukhannath* (male effeminate, transvestite, transsexual, hermaphrodite), *tafkhidh* (intercrural intercourse), *bidal, mubadala* (taking turn in active and passive homosexuality), as well as *nisa' mutarajjilat* (masculinized women) and *rijal mu' annathin* (feminized men), no medieval Arabic word exists for bisexuality, considered to be the neutral, most common practice, for heterosexuality, or even for sexuality. The contemporary Arabic word *jins*, used today to mean sexuality, did not acquire this connotation until the early twentieth century. Up to that time, *jins* (derived from the Greek *genus*) denoted type, kind, and ethnolinguistic origin. Its connotation of biological sex, national origin, and citizenship is a modern development, resulting from Arabic translations of Freud in the 1950s and of Michel Foucault's *History of Sexuality* in the 1990s.[75] Interestingly, the impact of these Western medical and theoretical ideas about (homo)sexuality on the Arab world has led to the replacement of the medieval Arabic terms of *liwat* and, to a lesser extent, *sahq* with *mithliyyah* (sameness) to mean homosexuality and *ghayriyyah* (differentness) to mean heterosexuality. The coining of these new Arabic terms was accompanied by that of *al-shudhudh al-jinsi* (literally, sexually rare or unusual), a translation of the Western concept of homosexuality.[76] The notions of sexuality and heterosexuality, and the categorization of homosexuality as sexual deviance appear thus to be some of the Western imperial legacies to the Arab world today. Ironically, and despite its promise of "modernizing" and "liberating," the hegemony of the Western cultural and intellectual capital has ended up erasing the flexible medieval Arabic model of sexuality and imposed instead a heterosexual binary view of sexuality onto the Arab world.

The surprisingly positive valuation of lesbianism and homosexuality in medieval Arabic literary writings (in comparison to the medieval West) is most likely a consequence of the general commendation of eroticism and (hetero)sexual practice in Arab and Islamicate discourses. Not only is sexuality explicitly celebrated in a large number of medieval Arabic scientific and literary texts but sexuality is positioned at the very heart of religious piety. In fact, it has been argued that "sexual activity is an important form of worshipful pleasure."[77] In contrast to medieval Christianity, sex is not a sin in Islam and heterosexual desire (in marriage or concubinage) is viewed as both licit and desirable. The Qur'an itself describes Paradise in sexual terms and proclaims the primacy of physical sensual pleasures.[78]

It is worth noting that the principal, most vehemently condemned sexual sin in the official Islamic discourse is adultery (*zina*), not homosexuality (*liwat*). *Zina* is defined very specifically in Islam as vaginal intercourse between a man and a woman who is neither his lawful wife nor his concubine. Much more than same-sex desire, *zina* is emphatically and unambiguously condemned in both the Qur'an and the Sunnah, and has traditionally been the focus of Islamic scholars and of jurisprudence. Interestingly, the interest in *zina* seems to have encouraged, at least partly, the acceptance of *liwat* in Islamicate societies. In fact, in his chapter on "lesbianism" in his fourteenth-century *Rushd al-labib ila mu`asharat al-habib* (*An Intelligent Man's Guide to the Art of Coition*), Ibn Falita (d. 1362) compares *sihaq* and *zina* and underscores the social advantages of the former over the latter. He writes: "Know that lesbianism insures against social disgrace / While coition is forbidden except through marriage."[79] In that perspective, Everett Rowson has observed that "because of the cult of female virginity and the dependence of a man's honor on the chastity of his female relations, heterosexual philanderers were in fact playing a more dangerous game than *lutis*, and an argument could be made for a shift over time in the weight of societal disapproval towards the former and away from the latter."[80] Because the Qur'an does not prescribe a specific punishment for homosexuals, Islamic jurisprudence tended to analogize (*qiyas*) homosexuality to adultery for the purposes of punishing homosexual acts. Moreover, as *liwat* was specifically defined as anal penetration by a penis, and since lesbianism was considered not to involve penetration by a man, it was generally agreed that *sahq* merited a lesser punishment than *liwat*.[81] In most legal compendia of *fiqh* (Islamic jurisprudence), *sahq* is not even regularly addressed.

Despite the severity of Islamic law toward homosexuality, it appears that in practice homosexuality was tolerated within Muslim societies. During the early Abbasid period (ca. 750–850), for instance, homosexuality was broadcast among the fashionable misbehaviors of the time, along with wine drinking, gambling, cockfights, and dogfights.[82] In the caliphate court of ninth-century Baghdad, the tradition of the *ghulamiyyat*, singing slave-girls who cross-dressed as boys (at times even with painted mustaches), became the cultural fashion to be imitated by upper-class women of the city.[83]

But it is especially during the Mamluk period (1249–1517) that homosexuality became a veritable cultural fashion of the Islamic world, as many of the caliphs themselves maintained homosexual lovers. Verses celebrating homosexuality became more popular than those praising heterosexuality.[84] Same-sex behaviors became especially trendy, if not the norm, in intellectual circles, and in caliphate courts throughout the Islamicate world. The public role of male effeminates as court jesters in caliphate courts may have also secured the visibility of alternative sexual practices and hence officially sanctioned a certain degree of tolerance toward them.

In an attempt to emulate and surpass the courts of the Abbasids, the Umayyads of al-Andalus (756–1031) boasted their own tolerance of alternative sexualities. In Islamic Spain, homoerotic verses competed with and perhaps exceeded the production of heteroerotic poetry. The rulers themselves were both producers of such verse and vocal partners in same-sex love relations. Al-Mutamid, eleventh-century king of Seville, wrote to his male page: "I made him my slave, but the coyness of his glance has made me his prisoner, so that we are both at once slave and master to each other."[85] As the survival of this and other such verses reveal, homosexual relations were not kept a secret but were sung in courts, as well as in other milieus of Muslim Spain. In addition, it must be pointed out, the fact that "much of the most popular gay erotic poetry is written in a vulgar Arabic dialect containing many Romance words and expressions [suggests] that it was composed in a milieu familiar with if not consisting partly of Christians."[86] The cultural encounters between Muslims and Christians in al-Andalus thus not only promoted amorous liaisons between the two groups,[87] but also ensured cultural exchanges and the transmission of erotic verse to the West.

The case of Wallada (d. 1087 or 1091) deserves mention here. Daughter of the last Umayyad caliph in Muslim Spain (al-Mustakfi), Wallada unquestionably stands as the prototype of the unparalleled refinement of the Andalusian aristocracy in the eleventh century and of women's unsuspected sexual freedom. Hostess of a literary salon in eleventh-century Cordoba, Wallada defied conventional societal expectations as she is said to have openly entertained two male lovers (Ibn Zaydun and Ibn `Abdus) as well as one female lover (Mohja). While critics disagree as to whether Wallada may indeed be considered an Andalusian Sappho,[88] and while we cannot equate a poet's persona, the literary motifs used, and what real life was like for medieval Andalusian women, Wallada's story nevertheless serves as an important reminder that same-sex desire between women in the urban, courtly Islamicate literary world was far from absent.

A Brief Literary History of Medieval Arabic Erotic Texts

There is a surprisingly large literature (composed in Arabic, Persian, and Turkish) on same-sex practices in the medieval Islamicate world. Most of it is very difficult to access in bookstores and libraries worldwide; the majority has not been translated into Western languages, and because of the contemporary Middle Eastern political and social attitudes toward gender, very few of these works have been examined in criticism either within or outside of the Arab Islamicate world.[89]

The earliest extant Arabic homoerotic poetry dates from the late eighth century with the writings of Iraqi judge Yahya Ibn Aktham and poet Abu Nuwas (d. 815), the latter being traditionally considered "the principal originator of homoerotic poetry in the Muslim environment."[90] Much of the information on homosexuality in the medieval Arabic tradition may be gathered from what Arabists call the belletristic tradition (*adab*), namely, collections of poetry and anecdotes. As a literary genre that developed at first in the sophisticated urban environment of eighth-century Baghdad and that was sponsored by the Abbasid caliphate, *adab* was especially interested in promoting *zarf* (refinement, elegance), love as a science, erotology, and in exploiting the far reaches and power of linguistic formations. The semiscientific view of love, characteristic of *adab* in the Abbasid period and later found throughout the Islamicate world, including Muslim Spain, resulted in the composition of numerous treatises on love and topics such as music, singing, and dancing slave-girls. *Adab* anthologies are important not only as literary writings, but because they give us insights into the attitudes held by urban, elite, and mostly male writers and readers of the period.[91] One of the key subcategories of the *adab* tradition is the genre of *mujun* (profligacy) which contains books known as *kutub al-bah* (treatises on copulation). These are sex manuals interspersed with erotic tales that "flouted societal and religious norms."[92] Texts in the *mujun* tradition focus mostly on male alternative sexualities, but many include a chapter devoted to lesbianism and speak about female eroticism under other subheadings as well. It is the various chapters and passages on lesbianism of these larger *adab* texts that will be especially relevant to *Crossing Borders*.

Space allows us to mention here only some of the most prominent examples of this literary tradition: (1) Abu al-Faraj Ibn Muhammad al-Isfahani's tenth-century compilation, *Kitab al-aghani* (Book of Songs), which contains key information about songs and melodies, and offers anecdotes about poets, musicians, and personalities from the pre-Islamic era to the Abbasid period;[93] (2) the late tenth-century collection by Ibn Nasr al-Katib entitled *Jawami` al-ladhdha* (*The Encyclopedia of Pleasure*) and its multiple rewritings throughout the centuries, most importantly by Ahmad al-Tifashi in the early thirteenth century (*The Delight of Hearts*) and Ibn Falita in the middle of the fourteenth century (*An Intelligent Man's Guide to the Art of Coition*); (3) the early eleventh-century anthology by a religious scholar named Abu al-Qasim al-Husayn Ibn Muhammad al-Raghib al-Isfahani entitled *Muhadarat al-udaba' wa-muhawarat al-shu`ara' wa-al-bulagha'* (Lectures by the Literati and Conversations in Poetry and Eloquent Speech); and (4) the eleventh-century philological work written by an Iraqi religious judge named Abu al-Abbas Ahmad b. Muhammad al-Jurjani (d. 1089) entitled *al-Muntakhab min kinayat al-udaba' wa isharat al-bulagha'* (Anthology of Metonymic Devices Used by the Literati and Allusions in Eloquent Speech).[94] It may seem peculiar today to think of Muslim judges as authors of *mujun* literature, but this type of composition was considered a valid literary genre and does not reflect necessarily the sexual orientation or practices of its author nor the degree of permissibility such behavior had in its society.[95] In fact, one of the conventions of *mujun* is precisely the use of religious language to flout religious norms.

Another important genre that scholars have examined in their research on same-sex desire in medieval Arabic literature is that of the *wasf* tradition, or epigrammatical description in verse.[96] This poetical genre focused on multiple topics, including the comparative merits of boys and girls, of virgins and nonvirgins, of beardless boys and maidens as sex partners, and even of boys' jealousy and women's jealousy of male lovers. As far as sexual orientation is concerned, the tradition of *wasf* varied in its evaluation. At times, it showcased the advantages of heterosexuality as in al-Jahiz's (d. 868) *Kitab mo-ufakharati al-jawari wa al-ghilman* (*Boasting Match over Maids and Youths*) and *Tafdil al-batn `ala al-zahr* (*Superiority of the Belly to the Back*);[97] at others, it upheld a bias toward homosexuality as in Ibn Falita's fourteenth-century *Rushd al-labib ila mu`asharat al-habib* (*An Intelligent Man's Guide to the Art of Coition*) which includes a chapter heading referring to the "greater excellence" (*tafdil*) of boys over slave girls.[98]

Last, but not least, the framed narrative tradition of *Alf layla wa layla*, or the *One Thousand and One Nights* (also known as the *Arabian Nights*), is another important genre that is essential to any study of sexuality in the medieval Arabic world, especially as it relates to the lower levels of society who are never represented in other texts. As we will see in the following chapters, tales from this work which have circulated orally and in performance as early as the ninth century, but for which no written manuscript has survived prior to the early fourteenth century, give us key insights into alternative sexuality and female same-sex practices in the Islamicate world.

Orientalism and Challenge of Locating Arabic Erotic Materials

Despite the unquestionable value that texts such as these have for an investigation of alternative sexual practices in the medieval Arab world, and despite their overall importance in Arabic literary history and the promise they hold for a reevaluation of gender in the Arab Islamicate world, these works remain little known except by a select group of scholars. In fact, because of the sociopolitical climate in the Arab world today, and because such texts paint women with unexpected agency over their social and sexual lives and have thus the potential to become powerful sociopolitical models of resistance for contemporary Arab and Muslim women, many are often silenced or censored. They are also at times unedited, unpublished, and difficult to access not only in manuscript, but even in libraries and bookstores across the Arab world. One of the main challenges of the present study is precisely that of locating and obtaining copies of the relevant material. Understanding these difficulties and appreciating who is permitted to have access to Arabic materials on alternative sexuality provide a glimpse of the political and social potential for subversion that these documents possess.

My research in Egypt (summer 2002) revealed that even though some editions of medieval Arabic erotic writings, such as the *Encyclopedia of Pleasure* do indeed exist, they are not made available or sold to Arab/Muslim women.[99] A conversation I had with the assistant manager of a major bookstore in Alexandria (Egypt) illustrates the current status of erotic writings in

the Arab world. After handing me a greatly censored copy of Abu Nuwas's poetry (Abu Nuwas is considered to be the father of Arabic erotic poetry and is
mentioned regularly throughout the *Encyclopedia of Pleasure*), and after I de-
clined the book on this basis, the manager looked at me with shock mixed
with suspicion; he then proceeded to politely explain to me that he indeed
had the uncensored version in the back room of his store, and simply added
"but I will certainly not sell it to you." This conversation clarifies for me the
fact that erotic writings, though available in some Arab bookstores, are not for
the consumption of "proper" Arab and Muslim women.

I first obtained the only Arabic edition of the *Encyclopedia of Pleasure* that
exists (to my knowledge) through the intercession of an Arab male friend living in New York City who knew a Cairo bookshop owner who sold him this
volume in secret. At the same time that I discovered the existence of the Arabic edition of the *Encyclopedia of Pleasure*, I found out that it was published
in Damascus (Syria) by Dar al-kitab al-arabi (Arabic Book Press) in a series
entitled Adab al-jins `inda al-`Arab (The Erotic Writings of the Arabs) which
to date includes six titles on Arabic eroticism. I also quickly understood that
Arabic erotic treatises were more widely available in specialized bookstores in
the West (London and Paris in particular) than in the Arab world.

The initial moment of celebration at getting the Arabic edition of the *Encyclopedia of Pleasure* was quickly tempered when I actually examined the text.
The name of the press had been carefully blackened out, as was the date of
publication. The entire book was printed in black ink on white paper, over
which were superimposed prints in red ink of large trees. Most likely, this represented a (cheap) attempt at avoiding censorship by making quick identification of the book's subject matter difficult and ultimately the reading of the
entire book quite challenging. The superimposition of text and image, of
black ink over white paper, and of large red drawings over everything, literal-
ized for me the multiple layers of veils that the Arabic erotic texts had undergone over time. Last, this Arabic edition, perhaps because it was based on an
incomplete manuscript, did not contain several of the chapters found in the
English translation (particularly those dealing with same-sex relations).
Clearly, though available, the Arabic *Encyclopedia of Pleasure* continues to
evade us, its erotic content having been judged ideologically too subversive,
too dangerous to fall into the hands of just anyone. Until today, the *Encyclopedia of Pleasure* remains known primarily through an English translation, the
1977 Canadian Ph.D. dissertation of Salah Addin Khawwam, translated by
Adnan Jarkas and Salah Addin Khawwam and published by Aleppo Publish-

ing in Toronto. The presence of this English translation should not deceive us into thinking that this text is readily available. Quite the opposite. Aleppo Publishing has since gone out of business; none of the translators is to be found in any scholarly listings or directories; no information is given on the university where the dissertation was submitted and defended; the book is utterly unavailable for purchase anywhere, and only three copies of this dissertation are available in libraries worldwide: the Library of Congress in Washington, D.C., Columbia University, and the School of Oriental and African Studies (London).[100]

The difficulty of accessing medieval Arabic writings on alternative sexualities should not be understood to be a specific problem of the Arab world because of its contemporary political and social restrictions; it manifests itself also in the West, though under a different guise. Similarly to the *Encyclopedia of Pleasure*, the English translation of Shihab al-Din Ahmad al-Tifashi's thirteenth-century *Nuzhat al-albab fima la yujad fi kitab, The Delight of Hearts* by Edward A. Lacey,[101] has ended up ghettoizing this important Arabic text. Even though it is almost certain that this medieval Arabic work was addressed to a much wider audience, its contemporary English translation is published by an exclusively male gay press (Gay Sunshine Press) and is thus likely to be known primarily by a gay audience. Moreover, Lacey has taken the liberty to excise from his work the chapter on lesbianism as well as other sections dealing with heterosexuality because of budgetary concerns and press policy, which dictate that Gay Sunshine Press address exclusively male gay literature.[102] The manipulations that *The Delight of Hearts* has thus undergone have transformed this important text almost beyond recognition. Not only has this English translation (the only one available) utterly erased lesbian voices in the medieval Arabic tradition, but it has also presented sexual divisions that were certainly not present in the medieval text. Translating only the sections on gay men's sexuality has hence introduced a modern and Western perspective on the medieval Arabic work that places sexual orientations and their various practices on a continuum of behaviors.[103]

A Cross-Cultural Approach to Same-Sex Love Between Women

In the following chapters, I will demonstrate that Old French literature may be usefully considered a palimpsest, a textual surface that both obscures and reveals signs of multiple contacts (and conflicts) between medieval France and the Islamicate world.[104] By unraveling what lies just beneath the surface of French textuality, beneath its Western and heterosexual veneer, *Crossing Borders* will recapture alternative female same-sex sexual voices, long thought to be absent because they are dressed in Oriental garb. *Crossing Borders* purports also to recover those references to the Arabic tradition and to alternative sexual practices in Old French texts which the medieval Western audience would have heard, but which we (the contemporary audience) no longer recognize because we have lacked the critical cultural (and at times linguistic) tools to identify them. Only by reconstructing the multicultural context in which medieval French literature was composed is it possible to hear the heretofore silenced voices of premodern European female homoeroticism.

We will see in Chapter 1 that the medieval Arabic erotic tradition permits the deciphering for the first time of various images, terms, and rhetorical devices (military metaphors in particular) in Old French texts that have thus far appeared ambiguous or obscure (Etienne de Fougères's *Livre des manières*). Chapter 2 demonstrates the extent to which the Arabic tradition has offered a repertoire of themes, of tales, and of vocabulary for medieval Europe which permitted the expression of same-sex desire and sexuality between women (the *Yde et Olive* stories). Chapter 3 demonstrates how medieval French narrators represented same-sex desire between women through the safer discourse of friendship. A comparison between Jean Renart's thirteenth-century romance *Escoufle* and the framed tale of Qamar al-Zaman and the Princess Boudour from the *One Thousand and One Nights* reveals that the numerous repeated references in Old French texts to material goods, silk cloth, precious stones, and luxury commodities coming from the East are not to be read as ornamental, empty signifiers without any bearing on the interpretation of the romance. Rather, such allusions function as veritable narrative strategies that point to unsuspected and veiled expressions of intimate desire between women in Old French writings. Finally, Chapter 4 extends the meaning of intertextuality and cross-cultural literary encounters between the Arab world and medieval France to include the social and the cultural. We will see in particular how Arab cultural and social practices contributed to the development of the French literary lesbian's social identity. In that chapter, Arabic resonances in Jean Renart's *Escoufle* will be shown to far exceed specific linguistic or thematic borrowings and to reside rather in the development of alternative urban, socioeconomic spaces that are conducive to same-sex sexual practices between women.

CHAPTER TWO

Crossing Linguistic Borders

Etienne de Fougères's *Livre des Manières* and Arabic Erotic Treatises

> *A willingness to descend into that alien territory split-space of enunciation may open the way to conceptualizing an international culture, based not on the exoticism or multi-culturalism of the diversity of cultures, but on the inscription and articulation of culture's hybridity.*
> —Homi K. Bhabha

> *These turns of phrases [words designating the male and female parts and copulation] are there to be used. If it was generally believed that they were not supposed to be uttered, they would have had no meaning in the first place or would have already been removed from the language for reasons of probity and to protect its purity.*
> —Al-Jahiz

IRONICALLY, IT IS to a twelfth-century Anglo-Norman bishop and chaplain that we owe the earliest extant and most explicit depiction of lesbian sexual practices in French literature. Etienne de Fougères is indeed credited with writing the least ambiguous portrait of same-sex sexual practices between women in the entire French literary Middle Ages. The most striking elements in Etienne's account of lesbianism are undoubtedly the erotic military metaphors and unfamiliar linguistic terms that permeate seven stanzas of his *Livre des manières* (ca. 1174). As I decipher the eroto-military tropes and linguistic innovations of Etienne de Fougères's depiction of lesbian sexuality, I will argue that though unique in medieval French literature, the erotic military images found in Etienne's text strikingly echo various passages from widely circulated Arabic erotic treatises.

Etienne de Fougères's *Livre des manières* is the earliest extant example in French of the medieval genre of estate literature (*états du monde*).[1] As a moralistic composition, this genre is intended both to justify and to rectify the actions of the various members of society. Etienne's *Livre des manières* divides society into two groups: those who belong to the upper estate or social level and thus hold power—that is, respectively, the king, the clergy, and the knights; then those who make up the lower estate and thus lack power—namely, the peasants, the bourgeois, and women. In fact, his entire poem is divided exactly into two parts to address these two main categories: vv. 1–672 (the upper estates) and vv. 677–1344 (the lower estates).[2]

Like his contemporary Marie de France, Etienne de Fougères was associated with the Anglo-Norman courts of Henry II Plantagenêt, where he served as the king's chaplain. Like Marie de France's *Esope*, Etienne's poem also invites a cross-cultural reading. For Henry II's courts have long been recognized as especially rich hubs to which Arabic scientific, material, and cultural goods flowed from scholarly centers in Sicily and Spain.[3] The multiple exchanges between Norman England and Norman Sicily insured in fact the regular presence of Englishmen at Sicilian courts. English scholars, translators, and administrators were encouraged to study in Sicily as the number of scientific and literary works dedicated to Henry II seems to suggest.[4] Moreover, Etienne de Fougères's dedication of his *Livre des manières* to the countess of Hereford (vv. 1205–24) is further evidence that his work is connected to the matter of Araby. The Cathedral of Hereford is indeed recognized to have been a major center for the translation and transmission of Arabic scientific (and literary) learning in the twelfth century. Its important school and library drew Western scholars of Arabic science, many of whom having returned there to teach after their trips *arabum studia* (Walcher of Malvern, Roger of Hereford, and Adelard of Bath, among others). The Cathedral of Hereford was also the teaching center of Petrus Alfonsi's astronomical lessons based on Arabic scientific findings in the first quarter of the twelfth century, that same Petrus Alfonsi, author of the *Disciplina Clericalis*, who was responsible for the introduction of a significant amount of Arabic literary material into the

West.[5] Etienne was therefore living in a milieu that had repeated contact with Arabic scientific, cultural, and literary traditions either through scholars and translators, or at least merchants and returning crusaders. The association he establishes with the Cathedral of Hereford is an indication that he was familiar with Arabic scientific and literary writings, including undoubtedly their important homoerotic elements.[6] In this chapter, we will see that the first portrait of lesbian sexuality in medieval French literature may be considered a veritable hybrid composition between East and West, a polyphonic text that weaves Arabic homoerotic material with French generic conventions. Etienne de Fougères's seven stanzas on the lesbian stand thus as a prime example of the types of compositions produced in the cross-cultural milieu of mid-twelfth-century Anglo-Norman France.

The seven stanzas depicting the lesbian in Etienne de Fougères's *Livre des manières* occupy an intriguing space in the overall economy of the work and of the genre as a whole. For the genre of estate literature to which Etienne's text belongs does not address women. Though placed at the very bottom of the social hierarchy, after the peasants, the very insertion of women as a category in Etienne de Fougères's work and the fact that they are permitted to occupy a total of seventy stanzas in the text are in themselves noteworthy. Not content simply to add women to his moralistic view of the social makeup, Etienne subdivides the section on women into three portraits: first, the "bad, aristocratic woman" who receives a particularly misogynist description (vv. 977–1096); second, the lesbian whose sin is dubbed "vile" ("lei pechié," v. 1097) (vv. 1097–124); and, finally, the "good woman" ("bone fame," v. 1133) whose main representative is the Countess of Hereford, to whom the entire poem is dedicated (vv. 1125–224).[7] It is interesting to observe the placement of the highly erotic portrait of the lesbian which is situated neither at the very bottom of the social hierarchy (as we may have expected), nor before the depiction of the "bad, aristocratic woman." Curiously, in this text, the portrait of the lesbian is inserted between the two extremes of the bad and good woman.[8]

This is how Etienne depicts the lesbian in his *Livre des manières*:[9]

De bel pechié n'est pas merveille,	There's nothing surprising about the "beautiful sin"
Des que Nature le conseille,	When nature prompts it,
Mes qui de lei pechié s'esveille	But whosoever is awakened by the "vile sin"
Encontre Nature teseille.	Is going against nature.

Celui deit l'en chiens
    hüer,
Pieres et bastons estrüer;
Torchons li devreit [l'en]
    rüer
Et con autres gueignons tüer.

One must pursue [him]
    with dogs,
Throw[ing] stones and sticks;
One should smite him with
    blows
And kill him like any other cur.

Ces dames ont trové
    i jeu:
O dos trutennes funt
    un eu,
Sarqueu hurtent contre
    sarqueu
Sanz focil escoent lor
    feu.

These ladies have made up
    a game:
With two bits of nonsense they
    make nothing;
They bang coffin against
    coffin,
Without a poker to stir up their
    fire.

Ne joent pas a
    piquenpance,
A pleins escuz joignent sanz
    lance
N'ont soign de lange en
    lor balance,
Ne en lor mole point de
    mance.

They don't play at "poke in the
    paunch"
But join shield to shield without
    a lance.
They have no concern for a
    beam in their scales,
Nor a handle in their
    mold.

Hors d'aigue peschent au
    torbout
Et n'i quierent point de ribot.
N'ont sain de pilete
    en lor pot
Në en lor branle de pivot.

Out of water they fish for
    turbot
And they have no need for a rod.
They don't bother with a pestle
    in their mortar
Nor a fulcrum for their see-saw.

Dus et dus jostent lor
    tripout
Et se meinent plus que le
    trot;
A l'escremie del jambot

In twos they do their lowlife
    jousting
And they ride to it with all their
    might;
At the game of thigh-fencing

S'entrepaient vilment l'escot.	They pay most basely each other's share.
Il ne sunt pas totes d'un molle: L'un [e] s'esteit et l'autre crosle, L'un[e] fet coc et l'autre polle Et chascune meine son rossle. (stanzas 275–81)	They're not all from the same mold: One lies still and the other grinds away, One plays the cock and the other the hen, And each one plays her role.

Paradoxically, and as Robert Clark has accurately observed, what predominates in these seven stanzas on lesbian sexual practices is "the ever-present but always absent phallus":[10] the absence of any "lance," or its multiple synonyms in the text, "poker," "pointer," "handle," "rod," "pestle," "fulcrum." Throughout these stanzas, therefore, and just as the authors of the *Yde and Olive* stories do one and two centuries later, Etienne de Fougères attributes to lesbians a phallocentric sexuality.[11] In this text, lesbian sexual acts are understood in terms of heterosexual relations, which the two women are presumably attempting to replicate.

At the same time, one must observe the usage and role of the other military metaphors in stanzas 278 and 280: the joining of the two shields in stanza 278 ("join shield to shield without a lance") and the joust in both stanza 278 ("They don't play at jousting") and in stanza 280 ("At the game of thigh-fencing"). If as Robert Clark pointed out, the "lance" (in stanza 278) represents indeed the absent phallus, the "shields" in the text are evidently a metaphor for female sexual organs. As a consequence, the "joust" would represent a highly erotic and explicit scene of lesbian lovemaking. The absence of the "lance," combined with the image of two "shields" banging against each other (stanza 277) in a sexually charged "tournament" (stanza 278) thus elaborate a type of sexuality that is inherently idiosyncratic and lesbian, certainly a sexuality that is distinct from heterosexual norms.

While some critics have recognized the uniqueness and originality of Etienne's military description of lesbian sexuality,[12] others have claimed that such verses could not have been written by a bishop and that they must be considered a product of scribal interpolations. Charles-Victor Langlois for instance has observed that the detailed depiction of "acts against nature" in Etienne's text is "quite useless, display a shocking obscenity." He alleges further that the depiction of such acts is "written in a sarcastic and joking tone that contrasts strikingly with the rest of the book and which, no matter what the freedom of the period might have been, would have seemed more than odd at the hand of a bishop." In other words, the seven stanzas on the lesbian "display all the traits of an addition to the original text."[13] Langlois's assumption that Etienne's original text may have been written in Latin (no longer extant) and that the French text that has survived has suffered from important scribal alterations[14] may not be the only conclusion to be drawn from the poem. Nor is Anthony Lodge's interpretation convincing when he remarks that the lesbian episode is nothing but a humorous insertion within the text, fabliau-like, meant to entertain the audience, even as it edifies.[15] In their effort to extirpate Etienne from the responsibility of having authored the earliest extant, most detailed and explicit depiction of lesbianism in French literature, critics have pointed to the fact that the single surviving manuscript (dating from the early thirteenth century)[16] is poorly written and that the entire text, and especially the seven stanzas on the lesbian, contain words of unclear etymology that are unattested elsewhere in medieval literature.[17] Such a text could not have been composed in earnest by someone as educated, highly regarded, and greatly admired a bishop and literary writer as Etienne was.[18]

Etienne's Arabic Intertexts

I will argue that Etienne de Fougères's military depiction of lesbian practices is informed by two Arabic treatises dating from the tenth and eleventh centuries, thus written earlier than Etienne's *Livre des manières*. They are the late tenth-century *Encyclopedia of Pleasure* (*Jawami` al-ladhdha*), written by Abu al-Hasan Ali Ibn Nasr al-Katib,[19] which is considered to be the earliest example of Arabic homoerotic compilations, and the eleventh-century philological work entitled *al-Muntakhab min kinayat al-udaba' wa isharat al-bulagha'* (An Anthology of Metonymic Devices Used by the Literati and Allusions in Eloquent Speech) written by Iraqi religious judge Abu al-Abbas Ahmad Ibn Muhamad al-Jurjani (d. 1089). These two works provide us with some of the most crucial insights into the literary representation of the medieval Arab lesbian, and constitute key, unacknowledged intertexts of the *Livre des manières*.

Before I discuss the striking linguistic, metaphorical, and cultural crossings between Etienne's *Livre des manières* and these Arabic literary texts on lesbian lovemaking, one observation must be made with regard to the Arabic erotic tradition. As may be clear from the title of al-Jurjani's *An Anthology of Metonymic Devices Used by the Literati and Allusions in Eloquent Speech*, erotic material in the Arabic tradition is not confined to a specific genre. If Arabic erotic writings are most typically included in the literature of *mujun* (profligacy) and in *kutub al-bah* (treatises on copulation),[20] they are present in seemingly more "serious" texts, such as in al-Jurjani's work on linguistic metaphors. And indeed, *An Anthology of Metonymic Devices Used by the Literati and Allusions in Eloquent Speech*, despite its focus on language, is a particularly rich reservoir of information on homosexuality in the Arabic literary tradition. Focusing on the use of indirect expressions among the literati and orators, and in an effort to display his erudition and mastery of the Arabic lexicon, al-Jurjani quite naturally turns his attention to euphemisms used for various forms of illicit sexual practice, including active and passive male homosexuality (respectively, *liwat* and *ubna* or *bigha*), lesbianism (*sahq*), adultery (*zina*), male homosexual prostitution (*ijara*), male masturbation (*jild*), and intercrural intercourse (*tafkhidh*). While the overall organization of al-Jurjani's text might baffle the Western critic, Everett Rowson has demonstrated that the "impression of incoherence" that results from the classification system at work here is attributable to various cultural assumptions. These assumptions are twofold: what constitutes illicit sexuality (choice of partner, activity, or social context), and a conception of sexuality that views it primarily in penetrative and nonpenetrative terms.[21] More important for our purposes is the strategy (adopted by al-Jurjani) of discussing the topic of sexuality in books whose primary focus lies elsewhere. This technique reveals one of the ways in which some Arabic conventions on homosexuality may have been transmitted to the West in the Middle Ages, namely, embedded in various rhetorical, poetic, legal, medical, or scientific treatises.

The "lance," "shield," and "joust" as erotic metaphors will become commonly used in French from the thirteenth century onward. We find them used, for instance, in *Le Tournoi des dames* by Hue d'Oisy and *Le Tournoiement as dames de Paris* by Pierre Gentien where they describe women's involvement and skill in joust.[22] At the end of the twelfth century, however, such eroto-military metaphors were still atypical in French writings. They were, on the other hand, quite conventional throughout the

Arabic literary tradition.[23] Central to this study is the fact that as early as the tenth century, in Arabic literature, the word "shield" was understood to represent the vulva. For example, in the tenth chapter, "Lesbianism," of his *Encyclopedia of Pleasure*, Ibn Nasr writes: "Your vulva became like a shield."[24] The penis, not surprisingly, comes to be referred to in Arabic erotic writings as both the "lance" and the "sword."[25] Once this basic eroto-military semantic field was established, the joust (or war or tournament) metaphor logically followed and came naturally to mean lovemaking. These eroto-military metaphors were repeated verbatim from one century to the next, from one writer to the other throughout the Arab world.

The military metaphors that we find in Etienne's text and that appear so new and original to Western critics can easily be traced to specific lines of any number of Arabic erotic treatises. They repeat in fact verbatim some key metaphorical, if not linguistic, conventions of the Arabic homoerotic tradition, such as those we encounter in al-Jurjani's *Anthology of Metonymic Devices*:

أبدين حربا لا طعان بها   إلا إلتقاء الترس بالترس

They [lesbians] manifest a war in which there is no spear-thrusting,
But only fending off a shield with a shield.[26]

Anyone who remains unconvinced of the obvious sexual connotations of the words "war," "spear-thrusting," and "shields" in this quotation need only compare their usage with Ibn Nasr's *Encyclopedia of Pleasure* from the previous century. This work, which was undoubtedly one of al-Jurajani's sources, presents the metaphoric military words in their literal garb:

What's the good of two vulvas rubbing against each other?
It is the penetration of the penis that is important.[27]

Clearly, al-Jurjani's "spear" and "shield" respectively provide thinly veiled euphemisms for explicit references to "penis" and "vulva" in Ibn Nasr's text. Similarly, al-Jurjani's "fending of a shield with a shield" refers to Ibn Nasr's "rubbing of the vulvas."

The same eroto-military metaphors appear again in an early thirteenth-century Arabic text written by a Tunisian author named Shihab al-Din Ahmad al-Tifashi (1184–1253) and entitled *Nuzhat al-albab fima la yujad fi kitab*, which has been translated as *The Delight of Hearts Or, What One Can-*

not Find in Any Book. Although this text is written slightly later than Etienne de Fougères's time, its importance cannot be underestimated, because it shows the extent to which the military metaphors used to describe lesbian lovemaking since at least the tenth century had become conventional in the Arabic homoerotic tradition of the thirteenth century:

هيجن حربا لا طعان بها   إلا قراع الترس بالترس

They invented a tournament
In which there is no use of lance,
Hitting only with great noise
One shield against the other.[28]

Speaking of lesbian lovemaking as the banging of shields/rubbing of vulvas without the use of a lance is so embedded in the Arabic homoerotic tradition that it may be considered one of its most identifying trademarks. Even the word for "lesbian" in Arabic, *sahq*, evokes this rubbing (grinding) behavior. The word *sahq*, from the root *s/h/q*, means "to grind" (spices) or "to rub," while lesbians are referred to as *sahiqat, sahhaqat,* or *musahiqat*, meaning literally "those who engage in a rubbing behavior, or who make love in a rubbing fashion." But more significant than the rubbing metaphor which is found also in Greek antiquity (*tribades*) is the military image of the "shields" to refer to women's vulvas. This metaphor is characteristic of Arabic erotic writings and is striking in the context of Etienne de Fougères's stanzas. Thus, when readers familiar with Arabic homoerotic metaphoric conventions read in Etienne de Fougères's *Livre des manières* that women join one another shield against shield, as though in a joust without a lance (as we saw in stanzas 278 and 280), they cannot fail to recognize the Arabic intertextual references interwoven throughout the Old French poem.

Linguistic Crossings

The striking metaphorical echoes between Etienne de Fougères's *Livre des manières* and Arabic literary descriptions of lesbian sexuality do not end here. They are present throughout the seven stanzas under study here, although they do not come through clearly in the modern English translation. Critics of Etienne de Fougères often comment on the unfamiliar vocabulary encountered in the section on the lesbian and have gone so far as to question Etienne's authorship of these stanzas. However, the vocabulary used to describe the lesbian that sounds unusual to the Western ear resonates differently for the critic attuned to the multicultural milieu of the twelfth century. All that appears unusual today in this text seems so only because it belongs to a different cultural tradition. The eroto-military metaphors are, as we saw, an example of this phenomenon. Another example occurs in the last line of stanza 277: "Sanz focil escoent lor feu," translated as "Without a poker to stir up their fire." The cross-cultural reading of the *Livre des manières* proposed here would suggest that the translation of "escoent lor feu" as "to stir up their fire" reduces the tremendous ambiguity of the Old French verb *escoer*, which results in silencing the Arabic literary tradition that stands evident behind this line. *Escoer* is indeed one of those Old French verbs that has multiple significations. It means "to deliver, to agitate, to preserve, to avoid, to protect" and also "to cut the tail" or "to castrate" (and these two last significations, "to cut the tail" or "to castrate," are the primary meanings of the verb *escoer*).[29] The use of *escoer* with "fire" is uncommon; but its association with a "poker" may explain the selected English translation, for a poker stirs up a fire, after all.

The ambiguity of the Old French verb invites another translation. In fact, I would suggest rendering this line as "They deliver themselves from their fire without the use of a poker." This translation is not only linguistically and grammatically permitted, given the ambiguity of the Old French verse, but it illuminates further Etienne de Fougères's indebtedness to the Arabic erotic material. In translating this line thus, one aligns Etienne's French text with the medical definition of lesbianism as it was known in the medieval Arab world, and as summarized in Ibn Nasr's *Encyclopedia of Pleasure*: "Lesbianism is due to a vapour which, condensed, generates in the labia heat and an itch which only dissolve and become cold through friction and orgasm. When friction and orgasm take place, the heat turns into coldness because the liquid that a woman ejaculates in lesbian intercourse is cold whereas the same liquid that results from sexual union with men is hot. Heat, however, cannot be extinguished by heat; rather, it will increase since it needs to be treated by its opposite. As coldness is repelled by heat, so heat is also repelled by coldness."[30]

Ibn Nasr is here repeating the medical causes and treatment of lesbianism as they were understood during his time, claiming that lesbianism is a condition whereby heat is generated in the labia and can be reduced only through friction and orgasm with another woman. The reduction in heat cannot be achieved through intercourse with a man since the man's liquid is hot and as Ibn Nasr reports, "heat . . . cannot be extinguished by heat." Friction between two vulvas, on the other hand, is effective in calming the original heat because it results in the ejaculation of a cold liquid. Returning to Etienne de Fougères's text, we now recognize that given the context of "sanz focil escoent lor feu" (it is between two sections strongly reminiscent of the Arabic tradition since they both evoke the banging/rubbing of shields and include the military metaphors discussed earlier), "escoent lor feu" more likely refers to the extinction of fire (and therefore the reaching of orgasm), rather than to the stirring up of fire that the two women seek to achieve in their union. A lack of awareness of the Arabic homoerotic tradition that informs Etienne de Fougères's seven stanzas in the *Livre des manières* evidently leads to either (unintended) mistranslations or obscurities in the text. These mistranslations lead to further silencing the multicultural dimension of medieval society and further eliding the sisterhood of the Arab and French lesbian in the Middle Ages.

The most revealing example of interlinguistic crossings between the French and Arabic homoerotic traditions has to do with the usage of two words in Etienne's text, "trutennes" and "eu" in stanza 277, for which critics have found no clear etymology and which remain unattested elsewhere in medieval literature.[31] I would like to propose that these two terms may well be transliterated Arabic words. That Etienne de Fougères included two Arabic words in his poem would offer undeniable proof of his familiarity with elements of Arabic homoerotic literature. I recognize the tremendous problems involved in making a case for transliterations of Arabic terms into romance (in this case Old French), for there can never be absolute certainty. However, and especially given my analysis of the parallelism in the eroto-military metaphors used, and given the fact that these words are unattested in French, the hypothesis of Arabic terminology is worth considering.

It should also be pointed out that the presence of transliterated Arabic words in Etienne de Fougères's text, while striking in the context of a literary work, is not surprising when compared to the survival of Arabic and Arabic-derived terms in European languages in general. After all, the establishment of the Umayyad caliphate in medieval Spain and the Arabization of the Iberian peninsula have led to the adoption of many Arabic words related to philosophy, medicine, astronomy, chemistry, flora, colors, buildings, official titles, business, crafts, and musical instruments. In fact, because there were no

Latin equivalents for the new technical developments introduced by the Muslims in al-Andalus, Arabic words were simply co-opted and Latinized. A similar argument can be made for the vocabulary of lesbianism and same-sex attachments for which there was no available language. Because lesbianism was to remain unnamed throughout the European Middle Ages, it is very possible that medieval authors resorted to Arabic terminology when depicting same-sex relations. In this sense, the use of transliterated Arabic words in the *Livre de manières* may be likened to the adoption of Arabic technical vocabulary in the sciences.

I suggest that the word *trutennes* comes from the Arabic word *turrah* from the root *t/r/t* (the ending "ennes" is the grammatical ending for the dual form), which literally means "forelock" and thus by extension "mons." Although the word *t/r/t* is not used in any of the three Arabic homoerotic treatises cited above, I have found this word used in another erotic Arabic text entitled *Rushd al-labib ila mu`asharat al-habib* (*An Intelligent Man's Guide to the Art of Coition*), dating to the fourteenth century and written by Ahmad Ibn Muhammad Ibn Falita (d. 1362).[32] The word *t/r/t* is used in this work to refer to the mons of the beloved (both male and female). Even though this term occurs in a text that postdates Etienne de Fougères's work, it was likely a familiar word in Arabic erotic treatises, since Ibn Falita's writing, like that of all his predecessors, is only a compilation of sexual knowledge in the Arab world, up to the time of its composition.[33]

The word *eu* in the same line ("O does trutennes funt un eu") appears to be an onomatopoeia, attested both in Old French and in Arabic, that would reflect the moaning and panting associated with lovemaking and pleasure as well as the ultimate fulfillment of desire in orgasm. The line would thus signify: "In addition to the rubbing of two mons, they make moaning and gasping sounds." In the Arabic erotic tradition, these moans were believed to be essential to lesbian lovemaking. In fact, they were thought to be one of the foundations of lesbian knowledge and were an integral part of the training of future lesbians. Al-Tifashi writes that between lesbians attention was regularly paid to "this music of love that the breath produces as it escapes the throat and passes through the nostrils."[34] Similarly, one of the pieces of advice given by an experienced lesbian mother to her daughter is precisely about these moans: "You should snort heartily while wriggling lasciviously."[35] A bit later in the text, al-Tifashi speaks of "wheezing, panting, purring, murmurs, heartbreaking sighs."[36]

The use of these two transliterated Arabic words ("trutennes" and "eu") in Etienne de Fougères's poem and the quasi-verbatim rendering of various military erotic metaphors that I discussed earlier in this chapter suggest two possible ways of conceiving the question of the accessibility of the Arabic material in Europe and the likely channels of transmission. One could argue that Arabic homoerotic literature was available to the medieval West, and Etienne de Fougères was familiar with the Arabic literary tradition of lesbian eroticism; or alternately that Etienne was familiar at least with some foreign "dirty words" (*trutennes* and *eu*). In other words, it is possible to envision that in parallel to a high cultural literary or scientific register of transmission, there also existed a nonlearned level of transfer from the Islamicate world to Europe. Travelers, crusaders, pilgrims, and merchants may have been instrumental in this lower register of cultural transmission, just as scholars and translators secured the transmission of the scientific material.[37] Through travelers, merchants, crusaders, and pilgrims, Arabic dirty words, in authentic or butchered forms, may well have crossed the borders between East and West, and given voice to the heretofore silenced "vile sin." Whether Etienne de Fougères learned about Arabic eroto-military metaphors through the scientific high cultural register or through nonlearned channels, his inclusion of Arabic terms and images of lesbian sexuality in his poem testifies to the reality of cross-cultural relations between East and West in the Middle Ages and suggests that Arabic homoeroticism was central to the literary construction of lesbian desire and sexuality in medieval France.

Le Livre des manières: Polyglossia and the Contact Zone

That the *Livre des manières* should exhibit Arabic intertextual and interlinguistic resonances is not surprising, for after all, the entire text invites a polyphonic reading. As such, it is one of multilayered resistance. We must note from the outset that the insertion of the category "women" in the genre of estate literature, a tradition from which they are traditionally excluded, may be viewed as the introduction of textual fragmentation in the genre as a whole. Women, considered by medieval theologians to be a deviation of the moral order, are in Etienne de Fougères's text the very signal of sexual and moral confusion. Not only do they introduce social and sexual disorder, but they also disrupt the authoritative language of estate literature and transgress established social, moral, and (hetero)sexual order. Similarly, the presence of the figure of the lesbian in Etienne's work and her placement in an intermediary position between the bad and the good woman, rather than at the very bottom of the social hierarchy as we might have expected, unsettles the overall syntax of the text. The semantic confusion and syntactical diversity that permeate the *Livre des manières* invite us to question the conventional coherence and stability of generic, social, and sexual hierarchies. Ultimately, they undermine the homogeneity of the social makeup and signal disruptions yet to come in the overall economy of the text.

It is indeed in the context of the insertion of social (women) and sexual (lesbian) minorities in the *Livre des manières* that Etienne's plurilingualism must be considered. If thus far, estate writings had been composed in Latin, Etienne de Fougères is credited for being among the first to write an estate work in the vernacular. By choosing French over Latin and by inserting Arabic rhetorical devices, images, and linguistic terms in his text, Etienne privileges polyglossia over monoglossia, diversity over homogeneity. He thus points to the linguistic and cultural diversity of the Anglo-Norman courts in which he thrived, a place in which Latin, Old French (Anglo-Norman), and Arabic were present simultaneously, interacted with, and subverted one another. Ruth Kennedy and Simon Meecham-Jones have recently argued that "in twelfth-century Britain, to choose to write in any particular language was, inescapably, to make an ideological statement about the purposes of the text and the author's relationship to the structures of power."[38] If this observation is true, then the plurilingualism (both explicit and implicit) that informs the entire text of the *Livre des manières* puts in question the notion of "father-tongue" (Latin) and underscores the pluralistic, hybrid, and linguistically diverse culture that characterized Henry II Plantagenêt's courts in the middle of the twelfth century. More important, the polyglossia that permeates the *Livre des manières* points to the limits of Latin to maintain an idealized linguistic order through a social, heterosexual harmony. For if as Bakhtin has shown, polyglossia signals the simultaneous death of two long cherished myths—"the myth of a language that presumes to be the only language, and the myth of a language that presumes to be completely unified"[39]— the use of the French vernacular and the insertion of Arabic linguistic and metaphorical motifs in the *Livre des manières* expose the passing of Latin as a uniquely unifying language. At the same time, Etienne questions the very idea of social categorization based upon binary terms or heterosexuality. In a period of social and political upheaval such as the one that marked the reign of Henry II Plantagenêt, Etienne de Fougères's work may be considered a hybrid literary and linguistic form, innovative because it mixed high and low,[40] official and vernaculars, French and Arabic, heterosexual and homosexual. His work heralds a new form of sociosexual contestation within the discursive economy of Old French literature. As medieval farces will accomplish decades later, Etienne de Fougères's *Livre des manières* dialogizes and hybridizes medieval French writings and shows how the dominant, unifying, and male language with its attending heterosexual concerns is contested by other languages and sexual practices from subordinated groups.

Etienne de Fougères's work may thus be considered a prominent example of a composition produced in the contact zone between the Anglo-Norman courts and Arab Islamicate cultures in the Middle Ages; as such, it hints at the multiple and unrecognized multilinguistic and multicultural encounters between these societies in the middle of the twelfth century. Because the *Livre des manières* is a heterogeneous, bilingual construction, it invites different readings from "people occupying different positions in the contact zone."[41] As it deploys French and Arabic semantic and rhetorical systems, it resonates differently for bilingual speakers than for monolingual speakers of either language. Furthermore, because it depicts different modes of sexual practice, it likely resonated differently also to straight and gay members of the audience (medieval or modern). It is precisely due to these multilayered systems of representation and of linguistic expression that the *Livre des manières* has been thought by some critics to have been emended by a careless scribe and possibly not even written by Etienne himself. In the absence of any archival or philological evidence to the contrary, our reading suggests that the *Livre des manières* is in fact a coherent work and that the juxtaposition of low (vernacular, Arabic dirty words, military metaphors, sex, lesbian) with high (estate literature, moral writings, Latin, heterosexuality) languages does not result in cacophony. Rather, it gives us a glimpse of the multicultural milieu in which Etienne was writing and of the potential for resistance to the social, linguistic, and sexual orders when the subaltern (social, sexual, and linguistic) is allowed to speak.[42]

Cross-Cultural Differences: Etienne de Fougères and Ahmad al-Tifashi's *The Delight of Hearts*

Even as Arabic rhetorical and linguistic tropes enrich and inform our reading of Etienne de Fougères's *Livre des manières*, and even as Arabic intertextuality invites us to consider the extent to which medieval French writings about female homosexuality are more prevalent than hitherto believed, it is important to remember that the explicitness of the French tradition pales in comparison to that of Arabic writings. For indeed, equally significant to this analysis is the absence, in Etienne's poem as in other medieval writers' works, of other fundamental Arabic homoerotic metaphors. For in the end, only fragments of Arabic writings (and only a few fragments) describing *explicitly* lesbian practices were assimilated into the nascent vernacular literatures of Europe. Though no less phallocentric than their French counterparts and though written likewise from a male (not lesbian) perspective, the medieval Arabic treatises on homosexuality (for example, the *Encyclopedia of Pleasure* and *An Anthology of Metonymic Devices*) are by far more detailed, direct, and explicit than any depiction of lesbianism found in the French Middle Ages, including that of Etienne de Fougères. Thus, while Etienne's description of lesbianism is both original and explicit in the context of the French erotic tradition (there is probably nothing as unambiguous in French until the eighteenth century with the marquis de Sade and Restif de la Bretonne), it remains limited when compared to any of the Arabic homoerotic treatises.

An examination of a key passage from Ahmad al-Tifashi's *The Delight of Hearts* demonstrates the great differences between the medieval Arabic and French traditions in their treatment of homoeroticism and alternative sexualities. Even though al-Tifashi's treatise, as pointed out earlier, was written later than Etienne de Fougères's text, it represents nevertheless an excellent compilation of earlier Arabic writings on homosexuality, some of which have been preserved (such as Ibn Nasr's *Encyclopedia of Pleasure* and al-Jurjani's *Anthology of Metonymic Devices*), while others are attested only through his extensive references to them. The erotic metaphors that pervade *The Delight of Hearts* stand thus as a key synthesis of the ways in which alternative sexualities were viewed in the Islamicate world and provide us with an unsurpassed reservoir of information on the sexual metaphoric conventions in the Arabic tradition up to the thirteenth century. Etienne de Fougères may well have been familiar with any number of Arabic texts to which al-Tifashi refers, which existed in the twelfth century but have since disappeared.

The following account of lesbian sexual practices permits us to grasp the very different descriptive modes that animate French and Arabic texts on female homosexuality:

و من شرطهن: أن تكون العاشقة أعلى و المعشوقة أسفل، إلا إن كانت العاشقة نحيفة الجسم و المعشوقة بدينة، فإمن حينئذ تُجعل النحيفة سفلى و البدينة عُليا، ليكون ثقل جنبها أشفى فى الحك و أمكن لذلك.

و صفة عملهن: أن تنام السفلى على ظهرها و تمد فخذها الواحد و ساقها، و تضم الاخر و تفرج عن فرجها مائلة لاحدى شقها. و تأتى العُلياء فتحتضن الفخذ المشتال و تضع أحد شفريها بين شفرى السفلى و تحك ذاهبة و جائية فى طول البدن، سفلا و علوا. و لذلك يشبهونه بسحق الزعفران، لأن الزعفران كذلك يُسحق على المنال.

و إذا بدأت بوضع الشفر الأيمن، مثلا، حكت به ساعة ثم تحولت فحكت بالأيسر، ولا تزال كذلك إلى أن تقضى المرأتان نهمتيهما.

فأما إطباق الشفرين فإنه لا منفعة فيه عندهن و لا متعة به. و سبب ذلك ان محل اللذة يبقى فارغا من شاغل، و ربما استُعين فى العمل بقليل دهن بان ممسك.

The tradition between women in the game of love necessitates that the lover places herself above and the beloved underneath—unless the former is too light or the second too developed: and in this case, the lighter one places herself underneath, and the heavier one on top, because her weight will facilitate the rubbing, and will allow the friction to be more effective. This is how they act: the one that must stay underneath lies on her back, stretches out one leg and bends the other while leaning slightly to the side, therefore offering her opening (vagina) wide open: meanwhile, the other lodges her bent leg in her groin, puts the lips of her vagina between the lips that are offered for her, and begins to rub the vagina of her companion in an up and down, and down and up, movement that jerks the whole body. This operation is dubbed "the saffron massage" because this is precisely how one grinds saffron on the cloth when dyeing it. The operation must focus each time on one lip in particular, the right one for example, and then the other: the woman will then slightly change position in order to apply better friction to the left lip . . . and she does not stop acting in this manner until her desires and those of her partner are fulfilled. I assure you that it is absolutely useless to try to press the two lips together at the same time, because the area from which pleasure comes would then not be exposed. Finally, let us note that in this game the two partners may be aided by a little willow oil, scented with musk.[43]

This detailed account of lesbian sexuality in *The Delight of Hearts* certainly stands in stark contrast to the current political climate in Arab Islamicate countries and explains, partly, the tendency to occlude the Arab-Muslim lesbian in most contemporary writings, critical or otherwise. But it certainly also stands in marked contrast to any description of lesbian sexuality in French literature, at least up to the eighteenth century.

Certainly, a few details in al-Tifashi's account of lesbian practices evoke some lines of Etienne's description (once again, al-Tifashi is not Etienne de Fougères's direct source in these instances, because his treatise was written slightly later than Etienne's. However, there may very well have been intermediary sources known to Etienne that are now lost or not yet edited). For instance, the uncommon Old French phrase "escremie del jambot" or "thigh-fencing" (stanza 280) seems reminiscent of the insistence on the positioning of the legs in the Arabic erotic treatise. The balancing of the two women in the act of love and their effort to rub only one labium at a time strongly resonates with the third line of stanza 278, "n'ont soign de lange en lor balance," and with the last line of stanza 280, "s'entrepaient vilment l'escot." The similarity between these lines and the Arabic treatise is, however, once again lost in the translation. The third line of stanza 278 may be more accurately rendered as "they do not need a tongue in their balancing act," and the last line of stanza 280 as "they go at the game of thigh-fencing one person at a time." These translations have the advantage of evoking much more explicitly the truly balancing and serial act of lesbian lovemaking in al-Tifashi's text.

Yet, and once again, these parallels are allusive at best. For the most part, and despite their recognized explicitness, the metaphors we find in Etienne de Fougères often remain ambiguous (perhaps intentionally so), and they never match the unsparing details or at times the unabashed and blunt literalness of the Arabic treatises and the Arabic erotic tradition in general.[44] In other words, even as we herald Etienne de Fougères as the first author of lesbian sexuality in French literature, and even as we point to his use of Arabic metaphorical and linguistic conventions, we must also note the vast differences between the two traditions.

But the greatest difference between the French and Arabic tradition on female same-sex practices does not lie in the degree of detail or explicitness of one text versus another. It resides rather in what we can surmise about the attitudes held by each culture toward lesbianism and lesbian sexualities. It lies in what we can infer from each of these cultural productions about audience expectations and reception. If we examine once again the very inclusion of women as a category in Etienne de Fougères's *Livre des manières*, we get a glimpse of the very different stance toward both women and female same-sex practices that animates this text, in contrast to Arabic writings on homosexuality.

In her article on the position of women in the *Livre des manières*, Jeri Guthrie has argued that if women are included in this text, they are ultimately also excluded from it since their sole accepted function is biological, the bearing of children.[45] Besides their maternal role, women are otherwise banished from the economic sphere of society. I will add that if lesbians more specifically are included in Etienne de Fougères's text, it is ultimately better to exclude them. For once they move from the outside to the inside of Old French writings, medieval French lesbians are consigned to the margins[46] and are never permitted to take center stage in the text. In fact, the very positioning of the seven stanzas on the lesbian between the "bad" and "good" woman seems to literally enact her textual imprisonment within other (excluded) social categories. This reading lends support to Robert Clark's conclusion that Etienne de Fougères's seven stanzas on the lesbian participate in the formation of both a "persecuting" and "homophobic discourse"[47] against women who claim to find sexual satisfaction with each other, outside of sanctioned marriage.

Moreover, the polyglossia that we discussed above that permits a richer understanding of Etienne's text has as its corollary the very possibility of excluding the Old French lesbian from public discourse. For the use of Arabic, all the while providing a language (albeit indirect because it was metaphorical) for speaking the unspeakable, may also be understood in Etienne's text as the language of the obscene.[48] Similar to the use of Latin today that allows obscenity (naming anatomical parts, sexual activities, and sexual behavior in general) to be spoken in polite company,[49] Arabic may have served in the Middle Ages as a medium for verbalizing the silent, vile sin (*lei pechié*), safer precisely because it hides at the same time as it reveals, more effective than Latin would ever have been.

Finally, the very fact that the *Livre des manières* has been preserved in only one manuscript makes us wonder what its reception was in the Middle Ages. Did this text, because of its overt description of lesbianism, not enjoy a wider circulation in the Middle Ages, or on the contrary was it purposely destroyed *because* of its popularity? While the contemporary state of scholarship is unable to provide us with a clear answer to this question, it remains interesting nevertheless to speculate as to the reasons why most of the French texts that we will be examining in this project, texts that depict same-sex desire among women, have each been preserved in only one manuscript.

Interestingly, and in contrast, the medieval Arabic sexological tradition has for the most part been preserved in multiple manuscripts. This in itself is an indication that Arabic writings on alternative sexualities commanded tremendous respect from patrons in medieval courts and cities alike throughout the Islamicate world. Moreover, and again in contrast to the status of women and lesbians in the work of Etienne de Fougères, it appears as though in the Arabic tradition, lesbians regularly occupied a space (a chapter) in writings addressing the question of sexuality. Certainly, each of the Arabic texts under consideration devotes a much larger space to men and to male homosexuality than it does to women or lesbians. Nevertheless, lesbians remain visible in most of these Arabic texts; they consistently occupy an independent chapter that is labeled with as much clarity as other chapters within the same work. The very common strategy in Arabic writings of juxtaposing various forms of sexual practice, and of considering each of them as a literarily or culturally legitimate subject matter, indicates therefore that homosexuality, in opposition to its contemporary status in the European Middle Ages, was not simply viewed as an anomalous form of sexuality that required a separate (and ghettoized) treatment. Rather, throughout Arabic literary writings on sexualities, lesbianism was considered as one among multiple types of sexualities and consequently received both space and voice in the overall economy of a given text.

Conclusion

I hope to have demonstrated in this chapter the extent to which the first literary portrait of lesbian sexuality in the Old French tradition is indebted to the Arabic literary homoerotic tradition. Informed by key Arabic metaphorical, rhetorical, and linguistic conventions, Etienne de Fougères's depiction of lesbianism stands as a prime example of medieval cross-cultural writings and of East-West hybridity. Generally speaking, however, linguistic intertextuality such as the one we identified in Etienne de Fougères's text occurs relatively rarely in other medieval French texts. Despite the access of the West to Arabic homoerotic literature, it appears that there has been, because of the subject matter, a process of selective borrowing, or perhaps even at times of straight-out violent silencing, in the material that was absorbed. Those aspects of love and desire that dealt with male, but even more so, female homosexuality, were more readily rejected, especially from the twelfth century on, with the increasing tendency toward heteronormativity. One might say that some form of censorship took place at some level, though it is hard to pinpoint at which one—at the level of the translators, of the poets themselves, or of the scribes. What is evident, however, is the growing erasure of explicit literary metaphors and devices characteristic of Arabic lesbian desire from the Western homoerotic tradition. This does not imply by any means that the vernacular literatures of medieval France, especially those depicting lesbian sexuality, lacked Arabic resonances altogether. We will see in the following chapters that rather than borrowing specific sexual tropes or linguistic terminology from the Arabic tradition, medieval French authors more frequently resorted to Arabic tales and thematic motifs, invoked the growing imports of Eastern luxury material goods to medieval France, or depicted lesbian-like Eastern urban cultural practices. Thanks to these varied detours via the Islamicate literary, social, and cultural traditions, the medieval French lesbian enjoyed a literary existence in the Middle Ages, and medieval French writers, through the safety of Arabic intertextuality, perpetuated the "vile sin" and continued thus to speak the unspeakable.

CHAPTER THREE

Crossing Sartorial Lines

Female Same-Sex Marriage in *Yde et Olive* and
The Story of Qamar al-Zaman and Princess Boudour
from the *One Thousand and One Nights*

> *When, after all, is a kiss ever just a kiss?*
> —Carolyn Dinshaw

> *The presuppositions we make about sexed bodies . . . are suddenly and*
> *significantly upset by those examples that fail to comply with the*
> *categories that naturalize and stabilize that field of bodies for us within*
> *the terms of cultural conventions. Hence, the strange, the incoherent,*
> *that which falls "outside," gives us a way of understanding the taken-*
> *for-granted world of sexual categorization as a constructed one, indeed,*
> *as one that might be constructed differently.*
> —Judith Butler

IN COMPARISON TO the explicitness that characterizes accounts of lesbian
sexual practices in the Arabic tradition, very few French medieval literary
texts *explicitly* treat lesbianism or lesbian sexuality.[1] Much more frequently,
the medieval French literary tradition addresses the question of homosexuality and lesbianism via cross-dressing, a phenomenon that Michèle Perret
has dubbed second-degree homosexuality.[2] My goal in this chapter will be
to investigate these indirect manifestations of same-sex desire between

women in medieval writings. By focusing on instances of cross-dressing in a selection of Old French texts, we will see that female transvestism functioned as a textual/sexual strategy that permitted the exploration of same-sex desire between women. We will also see that crossing sartorial lines gave medieval French authors license to put into question (safely) the "naturalness" of gender roles and conventional paradigms of heterosexuality. Our reading will be complemented and enriched by an investigation of the complex web of intertextual resonances that medieval French works of cross-dressed heroines weave with Arabic tales of female transvestites. As we explore the ways in which some French narrators adapted, recast, and molded Arabic tales of cross-dressing to reflect the cultural milieu in which they lived and to suit the tastes of their largely aristocratic and Christian audience, we will uncover the censorship that some of the most explicit and ultimately threatening aspects of Arabic lesbianism underwent in the process. More significant than the parallels, the differences between the French and Arabic texts will be considered at the end of this chapter, as they reveal the divergent attitudes toward female same-sex love and unions in the two literary and cultural traditions.

Cross-Dressing and Second-Degree Homosexuality

If women cross-dressers were generally viewed with suspicion in both medieval Arabic and French history and chronicles,[3] the situation is more ambiguous in literary depictions of transvestism, where instances of cross-dressing are abundant. French fabliaux, miracle plays, and hagiographic literature offer striking examples of female to male cross-dressers.[4] In addition, the hero(ine) of several thirteenth- and fourteenth-century French romances is a woman disguised as a knight. The best-known examples include the character of Silence in *Le Roman de Silence*, the story of Blanchandine in *Tristan de Nanteuil*, and the story of Grisandole in *L'Estoire de Merlin*.[5]

Similarly, the Near Eastern tradition has an important history of female cross-dressers that dates back at least to the pre-Islamic era. The survival of some hadiths (sayings of the Prophet Mohammed) condemning effeminate men and masculinized women and of the names of famous cross-dressed women from the sixth and seventh centuries are all testimony to the fact that transvestites were prevalent from the early days of Islam.[6] Unfortunately, much of the poetry and literature written about these early transvestites has not been preserved. In fact, it is not until the Abbasid period (ca. 750) that the term *ghulamiyya* (pl. *ghulamiyyat*) is coined, a feminized form of the word *ghulam* (boy, slave, eunuch). The eighth-century poetry by Abu Nuwas (763–814) remains the most famous example of an entire literary genre (*ghulamiyyat*) in which the beloved is a woman (a female entertainer) dressed as a man.[7] Moreover, the tales of *Alf layla wa layla* (*One Thousand and One Nights*) and the Islamic and pre-Islamic Arabic folk romances (*siyar sha`biya*) offer countless examples of women warriors and Amazons. The story of Ibriza and Sharkan (embedded in the tale of King Umar al-Nu`man) in the *One Thousand and One Nights*; Princess `Ain al-Hayat in *Qissat Firuz Shah*; the characters of Queen al-Rabab, al-Ghayda', Gamra, and Nitra in the *Romance of `Antar*; Princess Fatima and Aluf in *Dhat al-Himma*; Princess Turban in *Hamza al-Bahlawan*; and the female army of Munyat al-Huda in the *Sirat Sayf ben Dhi Yazan* are just some of the most celebrated examples.[8]

The presence of one (or more) cross-dressed heroine(s) in both French and Arabic texts gives rise to a multitude of ambiguous situations and invites an exploration and an interrogation of gender, sexual hierarchy, and power relations. In these literary works, homosexuality is indeed represented "in the second degree" (to use the phrase coined by Michèle Perret) in the sense that it is usually only suggested, never truly actualized or addressed directly.

Cross-Dressing and Same-Sex Marriage Between Women

In this chapter, I focus on a subcategory of French and Arabic works on cross-dressing, more specifically on texts that combine female cross-dressing with same-sex marriage and that describe how a cross-dressed woman marries another woman. This particular combination (cross-dressing and female same-sex marriage) occurs in a small corpus of Old French texts, most notably in three works from three successive time periods that retell the same narrative, specifically the story of Yde and Olive:[9] (1) one of the mid-thirteenth-century sequels of the verse epic poem *Huon de Bordeaux*, known as *La Chanson d'Yde et Olive*;[10] (2) its late fourteenth-century dramatic adaptation known as the *Miracle de la fille d'un roy*;[11] and (3) its fifteenth-century French prose epic adaptation preserved in *Les prouesses et faicts du trespreux noble et vaillant Huon de Bordeaux, pair de France et Duc de Guyenne*.[12]

While some critics have traced the genealogy of these three French texts to the myth of *Iphis and Ianthe* in Ovid's *Metamorphoses*,[13] I propose to compare the three French Yde and Olive narratives (verse, play, and prose) to what I consider to be their main Arabic literary and cultural intertext, namely, one of the tales from *Alf layla wa layla* (*One Thousand and One Nights*), known as *The Story of Qamar al-Zaman and the Princess Boudour*. Although the earliest extant manuscript of *Alf layla wa layla* dates to the early fourteenth century (Paris, BN 3609–3611), thus later than the earliest Yde and Olive text, there is a growing body of evidence that suggests that some of its tales circulated much earlier in the East and in the West, both orally and in writing. Nabia Abbott for instance has uncovered the existence of a written version of the *Arabian Nights* in the ninth century.[14] Similarly, al-Qurti (1160–71) writes about a famous collection of stories, known as the *One Thousand and One Nights*, at the end of the twelfth century; this collection is said to have circulated in Fatimid Egypt in the twelfth century.[15] And as scholars have now demonstrated, some of the tales from *Alf layla wa layla* were known in Europe as early as the first quarter of the twelfth century, translated into Latin, and woven into Petrus Alfonsi's *Disciplina Clericalis* (1120s).[16]

While the current state of scholarship does not provide us with any information concerning the transmission history of the tale of *Qamar al-Zaman and the Princess Boudour* which is of interest here, it is possible to assume nevertheless that it must have been familiar to both Eastern and Western audiences, as it is one of the eleven stories that made up the original nucleus of *Alf layla wa layla*.[17] In the absence of a written manuscript of this tale dating earlier than the fourteenth century, we may assume that its circulation was oral, like that of many tales of the Arabic storytelling tradition. In fact, because of the framed narrative structure of *Alf layla wa layla*, because it is a storytelling tradition, and because of its use of the dialect (instead of the high register of Arabic), the tales it contained often enjoyed a parallel oral circulation. As we will see, the tale of *Qamar al-Zaman and the Princess Boudour* offers numerous striking resonances with the French Yde and Olive narratives (as well as with Jean Renart's *Escoufle* which we will examine in the next two chapters) and invites us thus to expand our understanding of the literary encounters between the Arabic and French traditions. Tales from the Orient crossed the borders into Europe not necessarily written down and bound in a manuscript, but more often as oral stories heard in the Middle East, in Sicily or al-Andalus and repeated in multiple ways by different travelers. Their traces are more marked in some Old French texts than in others; but, as we will see, they can always be detected through cross-cultural comparative analysis.

The Yde and Olive Stories: Verse, Play, and Prose Renditions

Despite some key differences to which I will return shortly, the French Yde and Olive texts (verse, play, and prose) all tell a very similar story.[18] Yde's parents, King Florent of Aragon and Queen Esclarmonde, after many prayers to God and the Virgin Mary, finally conceive a daughter named Yde in the verse epic (Ysabel in the miracle play; Ide in the prose narrative). Yde's mother dies in childbirth and her father, still grieving some fifteen years later, decides to marry his own daughter since she alone among all women resembles her mother perfectly.[19] Yde, horrified at this incestuous plan, runs away dressed as man, and adopts the name of Ydé,[20] in order to avoid being recognized. The text then recounts the various adventures and challenges that the cross-dressed Ydé/Ysabel/Ide faces and overcomes, the details of which differ somewhat in the epic, play, and prose renditions. In the verse and prose epic versions, the cross-dressed heroine finally arrives in Rome where s/he successfully leads the king's army against the Spaniards who attacked his lands.[21] After one year, King Oton of Rome[22] decides to compensate Ydé/Ysabel/Ide by making her/him his heir and marrying her/him to his daughter (Olive) who, we are told, loves the cross-dressed knight. Ydé/Ysabel/Ide laments her fate but seeing no alternative, puts herself in God's hands. The wedding is celebrated. While in the play, Ysabel confesses her true sex to her wife on their wedding night, in the verse and prose texts, Ydé/Ide feigns at first an illness, but some fifteen days later, not able to think of any other pretext, confides her true identity to Olive who promises to keep her secret. Their conversation is overheard,[23] however, and both women are denounced to the king. In order to ascertain the truth of this revelation and before rushing to burn them both at the stake as his advisors recommend, the king sends for the two women and orders a ritual bath in which Ydé/Ysabel/Ide must bathe naked. At this point in the epic, an angel descends from heaven and announces that God has transformed Ydé/Ysabel/Ide into a man. The angel also predicts the king's imminent death, and the birth of Croissant, the son of Ydé/Ide and Olive.

In the play, the ending is more convoluted: God himself, who had already personally intervened on various occasions earlier in the text on behalf of Ysabel, sends Saint Michael disguised as a white stag to divert the witnesses from the bath. The angel reassures Ysabel about disrobing for the bath, revealing to her that God will reward her faith in him. The emperor, seeing that Ysabel indeed has the requisite male sexual organs, blesses the union of the couple. He also does not punish the monk who had revealed to him the same-sex marriage, thanks to the timely and combined intervention of God and the Virgin Mary. Ysabel's sexual transformation is not permanent in the miracle play, however, since the story ends with Ysabel's return to her former biological sex and with the double wedding of Ysabel to the emperor of Constantinople and of the emperor's daughter to Ysabel's father.

Several critics have noted the obvious interrogation of gender roles and of sexual identities that the three versions of the Yde and Olive narratives invite.[24] Obviously, they all destabilize the foundation of heteronormativity and challenge the notion of a stable binary sexuality. This effect is not achieved through cross-dressing alone, but by adding one transgression to another: cross-dressing, same-sex marriage, and transsexual (transgender) transformation. The impact of each of these disruptive elements is greatly intensified by their simultaneous presence in the text and is a manifestation of what Marjorie Garber has dubbed "the third term," which is not a term, much less a "sex," but rather "a mode of articulation, a way of describing a space of possibility. Three puts into question the idea of one: of identity, self-sufficiency, self-knowledge."[25] Sexual identity is here expanded beyond the heteronormative binary.

Crossing Sartorial Lines: Social and Linguistic Disruptions

I will add that the Yde and Olive narratives (in the verse and prose epic versions, more so than in the dramatic adaptation) also disrupt social norms and class hierarchy.[26] With each gender/sexual transgression, social and class categories are subverted. When Yde cross-dresses in order to escape from her father's incestuous desires and plans, she introduces a "category crisis," thus exposing "a failure of definitional distinction."[27] By cross-dressing and leaving home, Yde must put aside both her gender and her social standing as daughter of the king. In the verse and prose texts, and in contrast to the miracle play, Yde is often described as hungry, she associates with lower socioeconomic classes (the thieves in particular), and she even works as a squire for a German soldier.[28] Yde's social descent is powerfully articulated by the narrator of the thirteenth-century verse epic: "On l'a servie, mais ore servira" ("She used to serve; but now she herself will serve").[29] The symmetrical rhythm of this sentence (which has no equivalent in the miracle play), combined with the opposition between the past tense and passive voice on the one hand ("on l'a servie") and the future and active voice on the other ("servira") highlight Yde's social transformation from a princess who was waited on and respected to a lowly servant, completely dependent upon others' good wishes.

It is also interesting to note that in the thirteenth-century verse epic, like in the fifteenth-century prose rendition, social decline is accompanied by linguistic transformation, if not decay. Once cross-dressed, Yde uses a linguistic register that is becoming to her new and lower social status, utterly discordant with her previous princely state. When she fights the Saracen army, Yde yells: "A mort, chiennaille, / A mort, a mort!" ("die, pack of dogs, / die, die").[30] Even as it functions as a rallying cry to her army reminiscent of the epic genre, the use of the word "chiennaille" shocks the reader in the context of an epic where the hero(ine) had been described only lines earlier as "Damoiselle Yde" ("the maiden Yde") and "la bele" ("the fair one").[31] This radical change in linguistic registers, of which there is no evidence in the miracle play, becomes even more pronounced in the prose epic version, composed two centuries later. There, once Ide faces alone the thirty thieves in the midst of the forest, she yells to her opponents: "Fils de putains" ("Sons of bitches").[32] Such terminology, common in the Middle Ages in the context of aggressive male confrontations and in literary encounters between Christians and Saracens,[33] sounds discordant when placed in the mouth of a heroine whom the narrator continues to describe through feminine characteristics ("damoiselle," "la bele," "noble pucelle"). Nevertheless, such dissonance underscores the fact that as Yde/Ide transgresses one set of boundaries (by adopting male garb), she transgresses her socioeconomic class as well, with its attending linguistic decorum. She thereby reconfigures social, linguistic, and sexual identities previously conceived of as stable and unchallengeable and calls into question their inviolability.[34]

Cross-dressing and Female Homoeroticism

Furthermore, throughout the Yde and Olive texts, and in the verse and prose epic versions especially, cross-dressing gives rise to ambiguous situations in which the expression of female homoeroticism becomes possible. Staging a cross-dressed Yde/Ide allows the narrator to depict (safely) Olive's emotional attachment and erotic attraction.[35] In fact, in the fifteenth-century prose text, as soon as she lays eyes on Ide, Olive is immediately attracted to her/him: "moult volontiers la demoiselle Olive la regardoit si la print en son Coeur moult fort à aimer" ("Lady Olive enjoyed looking at her so much that she began to love her very much in her heart").[36] The use of the feminine direct object pronoun "la" in this sentence renders explicit the lesbian erotic attraction, even if the latter is evident only to the reader, not to Olive herself. The association of seeing and loving repeats the conventional rhetoric of love, familiar in the West at least since Andreas Capellanus's twelfth-century *De amore* (*The Art of Courtly Love*), and in the East with Ibn Da'ud's (ca. 868–910) *Kitab al-zahra* (The Book of the Flower) and Ibn Hazm's (994–1064) *Tauq al-hamama fi al-ulfa wa al-ullaf* (*The Ring of the Dove*).[37] As such, it may be considered part of an effort to portray the nascent same-sex desire between women (for which no readily available language existed) on the same model as that of the more familiar heterosexual courtly love.

While the thirteenth-century verse epic does not explicitly portray Olive's love at first sight for the cross-dressed Yde, it too underscores Olive's pleasurable gaze and suggests that it may well be an erotic one:

Olive l'a volentiers esgardee.	Olive enjoyed looking at her.[38]
Et Yde proie a la Vierge honoree	Yde prays to the blessed Virgin
Qu'ele le gart que ne soit acusee,	To protect him from being accused,
U se ce non, elle iert a mort livree.	For if she were, she would be put to death.
(vv. 6910–13)	

In these lines, it is impossible to discern with certainty what causes Yde's fears: Is she anxious over the discovery of her cross-dressing and its likely punishment? Or is her fear linked to Olive's pleasurable gaze? The anxiety described here is so great that it leads to grammatical confusion: The use of the direct object pronoun "le" where one expects "la" in Yde's prayer to the Virgin (v. 6912) reveals the extent to which same-sex desire shakes the very foundation of language. The juxtaposition of Olive's gaze and Yde's fear of being incriminated suggests that the reader might in fact be witnessing a nascent attraction of one woman toward another. If Yde is scared, it may well be because she has seen Olive's gaze on her, she has sensed Olive's desire, a desire that she perhaps also shares. Therefore, even though these verses do not explicitly state that Olive is attracted to Yde (as the fifteenth-century prose text will do), we are permitted nevertheless to interpret them as suggesting precisely that.

The intimate link between seeing and loving is reiterated, both in the thirteenth-century verse text and its fifteenth-century rendition a few pages later, when after witnessing Yde/Ide's prowess against the Spanish army first-hand from her window, Olive's initial attraction becomes full-fledged love. This is how this scene is described in the thirteenth-century verse text:

Yde fu mout resgardee et coisie,	Yde was much looked at and noticed,
Car des crestiax l'avoit veüe Olive.	For Olive had seen her from the windows.
Trestous li cors de joie li fourmie	Her entire body throbbed with pleasure
Et dist em bas, c'on nel e[n]tendi mie:	And she said in a low voice, so that no one could hear
"Mes amis iert. Ains demain li voel dire.	"He will be my friend. I want to tell him so tomorrow.
Ains mais ne fui d'omme si entreprise,	I have never been so taken by a man,
S'est bien raisons et drois que je li die."	It is right and fair that I tell him."
(vv. 7024–30)	

This scene, which will be repeated almost verbatim two centuries later in the fifteenth-century prose version, uncovers Olive's mounting desire for Yde and her plans to effect their union.[39] Olive's love is especially interesting to note because of its physical portrayal: "Trestous li cors de joie li fourmie" ("Her entire body throbbed with pleasure") (v. 7026).[40] The term "joie" ("pleasure") combined with the verb "fourmie" ("throb") exposes the very sensual, if not sexual dimension of Olive's desire.[41] Her desire is not simply homoerotic; it is sexual, in fact orgasmic. In addition, Olive's desire in the verse epic gives rise to an enterprising spirit, an active stance, and a deliberate mind. Olive never considers keeping her feelings secret; she does not envision being, like so many troubadours before her, a lover from afar. Rather, she deliberately plans on sharing her thoughts and her love with the worthy knight (Yde).

Olive's gaze from the window and her placement as a witness to Yde/Ide's chivalric deeds are significant because they portray the nascent same-sex love and desire between women on the same model as conventional heterosexual courtly scenarios. As a matter of fact, if Yde/Ide had been a biological male, Olive's gaze from the window, her admiration of her/his chivalrous deeds, and her ensuing love, as depicted here, would have been nothing more than another instance of the conventional courtly love that a princess feels for a worthy warrior. They would only be repeating multiple other scenes from well-known medieval romances in which fair maidens pine away for victorious knights and long to be united with them.[42] Such is the case, for instance, of Chrétien de Troyes's *Lancelot* where Queen Guenevere and her maidens marvel at the prowess of he who "carried the red shield" ("qui porte l'escu vermeil"), namely, Lancelot.[43] This is how the narrator describes the scene:

Et lor volentez est commune	They all had the same wish
Si qu'avoir le voldroit	Which is to have him each for
chascune;	herself;
Et l'une est de l'autre jalouse	And each is jealous of the other
Si con s'ele fust ja	As if she was already married
s'espouse,	to him.
Por ce que si adroit	This is because they find him
le voient	so skilled
Qu'eles ne pansent ne	That they do not
ne croient	believe
Que nus d'armes, tant lor	That anyone could do
pleisoit,	in arms
Poïst ce feire qu'il	What this one did, so much did
fesoit.	he please them.
(vv. 6025–32)	

Such a scenario is likely to have been familiar to the fifteenth-century audience of the Yde and Olive prose text, just as it would have been to its late thirteenth-century verse epic public. Both audiences are likely to have perceived the parallel that the scene of female erotic attraction in Yde and Olive draws with conventional courtly romance episodes in which maidens extol the extraordinary deeds of knights and are smitten with love for them. Olive's admiration and growing love for Yde/Ide is clearly aligned with heterosexual courtly conventions such as these.

However, and at the same time, Olive's attachment is utterly unsettling for it is not directed toward a man, as one would have expected, but rather toward another woman. Of course, Olive does not know that the man she loves is a woman, nor is she aware of the fact that the feelings she expresses transform her unwittingly into a lesbian.[44] Nevertheless, and notwithstanding Olive's ignorance, this scene demonstrates how in the medieval West, same-sex desire between women was constructed on the heterosexual model as courtly love. Equally important, Olive's homoerotic attraction questions the very idea that courtly love is necessarily or even exclusively heterosexual. Her example raises the very intriguing possibility that courtly love may not have always been commensurable with heterosexuality, and, therefore, that it might more fruitfully be understood as an androcentric system of structuring gender relations. As such, courtly love could function at times as an unsuspected system for the expression of same-sex desire between women in medieval Europe.

In addition to depicting Olive's desire in sensual, if not sexual, terms, and in addition to portraying her as an active, enterprising character, the thirteenth-century verse epic goes one step further in its account of same-sex love. It calls into question the presumed heterosexuality of marital unions. If Ysabel in the miracle play and Ide in the fifteenth-century prose text both agree to marry Olive without raising any objections other than their supposedly lower socio-economic class, Yde in the thirteenth-century epic poses yet another condition before agreeing to conclude the marriage:

Ains le prendrai volentiers et
    de gré
Se il li plaist et il li vient
    en gré.
(vv. 7074–75)

I will marry him happily and
    willingly
If it pleases him/her, and if s/he
    is willing.

Yde's request to obtain Olive's consent before concluding the marriage is striking not least because of the confusion in grammatical gender it entails. Even though it is Yde, and not Olive, who is the cross-dressed character, Olive is the one in the above lines who is depicted as grammatically male (v. 7074). Yde's appeal to receive Olive's (depicted as male) consent thus bespeaks the effort made to construct the same-sex marriage as a relation between a masculine pronoun (Olive) and a female character (Yde). The confusion over the main characters' genders is further reflected in the grammatical inconsistency that is highlighted in the following line where Olive is mentioned as both male and female. Continuing the tradition of Alain de Lille's *Natura*, same-sex desire is clearly associated here with grammatical perversion.[45]

Furthermore, the mere invocation of Olive's consent ineluctably situates the entire discussion of the same-sex union within the important marriage debate that raged throughout the twelfth century. This controversy, which pitted the church against the aristocracy, ended with the official establishment of the spouses' consent as the sine qua non for a valid Christian marriage.[46] Ironically, the significant changes that marriage underwent in the twelfth century from an aristocratic, family, and economic affair to a private, consensual association between spouses opened up an unsuspected space for the expression of same-sex unions, validated automatically when they are freely accepted. That Yde should solicit (and receive) Olive's consent to the proposed marriage thus places the same-sex union between women within the parameters of church legislation, validates their homosexual relation, and transforms it into a sacrament. In the *Yde et Olive* verse epic, just as homosexual desire is modeled on courtly love, same-sex union is modeled on church-sanctioned marriage.

Even though Ide in the fifteenth-century prose text does not require Olive's consent to finalize the same-sex union, the narrator highlights the irony of a lesbian marriage cloaked in aristocratic ceremonials, typical of heterosexual marriage: "depuis que Rome avoit esté premierement fondee ne fut sçeu que si grande feste y fu faicte, comme elle fut à l'assemblee des deux pucelles, dont on cuidoit que Ide fu homme" ("Ever since Rome was founded, there was never as great a celebration as there was for the wedding of the two maidens, for it was believed that Ide was a man").[47] Such an account of the marriage festivities cannot fail to elicit the reader's smile, for, here, the wedding celebration—the sign par excellence of official, social, public, and spiritual endorsement of heterosexuality—is precisely the very moment that irrevocably sanctions the lesbian relationship. That this should occur in Rome, the very seat of the church, and at the wedding of the daughter of the emperor himself, adds an even greater level of irony and playfulness to the entire scene.

Religious Sentiments and Same-Sex Love

Cross-dressing is not the only strategy that permits the exploration of same-sex desire in the Yde and Olive narratives. Religious sentiments become an equally fruitful space for the expression of female homoeroticism. While the heavy emphasis on religious concerns in the three versions of the story works on the one hand to deflect one's attention from the significant female homo-erotic subtext that is expressed therein, it also serves to highlight it.[48]

In the fourteenth-century dramatic adaptation, *Miracle de la fille d'un roy*, the interweaving of the religious with the homoerotic is perhaps best illus-trated when God in person intervenes to give Ysabel permission to marry and share her legally wedded wife's bed. God's validation of the same-sex marriage and of bed sharing is repeated three times in the play. First by God himself who charges Saint Michael to transmit the following message to Ysabel:

Et de par moy tu li diras	And you will tell him/her this from me
Que plus ne s'esmaie ne doubte,	That s/he should not fear nor doubt,
Mais dedans sa chambre se boute	But that s/he should enter into his/her room
Et se couche avec s'espousée.	And sleep/lie down with her wife.
(vv. 2438–41)	

The same message will be repeated a few lines later by Saint Michael to Ysabel (vv. 2452–53), and again by Ysabel herself to her faithful servant Anne (vv. 2478–79). Even though this message is intended to reassure Ysabel, it could have unsettled members of the medieval audience who may not have been familiar with the end of the narrative and who may not yet have known that the play would revert ultimately to heteronormativity. The grammatical gender ambiguity in God's own mouth is indeed striking. Since Old French (like modern French) does not distinguish between the masculine and femi-nine indirect object pronouns and uses *li* in both cases, and considering the fact that the play recounts a same-sex relationship, God's message may not have been reassuring after all. Could his words be interpreted to sanction the same-sex relationship between the two women? Even as God's advice to Ys-abel was intended to teach people to trust in God's mysterious ways, it must have also appeared for some members of the audience as an unexpected and threatening validation of same-sex love, if not of same-sex unions.

Similarly, in the thirteenth-century verse epic, Yde's reaction to the idea

of the same-sex marriage imposed upon her weaves together religious sentiments and homoerotic attraction:

Nostre Seignour a sovent reclamé:	She called often onto our Lord:
"Glorious Dix, qui mains en Trinité,	"Glorious God, who lives in Trinity,
De ceste lasse cor vous prengne pités,	Take pity on this weary body/heart,
Cui il convient par force marïer."	Who has to get married by force."
(vv. 7105–8)	

These lines certainly imply that were she allowed to choose, Yde would
not intentionally engage in the same-sex relationship that is about to take
place. The adverb "par force" in line 7108 underscores the fact that Yde, as a
dutiful Christian woman, would not knowingly uphold homoeroticism but
would actively champion heterosexuality. After all, Yde is *forced* into this marriage; she is *forced* into an alternative sexual relation; she is *forced* into actions
she herself decries.

At the same time, it is not possible to deny the overall ambiguity of religious sentiments over the status of lesbianism in this passage. In line 7107
above, the term "cor," meaning both heart *and* body, leads the reader to question Yde's emotional stance: Is Yde really *forced* into marriage with Olive as the
adverb "par force" suggests? Or is she experiencing erotic feelings towards her
soon-to-be legally wedded wife and is thus seeking God's succor?[49] The recourse to the religious motif here underscores, rather than eliminates the subversive sexual element. Such an interpretation corroborates recent scholarly
findings about the insertion of erotic expression in the midst of the most spir-
itually charged discursive moments both in Christianity and Islam (especially
in sufi literature).[50]

Yet, these textual spaces that invite an interrogation of gender roles and
of sociosexual identities must be seen as only a temporary interlude within the
economy of a text that ultimately affirms heterosexual norms and traditional
gender hierarchy (and social relations). As a matter of fact, even though the
Yde and Olive stories describe a same-sex union, that is a disruption of the
"normalcy" of heterosexual marriage, and despite the mental transgressive

"residue" that the text may leave in the mind of the audience,[51] binary hetero-sexual relations are ultimately upheld and validated.

The Wedding Night

The interlacing of the erotic and the religious in the fourteenth-century dra-matic adaptation, *Miracle de la fille d'un roy*, in contrast to the verse and prose epic versions of Yde and Olive, abruptly comes to an end on the wedding night which resolutely splits both discourses and subordinates the sexual to the religious. After praying with Anne and after being reassured by Saint Michael about the ultimate preservation of her honor (vv. 2472–85), Ysabel is only temporarily comforted. Distressed a few moments later, she turns to the Virgin Mary seeking guidance: "Doulce mére Dieu, que feray?" ("Sweet Mother of Jesus, what shall I do?") (v. 2562). Then, as though to preclude any sexually jeopardizing encounter with her newly wedded wife, and to avoid any potentially ambiguous and theologically compromising situation, Ysabel does not wait for fifteen days, like her homologue in the verse and prose epic ver-sions, to reveal the truth of her sex. She opts rather for immediate disclosure:

Dame, en vostre mercy me met.	Lady, I place myself in your mercy.
Pour le confort que m'avez fait,	For the comfort you showed me,
Vous vueil descouvrir tout mon fait	I want to reveal to you my entire story
Et ce pour quoy j'ay tel annuy.	And the reason why I feel such discomfort.
Sachiez conme vous femme suy,	Know that I am a woman like you,
Fille de roy et de royne.	Daughter of a king and a queen.
. . . . .	. . . . .
Et pour moy garder de diffame	And in order to protect myself from dishonor
Ne me sui point monstrée fame,	I did not show myself as a woman,
Mais conme homme m'ay maintenu,	But have dressed (or acted/appeared) as a man,

Et Dieu m'a si bien
    soustenu
	And God has helped me so
	    much

Et donné de sa grace
    tant
	And given me so much of his
	    grace

Qu'en lieu n'ay esté combatant	That in no place have I fought
Dont je n'aye eu la victoire,	Where I was not successful.

Dont je ly rens loenge et
    gloire.
	For this I give him thanks and
	    glory.

Or savez conment il
    m'est, dame,
	Now you know how it is with
	    me, my Lady,

Puis que je sui conme
    vous femme
	That I am a woman,
	    like you

Et que j'ai mamelles:
    tastez.
	And that I have breasts:
	    Feel them.

Pour Dieu
    mercy, . . .
	Have mercy on me, for God's
	    sake, . . .

(vv. 2581–608)	

In these lines, gender and social class are once again linked, though they are now in inverse relation to what we saw earlier: Ysabel's confession of her biological sex ("femme suy") is intimately associated with the revelation of her high social status ("Fille de roy et de royne"). This double exposure eliminates all suspense from the play, as the heroine is shielded henceforth from any social fall and sexual or carnal temptation. At this moment, and despite the preceding textual spaces devoted to cross-dressing, the text sides with the promotion of heteronormativity. Ysabel punctuates her entire confession with references to her infinite faith in God, her submission to his will, and her undeviating preoccupation with honor and reputation. Her proposition to her wife to touch her breasts ("mamelles") to ascertain the truth of the fact that her husband is in fact a woman (v. 2607), while suggestive, shifts the reader/viewer's attention from the visual to the tactile, all the while highlighting the deceptive nature of sight.[52] Gender as established by sight is revealed no longer to be *historia*, but *fabula*, a lie, a discursive construction.

The move from seeing to touching in an effort to reach some measure of "truth," or gender stability, is not taken up by the emperor's daughter. The proposition to touch the "mamelles" remains at the level of rhetorical, intellectual subversion of gender construction; it is not permitted to become a potentially intimate moment between the spouses. The emperor's daughter's response is interesting in this respect:

De ce ne convient plus parler.	There is no need to speak further of this.
Or vous mettez hors de soussi,	Put yourself at ease,
Car tout ce que m'avez dit cy	Because everything you have told me here
Je vous promet bien celeray,	I promise to conceal,
Et tel honneur vous porteray	And I will show you such honor
Con doit faire a son mari femme.	As a woman must show her husband.
En touz cas, ce vous jur par m'ame,	In all matters, I swear this upon my soul,
Ne ne vous aray ja mains chier.	Nor will I ever hold you less dear.[53]
(vv. 2612–19)	

It is certainly possible to interpret these lines as an endorsement of severely condemned forms of sexuality, as Robert Clark and Claire Sponsler have suggested.[54] After all, the emperor's daughter indicates that biological sex does not matter and that she is ready to uphold the sacrament of marriage despite the new information provided. I will add, however, that the emperor's daughter's response also works to maintain the ideology of phallocentrism and heterosexuality. The promise to continue to "honor" Ysabel as she would have, had Ysabel indeed been a man, maintains the emperor's daughter in a subordinate position not only in relation to biological masculinity, but also, and more importantly here, to any socially constructed or outward manifestation of masculinity.

The wedding night scene is markedly different in the thirteenth-century verse and fifteenth-century prose renditions of the story, where the reader senses the narrator's struggle between conformity to religious and social norms and the titillating temptation to describe the sexual proximity (if not promiscuity) of two women in bed. In the Yde and Olive verse and prose epics, the wedding night is not devoid of sexual content. First, and despite her understandable distress, Yde/Ide begins by "securely locking the door" ("la cambre a bien veroullié et fermee").[55] She then pretends to be ill, thus incapable of consummating their marriage that night. As Yde/Ide tells Olive of her sickness, she accompanies her words with hugs: "With these words, Olive was hugged" ("A ices mos fu Olive accollee").[56] The verb "accollee" (to hug) is repeated twice more in that same scene (for a total of three times), the next time by Olive. Let us note here that it is Olive, and not Yde/Ide, who pleads to have their wedding consummation put off for fifteen days after all the guests have left, saying that she is looking forward to "doing more" later; for now, she will be satisfied with kisses and with being "accolee":

Fors du baisier bien voel estre accolee,	Besides kissing, I don't mind hugs
Mais de l'amour c'on dist qui est privee	But as to the love that is said to be intimate
Vous requier jou que soie deportee.	I request to be exempt from it.
(vv. 7185–87)	

Relieved, Yde/Ide agrees, and the narrator adds that the two women kiss and hug: "They kissed and hugged each other" ("Dont ont l'un l'autre baisie et accollee").[57] Because nothing in the verse or prose epic specifies the kind of kiss or hug exchanged between the two women (sisterly? compassionate? respectful?), the reader must wonder what meaning to accord these affective acts: Do they represent conventional cultural practices in the Middle Ages, as often occurred between men to denote courtesy, peace, hospitality, or affirmation of feudal relations?[58] Or do these hugs and kisses between the two women have a sexual valence and are charged with an erotic subtext? In order to understand the meaning of "baisier" and "accoller" in this scene, we must compare them to their usage earlier in the text, where they had been invoked at several key moments to describe Yde's father's incestuous love for his daughter: "Mout souvent l'a accollee et baisie" ("he hugged and kissed her often").[59] At that time, the words "baisie" and "accollee" had been glossed by the narrator when reporting the barons' concern over their king's illegitimate behavior:

S'il le tenoit en sa cambre a celee,	If he had held her in a private room,
Ja ne seroit de Florent deportee	Florent would not have delayed
Qu'il nel eüst tantost despucelee.	He would have deflowered her immediately.
(vv. 6429–31)	

In these lines, the narrator points out the implicit sexual meaning of the king's actions.[60] If outwardly he hugs and kisses his daughter, his true wish is to enjoy her sexually, if not deflower her ("despucelee"). In other words, and from the very beginning of *Yde et Olive*, the reader has been warned that a kiss is *not* always *just* a kiss. Armed with this wider semantic range of meanings of affective acts, the reader must wonder whether the hidden, sexual connotations of "hugging" and "kissing" apply to Yde and Olive's encounters. Are their hugs and kisses to be read as an implicit affirmation of their sexual union?

This is what Diane Watt has suggested.[61] Without going as far, it is crucial to recognize nevertheless the sexual undercurrent of the words "baisier" and "accollee" for they may well have been key signifiers of lesbian sexuality in medieval Western literature. Far from being vaginal or focused on penetration, the expression of erotic encounters between women in the European Middle Ages appropriated and subverted the conventional terminology of affective relations.[62]

The likely sexual meaning of the signifiers "baisier" and "accollee" to depict Yde and Olive's encounter during their wedding night is supported by the following two lines from the thirteenth-century verse epic that appear to have disturbed some (medieval) scribes or readers. They are indeed partly (purposely?) effaced and are supplied by other manuscript readings:[63]

En cele nuit n'i [ot] cri ne mellee.	That night, there were no screams or fights.
La nu[i]s passa, si revint la journee.	The night ended, and the day shone.
(vv. 7191–92)	

The silence over the details of the wedding night of the female couple is a textual strategy that speaks eloquently of the efforts made to keep the sexual and the titillating representation of lesbianism bracketed. The homoerotic is not entirely silenced, however, as is evident in the use of the demonstrative "*that* night" to point to the lack of violence of the lesbian wedding night in which there were no screams or fights, in contrast perhaps to the heterosexual wedding night in which there may have been screams and fights. Not least, the (possibly) consummated lovemaking of Yde and Olive is implied in the use of battle metaphors ("cri ne mellee") that, as shown in Chapter 2, may well refer to the homosexual (military) language borrowed from the Arabic tradition. Finally, when King Oton asks his daughter about her wedding night, Olive's answer is conveniently ambiguous:

"Fille," fait il, "comment iés mariee?"	"Daughter," he said, "How is it to be married?"
"Sire," dist ele, "ensi com moi agree."	"Sire," she said, "the way I like it" (or "the way it pleases me.")
(vv. 7198–99)[64]	

But ultimately, Yde (just like Ide two centuries later) reveals her biological sex to Olive in the midst of apologies and prayers for mercy.[65] The affective transgressive dimension that had been present, however timidly and metaphorically, is henceforth banned altogether from the text. The text appropriates the cross-dresser as female, and erases completely the "third term" that had been introduced earlier in the epic.

Triumph of Heteronormativity

In the thirteenth-century verse epic, like in its fifteenth-century prose rendition, but in contrast to the fourteenth-century miracle play, the recuperation of the potential lesbian and her integration into heterosexuality begins with Olive's initial reaction to the revelation that her husband is in fact a woman:

Olive l'ot, s'en fu espoëntee. (v. 7216)	Olive listened, she was horrified.

In the prose text, the narrator writes, "Quant Olive entendit Ide: elle fust moult dolente" ("When Olive heard Ide, she was very miserable").[66] Curiously, Olive's distress has been greatly de-emphasized by critics. Yet, it echoes the Deuteronomic injunction against transvestism (Deut. 22:5) and reveals social anxiety about the dissolution of boundaries. Yde's/Ide's cross-dressing, which was threatening because it blurred or obliterated legible gender distinctions, is henceforth annihilated by Olive's reaction. Olive's normative voice utterly silences the transgressive preceding section and signals the return to sanctioned sexual and grammatical categories.[67]

The restoration of the normative is also heralded by the daring act of naming the same-sex love between women that had been portrayed. For indeed, and only in the fifteenth-century prose text, the narrator alludes to Yde and Olive's relation as "bougrerie," the early modern appellation for sodomy.[68] The usage of this term is especially noteworthy because it is one of its earliest occurrences in French. It is used already here in a legal and penal sense, and is associated with capital punishment.[69] Labeling the silent sin "bougrerie" in the fifteenth-century French text is thus tantamount to proclaiming Yde and Olive's death sentence, indeed the classic penalty for lesbians under the *lex foedissimam* (edict of Roman law) of 1400.[70]

Furthermore, the return to heteronormativity is ushered in through the appearance of an angel who reveals God's personal intervention in Yde's/Ide's affairs, and her timely sexual transformation into a man.[71] But perhaps even more important, the return to heteronormativity is affirmed by the angel's announcement that Yde/Ide and Olive successfully conceive a son named Croissant that very night:

> Et en cel jour fu Croissans
>   engenrés.
> (v. 7283)[72]

> On this day, Croissant was
>   conceived.

Clearly, not only does Yde/Ide receive a penis to reward her for her unswerving belief in God and her submission to his will, but it is a well functioning one too, we are swiftly reassured, as is evident in the efficiency with which the conception of the child occurs. The angel's statement is not simply a premonition; it is a speech act. Revealing the miracle is accompanied by its accomplishment. Croissant's conception is so significant that it takes narrative precedence over any information the audience may have hoped for about Yde's/Ide's successful sexual transformation. The transsexual miracle is far less amazing than it may appear at first sight however, for according to Western Galenic medical theories, it was believed that women's sexual organs were identical to men's, except they were inverted (the vagina was thought to be an inverted penis).[73] However, from the perspective of the audience of the epic or drama, most of whom were probably *not* familiar with premodern theories of medicine, it can be argued that an explicit depiction of the transsexual transformation might have been desired, if not expected. Such a description, in contrast to its Ovidian textual precursor, is absent however from all the stories that have preserved the Yde/Ide and Olive tale.[74] We do not see the growth of the penis on Yde's/Ide's body, which is especially surprising in the narrative economy of the epic, where the narrator had not shied away from elaborately describing Yde's/Ide's female body.[75] We do not hear Yde's/Ide's reaction to the unexpected "gift" of the penis. Is she shocked? Relieved? Surprised at least? Did she even want to be a man?[76] The question of gender identity is subsumed under that of sex; it is unproblematized as though it did not matter, or rather as if it was expected that Yde/Ide of course would have wanted to be a man if given a choice. After all, according to the theological and scientific teachings of the time, if given a choice, any woman would have wished to be a man.

In both the epic and prose versions of *Yde et Olive*, perhaps because they are concerned primarily with the question of lineage and with the foregrounding of marriage and procreation, there is a lingering presumption that male is better, that to wish to be a man (however unexplicitly or unconsciously since Yde/Ide never verbalizes such a longing), is perfectly "normal" and, culturally speaking, perfectly logical. Obviously, these assumptions undermine whatever disruption of, and challenge to, easy notions of binarism that transvestism may have invited at first reading. Underlying this assumption of male supremacy, women are scapegoated. The challenge or threat posed by cross-dressing is henceforth contained, as the epic moves unproblematically to the continuation of the Huon de Bordeaux family line. Diane Watt points out the advantages of such a narrative resolution for the male characters and in the context of an epic; in effect, such a resolution "provides not just Oton but also Florent [Yde's father] with a direct male descendant and thus enables the transmission of both their property according to the rules of patrilineage."[77] For the female characters however, the very possibility of alternative sexualities is scapegoated. The symbolic function of "transvestism *as* a powerful agent of destabilization and change, the sign of the *un*groundedness of identities on which social structures and hierarchies depend" is conveniently set aside and subordinated to genealogy and social heteronormativity.[78]

Finally, it is important to note the narrative construction of the epic and the way the story of Croissant is embedded within two sections both dealing with Yde/Ide and Olive (known in contemporary scholarship as *Yde et Olive I* and *Yde et Olive II*). The choice of ending the first part of Yde and Olive precisely at the moment of the sexual transformation and the birth of Croissant, and of returning to that story only about four hundred lines later is significant because it points to the narrator's effort to divert the audience's attention from sexuality to social normativity and sexual legitimacy. Just as the narrative had moved swiftly over the momentarily erotic behavior of the newlyweds, we note that immediately following Yde's/Ide's successful and rewarding sexual transformation, and immediately after Croissant's birth and his reaching his twelfth birthday (summarized in one line), the heterosexual couple leaves Rome to visit Yde's father, King Florent: "Congié ont pris, n'i ont plus atendu" ("They took leave, they waited no longer").[79] The reader's attention is hence deflected from the sexual transformation onto lineage and the successful continuation of the Huon de Bordeaux family line. The very space that could have been used by the audience to imagine the specifics of the sexual transformation (the erotic encounter between Olive and the now officially transsexual Yde/Ide) is replaced by a story that emphasizes family lineage (Croissant's life) and thus heteronormativity. And yet, one could have easily imagined a narrative that binds the two sections of the Yde/Ide and Olive stories before turning to their son. This order would have probably been more appropriate in the context of an epic cycle where narrative development is typically chronological and historically linear. During the Croissant episode, the transsexual Yde/Ide disappears from the text, and to some extent perhaps also from the reader's mind, and remains invisible until her lineage has been firmly established. In fact when s/he returns in *Yde et Olive II*, Yde/Ide has now fathered four sons and three daughters.[80] The displacement from the axis of sex and gender to that of lineage and social continuity reflects an anxiety over genealogy, fatherhood, and patriarchy. At the end of the epic, one fully measures the extent to which transvestism has been in fact only a temporary interlude within the economy of the text, and the extent to which questions about gender ambiguity have become displaced onto a sociopolitical axis.

In the miracle play, the reestablishment of the heterosexual status quo is manifested in the final double marriage that ends the play: Ysabel marries the emperor of Constantinople, while the emperor's daughter marries Ysabel's father.[81] Hence, it becomes clear that the erasure of gender and sociocultural distinctions that had initiated the entire play were temporary; at the end, the audience returns to the safety of the religiously and socially sanctioned happy heterosexual union. This drama supports Michelle Szkilnik's view that by the end of the fourteenth century, transsexual transformation in Old French literature is no longer allowed to remain permanent.[82] All possible gender ambiguity is effaced both from the textual remains, as well as from the audience's imagination.

Arabic Intertextuality

But it is especially in comparison to the Arabic literary tradition on crossdressing and female same-sex marriage that the extent of the heteronormativity of the medieval French texts can be fully appreciated. The comparative cross-cultural approach, in effect, allows us to grasp nuances in each text that remain hidden when one cultural discourse is examined alone, or is divorced from its multicultural context. While it is difficult, if not impossible, to trace the precise Arabic genealogy of the Yde and Olive narratives, it appears undeniable that the "author(s)" of these French texts were familiar with the Arabic literary tradition of homosexuality, as well as with a number of tales from *Alf layla wa layla*, or the *One Thousand and One Nights* (also known as the *Arabian Nights*).[83] In particular, they seem to be familiar with *The Story of Qamar al-Zaman and the Princess Boudour* which, as I pointed out at the beginning of this chapter, constitutes one of the main, heretofore unacknowledged, intertexts of the French Yde and Olive tales. There are important resonances between the two literary traditions that are apparent as soon as we compare the basic storyline of the Arabic text with its French rewriting.

The Arabic *Story of Qamar al-Zaman and the Princess Boudour*

The early part of the Arabic tale describes a story that is strikingly reminiscent of that of Yde and Olive, as it too combines cross-dressing and same-sex marriage. While cross-dressing was the solution to a father's incestuous desires in the French epic, it is a safety measure adopted by Boudour in the Arabic tale when she discovers that her husband has mysteriously disappeared from her side. In order to find her husband and to protect herself, and thanks to her resemblance to her lost husband, Boudour cross-dresses as him, and adopts his name, Qamar al-Zaman. She arrives at the Isle of Ebony where King Armanos abdicates in her favor and forces her to marry his daughter named Hayat al-Nefous or the Life of Souls. Qamar al-Zaman, who has worked as a gardener during his separation from Boudour, is finally discovered through his sale of vats full of olives, a condiment that, we are told, Boudour loves. She reveals the truth to King Armanos, and all ends seemingly in the most heteronormative and polygamous way: Boudour is reunited with Qamar al-Zaman, abdicates in his favor, and in addition gives him Hayat al-Nefous as a second wife. And the three of them live happily ever after.

The thematic echoes between the French narratives of Yde and Olive and the Arabic tale of *Qamar al-Zaman and the Princess Boudour* are obvious: cross-dressing, forced same-sex marriage, homoerotic encounters between two young women, and the return to heteronormativity in the end. In addition to this intertextuality at the level of themes, both traditions display intriguing resonances at the level of character names. In this respect, Francesca Canadé Sautman has observed that the place/people names and the geographic location of the Yde and Olive verse epic all point to the Islamicate world. She writes: "Many clusters around the same-sex change are centered in Spain and Italy, which is consonant with the mention of Aragon, Castille, and Barcelona in *Yde and Olive* and the use of the southern name Olive."[84] I would like to explore further Sautman's observation and show how the names of the main characters in the French Yde and Olive texts, while unusual in the French literary tradition, weave indeed an intriguing (and revealing) intertext with character names from tales of *Arabian Nights*.[85]

The name of Yde and Olive's son, Croissant, whose story had interrupted the epic at the moment of the sexual transformation, as we saw earlier, merits consideration. The first name Croissant (meaning "moon crescent") is atypical in French;[86] it is however quite common in Arabic and is used with great regularity throughout the Arabic literary tradition. In the *One Thousand and One Nights*, "Moon" (with its multiple synonyms and variations) is an androgynous name and, despite its grammatically masculine gender in Arabic, is given with equal frequency to male and female characters. In *The Story of Qamar al-Zaman and the Princess Boudour*, each of the title characters' names evokes the moon: Qamar al-Zaman (male) means "the Moon of the century," while Boudour (female) means "the Moon of Moons."[87] If the name "Moon" (and its derivatives) is androgynous throughout *Alf layla wa layla*, it is associated specifically with lesbianism in the earliest extant erotic treatise in Arabic, namely, Ibn Nasr's tenth-century *Encyclopedia of Pleasure*. This text reports indeed that lesbians prefer to "have intercourse with a woman . . . with a vulva . . . like a full moon."[88] It may thus be possible to argue that in Arabic literature, the name "Moon" was used at times as a symbolic code word for (homo)eroticism. The choice in the French verse and prose epics of naming Yde and Olive's son "Croissant" becomes of course significant and invites a cross-cultural (French/Arabic) reading of the narrative and of the expression of alternative sexuality therein.

A second intriguing resonance between the French and Arabic narratives is the name of the female character "Olive." Once again, the name "Olive," like Croissant and Yde which we will examine in a moment, is unusual in French literary history. In the Arabic *Story of Qamar al-Zaman and the Princess Boudour*, even though we do not encounter the name "Olive" per se, the olive motif is important at a key moment in the text as olives literally insure the reunification of the title characters at the end of the tale.[89] The choice of naming one of the French female characters Olive invites us therefore to consider the Arabic intertextual resonances of *Yde et Olive*, hinted at by Sautman. By naming Yde's wife Olive, French narrators are implicitly giving voice to another story, written (or recited) in a different language and belonging to another tradition. Garber's notion of the function of proper names as signifiers that "encode a whole story below the line, below the surface" is fundamental here.[90] It allows us to posit that the other story that stands "below the surface" of the French text is the Arabic *Story of Qamar al-Zaman and the Princess Boudour*. The name of Olive (or Croissant, or Yde as we will see) may hence be considered a narrative gesture that urges the reader to read "below the surface" of the text, "below the line," and to cross the borders between what is visible on the pages of the text (French, heterosexuality), and what is invisible, yet implicit (Arabic, female homoeroticism).

The power of signification of the name of the third main character of the French *Yde and Olive*, namely, of Yde herself, must also not be overlooked. Like the names of Croissant and Olive, that of Yde is highly unusual in the French medieval literary tradition. It is evocative however of the name of the first lesbian known to the Arabs according to Ibn Nasr's *Encyclopedia of Pleasure*, Hind Bint al-Khuss al-Iyadiyyah.[91] It is possible that the French character Yde/Ide was named after her Arabic homologue, "Iyadiyyah" (the final two syllables "iyyah" represent a diminutive suffix in Arabic).

Not only does Yde's name act as a powerful indicator of cross-cultural exchange, but the function that she occupies in the French epics also weaves an intertext with the Arabic tradition of *Alf layla wa layla*, and bears striking parallels to that of its main narrator, Scheherazade. Let us indeed recall that Scheherazade, through her tricks and wisdom (marrying Shahrayar and telling him tales), succeeds in saving both herself and all the other women of her city, condemned to die one by one the day after their wedding. Her wisdom and self-sacrifice lead to the liberation of all women (and ultimately the entire realm) from the endless wrath and jealousy of the all-powerful Shahrayar.

In striking parallel to Scheherazade, Yde also sacrifices herself in order to save both herself and at least one other woman (Olive) from the deadly desires of men. Yde flees to escape from her father's incestuous desires, and in the process, she rescues Olive from the violent desires of another man, the king of Spain (the narrator specifies that the latter had come to attack Rome precisely because Olive's father had refused to give him his daughter in marriage).[92] Yde therefore might be thought of as a Western Scheherazade, who,

like her Eastern counterpart, stands as a prime example of female empowerment achieved though sexual knowledge. Not least, Yde might also be considered a storyteller in her own right, as is evident in the new biography and
genealogy she invents at least three times to escape from the threatening situations she encounters. As a matter of fact, once cross-dressed, Yde gives three
different versions of her identity and familial background, successively to the
Germans (v. 6615), the thieves (v. 6740), and the king of Rome (v. 6833 and
vv. 6856–62). In this regard, Yde's empowerment, her reversal of established
social and sexual hierarchies and the multiple identities she adopts strongly
evoke Scheherazade's own storytelling. As such, Yde's cross-dressing and same-
sex adventures are part and parcel of the transmission of the *One Thousand
and One Nights* from the East to the West. As one of the first medieval Western lesbians, Yde stands as an eloquent voice that embodies the transfer of
Arabic cultural practices and alternative female voices from the Islamicate
world to medieval Europe.[93]

There is a reiteration of significant Arabic details in the French stories of
Yde and Olive: the adoption of Arabic (or Arabic-like) names and the striking
similarity in the functions of Yde and Scheherazade. Taken together, they
weave a web of intertextual and intercultural resonances with *The Story of
Qamar al-Zaman and the Princess Boudour* and invite our cross-cultural reading. At the same time, these resonances should not obscure the key differences
in attitudes toward homosexuality, cross-dressing, and same-sex marriage that
also distinguish the two traditions. It is these differences that will be our primary focus in the remainder of this chapter. We will see that all the while offering French narrators tales and thematic motifs that permitted them to
broach taboo subject matters (same-sex marriage, female homoeroticism, lesbian sexuality), the Arabic tradition of *The Arabian Nights* was not rendered
mimetically in French. In fact, far from faithfully translating *The Story of
Qamar al-Zaman and the Princess Boudour*, medieval French narrators adapted
the Arabic text, changed the emphases of key erotic scenes, and silenced its
open ending in order to render it more suitable to their European, Christian
audience. Just as I proceeded with the French text, I propose to examine three
crucial moments of the Arabic tale: the cross-dressing, the wedding night, and
the return to the culturally sanctioned polygamy at the end (which, it must
be pointed out, does *not* involve a transsexual transformation).

Cross-Dressing in *The Story of Qamar al-Zaman and the Princess Boudour*

In contrast to the function of cross-dressing in the French narratives of Yde and Olive, cross-dressing in *Alf layla wa layla* does not introduce a "category crisis," nor does it lead to Boudour's social and linguistic fall. In fact, even after she adopts male clothing and her husband's name, Boudour continues to occupy the same social position as she did earlier in the tale, that of the off-spring of a king. This is indeed how she introduces herself to King Armanos's messenger: "The messenger returned to king Armanos and informed him that this was a king's son."[94] It is also as the son of a king that her host, King Armanos, welcomes her to his city. More importantly, it is because of his/her high social class that he invites her/him to marry his own daughter, Hayat al-Nefous:

يا ولدي اعلم انني بقيت شيخ كبير و ما رزقت ولد ذكر قط ذكر غير بنت و هي بحمد الله تعالى تقاربك
في السن و الجمال، و أنا قد عجزت عن الملك، فهل لك أن تسكن أرضنا و تتوطن ببلادنا و ازوجك
بابنتي و اعطيك ملكي و استريح أنا.

> My son, know that I have become very old and I was not blessed
> with a male child, but only a daughter. She is, thanks be to God, of
> your age and beauty. I have become too old to reign. So if you
> [agree to] live in our lands and settle in our realm, I will marry you
> to my daughter and I will give you my realm, while I rest. (591)

The stability in Boudour's social identity means that this character will not need to prove herself a worthy knight or accomplish extraordinary deeds in order to recover a social standing lost to cross-dressing, as Yde does. It also means that cross-dressing in *The Story of Qamar al-Zaman and the Princess Boudour* is not a transgressive social act, as it will become in the process of translation into French. Rather, in the Arabic text, cross-dressing functions as a key narrative strategy that permits the storyteller to focus directly and explicitly on the erotic, if not sexual, ambiguities which encounters with a cross-dressed heroine necessarily elicit. In other words, cross-dressing in the Arabic text does not lead to a depiction of homosexuality in the second degree as is the case in the French tradition but becomes yet another instance of Arabic literary practice that consists in treating homosexuality openly and freely.

The Wedding Night in *The Story of Qamar al-Zaman and the Princess Boudour*

In contrast to the French miracle play in which Ysabel reveals her true sex to her wife immediately in order to avoid any sexually jeopardizing encounter, and to the French verse and prose epics in which the wedding night is spent feigning illness in order to avoid (lesbian) sex between Yde and Olive, the Arabic tale focuses from the outset on the two young women's sexual relation. This is how their wedding night is depicted:

ثم ادخلوا حياة النفوس ابنة الملك على بدور ابنة الملك الغيور و ردوا عليهما الباب و
اوقدوا لهما الشموع و الفوانيس و فرشوا لهما الفراش الحرير فدخلت بدور الى حياة
النفوس.

> They [the servants] made Hayat al-Nefous enter into the room where Boudour, daughter of king Ghouyour, was [sitting], and they closed the door on them. They lit candles and lights for them and spread their bed with silk [sheets]. Boudour entered into Hayat al-Nefous.[95]

The explicitness of the sexual encounter between the two girls is not evident in the English translation, for it rests on the use of the Arabic verb "dakhala" (to enter) twice in the above quote, first with the preposition "'ala" ("they made Hayat al-Nefous enter into the room where Boudour was") and then with the preposition "ila" ("Boudour entered into Hayat al-Nefous"). What must first be noted is the fact that the Arabic verb "dakhala"—meaning to enter, to penetrate—does not require the use of any preposition. The fact that the redactor chose to add not one, but two different prepositions with this verb must therefore make us pause.[96] In its first occurrence with the preposition "'ala," the audience is led to understand that Boudour is already in the room into which Hayat al-Nefous is led. The second use of the verb "dakhala" with "ila" comes therefore as a surprise since such a combination can only mean to penetrate into a physical space, or to penetrate sexually, to have intercourse. In the context of this scene, only the second meaning of "dakhala ila" is possible, leading us to conclude that Boudour and Hayat al-Nefous's initial encounter is utterly sexual.

While the redactor of the fourteenth-century Syrian manuscript of *Alf layla wa layla* does not further depict the lesbian wedding night, the power of such nondescription ought not to be overlooked. For it is indeed in its very "indescribability" that the impact of lesbian sexuality lies.[97] In the oral performance of the tale of *Qamar al-Zaman and the Princess Boudour*, the sexual encounter between Hayat al-Nefous and Boudour is likely to have been one of those key moments that would have invited further elaboration by the storyteller, or at the very least, stirred the imagination of the audience.[98] In contrast to the destiny of Yde and Olive's sexuality in the French thirteenth-century epic, which will be effaced by scribes or readers as we saw earlier, Boudour and Hayat al-Nefous's sexual relation will be expanded and amplified throughout the following centuries, leading to the detailed portrayal of lesbianism in Burton's English (1885–88) and Mardrus's French (1899–1904) translations.[99]

After their initial, overt sexual encounter, Boudour and Hayat al-Nefous spend the next two nights "kissing" and "caressing." This is how the redactor of the fourteenth-century Syrian manuscript depicts their intimacy:

جلست الى جانب حياة النفوس و قبلتها .

Boudour sat down next to Hayat al-Nefous and kissed her (*qabbalat-ha*). (592)

And on the following night:

فرأت . . .حياة النفوس جالسة فجلست بجانبها و طقطقت عليها و قبلتها بين عينيها.

When [Boudour] saw Hayat al-Nefous sitting, she sat besides her, patted/caressed her (*taqtaqat*) and kissed her (*qabbalat-ha*) between the eyes. (593)

The verbs "patted/caressed" (*taqtaqat*) and "kissed" (*qabbalat*) used in the Arabic tale evoke certainly the way Yde and Olive's encounter had been depicted by the Old French narrators of the verse and prose epics (kissing and hugging). We must note however that the meaning of the Arabic "kissing" differs from its French counterpart in that in the Arabic erotic tradition, "kissing" has a specific and overtly sexual connotation. This is indeed how "kissing" is defined in the *Encyclopedia of Pleasure*: "Kissing is a means by which sexual desire is aroused. . . . Kissing becomes more effective when it is accompanied by biting, pinching, sucking, sighing, and hugging. It is then that both the man and the woman burn with sexual desire simultaneously. . . . Kissing is the penis's messenger to the vulva. It is also said that kissing is an essential part of sexual union. . . . Kissing, like lubrication, facilitates sexual union. . . . Coition without kissing is imperfect."[100]

Kissing is here heralded as a key component of (heterosexual) foreplay, as a recommended accompaniment to sexual union, possibly as a euphemism for it. In fact, in the *Encyclopedia of Pleasure* kissing is considered one of five techniques to speed a woman's slow orgasm: "There are five ways of quickening a woman's slow orgasm. These ways are: kissing, smelling, biting, rubbing, beating."[101] Moreover, the Arabic erotic tradition enjoins the lover to apply the kiss on, or between the eyes, as a strategy aimed at speeding a woman's orgasm: "The areas to be kissed are: the cheeks, the lips, the eyes, the forehead, the area behind the ears, the bosom and the breasts."[102]

Seen in this light, Boudour's kiss and its placement between Hayat al-Nefous's eyes should be interpreted as an unambiguous reference to their foreplay, sexual relation, perhaps even orgasm. We are hence permitted to conclude that while the Arabic and French texts under consideration use the same semantic field and linguistic terms (kissing, hugging/patting/caressing) to portray female same-sex relations, the Arabic text is anchored in a socio-cultural context where such conduct holds a very precise sexual connotation. In this light, Boudour and Hayat al-Nefous's kisses, much more clearly than those between Yde and Olive, are to be interpreted as foreplay, sexual intimacy, intercourse.

Lesbian Sexual Intimacy and Cross-Cultural Differences

It is on the third night that Boudour reveals her biological sex to her wedded wife. This scene is important because it represents the moment at which the French Yde and Olive narratives differ markedly from the Arabic tale that provided their main storyline. An investigation of the key differences between the two traditions illustrates the extent to which medieval French narrators silenced some of the most daring homosexual features of the Arabic tale; it also exhibits the very divergent attitudes held by each of these traditions toward female homosexuality.

We must note from the outset that Boudour's revelation is not made by an apologetic or repenting cross-dresser as was the case with Yde/Ide in the

French epics. It takes place instead in the midst of an erotic and sexually charged scene. This is how the scene is depicted in Mahdi's edition:

قالت بكلام رقيق مؤنث و هو كلامها الحقيقى الغريزى و كشفت عن حالها . . . الى أن حكت لها ما جرى مع معشوقها زوجها قمر الزمان و اورتها فرجها وقالت لها أنا امرأة ذات فرج و نهود.

> [Boudour] spoke [to Hayat al-Nefous] in a soft, feminine voice, and this was her true, natural voice, and she unveiled the truth about her situation. . . . She told her what had happened to her and her beloved husband Qamar al-Zaman, and she showed her genitals and said to her [I am] a woman who has genitals (vulva) and breasts. (595)

While in the *Miracle de la fille d'un roy*, Ysabel suggests that her wife touch her "mamelles" ("breasts") as proof that she is indeed a woman, the Arabic text goes farther in the proofs that Boudour is willing to give. As a matter of fact, Boudour does not simply *offer* to show her female sexual characteristics; she actually *shows* them. She does not just show her breasts (*nuhud*); she also uncovers her genitals (*faraj*). In fact, it is that which she exhibits first. The unveiling of Boudour's private parts is repeated twice in this scene, as though the redactor wished to highlight the sexual moment, as well as to encourage the audience's (male, and undoubtedly also female) imagination concerning the implications of such a sexual exposition. As the text remains silent over Hayat al-Nefous's response to Boudour's stripping, the reader is permitted to conclude that she may not have been displeased by what she saw. Staging a female character who willingly (and titillatingly) uncovers her private parts and breasts thus becomes another step in the process of deepening the intimate contact between the two female spouses.

While in *Yde et Olive*, the revelation was overheard and rapidly divulged to the king, in the Arabic tale, Boudour's secret remains for the greater part of the tale known only to Hayat al-Nefous. The limited disclosure of Boudour's biological sex allows the sexual transgression by the two women to continue undisturbed. In fact, the greater permissiveness of the Arabic text (in comparison to the French narratives) toward lesbianism becomes even more pronounced in the scenes that *follow*, rather than precede, Boudour's revelation of her biological sex. Whereas in the Yde and Olive epics, the confession

became the space of panic and the beginning of the return to heteronormativity, it is not accompanied by any anxiety about cross-dressing in the Arabic
story or about the lesbian sexuality that had taken place. There is no anxiety
either about the necessity of maintaining visible, legible gender distinctions or
enforcing social hierarchy. There is no divinely ordained injunction against
lesbianism to worry about, no impending capital punishment and, as we will
see, no divine intervention to reestablish order in the midst of what must have
appeared as sociocultural and moral chaos to the medieval West.

In fact, in the Arabic tale, Boudour's revelation gives rise to an alternative
female space in which both women become equal and hence enjoy mutual
support and reciprocal intimacy. Boudour's revelation is met with mere surprise on the part of Hayat al-Nefous, not with panic or distress: Hayat al-
Nefous is "surprised at her story" (ta`ajjabat) writes the redactor of the tale
(595). More important perhaps, the revelation of Boudour's womanhood is
also met with pleasure: Hayat al-Nefous "was pleased (farahat) with the news"
(595). The fact that Boudour is a woman, not a man, puts Hayat al-Nefous
more at ease. The presence of the cross-dresser in the Arabic text, rather than
heightening anxiety as it did in the French tradition, opens up a space for dialogue between the two girls and ultimately increases their intimacy and pleasure. Immediately following the news about Boudour's biological sex, the
redactor writes that both women

ثم تحدثوا و لعبوا و تضاحكوا و ناموا.

spoke, played, laughed with each other, and slept. (595)

We must note here in particular the morphological choice of the verb
"tadahaku" ("to laugh with each other"), which in Arabic is a reciprocal verb
form that signals actions performed with others. The choice of this form lends
the entire passage a reciprocal tone, and thus for the first time in the homoerotic
interlude of this tale, the redactor signals Boudour's and Hayat al-Nefous's
sexual play, laughter, conversation, and overall pleasure in each other's company. It is as though while Boudour performed a male role, the redactor was
compelled to depict her in the conventionally male active position of kissing
and caressing Hayat al-Nefous. After Boudour's revelation, however, Hayat al-
Nefous becomes an equal partner in the relationship, both active giver and
passive recipient of the same-sex intimacy. The reciprocity inherent in the lesbian encounter stands thus in contrast to conventional portrayals of hetero-

sexuality or even male homosexuality which often pit an active (male) partner against a passive (female) one. Some might argue that the very fact that Boudour's biological sex must remain a secret to everyone but Hayat al-Nefous and the reader indicates that medieval Arab Islamicate society, just like French culture, did not condone lesbianism. If this may be true at a legal level, it is not so at a narrative and literary level. To the reader or listener, especially to the medieval lesbian in the audience, this tale must have provided a validation (albeit an imaginative one) for a way of life that differed radically from legally sanctioned sexual encounters.

Not only is Boudour and Hayat al-Nefous's intimacy highlighted *after* Boudour's revelation of her biological sex, but their marriage is finally consummated. Of course, it is not consummated in a heterosexual mode, but rather by destabilizing the association of heterosexual marriage with virginal blood. As a matter of fact, Hayat al-Nefous, in order to assuage her father's mounting concern over her prolonged virginity, stages her own defloration. She kills a chicken and spreads its blood over her own thighs and handkerchief. She also screams, repeating thereby the expected association of heterosexuality with violence and pain:[103]

الى قريب الاذان فقامت حياة النفوس اخذت دجاجة و قلعت سراويلها و صرخت بعد أن

ذبحتها و تلطخت بدمها و بلت منديلها. ثم أخفت الدجاجة و لبست سراويلها و نادت فدخلوا

عليها أهلها.

Hayat al-Nefous woke up before the morning call to prayer. She took a chicken, took off her pants, screamed after killing it and spreading its blood over herself and her handkerchief. She then hid the chicken, put her pants back on and called. So her family entered the room. (596)

As Hayat al-Nefous expected, the stained handkerchief is taken by King Armanos and his wife (and society at large) to be definitive proof of the consummation of their daughter's marriage. The proud parents rush to exhibit the bloody cloth, without worrying about the provenance of the blood. Ironically, the very moment that the two lovers are portrayed as maintaining heteronormativity is also the very space where binary sexual relations are exposed and where the very notion of stable identities is challenged. Judith Butler's analysis of homosexual marriage is particularly pertinent to this discussion:

"The replication of this heterosexual tradition in a non-heterosexual context brings into relief the utterly constructed status of the so-called heterosexual original. Thus, gay is to straight *not* as copy is to original, but rather, as copy is to copy. The parodic repetition of 'the original,' . . . reveals the original to be nothing other than a parody of the *idea* of the natural and the original."[104]

In the Arabic tale, the exhibition of the bloody cloth in the context of a homosexual marriage reveals that heterosexuality is critiqued, denaturalized, animalized. After all, marriage is legitimized here not by the virginal blood of a bride, but by that of a lowly farm animal, the chicken. Meanwhile, Boudour and Hayat al-Nefous are allowed to continue their intimate lives with each other, inadvertently blessed this time by the entire social system.

The End of the Story: Homosexuality Within Heterosexuality

Nothing disturbs the lesbian relation—neither Hayat al-Nefous's sexual maturity, nor Boudour's revelation of her biological sex to her partner and to the reader. Whereas in the French epic, the revelation of Yde's sex is closely followed by the threat of capital punishment and by the divine miracle (the transsexual transformation), in the Arabic tale, the revelation contributes to the development of the intimate relationship between the two women. As a matter of fact, each night thereafter, Boudour and Hayat al-Nefous live in the same bliss, tending to their emotional, intimate relationship, while awaiting the eventual return of Qamar al-Zaman:

الى الليل تدخل الى حياة النفوس فيتحدثوا و تشكوا لهل قلقها و شوقها الى معشوقها قمر الزمان.

At night, [Boudour] penetrates into Hayat al-Nefous. They speak
to each other and she tells her about her worry and her love for
Qamar al-Zaman. (596)

In this quote, the verb "dakhala" (to enter, to penetrate) is used again with the preposition "ila" that we discussed earlier, hence emphasizing the endurance of the sexual encounter between the two women, even after the revelation of Boudour's biological sex. Although the lesbian relationship is presented here as an ersatz for heterosexual relations (the two women's intimacy occurs seemingly only *because* they are waiting for Qamar al-Zaman's return), it seems clear nevertheless that a space is opened up for alternative emotional, if not sexual, satisfaction. In the Arabic tale, lesbianism is allowed to exist, is fostered even, within a frame of heterosexuality, while in the French texts we examined earlier, lesbianism is placed at the other extreme of heterosexuality.

It is only when Boudour recognizes Qamar al-Zaman as the vendor of olives that the lesbian sexual relation comes to a halt. At first reading, the end of the Arabic tale may be seen as a return not only to the androcentric model of marriage (Qamar al-Zaman and Boudour are reunited), but also, and in keeping with the cultural background of the *One Thousand and One Nights*, to polygamy: Hayat al-Nefous is given as second wife to Qamar al-Zaman. Moreover, the end of the text seems to herald the victory of patriarchy since, once reunited with her husband, Boudour abdicates in favor of the "true" man of the story, Qamar al-Zaman. The ultimate triumph of patriarchy is further manifested in the fact that Hayat al-Nefous is never consulted about becoming a second wife. However, once again, heterosexuality in the Arabic text is only a temporary interlude as lesbianism is never conveniently bracketed or completely and utterly contained and silenced. For when King Armanos asks Qamar al-Zaman to marry his daughter, Hayat al-Nefous, Boudour is the one who answers:

فقالت بدور و الله مثلي مثلها و ليلة لي و ليلة لها و اسكن أنا وإياها في بيت واحد لاني تعودت عليها.

So Boudour replied: By God, for me like for her; a night for me and a night for her. And I will live together with her in one house because I have gotten used to her [literally: I have returned to her repeatedly]. (609)

While, on the surface, these lines suggest that Boudour generously accepts the sharing of her husband with Hayat al-Nefous, they also hint at the fact that the women's relationship is far from coming to a halt at the end of the tale. Even as she adheres to the basic legal principles of polygamy ("one night for me and one night for her"), Boudour introduces an important departure from its conventions when she states her desire to live in the same house as Hayat al-Nefous. Her use of the verb "ta`awwad-tu," which means both "to get used to" and "to return repeatedly to," reveals that the main reason for refusing the very common practice of the separation of households may well be her desire to continue "returning repeatedly to Hayat al-Nefous."

Boudour's desire to continue sharing Hayat al-Nefous's house thus has significant implications for their same-sex relations. Not surprisingly, the survival of the lesbian relationship beyond the polygamous ending is the way Mardrus (the celebrated nineteenth-century French translator of *Alf layla wa layla*) will render the end of *The Story of Qamar al-Zaman and the Princess Boudour*: "Qamar al-Zaman governed his kingdom as perfectly as he contented his two wives, with whom he passed alternate evenings. Boudour and Hayat lived together in harmony, allowing the nights to their husband, but reserving the days for each other."[105]

Mardrus restates here explicitly what was depicted implicitly in the fourteenth-century Syrian manuscript that Mahdi edited. We must not disregard his translation out of hand, claiming it merely constitutes nineteenth-century Orientalist presuppositions and in no way reflects medieval viewpoints.[106] Such an end is in fact quite consistent with the double meaning of "ta`awwad-tu" in the Syrian manuscript and resonates very strongly with medieval Arabic erotic treatises which consider lesbianism as one form of sexual practice, alongside many others. The Arabic *Story of Qamar al-Zaman and the Princess Boudour*, in contrast to the French narratives of Yde and Olive, thus permits the survival of Boudour and Hayat al-Nefous's relationship, even as it places it within the parameters of heterosexuality and polygamy.[107] Whereas the French epic recuperates the cross-dressed Yde and silences the transgressive voice of the "third term," the Arabic tale does not interrupt the workings of this "third term," and allows a move toward a new structure where heterosexuality is viewed as only one possibility in a larger chain. The Arabic text thus, until the very end, permits border crossings, and reveals the intrinsic weakness of definitional distinctions. One may say that while her French sister, because of her transsexual transformation, is forced ultimately to embrace heterosexuality, the Arab lesbian, despite her heterosexual and polygamous marriage, is allowed to maintain her commitment and unfaltering faithfulness to her female partner.

Conclusion

This chapter has investigated instances of textual/sexual interconnections between medieval French and Arabic narratives of female cross-dressing. Our cross-cultural reading of the lesbian interlude in the three renditions of the Yde and Olive stories and the tale of *Qamar al-Zaman and the Princess*

Boudour from *Alf layla wa layla* has revealed the extent to which French narrators, all the while giving voice to female homoeroticism in ways strikingly reminiscent of the Arabic tradition, end up silencing the more disruptive sexual elements and revert ultimately to heteronormativity. This does not mean that the French Yde and Olive narratives are not subversive *within their own* literary and historical context or that cross-cultural research is equivalent to competitive cultural evaluation. It means rather that a cross-cultural, comparative intertextual analysis of Arabic and French renditions of the same story is valuable in providing a more nuanced reading of same-sex desire between women in the medieval East and West. By allowing us to ask new questions or to ask old questions in new ways, cross-cultural scholarship inevitably forces us to adjust our analysis of one cultural discourse taken singly. As they reveal the historical and ideological power structures that construct discursive representations of sexualities, cross-cultural sexuality studies give us a glimpse of what else could have been there in the French text, how else sexuality and homosexuality could have been described. Such an approach allows us to discover and decipher those blank spaces in medieval French textuality, those places where same-sex desire could have been inscribed but, in the process of border crossings, were rendered ambiguous or were simply effaced. Ultimately, such an investigation is valuable for the insight it affords us into the medieval creative (and censoring) process more generally.

CHAPTER FOUR

Crossing the Lines of Friendship

Jean Renart's *Escoufle*, Saracen Silk, and Intercultural Encounters

> *The love which you bear one another ought not to be carnal, but spiritual: for those things which are practiced by immodest women, even with other females, in shameful jesting and playing, ought not to be done even by married women or by girls who are about to marry, much less by widows or chaste virgins dedicated by a holy vow to be handmaidens of Christ.*
> —Saint Augustine

IF LESBIANISM WAS staged via cross-dressing and same-sex marriage in the Yde and Olive narratives, it is ushered in by a predatory bird (a kite) and its theft of a silk purse in Jean Renart's thirteenth-century romance *Escoufle* (The Kite; ca. 1200–1202). The scene of the kite's robbery is so crucial to the entire romance, and to the lesbian episodes that soon follow it, that the narrator calls attention to it specifically, as he defends in the epilogue his choice of the romance title (*Escoufle*) and justifies it against those detractors who consider it inappropriate ("c'on en tient a lait"):[1]

| Pour ce si dist que grant tort a | This is why I say that he is wrong |

Cius qui le non blasme
    et despise.
Se li escoufles n'eüst prise
L'aumosniere, on n'en
    parlast ja.
(vv. 9092–95)
	Who blames and despises the
	    title [of the book].
	If the kite had not stolen
	The purse, we would not speak
	    about it.

According to the narrator, the entire romance hinges precisely on the kite's theft of the silk purse (*aumosniere*). Without this crucial scene, the entire romance would have had no existence.

The narrator's defense of his title and his emphasis on the kite's theft of the silk purse make sense in the narrative economy of the romance. After all, the kite appears at a key moment in the text, shortly after Guillaume and Aelis (the central heterosexual couple of the romance) are forced to flee from Rome to Normandy in order to escape from Aelis's father's (the emperor of Rome) injunction against their marriage. While they stopped to rest near the town of Toul in Lorraine, a kite, suddenly descending from the skies and acting as a veritable deus ex machina, steals from Guillaume the silk purse containing the precious ring that Aelis had just given him as a token of her love. Guillaume, hoping to recover the valuable gift, pursues the kite, leaving Aelis asleep. The lovers are separated. Aelis wakes up to find herself alone, assumes that Guillaume has abandoned her, and decides to press forth to Normandy. As for Guillaume, after a few days pursuing the kite, he salvages both purse and ring but, upon his return, discovers that Aelis has disappeared. Thinking that she might have been caught by her father's men, he turns back toward Rome in search for her. During the seven years of Guillaume and Aelis's separation and search for each other, Aelis becomes a successful businesswoman in Montpellier where she establishes an embroidery workshop with a new female friend, Ysabel. She soon contracts two additional important friendships, one with the lady of Montpellier and another with the countess of Saint-Gilles, before being reunited with Guillaume at the end of the romance. The *Escoufle* concludes with the marriage of Guillaume and Aelis and their double crowning in Normandy and in Rome.

It should be clear from this brief overview that the scene of the kite represents indeed a turning point in the narrative economy of the romance, justifying the narrator's defense of his title in the epilogue. We might be tempted to attribute the discomfort presumably felt by the medieval audience toward the title of the romance to the fact that the kite held multiple negative associations in the medieval Western imaginary. Since classical antiquity, in the Christian tradition, as in didactic and allegorical writings throughout the Middle Ages, the kite was linked to the theft of farm animals and evoked the Devil.[2] Such an analogy could certainly have predisposed the medieval reader to view with suspicion Jean Renart's entire literary project. The author's defense of his title in the epilogue may thus be interpreted as a warning against judging the entire romance by its title alone and against any predisposition to spurn the text without reading what lies between its covers.

However, and more important, Jean Renart's defense of his romance title in the epilogue serves to draw our attention to the scene of the kite's theft and to underscore the fundamental changes in gender and social identities to which it gives rise. After all, the scene of the kite's theft of the silk purse represents a critical juncture in the romance as a whole that destabilizes the heterosexual paradigm, while marking the onset of alternative emotional attachments between women. As a matter of fact, the presence of both the kite and the silk purse sparks the heterosexual couple's seven-year separation and ushers in three female friendships with their associated configurations of gender and social trouble. It is the interjection of the kite and silk that gives rise to thousands of lines of narrative that relate the heroine's intimate encounters with other women.[3] In other words, the heterosexual lovers' separation, permitted by the bird's theft of silk, literally transforms the heretofore heterosexual narrative into a series of homoerotic female spaces and encounters.

In this sense, Jean Renart's warning at the end of the romance confirms the fact that the frame of the romance does not tell us the entire story of the *Escoufle*. This romance, like most others in medieval literature, begins and ends in a very conventional mode. It starts with count Richars's (Guillaume's father) crusade and pilgrimage to Jerusalem, both very legitimate goals for any able-bodied man at the turn of the thirteenth century when Europe was engaged in its crusading efforts in the Middle East. The romance ends in equally legitimate and praiseworthy pursuits, with the celebration of the heterosexual couple, crowned both in Normandy and in Rome. Such an ending implies that the couple, now united in marriage, is going to fulfill the expectations of the monogamous heterosexual family, produce lineage, and reaffirm the patriarchal order. Clearly, the paratextual apparatus (the prologue and epilogue)[4] upholds conventional morality and gender binarism, while endorsing patriarchy and normative sexuality.

Such a reading, like reservations about the title of the romance, might be especially undesirable because it could lead the reader to miss the key narrative development of the middle section of the romance. By warning us against misjudging his romance by its title (or by its paratext), the narrator of the *Escoufle* draws our attention to the middle section which describes Aelis's (mis)adventures, her alternative friendships, and the novel socioeconomic practices in which she engages. A careful reader of Jean Renart, Roberta Krueger, warns us similarly against focusing exclusively "on where the major protagonists of courtly romances eventually 'end up.'"[5] Only by examining the period of a maiden's autonomy before marriage can one indeed appreciate the multiple ways in which the genre of the romance, and more specifically of the "realistic romance" (to which the *Escoufle* belongs),[6] subverts conventional gender and social categories under the guise of upholding them. As we will see, it is precisely when the kite intervenes that heterosexual relations come to an end, and it is once they are (temporarily) put on hold that alternative friendships, same-sex female intimacy, and novel sociocultural practices begin to emerge. The title of the romance acts thus as the very (threatening) sign of its queerness.

The *Escoufle* and the Matter of Araby

I will add that the title of the romance is also a sign of the cross-cultural nature of the project as a whole.[7] In fact, I will submit that the *Escoufle* (like *Le Livre des manières, Yde and Olive, Floire and Blancheflor,* or Marie de France's *Fables,* for example) is a key example of medieval Western, hybrid writings, a product of the contact zone between the medieval European and Islamicate worlds. The very title of the romance, the scene of the kite's theft of a silk object, as well as the numerous references throughout the text to Saracen silk and to Eastern material goods highlight the textual indebtedness of the *Escoufle* to the matter of Araby.

After all, the key role that both kite and silk play in the *Escoufle* resonates with the equally critical role that another bird and another snatched object enclosed in silk play in an Arabic tale from the *One Thousand and One Nights,* a tale that is likely to have been familiar to Jean Renart and at least some members of his audience. I am referring here to *The Story of Qamar al-Zaman and the Princess Boudour* which I discussed in Chapter 3, with reference to the Yde and Olive narratives. This framed tale which, we will recall, is one of the eleven core stories known to have circulated in Europe as early as the twelfth century, recounts how while traveling, Qamar al-Zaman and Princess Boudour stop to rest by a meadow. Like Aelis, Boudour falls asleep. As he caresses her, Qamar al-Zaman sees a ring hanging at the end of a silk ribbon from his beloved's drawstring pants (Boudour does not give this ring as a gift to Qamar al-Zaman as Aelis does to Guillaume). While the intrigued Qamar al-Zaman examines the ring outside of their tent, a bird (not identified specifically as a kite) steals it from his hands and flies away. Just like Guillaume, Qamar al-Zaman follows the bird in an effort to recuperate his wife's property, and when he returns, he finds that Boudour (like Aelis) has disappeared. While in the *Escoufle*, after her separation from Guillaume, Aelis becomes a successful businesswoman and forms a series of three female friendships, in the Arabic tale, Boudour cross-dresses, takes on her husband's identity, and marries the daughter of King Armanos, Hayat al-Nefous.[8] Both in the French romance and in the Arabic tale, therefore, the separation of the heterosexual couple, permitted by a bird's theft and by the introduction of silk, leads directly to the establishment of alternative sexual practices between women. Both texts also end on a seemingly normative tone, with the reunification of the heterosexual couple and their official marriage.

Even though the Arabic tale and the French romance each depict the subversion of binary gender distinctions through different narrative strategies (cross-dressing in one and intimate female friendships in the other), both texts trace the onset of alternative gender and social identities to the same events, namely, a preying bird (a kite), and the presence of silk (a silk purse in the *Escoufle* and a silk ribbon in the Arabic story). These thematic and intertextual resonances between the *Escoufle* and *The Story of Qamar al-Zaman and the Princess Boudour* are crucial, as they invite us to reread the French romance and its depiction of female friendships through Arabic writings and cultural practices. Analyzing Jean Renart's *Escoufle* through the reading lens of the Arabic tradition permits us thus to decipher in new ways the affective and intimate friendships that Aelis develops with three women in the romance (Ysabel, the lady of Montpellier, and the countess of Saint-Gilles), and the uncertainty about gender and sexual roles that the French text, in parallel to the Arabic tale, emphasizes. Read from this perspective, the title of the French romance acts not only as a sign of the queer relations between women that are depicted therein, but also as a symbol of the hybrid, cross-cultural nature of the entire literary project.

The *Escoufle*, Eastern Silk, and Cross-Cultural Encounters

The relation between the Arabic tale and the French romance reaches beyond the intertextual resonances that we have just described. It extends to the economic ties that medieval France entertained with the medieval Arab Islamicate world, and by extension to the intercultural connections between the French narrative and Arab sociocultural traditions. In other words, and even though Jean Renart does not allude explicitly to any Arabic intertext (in contrast for instance to the multiple references to the Tristan and Ysolde legend), we must remain sensitive to the "fabric of implicit [Arabic] allusions"[9] and to the blending of Western and non-Western cultural traditions in the romance. The "implicit [Arabic] allusions" that permeate the *Escoufle* reside in the repeated references in the romance to material goods, silk cloth, precious stones, and luxury commodities coming from the East. Such allusions are not to be read as ornamental, empty signifiers without any bearing on the interpretation of the text. Rather, I argue, they hint at unsuspected and veiled expressions of cross-cultural contacts, and at times even of intimate desire between women.

In the *Escoufle*, silk, like the kite, plays a key role in destabilizing the overall narrative economy of the romance. It operates similarly to the way it functions in the courtly romances recently analyzed by Jane Burns in her *Courtly Love Undressed*.[10] By introducing into Western romance multiple references to Eastern material goods, silk defines Western hero(ine)s with a material identity coming from the East. In the case of the *Escoufle*, Aelis's entire life before her elopement with Guillaume and after her establishment in Montpellier, as well as throughout her stay in Saint-Gilles, is marked by silk and lavish clothes. While still a child, she had learned to embroider with gold thread and silk; in fact, the narrator describes her involvement in such activities with her *puceles* in her palace room in Rome (vv. 2060, 2967–71). Aelis is also often portrayed wearing silk clothes, at least until the moment of her elopement when she must exchange her silk tunic ("bliaut de Sire," v. 3991) for one made of Flemish wool ("drap flamenc," v. 3996) in order to conceal her identity (vv. 3990–96). Her mother gives her a precious ring with a magic green stone (vv. 3805–13) which Aelis encloses in an "aumosniere / d'un samit" (vv. 3828–29), a purse made of luxurious heavyweight silk imported into the West from Syria and Asia Minor. Even though the text does not specify the origin of this ring or of its stone, the reader may easily infer that they both came from the East since this was the provenance of precious stones and metals in the medieval West. Finally, throughout the *Escoufle* and whenever the narrator specifies the origins of material goods, it is often an Eastern one: "Besaces turcoises" ("bags from Turkey," v. 3590); "bliaut de Sire" ("a silk tunic from Syria," v. 3991); "vaissel d'or d'uevre turcoise" ("gold dishes crafted in Turkey," v. 8854).

The multiple references to Eastern goods in the *Escoufle* reveal the omnipresence of such commodities in Western Europe and the role that Middle Eastern culture (material and otherwise) played in the cultural, social, and political life of the medieval West. As far as the transmission of silk and embroidery from the East to the West is concerned, recent archaeological findings indicate that trade routes were more direct than heretofore believed, rendering the exchanges between the two civilizations less circuitous and the borders more porous. As a matter of fact, while it has long been thought that Oriental weavers and embroiderers were settled in medieval Italy and that it was from there (Luccha, Genoa, and Venice, in particular) that silk and gold embroidery techniques spread to the rest of Europe as early as 1160, the latest scholarly findings suggest otherwise. Recent scholarship has revealed that Italian merchants had settled in Northern Iran (in the city of Tabriz especially), and it was there that they learned gold embroidery and Eastern weaving techniques; it was also from Iran that they traded silk to Italy and from there progressively to the rest of Europe.[11] Moreover, Olivia Remie Constable has uncovered the crucial role played by al-Andalus (and the cities of Almería, Córdoba, and Zaragoza, in particular) in the silk industry as early as the eighth century, and in the diffusion of Andalusian gold, silk, and textiles to markets in the central and eastern Mediterranean, as well as to Western Europe in the twelfth and thirteenth centuries.[12] More recently, Kathryn Reyerson has unearthed the important position that the town of Montpellier occupied in the diffusion of gold embroidered textiles and techniques from the Southern Mediterranean and al-Andalus to Northern European markets.[13]

Aelis's lavish silk *aumosniere*, which will be stolen by the kite, stands therefore as an undeniable mark of imperial opulence and of imported Eastern luxury. As such, it marks her Western identity with a material wealth deriving from the East and fashions consequently hybrid gender identities. Not only does it set the stage for the development of Aelis's cross-cultural gender and social identity, but as a unisex symbol offered by Aelis to Guillaume as a token of love, it is also capable of crossing gender binaries. Once he recovers Aelis's silk purse from the kite, Guillaume will have it sewn in his pants ("en ses braiel," v. 7723), as a sign of his own ambiguous gender identity. In addition, silk permits the crossing of social lines since its transfer from Aelis to Guillaume cements the relation of a son of a count to the daughter of an emperor. Finally, the separation of the couple, permitted precisely by the transfer of the silk *aumosniere* from Aelis to Guillaume and its momentary loss to the kite, enables Aelis to step outside the heterosexual role expected of an imperial princess and its attending responsibility to ensure proper dynastic succession. In other words, the transfer of the *aumosniere de samit* from Aelis to Guillaume liberates Aelis from the gendered expectations of heterosexual marriage and casts her in a liminal space in which she fashions alternative identities and moves in new sociocultural geographies, at the crossroads between East and West.

It is thus perhaps not surprising that the scene of the kite and its theft of the silk purse is situated outside of Toul, a town in Lorraine that is midway between Rome (Aelis's inheritance) and Normandy (Guillaume's lands), and midway between Rome (Aelis's city of birth) and Montpellier (city in which Aelis establishes her highly alternative residence). Being geographically located in the middle of Western Europe halfway between Normandy and Montpellier, Toul acts as an intermediate liminal space, where all becomes possible including the transformation of Aelis from a heterosexual beloved into an active lover of women.

Aelis's Friendship with Ysabel: New Emotional and Social Scenarios

The first person that Aelis meets after the critical scene involving the kite is a young girl who will become her close friend throughout the romance, namely, Ysabel.[14] As soon as she sees her, Aelis voices a startling wish mentally at first, that of spending the night together in one bed:

Ce vait pensant bele Aelis	Fair Aelis began thinking
Ke bien porra la nuit	That the two of them could well
uns lis	spend the night
Souffrir a eles ii ensamble.	In one bed together.
(vv. 4885–87)	

A few moments later, she repeats that desire directly to Ysabel:

Ele prie ml't doucement	She gently asks
La meschine que o li gise.	The young girl to sleep with her.
(v. 5264–65)	

Though certainly unexpected, Aelis's desire to spend the night in one bed with Ysabel may be explained by the particular context of the scene. At this point in the romance, Aelis is a twelve-year-old girl who finds herself alone in the midst of Lorraine without any male protection, victim of the two trusted men she knew: her father and Guillaume. At twelve, the legal age of marriage in medieval society and the onset of puberty, Aelis had certainly reached an especially vulnerable stage in her life. This is precisely the age when Silence, heroine of the romance of the same title, wonders whether she should continue her life as a boy with the social advantages to which this gender entitles her, or if she should instead assume her female role.[15] As a girl alone in the midst of a medieval urban setting, like maidens lost in forests in courtly romances, Aelis could certainly become easy prey to passing men.[16]

Aelis's request to sleep with Ysabel is ambiguous, however. The ambiguity rests on the use of two polysemic terms in the above two quotations employed to express Aelis's desire to share Ysabel's bed: *lis* (v. 4886) and then *jesir* (v. 5265). According to Godefroy's Old French dictionary, *jesir* has the double meaning of "to rest" and "to sleep with someone, to cohabit," while the word *lis* means "marriage," in the sense of a husband and wife sleeping together.[17] Aelis's desire to spend this first (and future nights as she will soon add [v. 5271]) together in the same bed with Ysabel invites us therefore to consider a sexual, (homo)erotic interpretation. In fact, her request may be read as an alternative same-sex marriage proposal. If so, this wish places this romance squarely within the parameters of same-sex desire among women in the Middle Ages and Aelis in the lineage of the numerous unrecognized lesbians of medieval French literature.

Aelis's proposition to sleep in the same bed as Ysabel is especially astonishing because it (innocently?) voices one of the very behaviors explicitly condemned by medieval theologians and forbidden by the rules and regulations of women's monastic communities. These rules continued to be repeated from one century to the next, since Saint Augustine's fifth-century warning (cited as an epigraph at the head of this chapter), undoubtedly indicating that the perceived threat of women's friendships in convent settings continued to be felt. A seventh-century rule stated specifically that "young girls should never lie down together lest in some adversity of the flesh their warmth carries them off to sin."[18] Seven centuries later, the councils of Paris (1212) and Rouen (1214), in an effort to stamp out such relations "prohibited nuns from sleeping together and required a lamp to burn all night in dormitories."[19] Thirteenth-century monastic rules echoed the same prohibition against nuns sleeping in each other's cells, and, in addition, required them to keep their doors unlocked so that they might always be able to prove their innocence if need be.[20]

As it encodes ambiguously what religious discourse posed only in negative terms, Aelis's request to be lodged with Ysabel conflates the categories of the "designing damsel" and the "damsel in distress," both well known from Arthurian romance.[21] But while such ladies typically make their sexual requests to knights and in courtly settings, Aelis makes her appeal to another woman and in the context of a city. Moreover, while traditional damsels (designing or in distress) are regularly eliminated from Arthurian romance because they impede the trajectory of the male hero,[22] Aelis, once she makes her request to Ysabel, emerges truly as the central character of the romance, becoming the veritable (female) "knight" of the *Escoufle*, ultimately justifying the critical categorization of this romance as "feminocentric."[23]

The role and status of Aelis in the *Escoufle* and her relationship with Ysabel have been variously interpreted by critics. Most have opted for a nonsexual analysis except for G. Diller who proposed a sexual reading of the romance.[24] Adopting a social-constructionist view of homosexuality, Diller interpreted Aelis's friendships with other women as intimate sexual attachments and attributed them to her double victimization and disappointment by Guillaume and her father. If Aelis loves women, according to Diller, it is only by reaction, as a defense mechanism and in an effort to "cease being reduced by men to the level of a woman-object" and to "liberate herself from male domination."[25]

Though I question Diller's social-constructionist view, I agree with his perspective that Aelis's relationships with women ought indeed to be read as sexual ones.[26] Failing to recognize the erotic nature of Aelis's request and of the ensuing intimate friendships—first with Ysabel, soon with other women—or failing to acknowledge the ambiguity of these episodes means that one defines the lack of sexuality in Aelis's life subsequent to her separation from Guillaume as the lack of *hetero*sexuality. If lesbianism has been thought to be absent from premodern European literary production, it may well be because expressions of same-sex intimacy (such as we find in the *Escoufle*) have simply not been recognized as sexuality at all.[27]

If lesbianism remains latent in the *Escoufle*, it is on the other hand openly depicted in *The Story of Qamar al-Zaman and the Princess Boudour*. In the Arabic text, as discussed in Chapter 3, the separation of the heterosexual couple leads to the development of an intimate same-sex relation between Boudour and Hayat al-Nefous. While in the Arabic tale, same-sex marriage between the two women is permitted by Boudour's cross-dressing, the narrator of the *Escoufle* stages a same-sex intimate relation between women without recourse to cross-dressing. His originality lies in his recasting of a (Arabic) tale of cross-dressing into a romance of female friendships, spoken in a language that hovers at the borders between the sexual and the nonsexual, between love and friendship. The intertextual resonances between the Arabic tale from the *One Thousand and One Nights* and the *Escoufle* invite us thus to ask questions about Aelis that we may not have asked in a monocultural reading of the romance and permit us to envision novel interpretations of Aelis's sexual and social practices that we may not have considered.

My analysis of the *Escoufle* reveals that same-sex relations between women do not depend on cross-dressing. In fact, characters like Aelis who do *not* cross-dress can become involved in same-sex relations, just like those (such as Boudour, Yde, or Silence) who do. Women who do *not* cross-dress too can question binary gender roles by exploring the lines that distinguish female friendship from lesbian love. Aelis's emotional and sexual maturity from the moment of her separation from Guillaume to the establishment of her alternative friendships—respectively with Ysabel, the lady of Montpellier, and the countess of Saint-Gilles—urges us to interrogate her gender and ultimately her social categorization, and to ponder, in light of Arabic intertextuality, the implications of the implicit, yet ubiquitous, sexual overtones of her friendly request.

Like Aelis's ambiguous request to share her bed, Ysabel's initial response is a double entendre, perhaps in order to conceal the fact that she has indeed understood Aelis's implicit sexual invitation:

Dame, fait ele, vo franchise	My lady, she said, your nobility
Ne requiert pas que tex ancele	Can not require a servant
Com je sui gise a tel pucele	Such as I am to sleep with a young maiden
Come vos estes; n'est pas droiture.	Such as you; it is not right.
(vv. 5266–69)	

Ysabel's response, like Aelis's proposition, hovers between the sexual and the nonsexual, the legitimate and the illegitimate. Her reply both maintains the ambiguity of the verb *jesir* (lying down and sleeping together as a married couple) that Aelis had introduced and expands it with the observation *n'est pas droiture* (v. 5269). Let us recall that in medieval usage, *droiture* means not only "right," but also "the rightful position," including the one taken during (hetero)sexual intercourse. Since medieval law held a wide definition of aberrant sexualities and thus prohibited not only acts of sodomy, masturbation, or bestiality, but also wrongful sex positions between heterosexual couples,[28] Ysabel's remark on *droiture* refers not to heterosexual positions, but to the sexual illegitimacy of having two girls share the same bed. Her comment on the sexual inappropriateness of sleeping with Aelis uses, therefore, the terms of (nonnormative) heterosexuality in order to speak about alternative sexuality. If this demonstrates that medieval French literature lacked an established vocabulary to speak about female homoeroticism, it also reveals the fact that the expression of same-sex desire between women in Old French textuality was expressed through a detour. While at times, the detour was Arabic rhetorical devices (Chapter 2), at others, it was Arabic thematic motifs (Chapter 3). In the *Escoufle*, the strategy involves the recourse to Arabic thematic parallels (the kite's theft), Eastern material goods (silk and precious stones), as well as the mimicking and subversion of Western conventions associated with the most legitimate model of sexuality, namely, heterosexual relations.

In addition, Ysabel's remark on the *sexual* illegitimacy of sleeping in the same bed as Aelis points to the *social* illegitimacy of the request. The first lines of her response indeed move the *sexual* connotations of Aelis's plea to an emphasis on *social class*. A close reading of her words indicates that she is reacting with disbelief at the idea that Aelis would display so much generosity (nobility) as to consider an association between herself (*pucele*) and Ysabel (*ancele*). The contrast between these words is important as both *pucele* and *ancele* had very specific meanings in the Middle Ages. While *pucele* means any young unmarried woman, regardless of rank, and will come to signify exclusively a virgin,[29] *ancele* possesses a technical meaning in medieval charters and law. Drawing primarily on Mediterranean sources, Susan Mosher Stuard has argued that *ancilla* was "the Roman term for female chattel slave that remained in use through medieval centuries."[30] It soon came to refer to maidservants, a quasi-exceptional category in the tripartite sexual system of classification for women developed by Jacques de Vitry (d. 1240) and Franciscan Gilbert de Tournai (d. 1284) in their *ad status* sermons.[31] *Ancilla*, hence, encompassed those single women who were not free—single female slaves who lived and worked for their master and who had very limited rights in medieval society. Interestingly, Ysabel fits this description. She is the unmarried daughter of an unmarried mother (the narrator never calls Ysabel's mother a widow, and no information is ever provided concerning Ysabel's father), herself probably also a slave who has passed her unfree state to her daughter. Moreover, both Ysabel and her mother live in a warehouse belonging to a rich bourgeois and work for him (vv. 4964–74).[32] Ysabel's observation that it is not *droiture* that a *pucele* associates with (lives with, sleeps with, or, marries, depending on our interpretation of *jesir*) an *ancele* thus likely alludes to the prevalent debate in medieval society concerning the legal and social status of *ancillae*. As she translates the heterosexual terms of this debate into the homosexual context of her own fictive situation, Ysabel's comment may refer to the social instability that maidservants were accused of provoking and more specifically to the threat of sexual transgressions they were believed to pose to the medieval Western social order.[33]

Because of the possibly sexual meaning of *jesir*, Ysabel's astonishment at the potential alliance between a *pucele* (Aelis) and an *ancele* (herself) might even point to the question intensely debated within canon law about the right of slaves to marry. This was an especially pertinent topic in the year 1200 (circa the time when the *Escoufle* was composed) when marriage rites came to be considered church sacraments. The very invocation of history in the romance, while tempting us to read fiction as history, playfully points to the limits of history. For if the church validated a marriage between a free man and an unfree woman,[34] it said nothing about consent between two women of different social conditions, and nothing about the unintended and intriguing possibility of considering such consent to be an officially sanctioned marriage. The silence over same-sex consent and unions may have unwittingly opened a space in which the narrator of the *Escoufle* could safely imagine the alternative social and gender configurations that suddenly became possible under new church legislation.[35]

Reread in this light, Aelis's request to *jesir* with Ysabel may be interpreted as the verbal (thus valid) consent by a free woman (Aelis) to contract an intimate relation with an unfree woman (Ysabel). Under medieval law, this consent (if we set aside for a moment the fact that it is given for a same-sex relation and not a heterosexual one) legitimizes their bond, permits their cohabitation and sets Ysabel free.[36] If canon law did not give full parental rights to a free man who married an unfree woman (her children continued to belong to her master), thereby limiting the total number of men who married *ancillae*, the question of children is not at issue between Aelis and Ysabel. Therefore, Ysabel stood to gain everything from an intimate (marital) association with Aelis, hence her wonder at Aelis's nobility and generosity ("vo franchise," v. 5266). Ysabel's emphasis on social class may thus be read primarily as a comment on the extraordinary liberating potential of a (same-sex) liaison with a free individual. An alliance (between women), imagined to have the same consequences as a heterosexual marriage, could become the very door to freedom for the *ancele* Ysabel.[37]

And indeed, the same-sex relation that develops from this moment forward between Aelis and Ysabel affords Ysabel an unexpected upward social and economic mobility. Freed from her *ancilla* status, she is richly clothed by Aelis with a new dress ("robe novele," v. 5341); she sleeps with Aelis in the same bed as *jesir* is no longer a prerogative of heterosexual unions, but remains until the end of the romance when Aelis and Guillaume are reunited, the exclusive privilege of same-sex relations between women. Moreover, Ysabel's social promotion represents a veritable manumission of her *ancilla* state. She is never referred to by this name again in the romance. She freely leaves Toul with Aelis, settles down in Montpellier and trades the poor household ("povre ostel," v. 4924) she shared with her mother for a comfortable furnished house with a front yard and a garden in the back (vv. 5473–75). Through her relationship with Aelis, Ysabel partakes of the material wealth of her companion and participates fully in the establishment of the new embroidery workshop/beauty salon. Even the poor *gimples* (wimples) she sews acquire a higher status as they are sold on an equal footing with the more luxurious embroideries that Aelis confects.[38] Ysabel's mother participates in the material advantages gained from this lesbian relationship. Aelis leaves her mule with her as a retribution for their lodging (vv. 5313–17); later in the romance, she will sell the mule with great profit. The same-sex relation that develops in the *Escoufle* expresses, therefore, the very tempting possibility of (imaginary) freedom for those women in the Middle Ages, those *ancillae* and maidservants who were single and unfree "by law and custom."[39]

Ysabel's upward social mobility goes hand in hand with the development of the young girls' erotic relationship. It does not take long for Ysabel and Aelis to engage in more intimate activities. If Ysabel begins by placing herself in bed with Aelis *souvine* ("on her back," v. 5273), she likely remains in that position only momentarily for soon thereafter she agrees to accomplish all of Aelis's wishes:

. . . ele li dit	She tells her
Qe'ele fera sans	That she will accomplish
contredit	completely
Sa volenté, comment k'il aille.	Her wish, whatever it is.
(vv. 5291–93)	

Ysabel's willingness to submit to Aelis's desires is described as being the result of Aelis's more convincing nonverbal arguments:

Ele se traist plus deles li,	She moves closer to her
Si la baise, estraint	She kisses her, embraces and
et acole.	hugs her.
(vv. 5288–89)	

As the couple transgresses social and sexual lines, the narrator violates the linguistic register specific to love and collapses descriptions of same-sex female friendship with those of heterosexual love. As a matter of fact, the behaviors that Aelis and Ysabel engage in borrow the vocabulary that pertains to heterosexual intimacy, all the while remaining at the threshold of genital activity.[40] The verbs used here, *baise, estraint,* or *acole,* recall the terms that characterized Yde and Olive's relationship which I discussed in the previous chapter. Like them, these verbs invite and resist a sexual reading. After all, these are terms that are commonly used throughout medieval literature to depict both sexual and nonsexual bonds, to describe lovers and friends, legitimate and illegitimate relations; they can be read both sexually and not, metaphorically and literally. Far from explicitly choosing one meaning over another (be it friendship or love), the text maintains a veil of ambiguity over the relationship described and blurs the precise nature of the bond between the two women. By remaining equivocal as to the extent of the two girls' relationship, the narrator leaves the reader wondering, and hence imagining, what exactly went on in the privacy of their bedchamber.

In addition to the ambiguity of the vocabulary used to describe the relation between Aelis and Ysabel, the narrator couches the same-sex love pursuit in terms of a heterosexual (courtly) quest ("la conquiert," v. 5291).[41] Yet, this image, used to reinscribe within the lesbian relation the traditional heterosexual hierarchy of active (male) and passive (female), as well as the active/passive model associated with male homosexual activity, is also the very means of its subversion.[42] For in the *Escoufle,* there is no active male hero (heterosexual or homosexual). Rather, it is Aelis who performs this role, having become the sole active female heroine of the romance. Another moment of the veritable mimicking and undermining of heterosexuality is achieved by locating the first moment of the two girls' intimacy on the very bedsheets on which Aelis and Guillaume had slept the night before (vv. 5242–49). In a very literal and physical sense, the lesbian friendship is superimposed on the heterosexual bed.

Aelis and Ysabel's relationship continues to develop in equally ambiguous terms even after they leave Toul and begin their voyage north to Normandy, then south to Montpellier in their long quest for Guillaume. Ysabel quickly becomes a loyal friend ("amie et feeille," v. 5396); she serves Aelis and provides her with "so much solace, so much pleasure" ("tant de soulas, tant de delit," v. 5400); Aelis "enjoys herself in so many ways" ("ml't par se deduit bien et bel," v. 5402) that she soon feels less pain and anger (v. 5464); the "friendship" between the two girls develops so happily that Ysabel's "only pleasure is to be with the fair maiden" ("Or n'est il deduis se cil non / Que d'estre o la france pucele," vv. 5476–77). The main verbs used here to depict the affective relation between Aelis and Ysabel (*soulas, delit,* and *deduit*) display the same implicit sexual register as *jesir, acoler, estraint,* and *baisier* discussed above. Like *deduire* which can denote both "to enjoy" and "to make love to someone," *soulas* and *delit* possess both sexual and nonsexual connotations; they can be used to mean "pleasure" in a physical and in an emotional sense.

Regardless of the precise nature of Aelis and Ysabel's relationship, it remains clear nevertheless that their bond up to that moment in the romance is characterized by "exclusivity in affection,"[43] precisely that very loyalty and closeness that developed in monasteries and *beguinages* and which Augustine and monastic rules condemned repeatedly. If such intimate friendships could develop in all-female communities and if these became key spaces for the development of alternative forms of eroticism between women, the originality of Aelis and Ysabel's relation lies in its localization outside established religious spaces or formal groupings, in the context of the developing European urban and bourgeois milieus of the thirteenth century.

The narrator of the *Escoufle* seems to be fully aware of the sexual ambiguity created and to revel in it. By playfully interrupting it at some key passages, the narrator heightens the emotional charge of these scenes. Such is the case when, immediately following the lines cited above that describe Aelis's pleasure in Ysabel's company: "Ml't par se deduit bel et bien" ("[She] enjoys herself in so many ways," v. 5402), the narrator comments on the efforts deployed by the two girls in their search for Guillaume, observing: "Et ml't le quisent sagement" ("They searched for him wisely," v. 5403). The adverb *sagement*, following on the heels of *deduit*, puts an abrupt end to the audience's imagination and any effort to understand the nature of the friendship between the two girls. Should their *deduit* be considered *sage*, or is it to be interpreted differently? The opposition between *sagement* and *deduit* highlights the two competing events in the girls' lives: the quest for Guillaume (verbally and socially dubbed *sage*) and the development of the same-sex intimate affair (left unspoken, perhaps purposely silenced).

Shortly thereafter, the narrator once again deflects our attention from the eroticism of the two girls' relation and the pleasure they are having in each other's company and refocuses it on more legitimate, socially appropriate concerns. After commenting on their *deduit*, the narrator describes Aelis as a *pucele* ("young girl" or "virgin," v. 5477). This characterization catches the reader off guard for Aelis's virginity is unlikely to have been part of one's thinking at this moment in the romance. Calling Aelis a *pucele* precisely at the moment of describing the girls' pleasure teases the reader and confounds any attempt at drawing clear conclusions about Aelis and Ysabel's relationship. The normative reading of the romance thus competes very powerfully with the nonnormative interpretation.[44]

Aelis's Friendship with the Lady of Montpellier: Lesbianism and Gift Exchange

The alternative relationship that Aelis builds with Ysabel is only the first in a series of three that are depicted in the *Escoufle*. The next friendship that she initiates is the one she launches with the lady of Montpellier, shortly after she meets Ysabel and after they both establish themselves as businesswomen in Montpellier. Aelis's decision and desire to have more than one friend puts into question the exclusivity of affection characteristic of medieval religious women writers discussed above; it also interrogates traditional courtly love scenarios in which a knight is preoccupied with one woman only. Even as it takes its inspiration from women's homoerotic religious discourse and courtly love literature, the *Escoufle* does not reduce Aelis's intimate liaisons with other women to either model. The multiplicity of female spaces and of emotional attachments among women staged in this romance creates an alternative social system in which women engage in same-sex practices under the guise of friendship.

One might trace the very first steps in the development of Aelis's friendship with the lady of Montpellier to the moment when she resolves to present her with a gift. This scene may be considered to be Aelis's effort to create a space for female intimate relations within the urban milieu of medieval Montpellier where she has settled. In fact, Aelis explains that her decision to offer a gift is prompted by the indifference of some women toward her in church (the lady of Montpellier does not speak to her), and that, in contrast to some, the lady of Montpellier does not buy her lavishly embroidered goods. It is thus neither as a businesswoman nor as an embroideress that Aelis goes to visit the lady of Montpellier.[45] Rather, she goes there seeking the lady's friendship, speaking to her already as a future friend: "cel qui ml't se fait s'amie" ("She who acts greatly as her friend," v. 5643). Clearly, the presentation of the gift is depicted as Aelis's attempt to overcome psychological, social, and economic hostility from some women, as well as her desire to establish a personal bond with the lady of Montpellier. In this sense, Aelis may be considered a thirteenth-century urban reincarnation of Marie de France's courtly female characters in the *Lais* (ca. 1170) who depend on other women in order to surmount the social, psychological, or familial obstacles they face.

The notion of a gift as a token of friendship should make us pause for a moment.[46] In medieval epic, gifts were exchanged in order to bind social and political relations between men; they expressed *largesse* between a lord and his liege vassals, created strong ties of loyalty, conferred honor and prestige upon the giver, and initiated a cycle of return giving. In medieval romance, gifts cemented relations between lovers and at times took place in one-sided heterosexual attachments. The *Escoufle*, on the other hand, describes a situation that evidently falls outside these conventional situations privileged by either epic or romance. Aelis's presentation of a gift to the lady of Montpellier recounts a situation in which the gift is offered in a nonheterosexual context (from one woman to another), does not confirm a love relation (Aelis claims she wants to be the lady's *friend*, v. 5643), and is not meant to facilitate homosocial bonding through *largesse*. Rather than a gift that establishes (male) unity, that binds men to one another, or that upholds relations among heterosexual lovers, Aelis's present may be more usefully thought of as a "friendship gift" whose intent is to establish relations between women. As such, it gives rise to alternative social and gender scenarios, legitimizes an entirely different system of female solidarity, of emotional and also of sexual bonds between women. Yet, and even as it distinguishes itself from them, the friendship gift is created by taking the homosocial and heterosexual versions of the gift as its model.

Aelis's gift to the lady of Montpellier possesses unquestionable market value. It consists of a luxurious gold embroidered silk purse ("une ml't riche aumosniere / d'orfroi," vv. 5561–62) and a belt embroidered with rich gems ("Anelet et bocle et mordant / Fist faire d'or en la çainture" ["She placed a ring, a buckle and a fastener / made of gold on the belt"], vv. 5578–79). Both belt and *aumosniere* are embroidered with the coat of arms of the lady's husband, the count of Montpellier (vv. 5560–69). The choice of this decoration is deliberate as Aelis hopes that by appealing to the presumed love between the heterosexual couple, she would have more success constructing the same-sex (friendly) relationship she seeks:

Ml't devra chier tenir le don,	She should hold dear the gift,
Car c'iert des armes son baron	For both the purse and the belt
Et l'aumosniere et li tissus.	Are embroidered with her
	husband's coat of arms.

(vv. 5567–69)

If luxury garments are often understood in the medieval imaginary to be located in and associated with the bedchamber and its delights,[47] the *aumosniere* and belt, both luxuriously produced and embroidered with the husband's coat of arms, bespeak of the presumed intimate delights between the lady of Montpellier and her husband. At the same time, these gifts presented by a woman to another woman create a fantasy about the potential pleasures of friendship that may develop between the two women. They may suggest that the delights of female friendship could parallel those of the heterosexual courtly couple. As Aelis appeals through her gift to the presumed love between the count and lady of Montpellier, she demonstrates the extent to which the representation of women's friendships models itself on heterosexual relations, while hinting at the possibility that heterosexual love might at times have served as a foil to female intimate friendships.

Aelis's initiation of a female intimate liaison with the lady of Montpellier through gifts is successful. Very quickly, the lady of Montpellier is herself drawn into the cycle of gift exchange and transfer. In fact, in return for the material commodity received, she grants Aelis her solemn protection:

[. . .] Ja mar arés doute	Do not have any worry
D'ome qui en la vile viengne,	No man who comes to the city
Ne ja tant comme il i remaingne	However long he may stay

Ne vos diront pis de vo non.	Will dishonor your name.
(vv. 5724–27)	

Granting Aelis protection in exchange for a (friendship) gift places the lady in the position of a feudal lord who promises protection in exchange for his vassal's military service (Aelis's gift). But these lines could also be interpreted inversely, as positioning the lady as the liege vassal (and not the lord) who promises to protect Aelis's (her lord) social status in exchange for the latter's *largesse*. Whichever way we choose to interpret these verses, we ought not be surprised to find the model of feudal exchange and reciprocal service invoked here, since, after all, the friendship gift reenacts gift exchange in feudal society, even as it distances itself from it. As such, the exchange of friendship gifts becomes the central ritual that binds together the new community of women friends that Aelis is forming. However, the fluid exchange of positions between Aelis and the lady, who can be viewed each in turn as a lord or a vassal, disrupts the hierarchical gender and social stations inherent to the feudal (and courtly) model. Contrary to the hierarchy of feudalism and of heterosexual love that is supported and strengthened by gift exchange, the circulation of gifts among women gives rise to alternative social and emotional scenarios. Rather than sustaining hierarchy (as in feudalism and heterosexual love), friendship gifts in the *Escoufle* establish female intimate relations characterized by the equality of the partners and the flexibility of gender roles.[48]

In addition to promising Aelis her protection, the lady of Montpellier becomes actively involved in the new gift-exchange economy initiated by Aelis. Her involvement proceeds in two steps: first by ensuring the circulation of the gift that Aelis gave her; and second by presenting Aelis with a return, thank-you present.

If the lady of Montpellier graciously accepts Aelis's gift, it is not because it displays the coat of arms of her husband as our heroine had thought, not even because of its economic value, but rather because she plans to give it in turn to her own adulterous lover (the count of Saint-Gilles) as a token of her love and loyalty to him. In fact, no sooner does the lady accept Aelis's gift than she mentally offers it to her lover (shortly thereafter she will give it to him in person):[49]

La dame l'a ja son ami	The lady has given it already
Donee, et si ne la vit	To her friend; and yet he did not
onques.	see it (or her) yet.
(vv. 5698–99)	

We might be tempted to interpret the lady's mental transfer of Aelis's gift to the count of Saint-Gilles as the failure of Aelis's gift to achieve its intended goal. But, in fact, it is the very circulation of the gift that ensures its success. In the *Escoufle*, not only is Aelis's friendship gift circulated, but it is also recast more specifically as a love gift for a (adulterous) heterosexual liaison.[50] In other words, the gift that was intended for a woman ends up being the legacy of a man. Such transfer confirms the fact that in the *Escoufle* same-sex bonds between women are not absent, but they remain modeled on heterosexual relations (legitimate or not) and they persist in the shadows of heteronormative associations. They evoke in this sense the relation between Boudour and Hayat al-Nefous from the Arabic *Story of Qamar al-Zaman and the Princess Boudour* where the lesbian relationship is maintained at the end of the tale, under the cover of the harem, "protected" by the socially and politically legitimizing polygamous marriage.

It is only after the mental displacement of the gift from the lady to her (male) lover that the lady of Montpellier begins to respond explicitly to Aelis's request for friendship and to call her, for the first time, "friend": "Ceste moie novele amie" ("This new friend of mine," v. 5769). It is as though the social space for female friendships, and within it the relationship between Aelis and the lady, can take place only after the gift has been circulated and the friendship gift between women has been reinscribed as a heterosexual love gift.

For the lady of Montpellier, regarding Aelis as a friend translates into treating her as a lover. The lines following the lady's promise to safeguard Aelis's reputation complicate indeed the developing friendship and show that the line demarcating friendship from love is not drawn as neatly as we might have expected; it is in fact in danger of collapse. As the lady of Montpellier expresses her gratitude for Aelis's gift, she invites her to dinner and places her in the most distinguished seat at the table:

E[n] liu de signor et de per	In the seat of her lord and companion
Fist avoec li mangier la dame.	The lady had her [sit] to eat with her.
(vv. 5738–39)	

The first reading of this passage reveals how much the countess appreciates Aelis (and her gift) since she seats her in the place of honor, the one typically reserved for the *signor*, the lord, the husband of the house. This reading is quickly undermined, however, by the ambiguity of the phrase *en liu de* (v. 5738). While this locution means "in the seat of," it also signifies "instead of." This second meaning utterly transforms the implications of the scene and invites the reader to consider the countess's attention toward Aelis in a new light. For here, the countess treats Aelis *as if she were* her husband, *instead of her signor*.

Taking the place of the *signor* in the lines above, Aelis becomes, by the same token, the lady's *per* (v. 5738). This word, meaning "companion," has the connotation of equality. It highlights once again the fact that female friendship is characterized by the equality of the partners, in contrast to the inherent inequality of medieval marriage.[51] Another meaning of the word *per* according to Godefroy's Old French dictionary is "spouse" and seems often to be used to refer to the female spouse as a synonym for *moullier*, wife.[52] If the lady of Montpellier treats Aelis as her *per*, she considers her, therefore, as her equal (female) spouse, constructing their (friendly) relationship as a marital one.

The reader gets an even more precise inkling of the nature of the incipient "friendship" between the two women a little later in the same evening. Once dinner has been completed and the tables cleared, we are made privy to the lady's thoughts:

Ml't vousist bien avoir a oste	The lady would really have liked
La dame la bele Aelis,	To have Aelis as a guest
Et si que sa couche et ses lis	And that she would happily
Li fust mi partis volentiers.	Share her bed.
(vv. 5750–53)	

These lines are reported in free indirect discourse, indicating that it is impossible to know whether these are the lady's inner wishes, or whether she revealed her yearning to Aelis. What is clear to the reader, however, is that the lady of Montpellier's appreciation of Aelis's gift and her offer of friendship are not platonic but extend to a desire to keep her as a guest and . . . share her bed! The lady's intimate thoughts are made explicit in the above lines through the use of two synonyms—*couche* and *lis*. These signifiers refer to "bed" both in its intimate (*couche*) and physical (*lis*) sense and reveal that the lady is imagining, fantasizing about the emotional and physical intimacy that she might enjoy in her friendship with Aelis.

The same desire to share a bed had been voiced, we will recall, earlier in the romance by Aelis in her initial encounter with Ysabel. Here, it is the lady of Montpellier who initiates the invitation, albeit perhaps only mentally. The same-sex (sexual) proposition that she voices leads to mental, if not physical intimacy since the disclosure of the countess's intimate thoughts is immediately followed by the timely and discreet departure of all servants (vv. 5754–55). Even though the narrator informs us that they go to eat, the staff's timely exit conveniently provides temporary privacy to the two ladies, as well as a titillating space for the reader's imagination.[53] The narrator seems to revel in drawing out the suspense of this scene. The reader wonders if the lady of Montpellier's wishes will be followed by their actual accomplishment; we are left to wonder what would happen if the two ladies were to find themselves in bed together.

The suspense around this friendship about to turn erotic is drawn out even longer after the servants' withdrawal, at the moment when Aelis asks permission to take her leave. To this request, the lady replies that she would like her to remain with her until the servants have finished their supper so that they may accompany her back to her house. The narrator playfully points out: "Ce la fist encore targier" ("This delayed her even more," v. 5761). This additional wait time lengthens the scene and ultimately increases the emotional charge of the intimate meeting between the two women. Yet, this private moment escapes representation; it is never described. The reader is left imagining what might have happened between the two women, knowing especially the countess's train of thought, wondering at what moment the servants will interrupt the scene again. These moments of privacy, however brief, may well have provided a mental relief to some audience members and a window into intimate encounters between women, far from established norms of heterosexual practices.[54]

It is again during this very short pause, which gives rise to the audience's erotic fantasy, that the narrator heightens the sexual tension of the scene. He does so by reintroducing the theme of the mutual exchange of gifts. While waiting for the servants to resume their service, the lady offers Aelis a gift, in return for the luxurious presents she has received:

Onques el mantel n'ot atache:	This coat never had any fastener
Bien amendera cest damage	This new friend of mine
Ceste moie novele amie.	Will easily repair this defect.
(vv. 5767–69)	

As it reenacts the medieval value of *largesse*, depicted in countless scenes of epics and romances in which a ruler bestows a robe on a knight, this scene superimposes an erotic dimension. For, as the lady participates in the cycle of giving, circulating, and returning gifts, she is unwittingly solidifying the emotional bond between herself and Aelis. In the lines just quoted, the lady reveals that the robe she is offering Aelis does not have the required metal "fastener" (v. 5767). She insists that the robe *never* had a fastener, indicating perhaps that it is a brand new one, and urging Aelis who is a skilled embroideress to repair this lack.

Rather than being insignificant details in the romance, the very mention of the robe and the absence of a metal fastener are signs of the hybridity that characterizes the romance as a whole. In the Arabic sexological tradition, the "unfastened robe" is one of the numerous metaphors used to depict alternative sexual practices, in this case heterosexual anal intercourse. This sexual metaphor is found in *Ruju` al-Shaykh ila sibahi fi al-quwati `ala al-bahi* (The Return of the Sheikh to His Youth Through Vigor and Coition), a work that has traditionally been attributed to Tunisian writer Ahmad al-Tifashi (1184–1253), author of *The Delight of Hearts* that I discussed in Chapter 2, or to Jalal al-Din al-Suyuti (1445–1505). These attributions have come under criticism, however, since the work contains some references to individuals who lived after these authors' death. More commonly today, *The Return of the Sheikh to His Youth* is credited to an Islamic Ottoman judge working under Suleiman the Magnificient, Ahmad b. Sulayman, better known as Ibn Kamal Pasha (d. 1533 or 1534) who, in fact, only translated the work into Turkish. Even though the current state of scholarship does not permit us to date precisely this work, the metaphors it lists are likely to have circulated in compilations dating earlier than the sixteenth century but that have since disappeared. Among the sixteen metaphors recorded for heterosexual anal intercourse in *The Return of the Sheikh to His Youth*, we encounter that of *hall al-izaar*, or the "unfastening the robe."[55]

Although the metaphor of "unfastening the robe" in the Arabic text is not specific to lesbian practices, it is one nevertheless that has an obvious sexual connotation. Read from an Arabic perspective, the lady of Montpellier's presentation of an "unfastened robe" to Aelis may hence be interpreted in sexual terms, as an invitation to Aelis to partake in sexual activity with her. The fact that the robe she offers never had a fastener may imply that she herself has never engaged in alternative relations before, but that she is willing to experiment with her new friend, Aelis.

The use of an Arabic metaphor of sexual practice in the *Escoufle*, like the use of military rhetorical devices in Etienne de Fougères's *Livre des manières* discussed in Chapter 2, points to the cross-cultural literary milieu in which the romance was composed or recited, and to the linguistic, thematic, and cultural hybridity of Old French writings on female homosexuality. It reveals also that the lady of Montpellier, like Aelis, is another instance of a Western character whose gender identity is at least partially fashioned in the East. The very invocation of an Arabic sexual metaphor in the context of this Western romance underscores the lady of Montpellier's cross-cultural identity and her interest in alternative sexual practices. While bilingual members of the Western audience would certainly have been attuned to the sexual overtones of the lady's presentation of an "unfastened robe," monolingual speakers would have reveled in the ambiguity of the text and of the friendship it describes. Whichever the case, it is evident that in the *Escoufle*, like in Etienne de Fougères's *Livre des manières*, Arabic functions as the language of the obscene, the language that permitted medieval Western narrators to speak lesbianism while keeping it silent.[56]

Aelis and the Countess of Saint-Gilles: Articulations of Difference

If the friendship between Aelis and the lady of Montpellier remains subordinated to the adulterous relation between the lady and the count of Saint-Gilles, the friendship that develops soon thereafter between Aelis and the countess of Saint-Gilles takes center stage in both women's lives. Aelis's liaison with the countess of Saint-Gilles is perhaps the most eloquent example of the success of the gift-exchange economy established through Aelis's relation with the lady of Montpellier. Contrary to her previous liaisons, the attachment she develops with the countess is not initiated by either party but is depicted as the unswerving result of the circulation of Aelis's gift to the lady of Montpellier and from her to the count of Saint-Gilles. For it is indeed the count's display of the *aumosniere* and the belt given to him by his mistress (the lady of Montpellier) that confirms his adultery to his wife (the countess of Saint-Gilles), gives rise to a marital dispute, and leads very directly to Aelis's voyage to Saint-Gilles and the third and final friendship between women in the *Escoufle*.[57] Evidently, the circulation of the friendship gift (the belt and the *aumosniere*) is instrumental not only in setting the stage for the development of Aelis's third intimate friendship, but also in establishing a network of women's associations and in solidifying their bonds especially in the face of marital troubles.

The conjugal dispute between the count and the countess of Saint-Gilles that results from the circulation of Aelis's gift is especially remarkable because it is a highly original variation and reconceptualization of the motif of the *mal-mariée* of the courtly love tradition. Like the *mal-mariée* Orable in the *Prise d'Orange* or the lady in Marie de France's lai *Yonec*, the countess of Saint-Gilles in the *Escoufle* is initially depicted as the young, attractive, and unhappy wife not of an older man, as in conventional versions of the motif, but of an indifferent count. The age difference typically encountered in the *mal-mariée* motif is here translated into an emotional distance between the spouses—both situations being common at a time when marital unions were contracted for familial and economic reasons. Like the *mal-mariée*, therefore, the countess of Saint-Gilles is expected to find comfort with a handsome young (male) lover. All the while implicitly alluding to this common motif of courtly literature, the *Escoufle* skillfully transforms the conventional heterosexual, adulterous plot of the *mal-mariée* into a same-sex, publicly validated story: the countess will find solace in a woman (not a man) friend-lover, and the same-sex union will develop not as an adulterous liaison, but rather as an openly contracted affair, encouraged by the count himself.

If the intimate liaison between women becomes the agreed-upon solution to the count's adultery, it is because it has been reconceptualized in socially acceptable terms and situated within sanctioned social categories. In fact, the entire episode of the Saint-Gilleses' altercation may be read as a veritable process of negotiation between the spouses as to how to name intimate relations between women and ultimately how to render them socially admissible. Four principal terms are proposed.

The first term proffered to speak about the same-sex relation between women is suggested by the count himself, in response to his wife's jealous outcry and in an attempt to find a solution to the marital dispute. He urges her to do "the same" as him:

Dame, fait il, faites autel,	Lady, he said, do the same,
S'il vos grieve de rien u poise.	If it does not bother you to do so.
(vv. 5913–14)	

The count's response and invitation to his wife to do *autel* is highly ambiguous. For what does he mean by doing the same as he does? Is he simply inciting his wife to have a belt and *aumosniere* sewn for herself by the same seamstress who made the ones he now wears, as he tries to explain to his aggrieved wife (vv. 5929–35)? Or do his words encourage a sexual reading, as his wife's interpretation seems to suggest?

The countess's reply echoes the ambiguity of her husband's proposition perhaps in order to conceal the fact that she has indeed understood the layering of ambiguity in her husband's invitation to behave like him. For, after all, acting like him does not only mean to have a belt and purse embroidered by the same woman (Aelis), it does not just suggest that she ought to engage in an adulterous liaison, but it also appears to entreat her to get involved in a relationship with another . . . woman. The countess's response and her use of the word *çainturiere* reveal that she has understood her husband's proposition to be precisely that:

> Certes, fait ele, en mon lignage   For sure, in my lineage
> Ne sai jou nule *çainturiere*.   I do not know any *çainturiere*.
> (vv. 5918–19, emphasis mine)

The use of the word *çainturiere* is noteworthy because it points to the well-known association of sewing and loving, common in the lyric genre of the *chanson de toile*.[58] The countess thus may be using the term *çainturiere* as a euphemism both for a woman who embroiders belts and for one who is proficient in the techniques and manners of love. When she claims that her family has no *çainturiere*, she may be pointing to the fact that her family lineage does not include belt makers, but more importantly that the female-female intimacy that her husband invites her to engage in is equally novel in her family.

Interestingly, the first lines of the countess's response do not reject outright the notion of a female homoerotic relation, suggesting perhaps that such intimacy between women was more common than we might have been led to believe considering the clerical and theological condemnations of female intimate friendships. Yet, even as she understands her husband's implied suggestion and even as her first reaction is not to be offended by it, the countess quickly changes her response. She adopts instead the role of the cheated wife who patiently endures her husband's adultery and scolds the count for making such a *lait* proposition.[59]

> Et quand jou sueffre en   And when I
>   tel maniere   endure so
> Vostre volenté et ma honte,   Your wish and my dishonor

Jou ne voi pas de quel aconte	I do not see how
Vos m'en deüssiés dire lait.	You can say ugly/evil things to me.
(vv. 5920–23)	

Recognizing the failure of the words *autel* and *çainturiere* to resolve the marital dispute, the count introduces a third term, *pucele*, in a last effort to exonerate himself both from the immorality of his own adulterous relation with the lady of Montpellier and from his homoerotic suggestion to his wife. He hence beseeches his wife to invite Aelis (and Ysabel) to come live with her, as her *pucele*:

Mandés li qu'ele viegne cha	Invite her to come here
Et s'amaint o li sa	And to live here with her
compaigne.	companion.
Si li priés qu'ele remaigne	Ask her to stay
Entor vous, s'ert vostre pucele	Around you, as your maiden.
K[e] il n'a si preu ne	For there is none as skilled or
si biele,	as beautiful
Si com on dist, en tot le raine.	In the entire realm, as I am told.
(vv. 5948–53)	

Inviting Aelis to live with the countess of Saint-Gilles as her *pucele*, maidservant, or lady-in-waiting, as aristocratic women were wont to surround themselves with in the Middle Ages, reflects the count's effort to refocus his wife's attention onto more socially suitable plans: to surround herself with a desirable lady. The shift from *autel* (v. 5913) to *çainturiere* (v. 5919) to *pucele* (v. 5951) represents veritable linguistic and conceptual switches that radically recast the conjugal dispute and the count's sexually explicit proposition into something more socially admissible. And it is precisely the more socially acceptable solution of *pucele* rather than *autel* and *çainturiere* that ultimately pacifies the countess.

This scene foreshadows Raison's discourse in Jean de Meun's section of the *Romance of the Rose* (ca. 1270) and her discussion of the complex dyad *coilles* and *reliques* (vv. 7107–20). Without going as far as Raison, who highlights the fact that words are empty signifiers, the narrator of the *Escoufle*, through the three rhetorical devices used in this scene, points to the unquestionable advantages of linguistic conventions and lack of linguistic mimetism for depictions of alternative intimate relations between women. In contrast to sodomy, the absence of any single commonly accepted and recognized term to speak exclusively of lesbian relations in the Middle Ages ought not to be interpreted as a proof of the absence of such liaisons in the premodern period. Rather, and as the series of semantic decenterings or of word substitutions demonstrates, same-sex homoerotic relations were expressed through code words (*pucele*),[60] which both validated such relations and safely occulted them. In other words, eroticism between women, far from being silent in the European Middle Ages, was expressed indirectly and implicitly in ways that permitted lesbianism to be at once voiced and unspoken, visible and invisible, and that ultimately allowed women to be both friends and lovers.[61] Recoding lesbian liaisons as relations between *puceles* not only provides us with a renewed understanding of the category *puceles* in the Middle Ages, but it also blurs any distinction between love and friendship and keeps us at the threshold of interpretation.

The linguistic substitution of *autel* to *çainturiere* to *pucele* is accompanied by a fourth and final shift in the description of the countess's future companion that teases us into believing we have reached a clearer understanding of the nature of the relationship between women that will soon take place. When the countess of Saint-Gilles sends her messengers to seek Aelis, she does not speak of her as *çainturiere* or *pucele*, but rather as *amie* (friend):

Or la me salüés m'amie	Greet my friend
Ke onques ne vi.	Whom I have never seen.
(vv. 5982–83)	

Rather than bringing us closer to naming the relationship about to develop between the two women, the use of the word *amie* evades the whole question of speaking the unspeakable, of naming the silenced sin. Could the term *amie*, like *pucele*, have been one of those signifiers in the Middle Ages which denoted same-sex love between women? Inviting Aelis as a "friend" interrogates once again the very notion of friendship between women throughout this romance, urges us to reread depictions of friendships in other medieval texts and to reflect upon the very porous borders that distinguish friendship from love.

In addition, the second line of the countess's invitation in the above quotation is striking because it literally describes the developing same-sex female friendship between the two women along the same lines as Jaufre Rudel had depicted his love for the princess of Tripoli or as the Emperor Conrad for Lienor in Jean Renart's other famous romance, *Le Roman de la Rose ou de*

Guillaume de Dole, namely, as an *amor de lonh* or love from afar. In this light, Aelis becomes the friend from afar, the never-seen friend, but the one who already occupies the countess's heart. If geographical distance was great between Jaufre Rudel and the lady from Tripoli or between Conrad and Lienor, it is not so between Aelis and the countess of Saint-Gilles. The difference in this case is not so much geographical as it is social.[62] Aelis does not go to the Saint-Gilles household as an imperial princess, an aristocrat, or even a successful bourgeois businesswoman, but rather as a lady-in-waiting. But if she is demoted from bourgeois to maiden, Aelis is elevated at the same time from the status of lady-in-waiting to that of desired (lesbian) beloved.

The friendship-love relation between Aelis and the countess of Saint-Gilles does not take long to develop. In fact, it soon becomes exclusive and autonomous:

> Toutes sont i et cors et
> ame.
> Ne lor membre mais de
> Guilliaume.
> (vv. 6170–71)

> They are all one body/heart and
> soul.
> They no longer remember
> Guillaume.

These lines serve to contrast sharply the unity of the women's liaison to the heterosexual relation with Guillaume, whom the female friends have by now forgotten. This is evident at the stylistic (and visual) level, where a plural feminine (*toutes*)[63] is opposed to a singular masculine (*Guillaume*), and where the affirmative voice (*sont*) to speak of the liaison between women is contrasted to the negative voice (*ne . . . mais*) used to refer to the heterosexual union. But it is the description of the complete harmony between the women that is especially remarkable here. The ladies are now all one in body/heart and soul (v. 6170). Such a unity between women is remarkable because it recalls the very common medieval view of heterosexual marriage of the husband (like Christ) as head and the wife as body.[64] In the *Escoufle*, however, the narrator destabilizes the traditional associations of man as spirit (*mens*) and woman as body (*carno*) affirmed in the Bible (Ephesians 5:28, 5:22–23) and popularized by Augustine, Jerome, and twelfth-century theologians including Bernard de Clairvaux. For here it is the relation between women that is associated with the spiritual (*cors et ame*), while that with Guillaume is relegated to the domain of the physical, of the body, as the ambiguity of the word *membre* ("to remember" but also the "male sexual organ") indicates.

The fourth and final term *amie*, used to describe Aelis and to validate the nascent relationship between Aelis and the countess, quickly acquires sexual implications. This is clear in the special welcome that Aelis receives from the countess upon her arrival in the Saint-Gilles household:

Or ne fu pas ce fait
    de feme
	No other woman was ever
	    treated

Que la gentix contesse
    en fait:
	In the way the noble countess
	    did [Aelis]:

El la baise, puis si la lait	She kisses her, then let

As autres puceles
    baisier.
	The other young women
	    kiss her.

Lors l'enmaine pour aaisier	Then she takes her to relax

En ses cambres par la
    main nue.
	In her bedroom, holding her
	    with her naked hand.

(vv. 6122–27)	

The friendship that evolves between the two women is marked by kissing: the countess kisses Aelis and allows her maidservants to do the same. She then leads her to her room and provides for her needs with her "naked hand" (v. 6127). The expression "naked hand" models once again the expression of same-sex desire between women upon heterosexual courtly and feudal scenarios. But if feudal homage is characterized by the joining of hands between two men (the lord and his vassal), and if courtliness is often described as uniting the hands of a woman to those of a man, friendship between women is defined as the joining of the hands of two women.[65] The extraordinary welcome that Aelis receives from the countess renders the latter's kisses suspicious and destabilizes our understanding of the nature of the women's friendship.[66]

The seductive nature of the kiss between Aelis and the countess becomes even more pronounced when compared to the one which soon follows, this time between Aelis and the count of Saint-Gilles. For he too participates similarly in welcoming Aelis; and he does so by first asking permission from his wife (to avoid her jealousy, v. 6141) to kiss the newly arrived maiden. In contrast to the kissing scene above where the accent was placed on the kiss givers (the countess and her maidens), the following description focuses on Aelis as a recipient of the count's kiss:

El ne guenci onques la teste,	She did not turn away her head,
Ains soufri le voloir le conte	Rather, she suffered the count's desire
Bonnement, onques n'en ot honte.	Willingly, without any shame.
(vv. 6142–44)	

The heterosexual kiss described here, seemingly in parallel to the kisses between women, is titillating and far from innocent. At the same time, however, the introduction of the concept of "shame" in the last line (albeit to deny its presence) introduces a new element that was absent from the previous scene. It invites the reader to question the type of kiss Aelis receives from the count as well as the latter's intentions. In addition, the choice of the verb *soufri* and the observation that Aelis does not attempt to dodge the count's kiss seem to suggest that we are witnessing a forced kiss, not a mutually exchanged gesture of affection. The reader wonders why the count had asked permission from his wife and not from Aelis herself, if his intention was simply to give a "friendly" kiss. The very real possibility that Aelis, as a consequence of her move to the Saint-Gilles household, must henceforth submit to the *droit du seigneur* must be considered, with all the violence (physical and psychological) that this custom entails. The kiss that Aelis receives from the count of Saint-Gilles may be a manifestation of the conflation between (heterosexual) eroticism and violence or rape in medieval literature (and in the *pastourelles* in particular) that has been studied by Kathryn Gravdal.[67] This heterosexual kiss, made possible because of the (apparent) class difference between Aelis and the count, may be considered heir to the sexual violence to which countless medieval maidens were subjected.

A comparison between the two scenes of kissing highlights the fact that Aelis did not appear to be forced when kissed by the countess and her maidservants; she did not attempt to avoid the kisses bestowed upon her and no reference to shame was made. Could the kisses between women have been more pleasurable to her than the heterosexual ones? Or were kisses between women, be they due to friendship or love, considered to be less threatening to a medieval Western patriarchal society than kisses that took place in the context of heterosexual adultery? While the precise nature and meaning of kissing remain ambiguous in this scene as in previous ones, it is clear nevertheless that this physical manifestation of desire plays a central role in the ambiguity of the text and contributes to blurring even further the lines between friendship and erotic desire, between lesbian love and heterosexual relations.

Conclusion

Reading the *Escoufle* through the Arabic *Story of Qamar al-Zaman and the Princess Boudour* and through Arabic metaphorical tropes has allowed us to unearth expressions of female same-sex love and desire in the thirteenth-century French romance. By inserting continuous references to Arabic material culture and introducing Arabic thematic motifs and metaphorical conventions in his text, the narrator of the *Escoufle* invites us to cross the borders between the French romance and the Arabic sexological tradition. In so doing, the narrator urges us also to cross the lines of friendship and to realize that the borders between same-sex friendship and same-sex love are more porous than we might have imagined. Intimate bonds between medieval French female heroines, reconceptualized and verbalized through the Arabic tradition and through the subversion of key Western conventions, are enunciated, though they consistently remain couched in an implicit, ambiguous language that defies all attempts to differentiate clearly the discourse of love from that of friendship, the declaration of heterosexual love from that of homosexual intimacy. The absence of clearly demarcated categories of homosexual and heterosexual desire is not to be decried, however, since it may have authorized some female members of the audience to contemplate the (socially) unacceptable fantasy of lesbianism in an acceptable way.[68]

The significant role that Arabic literature and metaphorical devices plays in the *Escoufle* does not lie solely in the depiction of same-sex intimate relations between women, as we have seen in this chapter. It resides also in the incorporation into the French romance of various Arabic social and cultural traditions. These traditions are essential to the portrayal of Aelis's social identity in the *Escoufle*. We will now turn to this question, and demonstrate how, as the narrator crosses the borders between French and Arabic, romance and *mujun*, friendship and love, he creates characters whose social identity is also a veritable hybrid between Western and Eastern cultures, at once queer and cross-cultural.

CHAPTER FIVE

Crossing Social and Cultural Borders

Jean Renart's *Escoufle* and the Traditions of *Zarf, Jawari*s, and *Qayna*s in the Islamicate World

> *We need to recognize how fully, if invisibly, the lesbian has always been integrated into the fabric of cultural life.*
> —Terry Castle

BECAUSE REPRESENTATIONS OF same-sex love and desire are intrinsically linked to constructions of social identity, my cross-cultural reading of medieval lesbianism cannot conclude without an investigation of the medieval lesbian's social identity, as it is depicted in literary texts. This topic remains hardly broached in either literary or historical scholarship, even in studies devoted to marginal groups (including women). And yet, as we will see, just as they determine the social identity of marginal groups, Western clerical presuppositions about women and single women especially play an important role in the production of the social identity of the medieval French literary lesbian.

In this chapter, we will examine the depiction of Aelis's social identity in Jean Renart's *Escoufle* (ca. 1200–1202), and we will see how the narrator of the thirteenth-century French text inscribes history into his fiction and invites us to read Aelis's social function through the lens of prevailing clerical systems of classification for women. We will demonstrate that Aelis's occupations in Montpellier and the fictive social spaces that she creates both there and at Saint-Gilles establish what we may call a mirage of historic mimetism, a narrative that both reflects and refracts aspects of thirteenth-century French social life. Aelis's social identity, while resonating with medieval clerical discourses on women's proper place in European society, cannot be contained or be reduced to them. In fact, new interpretations emerge as soon as we compare Aelis's social function and the spaces she inhabits in the *Escoufle* with those occupied by some women in medieval urban Islamicate society. It is only by contextualizing Aelis's occupations within both Eastern and Western traditions that we will be able to grasp the complexity of Aelis's truly hybrid and cross-cultural social identity.

Jean Renart and New Sociocultural Geographies

After two years of crisscrossing Europe searching for Guillaume (v. 5405), traveling from East (Toul) to North (Normandy) to South (Montpellier), both Ysabel and Aelis decide to halt their quest (vv. 5416–17), to settle down in Montpellier (v. 5451), and to open a new business from which they can both earn a living (v. 5454).[1] This decision represents a turning point in the personal development of Aelis both as a character and as a single woman involved in an intimate liaison with another woman.[2] The blurring of gender identities and of binary constructions of emotional attachments (love versus friendship) that I discussed in Chapter 4 is accompanied by the development of alternative and highly marginal social spaces, at least seen from a Western cultural perspective. Roberta Krueger points to the moment of Aelis's relationship with Ysabel as the veritable turning point in the romance and notes that Aelis's arrival in Toul marks her entrance into "a new liminal space marked by private domesticity, variable economic status, ties with women, and urban settings."[3] If we distinguish for a moment the turning point in Aelis's "domestic" or *personal* gender identity (her lesbian relationship with Ysabel) from the development of her *social* identity (the departure from Toul, the establishment of the household business in Montpellier, and her move to Saint-Gilles), we note that in the *Escoufle*, the development of alternative social spaces is depicted as the logical consequence, as the inescapable result, of alternative gender identities.

This relation of cause and effect between the personal and the social is manifest in the description of Aelis and Ysabel's departure from Toul in search for Guillaume, shortly after their first night together in bed. Throughout their travel, they go on foot (Aelis leaves her mule to Ysabel's mother, v.

5313), they do not lower their eyes as contemporary conduct manuals advised women to do,[4] they do not cross-dress, but don their women's clothes without any male escort, and without any attempt to cover up their particularly vulnerable social situation:

El ne se repounent ne mucent,	They do not disguise or hide,
Ains vuelent bien que on les voie.	They do not mind being seen.
(vv. 5328–29)	

In fact, Ysabel is richly dressed since Aelis has taken care to outfit her opulently:

Ele ot vestue richement	She [Aelis] has richly dressed
Ysabel de robe novele	Ysabel with a new dress
Cote ot tot d'un et cape bele	The tunic was all of one color; the nice cloak
Et coterel d'un drap mellé	And the coat were of a multicolored woolen cloth
Dont li giron furent ml't [sic] lé.	[and] the skirt was very wide.
(vv. 5340–43)	

The description of Ysabel's dress is striking not because it is such an extraordinary contrast to the rags she wore when Aelis first met her, but because such a transformation erodes, rather than maintains, established class distinctions. Stripped of the poor clothes that marked her as economically disadvantaged and socially marginal, Ysabel is now dressed in lavish, multicolored, and ample clothes that blur the distinction between lower-class and bourgeois states.[5] As she crosses the sartorial lines that identified her with the lower socioeconomic classes and dons opulent clothes, Ysabel acquires a new social body made of cloth and, consequently, also a new public identity. In so doing, she embodies the social threat posed to the old nobility by the rising wealth of the urban bourgeoisie to which Ysabel and Aelis will soon belong. This dress falsely marks Ysabel as a member of a social elite (rising bourgeoisie) and depicts "the kind of conspicuous consumption among lower ranks that royal decrees sought historically to curtail."[6] In other words, Ysabel's clothing, bestowed upon her through Aelis's *largesse*, is a fictive example of those novel trends that augmented anxiety in medieval France about the visual confusion of social ranks. It is the threat of such erosion of class (and gender) distinctions that will lead both kings and preachers to promulgate the first sumptuary laws, which in turn will give rise to the urban legislation of dress and class boundaries in the mid-thirteenth century.[7]

Ysabel's new dress recalls Enide's transformation from the daughter of a poor vavasor to a wealthy countess through her marriage to Erec at the beginning of Chrétien de Troyes's *Erec et Enide*. But while Enide's luxurious garments were presented to her by the queen, in front of an approving assembly of male courtiers and as a material sign of her heterosexual union, Ysabel's dress is given to her in private (the reader does not witness the actual transfer of luxury clothing from Aelis to Ysabel), as a marker of a social class to which she does not belong by birth, and as an affirmation of the alternative, homosexual liaison in which she has engaged. As she adopts lavish clothes, Ysabel might be considered "socially cross-dressed." It is precisely this new socially cross-dressed status that legitimates the new type of *conjointure* developed in the *Escoufle*, one that is made possible by the emotional union and business relation between two women. The scene of Aelis and Ysabel's travel from Toul to Montpellier thus highlights the fact that the transgression of heterosexual relations is primarily also a transgression of established social lines.[8]

In comparison to other romance heroines who cross-dress, Aelis and Ysabel might be considered far more threatening characters precisely because of Ysabel's transgression of social borders. In fact, it is likely that both Aelis and Ysabel would have appeared less threatening had they cross-dressed, for cross-dressing would have theoretically turned them into men and thus justified their independence. Ironically, the absence of cross-dressing in the *Escoufle* leads to the establishment of a more subversive scenario than its presence allows in other texts, for it puts into question both gender *and* social identities. But more important perhaps, Aelis and Ysabel are more subversive because the social occupations in which they will engage, first in Montpellier and later in the Saint-Gilles household, cross the lines that seem to matter most in the medieval West, namely, those of social class and the prescribed sociocultural practices for women.

Aelis's Montpellier Business in the *Escoufle*

Aelis's establishment as a businesswoman in Montpellier, and a successful one at that, represents a move from an aristocracy whose wealth is calculated in terms of land possession, feudal recognition, and inheritance by birth right to a bourgeois economy characterized by the exchange of goods, the accumulation and transfer of money, and shrewd marketing strategies. If historically in the West, powerful women were typically queens and nobles, Aelis's agency, her financial and social success, are all the more remarkable since she is acting as a bourgeois woman and no longer as an aristocrat. Emmanuèle Baumgartner has remarked that Aelis in the *Escoufle* (just like Fresne in *Galeran de Bretagne*) achieves her happiness through her own work, rather than from the more traditional family inheritance ("droit d'ancesserie").[9] In fact, Aelis notes that her need to labor with her "two hands" (vv. 5436–37) is due to the loss of her social status following her elopement (vv. 5431–33). She points to this as her "sin" ("péchié," v. 5426) which, curiously, does not refer to her same-sex relation with Ysabel, but rather to her fall from aristocracy (v. 5420). Aelis hence goes on foot, instead of riding her mule (vv. 5421–22), and establishes herself as a working woman instead of living on her private, inherited income. Settling in an urban Montpellier household may be read as the staging of Aelis's new social identity, one that is compatible with her alternative same-sex sexual practices. As she nourishes her intimate relationship with Ysabel, she fashions herself into a businesswoman in Montpellier.

To Ysabel, who proposes to earn their living sewing towels and wimples ("touailes, de guimples faire," v. 5454), Aelis replies that she will contribute to their livelihood through her luxurious embroidery:

Fait Aelis: "S'en iert mes deus.	Aelis said: "We will both do that [work].
Bien sachiés que jou referoie	Please know that I will embroider
Joiaus de fil d'or et de soie;	Luxury accessories with gold thread and silk;
K'il n'est feme ki tant en sache:	No woman knows as much as I do
D'orfrois, de çainture, d'atache,	About gold embroidery, belts and fasteners,
De ce faire ai je tot le pris.	I am renowned for doing this.
(vv. 5456–61)	

The insistence on Aelis's exceptional skills at fashioning accessories, at embroidering silk with precious stones and gold thread, is intriguing because it runs counter to the way women's work was perceived by medieval Western clerics, as an invention of the devil, as an alienation of the body and the soul. This kind of condemnation was especially virulent when women's work "brought them status and prestige,"[10] something that Aelis's business quickly achieves. Moreover, Aelis's business is unusual if only because medieval romances typically describe nonworking women, or if working, involved in unpaid jobs. As a matter of fact, if embroidery is the most traditional occupation of noble women in medieval romance,[11] their end products are never remunerated; more often they are given away as tokens of love (Soredamors in *Cligès*; Fresne in *Galeran de Bretagne*) or offered as gifts to the church (Lienor in Jean Renart's *Roman de Guillaume de Dole*). Aelis's embroidery workshop on the other hand, being a privately owned and operated one and participating in the "household economy" typical of most crafts and trades in the Middle Ages, is a full-fledged business and a financially lucrative one. Rather than its conventional association with the decorative and the adornment and fetishizing of women, the literary depiction of embroidery in the *Escoufle* gives rise to Aelis's social mobility and financial sovereignty.[12]

Aelis's social success is indeed rapidly achieved as she becomes quickly acquainted with the knights and nobles of Montpellier:

Ele a lués droit la grace eüe	[Aelis] quickly received the favors
Des chevaliers, des damoisiaus.	Of knights, and of young noblemen.

(vv. 5486–87)

As a fictional bourgeois businesswoman, Aelis defies the ideological presuppositions of women's proper role in medieval society. She enacts a new fate, albeit an imaginary one, for secular women who no longer need to be restricted to or constrained by marriage, heterosexuality, or the private arena; she inaugurates instead an innovative public, social, and lucrative space, that is also as we will see a cross-cultural one.

As she gains social status and prosperity, Aelis becomes like one of those autonomous literary single women in the Middle Ages, discussed by Krueger, who existed socially independent from a male protector (husband, father, lord, lover) and family supervision.[13] Aelis's independence and affluence are especially remarkable because luxury trade (such as that of silk and precious stones) was known to require not only skills but also investments, capital, and commercial organization, all more readily available to married and widowed women than to single women such as Aelis.[14] Even though such practical details are missing from the romance, it appears that our heroine has sufficient available resources to set up her business, perhaps through the jewelry she had remembered to take along with her when she escaped from her father's house in Rome (vv. 3790–95). The expendable wealth that Aelis brought with her functions similarly in the romance as the dowries that medieval women would have used to offset their business costs.

Aelis's achievement leads both to increased social recognition and surprising financial prosperity. In fact, the narrator insists on how well remunerated Aelis is for her embroidery:

Il ne li donent pas a conte	They do not give her money
Les deniers; ml't croist et engraigne,	Sparingly; her extreme kindness
Por ses joiaus et por s'ouvraigne,	Increases and augments the wages
Le loier sa grans gentelise.	Of her precious stones and her business.
Ne cuidiés pas c'on li eslise	Do not even think that one can point to
Mauvais argent quant on li done:	Defective money when she is given any:
Cascuns li baille et abandoune	Everyone gives her and hands her
De l'avoir tant com ele veut.	As many riches as she wants.
(vv. 5492–99)	

Aelis's financial success firmly situates her work beyond the traditional medieval female domestic role of family food provider and beyond reproduction. It represents a fictive departure from what we know of women's work in medieval towns. Sharon Farmer has indeed pointed out that in thirteenth-century Paris, most migrant women worked in the lowest paid sectors of the economy as domestic servants or unskilled laborers.[15] Similarly, Kowaleski and Bennett, building upon the groundbreaking work of Marian K. Dale's study of silk workers in fifteenth-century London, have argued that with the notable exception of female dominated guilds in Rouen, Paris, and Cologne, "most women in medieval towns worked as domestic servants, petty retailers, spinsters, midwives, prostitutes, and the like, all occupations never recognized as skilled, much less organized into gilds."[16] In the *Escoufle*, therefore, it is noteworthy that Aelis and Ysabel, two single women without a male connection to an established trade, are able to set up a successful private embroidery business, a business under their sole control, outside Paris, Rouen, or Cologne.[17] As it crosses the borders between history and fiction, the *Escoufle* inaugurates an intriguing new fictional image of medieval business women.

Lesbianism and Prostitution

As we admire Aelis's skilled, prestigious, and lucrative craft, we must wonder why Aelis (in the above quotation) is paid more than the actual price of the services she renders and in what ways her "grans gentelise" ("extreme kindness," v. 5495) augments her salary.[18] A close reading reveals the textual ambiguity surrounding Aelis's embroidery. It is curious indeed that the lines cited above that describe Aelis's financially lucrative business lack any direct reference to needlework per se. Embroidery is only referred to *implicitly* through words like "ses joiaus" (vv. 5489, 5494) and "s'ouvraigne" (v. 5494). The reader might be tempted to interpret these words to mean Aelis's embroidery, but in fact, they suggest other connotations. For, in addition to its conventional meaning of "luxurious gifts," "jewels," and "gems," the word "joiaus" is a euphemism often used in fabliaux and farces to speak of "female genitalia" and sexual pleasure, while the word "ouvraigne" is conveniently general and refers to all sorts of trades, including the sexual business.[19] As it describes Aelis's business and social identity, the text therefore lays out the provocative possibility that if Aelis is highly successful, and if she is paid more than the actual value of her embroidery, it may well be because she renders services over and above her needlework. These services are her "joiaus" (both her needlework and sexual favors) that she shares to her clients' liking ("C'est par son sens et ses joiaus / K'ele fait tex comme il devisent" ["Through her good manners and her jewels / Which she makes to their liking,"] vv. 5488–89) and that consequently increase her remuneration (v. 5493).

If the description of Aelis's services provides an ambiguous amalgam of skillful needlework and implicit sexual favors, the embroidery workshop that Aelis establishes in Montpellier may well have served, as some did in the Middle Ages, as a high-end private prostitution salon.[20] This interpretation corroborates what some medieval historians have revealed about the working conditions of urban women. In this regard, Sharon Farmer has noted that many migrant working women in thirteenth-century Paris had to supplement their meager income with wages from prostitution.[21] Moreover, Shulamith Shahar has pointed out that, throughout the Middle Ages, women (and at times men) kept brothels camouflaged as embroidery workshops and that successful prostitutes received their clients in their own homes and did not work in brothels, in contrast to lower-class ones.[22] The literary text opens us here a lens into medieval social practices, for we are permitted to interpret Aelis's lavish and fictional privately owned embroidery business as an instance of these historically documented and clandestine sexual trades.

The sexual connotations of Aelis's embroidery are also evident in the fact that for the first time in the romance, Aelis is referred to as "feme" (woman, wife) and no longer exclusively as she had been thus far, "pucele" (young girl, but increasingly virgin).[23] The term "feme" (an amalgam of the Latin *mulier* and *femina*, wife and woman) is revealing of the social and sexual transformation that Aelis undergoes when she moves to Montpellier. To call Aelis a "feme" precisely at this moment in the romance is to point very explicitly to her changed sexual status. Certainly, the word "feme" had already been used to describe the moment of Aelis's entry into the city, such as when the narrator pointed out that his heroine does not go unnoticed and that the public heralds her as the most beautiful woman in the kingdom ("la plus bele feme del raigne," v. 5480). The usage of the word "feme" in this verse does not yet reflect the change in Aelis's sexual state which will soon follow, since the term occurs in the context of an idiomatic expression.[24] A few lines later, however, and while describing Aelis's novel social space in Montpellier, the narrator calls her again "feme," this time with a more definite sexual meaning:

Avuec le grant avoir	Because of all the great wealth
qu'ele eut.	she received.
N'iert il si boine feme lors.	There was no better woman then.
Sachiés que c'est uns bons	Know that a good, beautiful and
tresors	prudent woman
De bone feme, bele et preu.	Is a great treasure.
(vv. 5500–503)	

The use of the word "feme" twice in these lines is significant. While the term appears here in the context of what seems to be a proverb or an aphorism (vv. 5502–3), suggesting that Aelis's social behavior is that of a good woman and fits within conventional morality, "feme" refers also very specifically to Aelis. And it is the specificity of its usage that lends support to the fact that the new social space created in Montpellier is one that has "initiated"[25] Aelis's sexual and social transformation from "pucele" to "feme." While the *Escoufle*, like most medieval literary texts, is not absolutely consistent in the usage of these terms, and while the narrator will continue to waver between "feme" and "pucele" when referring to Aelis in the remainder of the romance, it is still worth noting that the turning point from "pucele" to "feme" occurs at a key moment in the romance, precisely at the establishment of the Montpellier household business and the description of the (sexual) services Aelis renders to men therein.

The intimate relation between clothing (embroidery) and prostitution was implicit already in the way Aelis and Ysabel had been described when they departed from Toul on their voyage across France. Examining once again the description of Ysabel's dress reveals that it is depicted in precisely those terms that twelfth- and thirteenth-century preachers and theologians condemned as manifestations of luxury and inappropriate attachments to the material world. Maurice de Sully (bishop of Paris in the late twelfth century), Cardinal Jacques de Vitry, Dominicans Etienne de Bourbon, Humbert de Romans, Gilles d'Orléans, and the Franciscan Guibert de Tournai in the thirteenth century all echoed Tertullian's fourth-century call to women in his *Apparel of Women* (*De habitu muliebri* and *De cultu feminarum*) to "cast away the ornaments of this world if we truly desire those of heaven."[26] They reiterated Tertullian's condemnation of women's expensive clothes and decorative adornment as signs of their moral ruin and lasciviousness. Maurice de Sully in particular blamed women who walked with heads lifted up in order to be seen: "Celes qui . . . vont comme grue a petit pas, chiere levee que l'en les voie, cestes sont fornaises ardanz de luxure et sont mariees au deable et enfers est leur doaires, et si font meint ardoir entor euls par le jeu de luxure" ("Those women who . . . walk face uplifted as to be seen, these women are burning fires of licentiousness married to the devil, with hell as their dowry. They make many around them burn through their lustful tricks").[27]

The narrator of the *Escoufle* skillfully weaves history with fiction in his description of Ysabel's clothes. Her ornate attire flaunts the physical and sexual delights that are associated with the devil and which lead directly to hell. Her two-tone gown and her wide skirt distressingly betray the prevalent "anxiety over the deceptive excesses of elite women's trailing gowns."[28] Her clothing and luxurious adornments are especially dangerous because they obscure social differences and conceal the natural body underneath the seduction of lavish clothing. Finally, the fact that she and Aelis walk luxuriously dressed, without any disguise (they are not cross-dressed) and with their heads lifted without any shame, desiring to be seen, recalls precisely those elements that were severely condemned by medieval theologians.[29] The two women display a pride that is to be castigated, as it draws them into the public eye and links them to prostitutes.

Embroidery (prostitution) is only one of the multiple services proposed in the Montpellier workshop which includes also a beauty/barber shop (vv. 5508–11) and a literary salon (vv. 5524–29). In fact, soon, the primary and official function of the business as an embroidery workshop competes with the implicit and equally important additional services it renders.

We must be careful not to interpret the two women's involvement in several different crafts as demanded by their economic well-being and their survival,[30] since Aelis's embroidery business is financially lucrative and it seems clear that Aelis had readily available resources that allowed her to set up the business in the first place. Aelis and Ysabel do not engage in the additional occupations for financial necessity; rather, these tasks appropriately complement the implicit (sexual) work provided under the banner of embroidery.

In point of fact, Aelis's hairwashing business ought not be considered such an outlandish addition to the Montpellier business as we might think at first reading:

Si vit de ce qu'ele desert	She lived from what she earned
A laver les chiés as haus homes.	Washing the head (hair) of aristocratic men.
Ainc puis celi dont vos disomes	Since we told you her story
Feme si bien ne lava chief.	No woman ever washed heads (hair) as well.
Trop savoit bien venir a chief	She knew how to accomplish
De tot quanque feme doit faire.	Everything that a woman had to do.
(vv. 5508–13)	

Like the sexually ambiguous embroidery business, hairwashing invites at least two competing interpretations. First of all, it is one of the multiple services rendered by barber shops in the Middle Ages. And there is evidence that women worked as barbers in medieval towns, as indicated in the thirteenth-century list and regulation of Parisian guilds contained in Etienne Boileau's *Livre des métiers*.[31]

Even though the narrator of the *Escoufle* only mentions Aelis's hairwashing skills, medieval barbers did more than just that. In the medieval West, (male) barbers occupied an intermediate position between university trained physicians (*medicus*) and rural practitioners and healers. The very existence of women barbers represents a key surviving evidence of the role that women healers played in men and women's health care and medicine in the Middle Ages. These barbers tended to the physical needs of lay people in a more manual, practical way and were hence often associated with surgeons.[32] They took care of the hair, performed dental work, bled and worked on the visible parts of a person's body, since only the *medicus*, with his university training, could delve into and understand the inside of the body. It is not clear in the *Escoufle* what specific tasks Aelis performed in her barber shop, in addition to hairwashing. It is possible that she also acted as a female surgeon or healer. If so, the depiction of Aelis's work in the hairwashing/barber business could evoke the unparalleled opening up to women of medical teaching and practicing opportunities in Montpellier, following Count Guilhem VIII's famous 1180 edict that encouraged any foreigner to come and practice medicine in that city.[33] The literary Aelis may have profited, as some medieval European women likely did, from being able to take over one of the lower-level occupations that (male) barbers and surgeons used to render (hairwashing), but quickly vacated, following Guilhem VIII's edict, in favor of higher-level occupations in their upward move on the *medicus* professional ladder.

Yet, this interpretation of Aelis's hairwashing is not the only one suggested by the above lines. The insistence with which the narrator describes Aelis's skilled hairwashing (vv. 5510–11) and ability to do everything that a woman did (vv. 5512–13) highlights the ambiguity of the business she established. While no detail is given as to what constitutes "tot quanque feme doit faire" (v. 5513), we might infer that these activities are related to hairwashing. Interestingly, in the medieval West, barber-surgeons were not only associated with hairwashing, they also worked in tandem with bathhouses, which themselves were often a coverup for places of prostitution.[34] In other words, Aelis's beauty salon/barber shop maintains, if not confirms the overall (sexual) ambiguity of the embroidery business.

The sexual nature of Aelis's trade is manifest even in the very decoration of her household. Shortly after describing Aelis's skillful embroidery of silk and her much-appreciated hairwashing, the narrator points to the pleasure ("delit") that her clients receive from the adornments of her house, a description that one might mistake at first for a gratuitous detail concerning the comforts of Aelis's house:

. . . et si grant delit	. . . and her counterpane and her
Ses keutes pointes et si lit	bed
Enbelissent ml't son ostel.	That embellished her house
(vv. 5515–17)	Brought great pleasure.

The narrator mentions only the most intimate features of Aelis's house, the counterpane and the bed, and he does so immediately following the description of the embroidery and hairwashing services that Aelis provides. This juxtaposition leads the reader to wonder of what consists the "delit" that is mentioned at this juncture. Are the bed and counterpane pleasurable in an aesthetic sense because they are lavishly embroidered, made of the finest silk and hence give expression to Aelis's skillful embroidery? Or are they pleasurable in a more physical, sensual, and intimate sense because of the function they serve when the clients visit Aelis? These questions remain unanswered, heightening the reader's overarching uncertainty about the exact function of Aelis's Montpellier business.

Similarly, the third official branch of Aelis's embroidery workshop confirms the overall (sexual) ambiguity of the urban business and demonstrates the extent to which the social and economic space that Aelis develops in Montpellier is a highly unusual one, especially when read from a Western perspective. Not only does the house become the fashionable meeting place of bourgeois and knights:

Ele ot lués droit tot le	[The house] soon became the
repaire	home
Des borjois et des chevaliers.	Of the middle class and knights.
(vv. 5482–83)	

but it also becomes a successful literary salon where the uppercrust comes to mingle, to play chess and various board games, as well as to enjoy the oral entertainment (tales and romances) provided by Aelis:[35]

El les deduisoit bel et gent,	She entertained them well
Si lor contoit romans et	And told them romances and
contes;	stories;
Des autres gius n'estoit	The other games that are
nus contes,	mentioned in the tale
D'eschés, de tables et de dis.	[are] chess, board games, dice.
(vv. 5524–27)	

The addition of storytelling to the embroidery and overall sexuality of Aelis's business brings to mind the intimate link between sewing, desiring, and singing developed by the corpus known as the *chansons de toile* which will be composed some thirty years later (the *chansons de toile* are dated 1228–50).[36] But while the *chansons de toile* will estheticize the relation between sewing, desiring, and singing, making them the focus of a lyrical arrangement and displacing them to a courtly context, the *Escoufle* demonstrates that three decades prior to their poetic expression, these elements were already part and parcel of the genre of the realistic romance and may thus have also been manifestations of the urban existence of some European women at the turn of the thirteenth century.

Just as she excels in needlework and hairwashing, Aelis stands out as an accomplished hostess of her salon. In fact, Emmanuèle Baumgartner has observed that the embroidery business in the *Escoufle* extends far beyond mere survival; it is rather "a process of social seduction, the means of attracting the favors of knights and bourgeois, of triumphing over the indifference or disdain of the high nobility, of demonstrating perhaps that it is better to be a desired *çainturiere* rather than an ignored noble woman."[37] I will suggest that in the *Escoufle*, Aelis goes even further, for she successfully constructs a new type of social identity, one that transcends traditional categories of nobility and familiar occupations (*çainturiere*). Aelis becomes a financially independent *çainturiere* who displays the social status of a desired noble woman. The male clients she receives in her salon all belong to the noble or bourgeois classes, placing her at the center rather than at the margins of the most sophisticated social categories of her society.[38] Aelis achieves this idiosyncratic social state through her expertise at entertaining men ("deduit," v. 5524), at storytelling (v. 5528), as well as her embroidery and hairwashing skills.

Aelis's new social identity is defined by a constant search for pleasure. Our heroine's primary concern throughout the *Escoufle* is indeed to "plaire" which means both to please and to give (sexual) pleasure or satisfy (sexual) desires:[39] "Or est en[ten]tive la bele / De faire quanqu'a gens doit plaire" ("The beautiful [girl] was careful / To do whatever pleased people," vv. 5532–33). The ambiguity of Aelis's business is reflected in the ambiguity of the pleasures derived from the services received therein. The reader remains utterly unable to distinguish the satisfaction of intellectual needs (hearing stories, playing games) or the pleasures of esthetic and material possession (embroidery, hairwashing) from the fulfillment of physical or erotic desires.[40] What the narrator continuously insists upon nevertheless is the fact that Aelis's Montpellier urban household becomes the space par excellence of pleasure:

Il n'avoit a Monpellier tel
Ne de soulas ne de
   deduit.
(vv. 5518–19)

There were none in Montpellier
Equal to it in comfort and
   delight.

and a few lines later:

Son afaitement, son deduit
Prisent ml't cil qui l'ont
   hantee.
(vv. 5536–37)

Everyone who frequented her
praises her courtesy and her
   conduct

We recognize here the same polymorphous meanings of the words "soulas" and "deduit" that we encountered when discussing in the previous chapter the development of the friendly/erotic relationships between Aelis and the three main female characters of the *Escoufle*. The word "hantee" in the above citation sustains the ambiguity of the vocabulary of pleasure, since it means not only "those who frequented or visited Aelis" but also "those who had sexual intercourse with her."[41] Once again, the type of pleasure received in Aelis's household remains highly ambiguous and implicitly erotic. Just as it was not possible to draw a clear distinction between friendship and same-sex desire in the context of Aelis's liaisons with Ysabel, the lady of Montpellier, or the countess of Saint-Gilles (Chapter 4), it is challenging now to distinguish the professional from the private, the material possession of lavishly embroidered goods or the intellectual pleasures of a literary salon, or even the esthetics of a well-dressed hairdo from the more intimate pleasures offered on the luxurious bed of a courtesan.

If Ruth Mazo Karras's assessment is correct, that in the Middle Ages "the sexually active single woman was viewed in quite narrow terms—indeed, defined as a prostitute,"[42] then the sexual connotations of Aelis's services can only be interpreted as a coverup for prostitution and her as a prostitute. However, it must be emphasized that even though Aelis's fictional embroidery business stages multiple similarities with prostitution and even though her three-part business recalls that of a medieval prostitute, the character of Aelis escapes such easy social and sexual categorization. At no point in the romance is Aelis called "meretrix" which is the word used to refer to a professional prostitute in the Middle Ages; at no point does she receive payment solely for her sexual favors; and no mention is made of a commercial sort of (hetero)sexual activity. Any potentially compromising form of sexuality remains implicit in the text and carefully couched in the other official services that the business offers (embroidery, hairwashing, game playing, storytelling).[43]

In fact, while strongly inviting a sexual reading, the romance continuously resists such an interpretation. When Aelis wakes up to find that Guillaume is no longer by her side during their escape from Rome, she calls herself a "menestrel" (v. 4673) which can certainly mean a prostitute, but this meaning competes with the word's other less sexual connotations (itinerant singer or entertainer).[44] And Aelis herself struggles in that very scene to actively dissociate herself from any potential link with prostitution. For shortly after calling herself a "menestrel," she encounters a young man who tries to help her. She realizes at this very moment that the light clothing she is wearing (because of the heat, Aelis had taken off her outer garments while Guillaume was still with her and she had not put them back on) renders her situation especially compromising to anyone who would see them thus. Aelis hurriedly pulls her clothes over her thinly clad body:

Por ce k'aucuns nes truist	So that no one who would find
ensamble	them together
Ki i notast mal ou folie,	Would think it evil or lewd,
Ele se rafuble	She gets dressed and laces
et relie,	[her clothes]
Ml't plorant et pensive	While crying, thinking, and
et morne.	feeling wretched.
(vv. 4832–35)	

Aelis voices here the associations that the medieval audience would have made regarding single women without family or male protection. Such women become socially naked in the eyes of others, thus vulnerable to unfounded slander and associated with prostitutes and women of loose morals.[45] With Guillaume's disappearance, Aelis (in parallel to medieval single women or prostitutes) becomes visible; her social identity is threatened, and she becomes the potential victim of sexual violence and social blame. As she puts her clothes back on, Aelis literally conceals her social nakedness underneath a physical protective layer (her clothes) that affirms her honor and dissociates her from negative social categorization. While the narrator of the *Escoufle* warns us against equating single women (Aelis) with prostitutes in this scene, he teases us into making precisely this equation when reading Aelis's three-part Montpellier business.

In contrast to Ysabel, who is the object of the narrator's undisguised contempt, Aelis's social situation on the other hand is more complex. It falls somewhere in the middle of the high (professional) and low end of prostitution, far from the margins that medieval prostitutes were known to inhabit. Aelis's particular form of prostitution partly fits the category of "clandestine prostitution" which refers to those women who practiced on their own rather than in any officially recognized brothel.[46] In this sense, Aelis may be considered a full-time professional (embroideress) and occasionally a prostitute. But quickly, the question of financial need complicates such simple categorization since Aelis as we saw does not need the additional income to survive.[47]

If Aelis is not a prostitute in a commercial sense and not quite a clandestine prostitute, she may be a "sinful woman," similar to Mary Magdalen according to Karras's categories of prostitution.[48] This interpretation is particularly appealing because Aelis's religious intentions are moot at best. She does not go to church often and when she does, it is more out of a desire to increase her social recognition than an internal love or fear of God (vv. 5504–7).[49] But the category of "sinful woman" again becomes quickly inapplicable to Aelis who is soon thereafter praised for her beauty (v. 5480) and her wisdom (vv. 5596–5601). The reader's temptation to interpret Aelis's behavior univocally as that of a prostitute (professional, clandestine, or sinful) once again collapses.

Aelis and the Saint-Gilles Household

Aelis's Montpellier household business is not the sole sexually and socially ambiguous space that the heroine inhabits in the *Escoufle*. In fact, this social space and the complex social identity that Aelis acquires in the urban environment

of medieval Montpellier give rise to a second equally alternative social arrangement. We will recall that in the romance, Aelis's success in Montpellier leads to
her acquaintance and "friendship" with the lady of Montpellier which in turn
ushers her into the Saint-Gilles household. Invited there to become the countess's "pucele" and "amie," so that the countess could be "autel" (like) her husband, Aelis soon finds herself in the midst of a conspicuous social
configuration. The exclusively female community which she had come to join
quickly takes on novel traits, at least from a Western perspective. For contrary
to what we might have expected, the count does not disappear from the romance, nor does he continue undisturbed his extramarital affair with the lady
of Montpellier. Rather, he soon becomes an integral member of the all-female
community of the countess's entourage:[50]

Li cuens avoit une costume	The count had a custom
Qui li tournoit a grant	That brought him much
deduit	pleasure.
. . . .	. . . .
En la cambre u sont les puceles;	In the young girls' room
Si s'en va la jus avoec eles	He goes and sits with them
Mangier son fruit et aaisier.	And eats his fruit and relaxes.
(vv. 7016–23)	

The count regularly spends his evenings in the intimacy of the "puceles"
quarters, and is said to derive pleasure ("deduit") from their company. The use
of the word "deduit" evokes the same ambiguity that characterized the alternative liaison between Aelis and Ysabel (Chapter 4), or between Aelis and her
male clients in the Montpellier business discussed above. Just as it was not
possible to discern the pleasures of female friendship from those of same-sex
eroticism, it is equally impossible here to grasp the precise meaning of the
count's "deduit." Such blurring of meanings places the count's "pleasure" in
the maidens' company at the crossroads between casual friendship and sexual
satisfaction. The count's pleasure seems thus to be at once emotional, psychological, physical, and sensual.

Furthermore, and all the while evoking a gastronomical idiosyncracy, the
count's habit of eating his evening fruit (and pears specifically, as we are told,
v. 7075) with the maidens invites a sexual reading of the scene, rendering it a
literary heir to the prelapsarian moment of falling into sin. For the "pear" is
often evoked in the Christian Middle Ages as a synonym for "apple," the fruit

of sin par excellence, such as in the contemporary *Roman de la poire*: "Des puis qu'Adan mordi la pome, / Ne fumes tel poire trovee" ("Never since Adam bit into the apple / has such a pear been found").[51] When we read in the *Escoufle* that the count derived pleasure from eating his evening pear in the maidens' room, we are permitted to interpret this scene as indicating the inception of a new type of social structure within the economy of the text, where one (French) count obtains his pleasure (emotional and sexual) from the company of many women.

The sexual connotations of this scene and the role that Aelis plays therein become even more pronounced in the description of the remainder of the evening. This scene bears quoting in full:

Ml't le savoit bien soulacier,
La pucele bele Aelis.
(vv. 7024–25)

The young beautiful Aelis
knew how to relax him well.

Il se despoille por
    grater,
Et n'i laisse riens a oster
Fors ses braies; nis sa
    chemise
Li a cele fors du dos mise
Ki les autres vaint de
    biauté:
I surcot qui n'est pas
    d'esté
Li revest por le froit qu'il
    doute.
(vv. 7033–39)

He undresses in order to be
    scratched.
He removes everything
except his *braies*; the girl who
    surpasses
the others with her beauty
has removed his shirt from his
    back:
She dresses him with a winter
    coat
because of the cold that he
    fears.

Ses soulas, ses deduis
    envoise
Celes et ceus qui sont laiens;
(vv. 7044–45)

[Aelis] charms with her tales and
    her entertainments
everyone who is there.

Ele estoit toute desliie
En i frés vair pliçon sans
    mances,

She was completely undressed:
She had a sleeveless fur-lined
    tunic

Celes erent beles et blances	[her arms] beautiful and fair
De la chemise et bien tendans.	[could be seen] from the shirt.
Bien est rois qui ert atendans	Whoever was privy to her love and her beauty
A s'amor et a sa biauté.	Can be considered a king.
Ele a son destre bras geté	She had placed her right arm
Parmi l'emingaut du surcot	under the collar of the count's coat.
Le conte, qui son cief li ot	He had placed his head
Mis par chierté en son devant.	on her lap (bosom) out of affection (love)
Que qu'il atent en deduisant	while he waits for the fruit that is still not
Le fruit qui n'ert encor pas cuis.	cooked, enjoying himself.
(vv. 7048–59)	

This scene tempts the reader into participating voyeuristically, along with the immediate audience of these lines (the countess and her *puceles*) in the intimate encounter between the count and Aelis.[52] The latter, we are told, provides "ses soulas, ses deduis" not only to the count, her immediate partner in this scene, but also to all those present with them in the room (vv. 7044–45), including undoubtedly the medieval and contemporary audiences. Functioning as ocular witnesses to this bedroom encounter, each audience gazes at the central characters' suggested nakedness,[53] their intertwined positioning, and their ambiguous caresses. This scene is all the more titillating because it reverses the traditional hierarchy of (male) gaze and attending scopic pleasure. Here, the inscribed audience is made solely of women and it is they, rather than men, who are placed in the active position of gazing at the intimate couple. The (adulterous) heterosexual couple is henceforth reduced to the level of object of the female gaze and pleasure (v. 7044). By making the countess herself and at least two different audiences (an intra- and an extradiegetic one) from two different time periods (the Middle Ages and today) privy to this intimate scene, and by moving the private moment into the public eye, the narrator depicts a highly unusual social space within the medieval Western literary tradition. As we will see shortly, however, this scene is strongly reminiscent of common social interactions in the Arab Islamicate world, notably those taking place within the harem.

Equally important, the theatricalization of the intimate heterosexual encounter between the count and Aelis constitutes an early manifestation of "lesbian ghosting."[54] For all the while participating in the count's "deduit," the eye of the spectator is directed away from the figural center toward the spectral; that is, the other liaison staged outside the visual field. If the "figural" here is the heterosexual relation, the "spectral" is made up of the erotic union between Aelis and the countess of Saint-Gilles that I discussed in Chapter 4. This lesbian relation, known only to the female intradiegetic audience and the careful reader of the *Escoufle*, might be visibly absent from this particular scene, yet it is always present in the text and in the memory of the reader. The narrator skillfully displaces the visible part of the scene and urges us to do and undo representation by confronting the invisible. As a consequence, the audience must continuously negotiate between the visible and the invisible, the represented and the nonrepresented, the figural and the spectral. The heterosexual scene may hence be read as a visual erotic space in which the lesbian relation is at once visibly and invisibly spatialized. If the heterosexual relation is the only one that could be safely staged here, the lesbian relation constitutes nevertheless the most important extrascenic element that informs our reading of this scene. Aelis emerges clearly as a medieval example of the "ghost effect" analyzed by Terry Castle; she is "elusive, vaporous, difficult to spot—even when she is there in plain view, mortal and magnificent, at the center of the screen."[55] In the *Escoufle*, lesbianism is omnipresent at the very moment of its erasure from the text.

This scene allows the contemporary reader a rare glimpse into medieval intimate encounters, a look at an erotic space that is not exclusively heterosexual, if only because of the casual presence of a majority of women in the room.[56] The portrayal of the count surrounded by several women (we do not know their exact number) and caressed by only one of them, the one judged by all to be the most beautiful one, while his lawful wife seems to be happily relegated to the margins along with her *puceles* as passive witnesses to the pleasurable scene, is astounding to say the least. And yet, the narrator describes this scene nonchalantly, as though the household is used to such encounters, if only since Aelis's arrival in their midst.

Not least, this scene is unusual in the narrative economy of medieval (courtly) romance, because it runs counter to what medieval male clerics condemned for being a source of marital disharmony and social disorder. Aelis's caressing of the count seems indeed to enact the "intolerable evil," precisely that which one of the most influential clerics of the thirteenth century

(Jacques de Vitry, d. 1240) feared in female maidservants, namely, of stealing her lord's affection from his legitimate wife. Likewise, the count seems to personify one of those "miserable men" who "are exceedingly infected with this crime," that is of putting their maids before their wives.[57] The scene between Aelis and the count enacts therefore the threat that the introduction of female maidservants was thought to pose to medieval household stability, and it underscores male clerical anxiety about such practice.

This interpretation must be qualified, however. For the presence of Aelis in the Saint-Gilles household does not seem to have created marital instability. To the contrary, her entry into the Saint-Gilles household served to "cure" the count of his adulterous liaison with the lady of Montpellier, as well as to dispel the moral ambiguity of this affair. Coinciding indeed with Aelis's move to Saint-Gilles is the narrative closure of the tale of illicit love between the count of Saint-Gilles and the lady of Montpellier (this relationship is completely silenced in the remainder of the romance). Aelis's arrival has also replaced the adultery outside the home with an adultery within the home, perceived to be somehow less threatening because it institutes an unexpected harmony between the couple.

What results from the preceding discussion is that Aelis's social function does not become clearer after her move from Montpellier to Saint-Gilles. The social space that Aelis creates in Montpellier and in the Saint-Gilles household is not a new "integration into the collective" as Danielle Régnier-Bohler has suggested; it is not simply a reconstruction of the old structure, a new gynecaeum.[58] It is rather a new construction, a reconfiguration of the private and social spaces characteristic both of medieval Western European society and of French romance. Aelis's situation and living arrangements in Montpellier and Saint-Gilles demonstrate a level of female sexual, economic, and social autonomy far beyond those of female characters depicted in other courtly and realistic romances of the period.

Aelis's literary depiction further demonstrates that the status of unmarried, independent women living and working by themselves in medieval towns without any male control escaped easy categorization. In fact, there may have been no place and no name in medieval Western European literary culture for a single woman who is no longer a virgin, who is involved in a same-sex relation with another woman, and who continues to maintain erotically suspicious liaisons with men. She resembles a prostitute, yet is not associated with the conventional traits of prostitutes. Karras's remark that sexually active single women were viewed "in quite narrow terms" in the Middle Ages and quickly collapsed with prostitutes aptly applies to Aelis at the same time that this character escapes such a univocal characterization.[59]

Aelis's social identity is full of paradoxes. First, Aelis lives as a business-woman in a large city (Montpellier), yet, she does not appear to subsist fully in an urban environment; rather, her lifestyle mirrors that of aristocratic courtly ladies as well as their occupations. Second, she is involved in a same-sex relation with Ysabel as I demonstrated (Chapter 4), yet she remains at the heart of her (heterosexual) household-court as a desired *domna*. Third, Aelis lives as a single woman (with Ysabel), thus outside established social norms and independent of male or family control, yet no one attempts to control her sexuality or her behavior. Fourth, she is independent, prosperous, and she re-ceives men in her house; yet she is not described as a marginal woman and her house is not located at the periphery of society, but at its center. She is inde-pendent, creative, displays many "manly" characteristics;[60] yet the romance emphasizes her femininity through the focus on sewing and playing of amorous (erotic) games.[61] In this sense, Aelis maintains the gender tension al-ready portrayed through Chrétien de Troyes's female characters (the unmar-ried ones in particular) who are depicted at once as "privileged and displaced, subject and object."[62] But Aelis also expands this gender tension into what we might call a "social tension" which is a space at the crossroads of court and city, where she is both a single desiring woman and a desired beloved (a *domna*), an aristocratic lady and a businesswoman, a heterosexual prostitute and a lesbian lover. Even as the romance entices us to read fiction as history, it undermines the discourses of history with their established clerical systems of classification and their promotion of a monocultural social identity. The questions posed by the romance are: Who is Aelis? Where does she fit in the medieval Western social fabric? If these questions remain unanswered when the *Escoufle* is read solely from a Western perspective, new interpretations emerge when we examine Aelis's social identity through the lens of medieval Islamicate sociocultural traditions.

Arabic Intertextuality

If Aelis's social standing as it is depicted in both Montpellier and Saint-Gilles is innovative in the context of medieval Western literature and society, it ac-quires a new meaning when read against the backdrop of Arab Islamicate urban culture and social customs. Aelis's household in Montpellier and the complex amalgam of activities she engages in both there and in Saint-Gilles are strongly reminiscent of three Middle Eastern cultural and literary traditions, all intimately tied to silk clothing and gold embroidery, namely, the traditions of *zarf* (courtliness), of *qaynas* (singing slave-girls), and of homosexual refinement. These three cultural practices are important because they demonstrate the significant role that some women from the Middle East and Islamicate cultures (slave-girls especially) played in the public sphere, in the development of the literary and artistic sensibility of their society, and to some extent also in the economic and political dealings of their times.[63] I will begin by describing each of these practices in order to show the extent to which the social spaces that Aelis inhabits in the *Escoufle* may in fact be read as Western literary reconstructions and hybridizations of these Islamicate sociocultural traditions.

Zarf, Zurafas, Mutazarrifat

Zarf has been commonly translated as "refinement," "stylishness," or "courtliness." It is a cultural practice that began in Medina (Saudi Arabia) during the pre-Islamic and Umayyad eras, spread to the urban centers of Baghdad under the Abbasids from the eighth to the tenth century, and extended to the Islamic caliphate of Spain (al-Andalus) in Córdoba and Seville during the reign of the party-kings in the tenth century. This tradition promoted a nexus of behaviors that included an overarching sophistication at the levels of clothing, gastronomy, language, home decoration, as well as an intellectual atmosphere in which participants engaged in debates related to love, recitation of poetry, singing, dance, and storytelling. It was also a tradition that encouraged the development and circulation of the literature of *mujun* or libertinage that I have discussed in Chapter 1. Women, and especially slave-women (*jariya*, pl. *jawari*), played an especially prominent role in *zarf* through the literary salons that they held and to which they invited not only members of the aristocracy, but increasingly also the wealthy bourgeoisie, enriched by trade and international commerce.[64]

Much has been written on the development of *zarf* throughout the Islamicate world. The most important source of our knowledge of this movement remains undoubtedly *Kitab al-zarf wa al-zurafa'* (Book of Refinement and of Refined People), also known as *Kitab al-muwashsha'* composed by a tenth-century grammarian from Baghdad, Mohammed Ibn al-Washsha' (d. 936).[65] In it, he describes at length how the *zurafa*s (refined, courtly men) and *mutazarrifat* (refined, courtly ladies), those who subscribe to *zarf* behavior, adorn their homes with poetry that is sculpted on their house entrance doors, windows, ceilings, beds, tables, and sofas or use verses that have been luxuriously embroidered with gold and precious stones to decorate pillows, curtains, clothing, belts, rings, and even shoes. Throughout the Middle Ages, some women pushed the embroidery fashion so far as to use their own body as cloth. They thus painted a few lines of poetry with henna or a mixture of perfumes around their necks, on their feet, on their hands or on their cheeks.[66] Ibn al-Washsha' gives in his treatise a few famous examples of the types of verses sculpted by *zurafa*s on apples: "I come from the lover (male or female) / and I am given to the (male or female) friend."[67] Another famous example derives from Princess Wallada (d. 1087 or 1091; daughter of Umayyad caliph al-Mustakfi in Muslim Spain) who unquestionably stands as the prototype of the unparalleled refinement of the Andalusian aristocracy in the eleventh century, of women's emancipation therein, and unsuspected sexual freedom. Wallada openly entertained two male lovers (Ibn Zaydun and Ibn `Abdus) and one female lover (Mohja) and had the following two verses embroidered with gold thread on either side of her coat collar: "By God, I am fit for greatness, and stride along with great pride" and "I allow my lover to reach my cheek, and I grant my kiss to him who craves it."[68]

Without overgeneralizing the particular case of Wallada and the degree of women's social and sexual freedom in medieval Islamicate societies, it remains clear nevertheless that Middle Eastern women played a significant role in the development of *zarf*, of courtly customs and good manners not only within the Arabian peninsula and at the Abbasid courts in Iraq but also without, expanding the tradition of *zarf* to all major cities of the medieval Islamicate world in the East and in the West (Seville and Granada). Some of these women belonged to the Umayyad aristocracy, such as Sukayna Bint al-Husayn (d. 744), granddaughter of the Prophet, or Aisha Bint Talha (d. 718).[69] Both were famed for their extraordinary beauty, sharp intelligence, and quick wit. Both married multiple times, and were actively involved in politics and poetry. In addition, both were at the center of literary salons and of aristocratic courts and led discussions on astronomy, history, literature, and fashion, as well as religious matters. Some historians even report that these women pronounced judgments in matters of love and that their literary salons functioned in ways similar to those that will be headed four centuries later in France by Marie de Champagne and described by Andreas Capellanus.[70]

*Jawari*s, *Qayna*s

Most of the information about the *mutazarrifat*, those women promoting *zarf* and engaged in its growth and development, concerns slave-girls (*jawari*), and especially singing slave-girls, or *qayna*s. In his famous *Risalat al-qiyan* (*Epistle on Singing-Girls*), al-Jahiz (d. 868) defends the tradition of owning slave-singers by tracing the important role they played in the pre-Islamic era through the rise of Islam and the Prophet's time.[71] The origin of *zarf* and of literary salons, according to al-Jahiz, is to be found in the tradition of *ziyarat* (visitations), when men and women met to discuss various matters. During the *ziyarat*, "there was no veil between men and women. And since the veil did not exist, men and women did not just look at each other stealthily, but came together to discuss and stayed late together."[72] Al-Jahiz also notes, "the gaze they exchanged was not considered shameful or illicit during the pre-Islamic era or under Islam."[73]

Some of the most successful singing slave-girls (*qayna*s) have left traces in the historical records of the period. A few were prominent poets of the Abbasid period in Basra (Iraq), the most trustworthy transmitters of the oral repertoire, and the most accomplished performers and entertainers. At times, they even had their own singing schools and owned slaves.[74] The best known remain undoubtedly the three leading slave-girls of the Abbasid period, namely, `Inan (d. 841), Fadl (d. 875), and `Arib (d. 890), all of whom are cited in Abbasid historian, poet, and musicologist Abu al-Faraj al-Isfahani's (897–972) tenth-century *Kitab al-aghani* (Book of Songs).[75] `Inan, according to al-Isfahani, was a slave-girl raised and educated in Saudi Arabia. Not only was she beautiful, but she was "well educated, a good poet, and quick witted. She vied and contended with the master (male) poets of the period and she could hold her own among them."[76] Similarly, Fadl al-Sha`ira, or Fadl "the Poetess," was "considered to be the epitome of beauty, [who] set the standards for Arab singers for centuries to come," and she held her own literary salon till her death.[77] This is how Abu al-Faraj al-Isfahani depicts her: Fadl "was beautiful physically and in demeanor; she was well versed in literature, eloquent, notable for her quick, witty answers. She was accurate in her poetry rendering and there was no other woman poet who surpassed her in poetic eloquence."[78] *Kitab al-aghani* describes `Arib, one of the most famous poets, performers, and music instructors of the Abbasid period, in strikingly similar terms: " `Arib was a skilled singer, and a good poetess. She was a good calligrapher, was well-spoken, and possessed the utmost in loveliness, beauty, and gracefulness. She had a beautiful figure, was an excellent lutenist, and reached perfection in craft [of composition], knowledge of the modal system [modes and strings] and in the narration of poetry and literature."[79] In the pages devoted to her in *Kitab al-aghani*, `Arib is also praised for her skills at chess and backgammon, and she is identified as one of the prominent *ghulamiyyat* in al-Amin's Abbassid court (r. 809–13).[80]

*Qayna*s were not only literate, extremely well-educated slave-singers, they were also especially appreciated for the multiple pleasures they brought their audiences, and for the stimulation of three specific senses: sight, hearing, and touch. Al-Jahiz writes:

> Don't they offer men a variety of pleasures not combined anywhere else? . . . As soon as we discuss slave-singers, we note that three senses are associated, [and this without taking into account] the heart which is the fourth. [These are]: sight and [the pleasure of] gazing at a beautiful and desirable slave; . . . hearing and the pleasure of he who without any trouble enjoys alone the pleasure brought upon by the musical instrument; touch and the sexual desire as well as the desire for *bah* [sexual intercourse]. As soon as the *qayna* begins to sing out loud, all eyes turn to her intensely, all ears turn towards her. . . . Any intercourse with slave-singers is associated with the greatest seductive danger.[81]

*Qayna*s (like Japanese *geisha*s and Greek *hetaira*) were educated to provide entertainment through various skills: music (singing, composition, performing on a musical instrument), dancing, storytelling, and sexual pleasure. Eroticism was considered to be an integral part of the education of a *qayna* and was given equal attention as music or intellectual skills. In fact, al-Jahiz goes so far as to assert that the lack of chastity is an integral part of the character of a *qayna*, of her education and her business.[82]

Intellectual skills and game playing were also essential to a *qayna*'s repertoire, for the more skills she had, the more diverse the pleasures she could offer, and the more highly prized she was. The best-known literary *qayna* is undoubtedly the slave-girl Tawaddud (Showing Winning Love), also known as "Sympathy the Learned," eminent heroine of a tale from the *One Thousand and One Nights.*[83] In this story, the slave-girl is legendary not only for her beauty, singing skills, and game playing, but also and especially for her knowledge of all the known sciences of the time, including grammar, poetry, music, religious law, theology, mathematics, astronomy, philosophy, and medicine. This *qayna* is depicted excelling in scholarly discussions and surpassing the knowledge of (male) scholars patronized by the court. What Arab and Muslim historical and fictive women such as Tawaddud, ʿArib, ʿInan, Fadl, and others like them demonstrate is that singing slave-girls were not only defined by their sexuality, but were also well-educated young women, gifted poets, composers, and performers who became the great artists of their period and the repositories of its oral tradition. The role and function of *qayna*s resonate clearly with Aelis's sexually ambiguous Montpellier business. The social space in which Aelis evolves recalls that which *qayna*s inhabit, while not being reducible to it, as we will see shortly.

*Qayna*s participated actively in the literary salons of their period, or what in Arabic is called *majliss* (plural *majalis*). In Arabic, the term *majliss* has an added specific meaning that highlights the pleasure taken in intellectual debates and sensual encounters. Fatima Mernissi defines *majliss* as follows: "The word *majliss* comes from the verb *jalasa*, which means to sit down with the idea of relaxing motionless for some time, for the sake of pure enjoyment. The word *majliss* means a group of people with similar interests who meet in an attractive place, such as a garden or a terrace, for the sheer pleasure of conversing together and having a good time."[84] George Dimitri Sawa, in his study on music performance in the early Abbassid era specifies that the pleasure of the *majliss* was the pleasure of learning together, and contributing to "discussions and debates on music, history, theory, criticism, and aesthetics."[85] It is precisely the pleasure, sensuality, and intellectual atmosphere that permeated these *majalis* that echo in Aelis's embroidery business/literary salon in Montpellier.

Slave-singers, despite (or rather, *because of*) their social status as slaves, played a significant role in the medieval Islamicate world not only because they were freer to express themselves (in contrast to freeborn women), but also because of their superior intellectual skills and extraordinary beauty. Freed slaves especially could potentially achieve lucrative careers; some in fact rose to the top levels of society, marrying caliphs and kings.[86] In other words, and despite the well-rehearsed legal and religious prohibitions against Muslim women circulating in public urban spaces, one of the greatest achievements of medieval Muslim women lies precisely in their ability to circulate simultaneously in the private and public spheres and hence to cross socioeconomic borders. A slave-woman could gain financial means, prestige, and at times even respectability through her beauty, poetic and intellectual skills, and especially through her ability to conceive (*umm walad*). She could become part of a ruler's harem which was considered to be a promotion in Islamicate society, since it is often from within the harem that many women exerted considerable sovereignty.[87] It is thus misleading to read the harem (from an Orientalist and Western perspective) exclusively as a space of confinement and of subordination for women in medieval Islamicate societies. Without promoting the return of the harem or denying the obvious injurious connotations of such a cultural practice, it must nevertheless be recognized that within the context of the medieval Islamicate world, the harem was for many women also the space of social promotion, liberation, and political agency.

The most significant example of a slave who came to occupy politically and socially powerful positions from within the harem is undoubtedly that of Shajarrat al-Durr (d. 1259) or "Tree of Pearls," concubine of al-Malik al-Salih Ayyub, the last Ayyubid ruler of Egypt in the middle of the thirteenth century. After giving him a son, he gave her freedom, and she was pronounced Sultana of Egypt in 1249. She took on two titles: "Ismat al-dunya wa al-din" ("the Blessed of the earthly world and of the faith") and "Umm Khalil" ("Mother of Khalil," her son who died in infancy).[88] She may have ruled Egypt for only four months (November 1249 to February 1250), but her rule marked the official demise of the Ayyubids and the establishment of the Mamluk dynasty in Egypt which was to last for more than two centuries in Egypt and Syria (it would end only with the Ottoman conquest of Egypt in 1516). In the few months that Shajarrat al-Durr was sultana of Egypt, she had coins minted in her name and the Friday *khutba* (sermon) pronounced in her glory: "May Allah protect the Beneficent One, Queen of the Muslims, the Blessed of the Earthly World and of the Faith, the Mother of Khalil al-Musta`simiyya, the Companion of Sultan al-Malik al-Salih."[89] No official document left the palace without her signature.

Shajarrat al-Durr is best remembered for the unprecedented role that she played in the sixth crusade. When her first husband, al-Malik al-Salih Ayyub died on November 23, 1249, Shajarrat al-Durr concealed his death while waiting for the recall of her son and heir, Turanshah, from Iraq. She forged the late sultan's signature on official documents in order to maintain political and military stability. She defeated the French king, Saint-Louis, on February 19, 1250, at Mansura and ransomed him for one million bezants. Shajarrat al-Durr put an end to the crusaders' presence in Egypt, regained Damietta, and restored peace in Egypt. Yet, despite the extraordinary position she held in both Egyptian, Mediterranean, Western, and world political history, Shajarrat al-Durr's role has been downplayed by both Western and Arab chroniclers.[90]

In her *Forgotten Queens of Islam*, Fatima Mernissi has shown how the *qaynas'* intellectual proficiency not only permitted some to "climb the social ladder, but also raise their value in the slave market, and thereby subvert the ruling male hierarchy altogether."[91] And indeed it was the *qaynas'* beauty and intellectual skills that determined their price. Functioning as veritable commercial commodities and as "symbols of status," they were equivalent to "fine copies of the Quran, silk gowns, rare perfumes and crafted hilts."[92] Not surprisingly, some drew exorbitant prices. According to Jamal Eddine Bencheikh, a contemporary critic, the price of a first-class *qayna* in the eleventh century was 3,000 dinars. This sum is meaningful when compared to the yearly pension of a famous poet (such as Andalusian Ibn Zaydun, d. 1070), which was 500 dinars, and the daily salary of a construction worker (one dinar).[93] Some *qaynas*, such as Hubsiyya, ʿAwm's slave, drew 120,000 dinars.[94] Finally, al-Maʾmun, Harun al-Rashid's son and future caliph of Baghdad, did not hesitate to pay 1,000 dinars for a slave who was not only eloquent, and skilled in music and poetry, but who was also a superior chess player. For al-Maʾmun, playing chess sharpened his mind and prepared him for war, but playing chess with a woman had an added sensual pleasure that allowed him to combine the delights of the body with those of the mind and soul.[95]

The transfer of the *zarf* tradition from Saudi Arabia to Baghdad and later to al-Andalus is associated with *qaynas*, slaves, and the exchange of human gifts between ruling monarchs of the Abbasid caliphate in Baghdad and the Umayyads in Islamic Spain. Such is the case of Qamar, a singing slave-girl bought in the Middle East and sent as a gift for Prince Ibrahim al-Haggag of Seville. She played an important role in the transmission of sophisticated courtly etiquette, refined conduct, and good manners from the Islamicate East to the Islamicate West.[96]

In addition, the development of *zarf* in the Islamicate courts of Spain cannot be dissociated from the fierce desire of Andalusian courts to emulate and surpass the artistic, intellectual, and courtly achievements of their Baghdadi counterparts, as well as their social, military, and political successes.[97] Already since the ninth century, when the Iberian peninsula was becoming a refined urban society, Andalusian princes were prepared to pay any price to ensure that their own courts could compete with the most sophisticated ones in the East. And this is precisely what Abd al-Rahman II (822–52) did when he invited Baghdadi singer and musician Ziryab (d. 857) to introduce to his Córdoban court the ideals of *zarf* and to launch new fashions and new etiquettes in the areas of gastronomy, clothing, poetry, and music.[98] Ziryab is also credited for opening the first beauty salon in Córdoba where he taught new hairstyles and makeup and encouraged the use of toothpaste. Córdoban society thus learned everything that was fashionable in rival Abbasid courts. "Until his death in 857, [Ziryab] was an important influence in the transmission of Eastern Islamic culture to the outpost of Western Islam in al-Andalus."[99] His extraordinary achievements were continued by his daughter Hamduna who became a famous Andalusian singer and taught music.

Homosexual Refinement in Medieval Islamicate Society

As should be evident by now, the Arabic tradition of *zarf* is not a set of behaviors that defines a specific social class, but rather it cuts across all social classes: it characterizes some members of the aristocracy as it does singing slave-girls. It is not gender specific as it may be practiced by men as well as women. Finally, it is not exclusive to heterosexual relations but is regularly observed by (male) homosexuals as well, as Ahmad al-Tifashi describes in his famous thirteenth-century erotic treatise, *The Delight of Hearts*: "To have an elegant house that is for his own use only and of which he safely keeps the key. He must then place cages full of doves, cages full of birds which fly and sing gracefully. He will also place a chess board, books of poetry and of passionate love stories, volumes of illustrated legends and works on magic."[100]

The (male) homosexual, according to al-Tifashi, possesses and creates a private space in which intellectual and esthetic pleasures dominate. Not only does his house harbor volumes of literature, of (pseudo-)science (magic), of chessboard games, but it also rings of the music of birdsong, thus deepening the overall sensory pleasures of the space. Although the word *zarf* is not used throughout this description of the main traits of the homosexual, the details provided correspond nevertheless to the elegance, refinement, and sophistication inherent to the tradition of *zarf* described above, indicating that in the Arabic literary tradition, the (male) homosexual is a *zarif* by definition. In addition, because *zarf* is a code of conduct that is followed both by men (*zurafa*s) and women (be they *mutazarrifat, qayna*s, or *ghulamiyyat*), we may argue that medieval Arab courtly ladies were at times also lesbians; in other words, it is likely that *mutazarrifat*, like *qayna*s and *ghulamiyyat*, lived in homes decorated with a similar taste to that of elegant men (*zurafa*s), and that they evolved in private quarters filled with the same sensory and intellectual pleasures as those of the male homosexuals depicted by al-Tifashi.[101]

Reading Medieval French Romance Through Arab Sociocultural Traditions

Rereading the development of Aelis's urban embroidery business against the backdrop of the *zarf* tradition, of *qayna*s, and of (male and female) homosexual refinement is very useful because it permits us to better understand how the Arabic tradition of courtly manners becomes rewritten by Western hands. Let us begin by noting the remarkable parallels between the adornment of Aelis's Montpellier residence and that which characterizes the dwellings of *zurafa*s and homosexuals in the Arabic tradition. Even though *The Delight of Hearts* depicts the home of a male homosexual, the *Escoufle* reproduces much of its decorative features but situates it in the context of a lesbian household. Like the home of a typical *zarif* or *mutazarrifa* in the Islamicate literary tradition, Aelis's household displays extraordinary elegance, both physical and intellectual. Not only does it echo of storytelling (vv. 5524–27), it even has birdcages hanging from the windows, just like the domicile of the homosexual *zarif* in the Arabic tradition:

En bien vii kages ou en viii   Seven or eight birdcages
Pendent li oisel as fenestres.   Hang from her windows.
(vv. 5520–21)

In addition, Aelis's quarters provide entertainment to her guests/clients, consisting of various games, including chess: "D'eschés, de tables et de dis" ("chess, board games, dice," v. 5527). The reference to chess in the context of Aelis's Montpellier cross-cultural business is especially important as it highlights once again the integral role that Arabic material culture played in the medieval West. Not only is chess present in the description of the house of the homosexual as described by al-Tifashi, but chess is also known to have been a game in which *ghulamiyyat* excelled in the medieval Islamicate tradition.[102]

Equally significant is the fact that chess was a game that reached Western Europe precisely from its contacts with the Arabs and Muslims in the eighth century. Originally an importation from the Far East, chess was introduced first to Persia in 650 A.D., and with the spread of Islam, it reached North Africa and Spain (711) and penetrated into France during the military campaigns between the Moors and Charles Martel (688–741).[103] The presence of chess in Aelis's household (like that of silk) signals therefore the transfer of cultural traditions from the Far and Middle East to the West, as well as the integration of Arabic social customs (*zarf, ghulamiyyat, qaynas*, lesbian or lesbian-like courtly manners) within French romance.

Furthermore, the services that Aelis provides in her new business bear revealing resonances with those of the *qaynas*, even though Aelis is neither a slave nor a singer. Yet, her extraordinary beauty, her storytelling abilities that invite everyone to listen to her, the cost of her services, and the overall eroticism of the business suggest a salon that attempts to emulate those of the medieval Middle East or al-Andalus. Even Aelis's hairwashing services call to mind the graciousness of Middle Eastern beauty salons (perhaps such as those inaugurated by Ziryab in Córboba), rather than the services provided by lower-class women in France at the time. Hairwashing in the context of the *Escoufle* is associated with the elegance, the refinement typical of *mutazarrifat*, giving Aelis's business the prestige of Middle Eastern Islamicate culture and sophistication.

Aelis occupies a social function in Montpellier intriguingly reminiscent of that of *qaynas* or of aristocratic *mutazarrifat* in medieval Islamicate culture. Her literary salon entertains, gives pleasure, and privileges the three senses that are the hallmark of the *qaynas'* sphere of activity. Aelis indeed provides visual pleasure since all those present delight in the contemplation of her beauty:

Et cil cui si bel oel ravisent	And those whom her eyes notice
Cuident ester ml't plus que conte.	Consider themselves better than counts.
(vv. 5490–91)	

Aelis also treats her clients to the joys of touch not only through her embroidery but also through her hairwashing services:

Ainc puis celi dont vos disomes	Since we told you her story

Feme si bien ne lava	No woman ever washed heads
chief.	(hair) as well.
(vv. 5510–11)	

Finally, similar to a Western Scheherazade who elevates the pleasures from storytelling to the level of sexual fulfillment,[104] Aelis offers her audience auditory (and sexual) gratification through her captivating storytelling skills:

Tant lor disoit de ses	She told them so many of her
biax dis	beautiful stories
Que tos les fait a li entendre.	That she made them trust her.
(vv. 5528–29)	

While the character of Aelis shows multiple parallels to that of *qayna*s, we must be careful not to reduce her to this category. Perhaps the most important distinction (in addition to the fact once again that Aelis is neither a slave nor a singer) is that *qayna*s always worked for a master and brought financial advantages and social prestige to someone else. Aelis on the other hand, it must be emphasized, is independent; she works for herself and is her own mistress. In addition, Aelis's Montpellier business, even as it mirrors the cultural and social activities that characterize *qayna*s and *mutazarrifat*, remains an adulterated form of *zarf*, if only because the erotic meaning of her work remains implicit throughout.

We may thus say that while Aelis is unlike traditional medieval Western courtly ladies, and unlike medieval European working urban women or prostitutes as I showed above, she is not reproducing Islamicate social traditions either (be it that of *mutazarrifat*, *qayna*s, or female homosexuals). Rather, she takes elements from both Eastern and Western traditions and stands as an original example of a new cross-cultural social category, one that combines the social standing and refinement of some women in the Islamicate world with some of the stereotypes of the courtly lady. She emerges as neither one nor the other but gives a new meaning to both.

Saint-Gilles: A Western Harem?

Rereading the *Escoufle* through the lens of Arabic literature, culture, and social customs permits us to shed new light on the unusual social space created by Aelis's move to the Saint-Gilles household. Just as it was possible to rein-terpret Aelis's prostitution-like activities in terms of a well-established, fash-ionable, respected, and most often successful Middle Eastern social category (the *qaynas* and *mutazarrifat*), I would like to propose a rereading of Aelis's involvement in the Saint-Gilles household not just as a sinful act by an evil maidservant who steals the affections of a husband from his lawfully wedded wife (as Western clerics would have it), but rather as a manifestation of West-ern fantasies and reconstruction of an Eastern harem in the midst of Western society. For after all, the scene in the Saint-Gilles household that I examined above, namely, the portrayal of one man (the count of Saint-Gilles) involved in an explicitly sexual encounter with one woman (Aelis), under the happy and blissful gaze of many other women, immediately brings to mind the East-ern harem, at least as construed by the (medieval and contemporary) Western European imagination.[105]

It is no exaggeration to say that the Oriental harem represents one of the West's most recurring fantasies of the East. At the same time, the harem, still today, remains the least understood social structure of the Arab Islamicate world. In medieval French literature, representations of harems often occur in texts that promote an ideology of religious crusade and feudal conquest. Sharon Kinoshita has shown how the Eastern harem was rewritten by West-ern (male) authors as an earthly heaven, with all the lure of Saracen exoti-cism which tempted (male) heroes with "stasis and luxurious abandon."[106] Medieval French texts that incorporate a harem within their narrative most often describe the series of obstacles that (male) heroes have to penetrate and overcome in order to reach and save their beloved from an all-powerful polygamous husband (*La Prise d'Orange* and *Floire and Blancheflor* being per-haps two of the best-known examples). These French literary texts usually end with the reunification of the lovers and the conversion of the Saracen (oftentimes the woman, but not always) to Christianity. The Saint-Gilles household, it must be pointed out, does not describe such a harem, and the episode between the count and Aelis is divorced from the ideology of crusade and conversion that typically accompanies depictions of harems in Old French texts.[107]

The Saint-Gilles household differs also substantially from historically documented Middle Eastern harems. In Arabic, the term *harem* literally means that which is forbidden; it has quickly come to refer to the social space in which women were enclosed and by extension to the physical area of the household that was set off as a distinctly female space and occupied by wives, concubines, female relatives, and female servants. If in the West such a space was quickly imagined to be the very site of eroticism, of luxury, as well as of lesbian sexualities, and was cited as the "living" proof both of Islamic backwardness and of the subordination of Muslim women, such a perspective does not correspond to recent scholarly findings, as we saw earlier.

It is clear that neither the Old French view of the harem with its crusader ideology nor the potentially liberating perspective of the harem fully corresponds to the scene in the Saint-Gilles household portrayed in the *Escoufle*. For once again, what we have in the *Escoufle* is not an Eastern harem per se, but rather, I submit, an Eastern harem *as imagined* by the medieval West. The Saint-Gilles household proposes an intriguing new and creative construction that does not rely on the crusading/conversion associations that we are accustomed to from other Old French texts. It is novel also because it differs from the Western tradition of concubinage which was viewed with increasing ambivalence by church fathers since Augustine and well into the sixteenth century. If at times concubinage was tolerated by some canonists, it was only because it was understood to be exclusive of marriage. The situation depicted in the Saint-Gilles episode suspiciously combines marriage and cohabitation and hence dangerously points to an imported tradition, coming from the East.[108]

In addition, when the count's habit of eating pears nightly in the room of the *puceles* (the harem?) is read against the backdrop of the Arabic love tradition, this detail acquires new meaning, and the scene a more erotic connotation. For eating a pear like eating an apple does not evoke prelapsarian sin in Islamicate culture but reflects rather a healthy sexuality.[109] In the important tradition of the erotic symbolism of fruit characteristic of the Mediterranean Basin, Middle Eastern culture, and Islam, fruit is associated with Paradise, rather than with sin.[110] Poems describing fruit as metaphors of love were prominent since Abu Nuwas's eighth-century poetry and appear in al-Jahiz's ninth-century treatise on *qaynas*: "Women may be compared to perfumes and apples that we present to one another."[111] Other similar examples may be found in literary writings, such as the lines inserted in the tale of Nour in the *One Thousand and One Nights*, where each fruit is associated with a specific erotic function. This is what is written about pears in this tale:

> O young maidens, still virgins and a bit acid to the taste,
> O young ones from Mount Sinai, from Ionia, from Aleppo.
> Your beautiful hips, balanced,

Hanging from a very fine waist, you who are waiting
For your lovers who will eat you, have no doubt about it.[112]

If fruit is associated with sexuality in the Arabic literary tradition, it is a positive sexuality, not a negative one evocative of original sin. It is also a sexuality associated with the tradition of the *zurafas* and their refined eating manners.[113] In the context of Arabic literature, eating fruit implies the stimulation of the senses (taste, smell, touch, sight) which are considered to be especially crucial in the awakening of the appetites and of sexual arousal in particular. In the *Escoufle*, eating fruit in the company of maidens becomes thus a sensual detail that highlights the erotic connotation of the evenings that the count spends with the maidens.

The interpretation of the Saint-Gilles household as a harem-like social structure is buttressed by an analysis of the way the count stages Aelis's invitation to his household. The count's seemingly innocent suggestion to his wife that she invite Aelis to join their court as a "pucele," a lady-in-waiting, is especially interesting because it reenacts another scene from *The Story of Qamar al-Zaman and the Princess Boudour* from the *One Thousand and One Nights*. At the end of this Arabic text and as discussed in Chapter 3, once Boudour is reunited with her husband, Qamar al-Zaman, not only does she abdicate in his favor but she offers him her wife (Hayat al-Nefous) as a second wife. Such a proposition was viable because of the cultural context of the entire tale (the harem) which allowed Qamar al-Zaman to be legally wedded to two wives. And in fact, the lesbian relationship between Boudour and Hayat al-Nefous was permitted to continue, despite Qamar al-Zaman's return and the affirmation of heteronormativity, precisely because under Islamic laws, Qamar al-Zaman could marry both women. The Arabic tale ended with the lesbian relation embedded in the polygamous household of the harem.

In striking parallel to this Arabic tale, the count's proposition to his wife to take Aelis as her "pucele" unwittingly echoes Boudour's offer to her husband (Qamar al-Zaman) to take Hayat al-Nefous as a second wife. And similarly to the Arabic tale, the count's suggestion to his wife in the *Escoufle* authorizes (unintentionally perhaps) the development of the same-sex relation between Aelis and his wife (Chapter 4). In other words, the count sanctions the same-sex relation in the same way as Boudour had sanctioned the heterosexual relation between her husband and Hayat al-Nefous. Moreover, just as Boudour's invitation to Qamar al-Zaman to marry Hayat al-Nefous had transformed her monogamous same-sex household into a

polygamous one, the count's invitation to have Aelis join his wife utterly reconfigures the heretofore adulterous Saint-Gilles household into both a
same-sex one (the lesbian relation between Aelis and the countess) and a
cross-cultural harem.

There seems to be an awareness in the *Escoufle* that the establishment of
a harem (an importation from the East) and the erotic involvement between
the count and Aelis might lead to sociopolitical and economic disaster. This
is implicit in the way the count welcomes Aelis to the Saint-Gilles household.
After kissing her, he promises that:

. . . jamais n'avrons andui rien	. . . We both will never hold anything
Ki ne soit vostre tous jours mais.	That will not be also always yours.
(vv. 6156–57)	

The count pledges to Aelis a particular kind of relationship, one founded
upon the mutual sharing and division of all possessions. This promise is
provocative because it greatly surpasses the required largesse that structured
medieval society. Gifts given by a lord were important because they revealed
the giver's fortune, his economic power, as well as his personal qualities; they
contributed to increasing his public stature, especially when his gifts were
generous. Pledging to freely give Aelis half of his possessions the first time he
ever meets her is a gesture that exceeds largesse and goes beyond the generous
welcome in which this pledge is couched.[114]

If we take the count's promise literally, sharing everything with Aelis evidently includes partaking of her sexual favors since Aelis is actively intimate
not only with the countess, but also with the count. It could also be taken to
suggest implicitly that Aelis might become a competing heir to the count's inheritance. Given the fact that the Saint-Gilles couple is childless, introducing
Aelis as a sexual partner has indeed the potential to become particularly destabilizing for the family lineage. The promise to share everything therefore
poses a potentially considerable threat to the economic bases of Western Europe and to its system of wealth based upon family continuity, legitimate procreation, and cultivated lands.[115] Associating Aelis with the Saint-Gilles
household represents not simply the introduction of new alternative personal
relations within a (presumably) monogamous couple, but also the incorporation of cultural and economic structures, threatening both because of their

perceived Eastern origins and their disruption of Western European laws concerning procreation and legitimate succession.

The impending sociopolitical and economic disaster that the novel social structure enacts in the erotic encounter between the count and Aelis is averted by the narrator who skillfully shifts the focus of this highly subversive scene and reorients it toward legitimate heteronormativity. This scene quickly becomes an important turning point in the entire romance, as it ushers in the reunification of Aelis and Guillaume. It is at the very moment when the erotic content and cross-cultural dimension of the scene are at their peak that the count conveniently remembers the story that his falconer had told him earlier that day about the young man (who turns out to be Guillaume) who had gone hunting with him and his especially violent treatment of a kite:

En trestous les autres deduis
Li est des fauconniers menbré,
Mais de l'escouffle desmenbré
Ki fu ars une a une piece
N'orra il la verté a piece
Que qu'ele le sert et tient nu.
(vv. 7060–65)

And while [Aelis] serves him and holds him naked,
and in the midst of all the other amusement
He remembered the falconer
and the dismemberment (castration)
Of the kite that was completely burned
He is determined to hear the truth about it.

The sudden intrusion of the count's recollection reorients the developing erotic and cross-cultural scene toward a normative form of sexuality and signals the onset of Western narrative resolution.[116] The count's memory stands clearly as a veritable juncture in the romance that serves to introduce the falconer's tale and to usher in Guillaume himself, precipitating the recognition scene between Aelis and Guillaume.

The rhyming past participles "menbré" and "desmenbré" (vv. 7061–62) in the above lines are noteworthy for they masterfully unite the count's recollection ("menbré") to the violence of Guillaume's action toward the kite ("desmenbré"). More important, the wordplay in these lines highlights the thematic focus on the eroticism of the scene, while pointing to the potential violence that could result from the questionable erotic liaison between Aelis and the count and the harem-like structure their relationship introduced. In Old French, the word "menbré" not only means to remember, but refers also to the male sexual organ, while "desmenbré" means both to dismember and more specifically to dismember the only male sexual organ worth mentioning, the phallus. The count's recollection thus becomes a deft reminder of the only legitimate phallus that ought to occupy this scene, namely, Guillaume's. It also points to the very real punishment that could result for the count from his illegitimate sexual encounter with Aelis, that is, castration.[117] The linguistic irruption of the phallus ("menbré") and the threat of its dismemberment ("desmenbré") utterly put an end to all narrative developments on same-sex desire and female attachments,[118] as they silence alternative social structures in the *Escoufle* dangerously reminiscent of the East, including suspicious liaisons evocative of harems. They preface the reunification of the legitimate heterosexual couple (Guillaume and Aelis) and the crowning of the heroes in Rouen and in Rome.

Conclusion: Rereading French Romance

Rereading Aelis's household business through the lens of Arabic courtly culture allows us to qualify our earlier interpretation concerning Aelis's association with prostitution. It now becomes possible to situate her services within a new larger social context of courtliness, refinement, elegance, and sophistication. While medieval Western society did not offer women a viable category between single woman and prostitute, the Arabic tradition permitted them to occupy a respectable place between these social extremes. It afforded them a social position in which they could be at once single and sexual without being prostitutes, independent workers and courtly ladies, businesswomen and storytellers, sexual beings and admired ladies.

As it escapes easy labeling, Aelis's lesbian social identity may hence be more fruitfully viewed in terms of its hybridity. This hybridity is no longer interlinguistic or intertextual as was the case of other Old French lesbians discussed in earlier chapters, but it is primarily intercultural, sitting at the crossroads between European and Middle Eastern cultures and forming an intriguing conjunction of Arabic courtly motifs and Western urban and courtly elements. Such a cross-cultural combination places Aelis, one of the early forgotten lesbians of medieval French literary history, at the center and at the margins of medieval European society.

CONCLUSION

Beyond Orientalist Presuppositions

*Cultures are never unitary in themselves, nor simply dualistic in
relation of Self to Other.*
—Homi Bhabha

IF *CROSSING BORDERS* has demonstrated that love between women is more
prevalent in medieval French writings than hitherto believed, it is because we
have situated Old French literature in the multicultural context of medieval
Europe and read it through the lens of the cross-cultural contacts between
France and Islamicate civilizations and cultures in the Middle Ages. Old
French literary discourses on lesbianism have emerged as prime examples of
East-West hybridity, cross-fertilization, as well as cultural and literary exchanges. As polyphonic, dynamic constructions, and despite a heterosexual
veneer, they do not privilege one form of sexuality at the expense of another
or develop one single (Western) social and cultural practice. Rather, literary
texts discussed in *Crossing Borders* may be fruitfully considered a "crossing of
textual surfaces, a dialogue between several writings."[1] They juxtapose and in-
terweave multiple discursive voices: Western and non-Western; French and
Arabic; straight and gay; normative and alternative. Within this polyphony,
the French medieval literary lesbian emerges as truly cross-cultural; she is constituted as "other" not only sexually but especially linguistically, literarily, socially, and culturally. She is at once French and Arabic; her voice is one and
plurivocal; her depiction is heterosexual and homosexual (while not being reducible to bisexuality); her relations are (homo)sexual and homosocial.

The insertion of Arabic linguistic, thematic, and sociocultural traditions in Old French literature is important to consider because it invites us to reevaluate the nature of the threat posed by same-sex desire between women in the medieval West. In light of the preceding chapters, and especially our discussion of Aelis's cross-cultural embroidery business in the *Escoufle*, European clerical condemnations of same-sex love and desire between women do not appear to be solely due to the disapproval of erotic liaisons between women as manifestations of the "sin against nature" (*peccatum contra naturam*), to their perceived threat to the natural division of gender, or even to their disregard of religious (heterosexual) teachings. Rather, the denunciation of lesbianism by medieval Western theologians could at least be partly attributed to the *social* consequences that were feared to derive from the involvement of two women. In other words, if lesbianism was decried, it was perhaps because it was assumed to be a byproduct of the economic role that lesbian-like single women increasingly played in the developing urban economy of medieval Europe. It may be the power and independence that single women stood to gain from their emotional and business associations with other women that seemed menacing to conventional social and economic structures, especially when they competed with male spheres of activities, male earning potential, and hence male authority.[2]

Equally important, the insertion of Arabic interlinguistic, intertextual, and intercultural elements in Old French texts also represents the imaginary ominous irruption of (Eastern) unbridled public sexual encounters within the developing urban milieus of medieval France. It is the potential development of Western harem-like structures and alternative social geographies that were especially feared because they threatened Western social, public, and familial morality. Finally, it is possibly the alluring material pleasures and cultural sophistication of the East that clerics sought firmly to control when they decried same-sex love, friendships, or even women's business work. If lesbianism was considered a threat in the European Middle Ages, it is primarily because it took on the colors of the East.

Fragmented Cultural and Literary Transmission

This book has also pointed to the complex ways in which Arabic tales may have circulated in medieval France, inviting us to revise our notions of cultural and literary transmission. My discussion of the role played by the Arabic *Story of Qamar al-Zaman and the Princess Boudour* in the various Yde and Olive renditions, as well as in the *Escoufle*, strongly suggests that Arabic tales did not circulate (and likely did not even exist) in what we tend to think of today as "complete" and "full-fledged" versions. Arabic tales, firmly entrenched in oral tradition, were known primarily through their retelling in performance. Such stories, and framed ones especially, could thus only have been known and transmitted in smaller units or even in episodes. Hence, crossing the borders between Arabic and French does not mean that French authors translated or copied verbatim an available Arabic tale. Rather, it means that they culled some of its elements and wove them into a literary fabric to suit their audience's sensibilities and expectations and to conform to some of their period's generic and literary conventions. Jean Renart interlaced his *Escoufle* with only some scenes from the Arabic tale of Qamar al-Zaman and the Princess Boudour, while the authors of the various Yde and Olive narratives (verse epic, miracle play, prose rendition) evidently focused on other parts of the same story from the *Arabian Nights*. Such fluid adaptation may suggest that different parts of the Qamar al-Zaman and the Princess Boudour tale circulated in different forms in different parts of medieval France; or it may imply that each narrator was simply interested in a particular section of the same available tale. This process of selection, cross-fertilization, and transformation is central to the entire concept of cross-cultural literary transmission and production. For medieval French writers, Arabic texts (along with other cultural and literary traditions, including Latin, Celtic) were not models to copy blindly, but rather were examples to imitate, to subvert, and at times even to silence. If the exact line of transmission of Arabic tales to the West remains difficult if not impossible to trace, it is nevertheless fruitful to consider the very real and enriching possibility that medieval French writing is essentially a hybrid,[3] cross-cultural project.

At the same time, *Crossing Borders* has demonstrated the necessity of revising our understanding of the concept of intertextuality and its workings. Far from referring exclusively to linguistic and textual resonances, intertextuality points to the complex web of sociocultural codes that medieval French literary writings draw upon. It is precisely by taking into consideration the multiple manifestations of intertextuality, both its tangible aspects (language, rhetorical devices, textual motifs) and its less tangible ones (sociocultural traditions), that we have uncovered the critical role that Arabic literature and culture played in constructions of same-sex love between women in medieval French writings. The wider definition of intertextuality deployed here urges us to question the traditional dichotomy of "inside" and "outside" and to recognize the fact that Arabic literature and culture reside at the very heart of Old French textuality.

Implications of Cross-Cultural Research: Beyond Orientalist Presuppositions

Cross-cultural comparative research is not a neutral field of inquiry. Like any discipline, it does not produce objective knowledge; rather it has inherently political implications.[4] At the start of the twenty-first century, with the growing crisis facing the humanities, cross-cultural research between the medieval Arab world and medieval Europe is imperative because it calls into question the West's own view of itself and undermines its contemporary discursive self-presentation as secular, sexually liberated, and firmly positioned in the first world. Moreover, such an approach uncovers Western presuppositions of the sexuality of "third world women," whom Chandra Mohanty has described as follows: "This average third world woman leads an essentially truncated life based on her feminine gender (read: sexually constrained) and being 'third world' (read: ignorant, poor, uneducated, tradition-bound, religious, domesticated, family-oriented, victimized, etc.). [This image] is in contrast to the (implicit) self representation of Western women as educated, modern, as having control over their bodies and sexualities, and the 'freedom' to make their own decisions."[5]

This portrayal of Western feminists' perception of third-world women should not be assumed to be specific to the contemporary period, for as Mohanty points out, "Arabs and Muslims, it appears, don't change at all. Their patriarchal family is carried over from the times of the Prophet Muhammed. They exist, as it were, outside history."[6] The reductionism in the contemporary perception of third-world women has unfortunately often simply been projected back in time, with the assumption that the situation of Middle Eastern/Muslim women has always been the same, that they form a coherent group without any individuation, victims of an all-powerful patriarchal, legal, and religious system.

One of the main contributions of cross-cultural research is precisely its ability to destabilize the long-cherished Western assumption that Muslim and Arab women are an always already constituted coherent, stable category of sexually oppressed, sociopolitically subordinated objects, regardless of class, or of marginal and resistant modes of experiences. Another contribution of this research is its recovery of key primary materials on same-sex relations from the Islamicate world, materials that have long been assumed to be nonexistent, and when known, continue to be neglected or censored. Finally, cross-cultural comparative research is significant because it enriches medieval European writings and returns to them the multidimensional, plurivocal, and pluricultural depth that they undoubtedly possess.

The Ethics of Cross-Cultural Research

Taking into consideration the Arabic literary discourses on alternative sexualities has undeniable ethical considerations, for, after all, the primary Arabic texts that I have examined in *Crossing Borders* are some of the most important tools of resistance produced by medieval Arabic culture. As they propose a sharply different image of Arab/Muslim women, they reverse conventional and Orientalist presuppositions about Islamicate cultural practices and destabilize popular binary oppositions between Islam and the West. Since power can be understood *only* in the context of resistance (as Foucault has forcefully taught us), it is analytically and strategically important for us as critics to take into consideration these modes of resistance in the Arab Islamicate tradition. In their capacity to combat Western cultural imperialism, medieval Arabic discourses on sexualities ultimately have the potential to produce a change in the sociopolitical climate of the Islamicate world, as well as in the power politics and relations between the East and the West.

Uncovering the "othered" discourses on sexuality that are part and parcel of the Arab Islamicate cultural tradition is thus useful because it provides a point of departure for the elaboration of oppositional political strategy and new policies. In this sense, research in comparative sexualities studies has very crucial ethical and political implications for the contemporary Middle East. This research also has political implications that extend beyond this geopolitical area, since it forces Western (U.S. and French) self-images of Western sexuality to be more nuanced and context specific. Last, cross-cultural research promises to promote better cross-cultural understanding between two world areas (the West and the East) of increasing global significance, regions that have been entertaining tense relations, based on the former's proclaimed democracy (which includes the supposed liberation of women and their sexuality) and the latter's lack thereof (which is coterminous with female subordination and oppression). As it contextualizes East/West relations and their respective literary productions over the centuries, cross-cultural research promises to deconstruct such binary formulations, which increasingly threaten world peace.

Most significant perhaps, cross-cultural research (on sexuality in particular) puts into question the greater project of humanism "as a Western ideological and political project which involves the necessary recuperation of the 'East' and 'Woman' as Others."[7] As Foucault, Said, and Mohanty among others have pointed out, Western (man's) centrality can be maintained only by defining and constructing the "East" and the Islamicate world as peripheral.[8] One of the more powerful implications of cross-cultural research lies precisely in its potential to deconstruct the binary logic of humanist ideology and its attending vehicles of anthropomorphism, ethnocentrism, essentialism, and universalism. Herein lies its undeniable relevance both to the Middle Ages and to the contemporary world.

NOTES

PREFACE

1. Ruth Vanita and Saleem Kidwai, eds., *Same-Sex Love in India: Readings from Literature and History* (New York: Palgrave, 2000); Daniel Boyarin, *Carnal Israel: Reading Sex in Talmudic Culture* (Berkeley: University of California Press, 1993); Tova Rosen, *Unveiling Eve: Reading Gender in Medieval Hebrew Literature* (Philadelphia: University of Pennsylvania Press, 2003); Kathryn Ringrose, *The Perfect Servant: Eunuchs and the Social Construction of Gender in Byzantium* (Chicago: University of Chicago Press, 2003).

2. The notion of a horizontal and a vertical reading of texts, as well as the entire section on intertextuality and the intersection of textual surfaces, is indebted to Julia Kristeva's analysis of Bakhtin's reading of Dostoevsky's intertextual poetics. By "horizontal reading" Kristeva points to the relation between author-reader; while "vertical reading" is the relation between a text and other texts. See both her *Semiotica: Recherches pour une sémanalyse* (Paris: Seuil, 1969), 145–46, and her *Desire in Language: A Semiotic Approach to Literature and Art* (New York: Columbia University Press, 1980), 69. Bakhtin's analysis of Dostoevsky can be found in *Problems of Dostoevsky's Poetics*, ed. and trans. Caryl Emerson (Minneapolis: University of Minnesota Press, 1984).

3. This process of "écriture-lecture" is again described by Kristeva with reference to Bakhtin; see her *Semiotica*, 144.

CHAPTER ONE. CROSSING DISCIPLINARY BOUNDARIES

Note to epigraph: Catharine MacKinnon, "Does Sexuality Have a History?" in *Discourses of Sexuality: From Aristotle to AIDS*, ed. Domna C. Stanton (Ann Arbor: University of Michigan Press, 1992), 121.

1. Peter Abelard, "contra naturam, hoc est contra naturae institutionem, quae genitalia feminarum usui virorum praeparavit, et e converso, non ut feminae feminis cohabitarent," *Expositio in Epistolam Pauli ad Romanos I*, in *Patrologia cursus completus: Series Latina*, ed. J.-P. Migne (Paris, 1841–66), 178:806; cited in Louis Crompton, "The Myth of Lesbian Impunity: Capital Laws from 1270 to 1791," *Journal of Homosexuality* 6, nos. 1–2 (Winter 1980–81): 14.

2. Anastasius is cited in John Boswell, *Christianity, Social Tolerance, and Homosexuality: Gay People in Western Europe from the Beginning of the Christian Era to the Fourteenth Century* (Chicago: University of Chicago Press, 1980), 158.

3. "Vile affections" is the term that Saint Paul used in Romans 1:26 to speak of the pagans who reject God. While it is not entirely clear what Saint Paul meant by this phrase, it has been interpreted as same-sex behavior between women since Saint Ambrose (d. 397) and Saint John Chrysostom (d. 407). This interpretation was later repeated by Saint Anselm and Peter Abelard (d. 1142) in the twelfth century and by Albertus Magnus (d. 1280) and St. Thomas Aquinas (d. 1274) in the thirteenth. See Judith C. Brown, *Immodest Acts: The Life of a Lesbian Nun in Renaissance Italy* (New York: Oxford University Press, 1986), 6–7.

4. Jean Gerson, *Confessional ou Directoire des confesseurs* (n.d., late fifteenth century), in *Oeuvres complètes de Jean Gerson*, ed. Palémon Glorieux (Paris: Desclée, 1960), 1:85, cited in Brown, *Immodest Acts*, 19; emphasis mine.

5. Gregorio Lopez, *Las Siete partidas del sabio rey Don Alonso el Nono, nuevamente glosadas por el licenciado Gregorio Lopez* (1565; repr., Salamanca, 1829–31), 3:178, cited in Brown, *Immodest Acts*, 19; emphasis mine.

6. Cited in E. W. Monter, "La sodomie à l'époque moderne en Suisse romande," *Annales, ESC*, 29 (July–August 1974): 1029 (in Brown, *Immodest Acts*, 166 n. 5); emphasis mine.

7. Not all law codes in the Middle Ages agreed that lesbians should be burned. The earliest European statute to mention the death penalty for lesbians is a thirteenth-century French law code (Orléans, 1260) which states that other penalties should be applied to the first two offenses with burning only as a third and final resort. On this law, see Brown, Immodest Acts, 13; for a brief overview of what theological, canonical, synodal, and penitential writings and law codes say (or do not say) about female homoeroticism, see Derrick S. Bailey, *Homosexuality and the Western Christian Tradition* (Hamden, Conn.: Archon, 1975); Pierre J. Payer, *Sex and the Penitentials: The Development of a Sexual Code, 550–1150* (Toronto: University of Toronto Press, 1984); Ulrike Wiethaus, "Female Homoerotic Discourse and Religion in Medieval Germanic Culture," in *Gender and Difference in the Middle Ages*, ed. Sharon Farmer and Carol Braun Pasternack (Minneapolis: University of Minnesota Press, 2003), 292–95. In his "Myth of Lesbian Impunity," Louis Crompton has shown that in the Middle Ages, lesbianism was not perceived to be a lesser offense than male homosexuality and, likewise, was punishable by death. See also Edith Benkov, "The Erased Lesbian: Sodomy and the Legal Tradition in Medieval Europe," in *Same Sex Love and Desire Among Women*, ed. Francesca Sautman and Pamela Sheingorn (New York: Palgrave, 2001), 101–22; Marc Boone, "State Power and Illicit Sexuality: The Persecution of Sodomy in Late Medieval Bruges," *Journal of Medieval History* 22, no. 2 (1996): 135–53; Helmut Puff, "Localizing Sodomy: The 'Priest and Sodomite' in Pre-Reformation Germany and Switzerland," *Journal of the History of Sexuality* 8, no. 2 (1997): 165–95. On attitudes toward lesbianism held by various European countries at different periods of medieval history, see Brown, *Immodest Acts*, 12–14. In the case of the eighteenth century, Theo van der Meer has pointed out that women punished by death for lesbian relations

were usually found guilty of other offenses as well (religious inconstancy and heresy); see his "Tribades on Trial: Female Same-Sex Offenders in Late Eighteenth-century Amsterdam," *Journal of the History of Sexuality* 1, no. 3 (1991): 424–45. See also Brigitte Eriksson, "A Lesbian Execution in Germany, 1721: The Trial Records," *Journal of Homosexuality* 6, nos. 1–2 (1980–81): 27–40.

8. Karma Lochrie, *Covert Operations: The Medieval Uses of Secrecy* (Philadelphia: University of Pennsylvania Press, 1999), 199.

9. Wiethaus, "Female Homoerotic Discourse," 293.

10. On the invention of the category "sodomy" in the twelfth century, see Mark Jordan, *The Invention of Sodomy in Christian Theology* (Chicago: University of Chicago Press, 1997).

11. The only theologians who included women in their consideration of sodomy were Hincmar of Reims (d. 879), Peter Abelard, Albertus Magnus, and his student Thomas Aquinas; see Wiethaus, "Female Homoerotic Discourse," 293.

12. These views have been developed by Joan Cadden in *Meanings of Sex Difference in the Middle Ages: Medicine, Science, and Culture* (Cambridge: Cambridge University Press, 1993), 224; Brown, *Immodest Acts*; Harry J. Kuster and Raymond J. Cormier, "Old Views and New Trends: Observations on the Problem of Homosexuality in the Middle Ages," *Studi Medievali*, ser. 3, 25 (1984): 587–610; and John Boswell, *Same-Sex Unions in Premodern Europe* (New York: Villard Books, 1994).

13. The bibliography on male homosexuality in the European Middle Ages is growing rapidly. Except for Sautman and Sheingorn's volume *Same Sex Love and Desire Among Women in the Middle Ages*, which focuses explicitly on women, most of the articles in the other edited volumes on the queer Middle Ages address almost exclusively male homosexuality. See Louise Fradenburg and Carla Freccero, eds., *Premodern Sexualities* (New York: Routledge, 1995); Glenn Burger and Steven F. Kruger, eds., *Queering the Middle Ages* (Minneapolis: University of Minnesota Press, 2001); Karma Lochrie, Peggy McCracken, and James A. Schultz, eds., *Constructing Medieval Sexuality* (Minneapolis: University of Minnesota Press, 1997); Farmer and Pasternack, eds., *Gender and Difference in the Middle Ages*; Jacqueline Murray and Konrad Eisenbichler, eds., *Desire and Discipline: Sex and Sexuality in the Premodern West* (Toronto: University of Toronto Press, 1996); Josiah Blackmore and Gregory S. Hutcheson, eds., *Queer Iberia: Sexualities, Cultures and Crossings from the Middle Ages to the Renaissance* (Durham, N.C.: Duke University Press, 1999); and Gerald Herman, "'The Sin Against Nature' and Its Echoes in Medieval French Literature," *Annuale Medievale* 17 (1976): 70–87.

14. Brown, *Immodest Acts*, 9; emphasis in original.

15. In Vern L. Bullough and James Brundage, eds., *The Handbook of Medieval Sexuality* (New York: Garland, 1996), 191. The use of the term "lesbian" in this study will be discussed below.

16. This project thus confirms Steven Kruger's observation regarding the pressing need to read medieval Arabic texts side by side with European ones: "Medieval thinking about the sexuality of Christians is crucially different from, and yet intimately intertwined with medieval constructions of the sexuality of . . . Muslims." Steven Kruger, "Conversion

and Medieval Sexual, Religious, and Racial Categories," in *Constructing Medieval Sexuality*, ed. Lochrie, McCracken, and Schultz, 159. The important role that Arabic sexological and medical writings had on Western European knowledge about sexual practices and eroticism has been discussed in Danielle Jacquart and Claude Thomasset, *Sexualité et savoir médical au Moyen Age* (Paris: Presses Universitaires de France, 1985), chapter 3 in particular.

17. The concept of the "contact zone" was coined by Mary Louise Pratt in an influential article, "Arts of the Contact Zone," *Profession* 91 (1991): 33–40.

18. Michel Foucault, *The History of Sexuality: An Introduction*, trans. Robert Hurley, vol. 1 (New York: Vintage, 1980). This position of constructionism was popularized by nineteenth-century doctors and scientists, such as Hirschfeld, Havelock Ellis, and Krafft-Ebing. See also Jeffrey Weeks, *Coming Out: Homosexual Politics in Britain from the Nineteenth Century to the Present* (London: Quartet Books, 1977); David M. Halperin, *One Hundred Years of Homosexuality, and Other Essays on Greek Love* (New York: Routledge, 1990); John J. Winkler, *The Constraints of Desire* (New York: Routledge, 1990); and David M. Halperin, John J. Winkler, and Froma I. Zeitlin, eds., *Before Sexuality: The Construction of Erotic Experience in the Ancient Greek World* (Princeton, N.J.: Princeton University Press, 1990). Even Eve Kosofsky Sedgwick has followed this periodization in her *Epistemology of the Closet* (Berkeley: University of California Press, 1990) which focuses on the nineteenth and twentieth centuries, while her *Between Men: English Literature and the Male Homosocial Desire* (New York: Columbia University Press, 1985) begins with Shakespeare, thus with the Renaissance. Similarly, see Lillian Faderman, *Surpassing the Love of Men:Romantic Friendship and Love Between Women from the Renaissance to the Present* (New York: Morrow, 1981).

19. See John Boswell, "Towards the Long View: Revolutions, Universals and Sexual Categories," *Salmagundi* 58–59 (Fall–Winter 1983): 89–113; Jordan, *Invention of Sodomy*; Carolyn Dinshaw, *Getting Medieval: Sexualities and Communities, Pre- and Post-Modern* (Durham, N.C.: Duke University Press, 1999); Guido Ruggiero, *The Boundaries of Eros: Sex Crime and Sexuality in Renaissance Venice* (Oxford: Oxford University Press, 1985); Stephen O. Murray and Kent Gerard, "Renaissance Sodomite Subcultures?" in *Among Men, Among Women: Sociological and Historical Recognition of Homosocial Arrangements*, ed. Mattias Duyves et al. (Amsterdam: Sociologisch Instituut, 1983), 183–96.

20. David M. Halperin, *How to Do the History of Homosexuality* (Chicago: University of Chicago Press, 2002), 44. In 1983 George Chauncey had already pointed out that the assumptions underlying the construction of homosexual identity "oversimplify the complex dialectic between social conditions, ideology, and consciousness which produced gay identities, and they belie the evidence of preexisting subcultures and identities contained in the literature itself." See George Chauncey, Jr., "From Sexual Inversion to Homosexuality: Medicine and the Changing Conceptualization of Female Deviance," *Salmagundi* 58–59 (Fall 1982–Winter 1983): 115. More recently, Stephen Murray has called the modern denial of premodern homosexuality a case of nineteenth-century "special creationism" in his "Discourse Creationism," *Journal of Sex Research* 32 (1995): 263–65.

21. Karma Lochrie, "Desiring Foucault," *Journal of Medieval and Early Modern Stud-*

ies 27, no. 1 (1997): 9. A more extended critique of Foucault and his view of medieval studies may be found in her *Covert Operations*, 14–24.

22. Anna Klosowska, *Queer Love in the Middle Ages* (New York: Palgrave, 2005), 13. Other critics resisting the dogmatic readings of Foucault's *History of Sexuality* include Judith Bennett, Edith Benkov, Ruth Vanita, Tova Rosen, and Terry Castle, among many others.

23. Interestingly, even the index to J. N. Adams's *The Latin Sexual Vocabulary* (Baltimore: Johns Hopkins University Press, 1982) does not have an entry for "tribades" or lesbians.

24. Sautman and Sheingorn, *Same Sex Love and Desire*, 13. See also Terry Castle, *The Apparitional Lesbian: Female Homosexuality and Modern Culture* (New York: Columbia University Press, 1993).

25. Sautman and Sheingorn, introduction to *Same-Sex Love and Desire*, 2.

26. Foucault himself had already pointed to the distinction between identity and consciousness in an interview that was translated by James O'Higgins, "Sexual Choice, Sexual Act: An Interview with Michel Foucault," *Salmagundi* 58–59 (Fall 1982–Winter 1983): 11–12.

27. The archaeological information is cited in Marie-Jo Bonnet, *Les Deux amies: Essai sur le couple de femmes dans l'art* (Paris: Editions Blanche, 2000), 17.

28. Plato, *Symposium*, trans. W. R. M. Lamb, Loeb Classical Library (Cambridge, Mass.: Harvard University Press, 1925), 3:141.

29. This terminology is provided by Bernadette J. Brooten in *Love Between Women: Early Christian Responses to Female Homoeroticism* (Chicago: University of Chicago Press, 1996), 4–9, where she explains the different connotations of each of these terms. On female homosexuality in early Christianity, see also Boswell, *Christianity, Social Tolerance and Homosexuality* and *Same-Sex Unions*. On female homosexuality in the Greek period, see Geneviève Pastre, *Athènes et le "Péril saphique": Homosexualité féminine en Grèce ancienne* (Paris: Librairie "Les Mots à la bouche," 1987).

30. Brooten, *Love Between Women*, 5.

31. Contrary to what one might think, the usage of the word "lesbian" in the sixteenth century does not seem to have been a result of the rediscovery of Sappho's poetry. The first usage of the term "lesbian" in French occurs in Pierre de Bourdeille, Seigneur de Brantôme, *Vies des dames galantes* (Paris: Garnier Frères, 1841). It would not become commonly used until the nineteenth century, at which time the term seems to have referred to acts rather than to a group of people. Its earliest usage in English dates from the 1730s. See Emma Donoghue, *Passions Between Women: British Lesbian Culture, 1668–1801* (London: Scarlet Press, 1993).

32. Brown, *Immodest Acts*, 17.

33. Judith M. Bennett, "'Lesbian-Like' and the Social History of Lesbianisms," *Journal of the History of Sexuality* 9, nos. 1–2 (2000): 1–24.

34. Adrienne Rich, "Compulsory Heterosexuality and Lesbian Existence," *Signs* 5, no. 4 (1980): 631–60.

35. My work thus confirms Sautman and Sheingorn's view that the history of lesbianism is linked to the history of all women's struggles to assert independent lives (*Same Sex Love and Desire*, 11).

36. Other scholars have rejected the persistent distinction between medieval and

modern. They include Judith M. Bennett, "Medieval Women, Modern Women: Across the Great Divide," in *Culture and History, 1350–1600: Essays on English Communities, Identities and Writing*, ed. David Aers (London: Harvester Wheatsheaf, 1992), 147–75, and "Confronting Continuity," *Journal of Women's History* 9, no. 3 (1997): 73–94; Lee Patterson, "On the Margin: Postmodernism, Ironic History, and Medieval Studies," *Speculum* 65, no. 1 (1990): 87–108; Louise O. Fradenburg and Carla Freccero, "The Pleasures of History," *GLQ* 1, no. 4 (1995): 371–84; and Burger and Kruger, *Queering the Middle Ages*.

37. Wiethaus, "Female Homoerotic Discourse," 289.

38. A fourth promising area of research into medieval female same-sex practices may consider narratives of animal or monstrous spouses as spaces onto which Western anxieties about gender are displaced. Marie de France's *Lais* and the *Roman de Mélusine*, for instance, propose powerful instances of the deployment of alternative family and sexual configurations, and of resistance to medieval binary hierarchies and dominant heterosexual discourses. Furthermore, despite scholarly investigations of the "scandalous" content of French fabliaux which have focused on the definition of gender and sexuality, few have examined the homoerotic dimension of many of these texts. Gerald Herman has briefly addressed the use of the term "sodomy" in two fabliaux ("Du Prestre et du Chevalier" and "Du Sot Chevalier") in his "'Sin Against Nature.'" Fabliaux such as *Berengier au Long Cul, Les Quatre Souhais Saint Martin*, and *Le Sentier Batu* would merit queering in the future.

39. Karma Lochrie, "Mystical Acts, Queer Tendencies," in *Constructing Medieval Sexuality*, ed. Lochrie, McCracken, and Schultz, 195.

40. There is a large body of scholarship that investigates expressions of medieval lesbianism in the writings of mystics; in fact, it is probably the area that has contributed the most to our knowledge of medieval female homoeroticism. The following bibliography is not meant to be exhaustive. On the feminization of Jesus Christ, see Caroline Walker Bynum, *Jesus as Mother: Studies in the Spirituality of the High Middle Ages* (Berkeley: University of California Press, 1982). On the same-sex discourse of female mystics, see Wiethaus, "Female Homoerotic Discourse"; Bruce Holsinger, "The Flesh of the Voice: Embodiment and the Homoerotics of Devotion in the Music of Hildegarde of Bingen (1098–1179)," *Signs* 19, no. 1 (1993): 92–125; Ann Matter, "My Sister, My Spouse: Woman-Identified Women in Medieval Christianity," *Journal of Feminist Studies in Religion* 2, no. 2 (1986): 81–93; Lochrie, "Mystical Acts," 180–200; Kathy Lavezzo, "Sobs and Sighs Between Women: The Homoerotics of Compassion in the Book of Margery Kempe," in *Premodern Sexualities*, ed. Louise Fradenburg and Carla Freccero, 175–98; Amy M. Hollywood, *The Soul as Virgin Wife: Mechtild of Magdeburg, Marguerite Porete, and Meister Eckhart* (Notre Dame, Ind.: University of Notre Dame Press, 1995); Simon Gaunt, "Straight Minds/'Queer' Wishes in Old French Hagiography—La Vie-de-Sainte-Euphrosine," *GLQ* 1, no. 4 (1995): 439–47; Brown, *Immodest Acts*; and Walter Simons, "Reading a Saint's Body: Rapture and Bodily Movement in the Vitae of Thirteenth-century Beguines," in *Framing Medieval Bodies*, ed. Sarah Kay and Miri Rubin (Manchester: Manchester University Press, 1994), 10–23. The lives of saints (Sainte Douceline of Digne in particular) would benefit from future investigation into their representations of same-sex desire.

41. French literary texts (romances and plays) from the thirteenth century seem to have been particularly prone to such a theme. These texts typically stage a cross-dressed heroine; they describe her flight from ambiguous familial situations and her ability to adapt and succeed in new environments alone, especially with the help of a female friend. See Michelle Szkilnik, "The Grammar of the Sexes in Medieval French Romance," in *Gender Transgressions: Crossing the Normative Barrier in Old French Literature*, ed. Karen J. Taylor (New York: Garland, 1998), 61–88; Kathleen M. Blumreich, "Lesbian Desire in the Old French *Roman de Silence*," *Arthuriana* 7, no. 2 (1997): 47–62; Valerie R. Hotchkiss, *Clothes Make the Man: Female Cross Dressing in Medieval France* (New York: Garland, 1996); J. L. Welch, "Cross-Dressing and Cross-Purposes: Gender Possibilities in the Acts of Thecla," in *Gender Reversals and Gender Cultures: Anthropological and Historical Perspectives*, ed. Sabrina Petra Ramet (London: Routledge, 1996), 66–78; Robert L. A. Clark and Claire Sponsler, "Queer Play: The Cultural Work of Crossdressing in Medieval Drama," *New Literary History* 28, no. 2 (1997): 319–44; Susan Crane, "Clothing and Gender Definition: Joan of Arc," *Journal of Medieval and Early Modern Studies* 26, no. 2 (1996): 297–320.

42. Susan Schibanoff, "Hildegarde of Bingen and Richardis of Stade: The Discourse of Desire," in *Same Sex Love and Desire*, ed. Sautman and Sheingorn, 49–84, and Konrad Eisenbichler, "Laudomia Forteguerri Loves Margaret of Austria," in *Same Sex Love and Desire*, ed. Sautman and Sheingorn, 277–304.

43. The most important article in this controversy is undoubtedly Angelica Rieger's "Was Bieiris de Romans Lesbian?: Women's Relations with Each Other in the World of the Troubadours," in *The Voice of the Trobairitz: Perspectives on the Women Troubadours*, ed. William D. Paden (Philadelphia: University of Pennsylvania Press, 1989), 73–94.

44. The term Islamicate which I will use throughout this study was coined by Marshall G. S. Hodgson who defines it thus: " 'Islamicate' would refer not directly to the religion, Islam, itself, but to the social and cultural complex historically associated with Islam and the Muslims, both among Muslims themselves and even when found among non-Muslims." See his *The Venture of Islam: Conscience and History in a World Civilization* (Chicago: University of Chicago Press, 1974), 1:59. The advantage of this term is that it highlights the social and cultural dimensions over the religious. For reasons of variety, I will be using other terms (Arab, Eastern, Oriental, Middle Eastern, the Levant, Mediterranean), even though I recognize the anachronism, limitations, and problems associated with each of these words. The same limitations apply to my use of the terms "Western," "medieval France," or "medieval Europe" throughout this study.

45. On the hybrid culture of medieval Sicily, see Karla Mallette, *The Kingdom of Sicily, 1100–1250: A Literary History* (Philadelphia: University of Pennsylvania Press, 2005).

46. The term "clash of civilizations" was coined by Samuel Huntington in a now-famous article by the same title published in *Foreign Affairs* 72, no. 3 (1993): 22–49. It has given rise to a great number of critiques, most notably by Edward Said, "The Clash of Ignorance," *Nation* 273, no. 12 (October 22, 2001): 11–13.

47. *Funduks* (as they were called in Arabic and imported as *fondoco* in European southern ports) were commercial towns in which Christian merchants lived during their trade with the Orient. The city of Montpellier, for instance, is known to have had an

important presence in Antioch, Saint Jean of Acre, Tyre, and Alexandria. The participation of rulers in the establishment of *funduks* even while on crusades is amply documented (Guilhem of Montpellier was seeking to further his commercial interests in Palestine and Syria, as Jacqueline Liault has demonstrated [*Montpellier, la médiévale* (Nîmes: C. Lacour, 1990), 49–60]). On the *funduks* and their importance as spaces for cross-cultural exchange, see Olivia Remie Constable, *Housing the Stranger in the Mediterranean World: Lodging, Trade and Travel in Late Antiquity and the Middle Ages* (Cambridge: Cambridge University Press, 2004). On the crusades and cultural exchanges between East and West, see Carole Hillenbrand, *The Crusades: Islamic Perspectives* (London: Routledge, 1999).

48. There are a great many publications on the role that Arab sciences played in the development of the scientific fields in the West. The following references give just a glimpse of the material that is available. See John Tolan, *Petrus Alfonsi and His Medieval Readers* (Gainesville: University of Florida Press, 1993); Charles Burnett, *The Introduction of Arabic Learning into England* (London: British Library, 1997); Charles Burnett, ed., *La Transmission des textes philosophiques et scientifiques au moyen âge—Marie-Thérèse d'Alverny* (Aldershot, Hampshire, U.K.: Variorum, 1994); Dorothee Metlitzki, *The Matter of Araby in Medieval England* (New Haven, Conn.: Yale University Press, 1977); Alice Lasater, *Spain to England: A Comparative Study of Arabic, European and English Literature in the Middle Ages* (Jackson: University of Mississippi Press, 1974); Monica Green, ed. and trans., *The Trotula: A Medieval Compendium of Women's Medicine* (Philadelphia: University of Pennsylvania Press, 2001); Monica Green, *Women's Healthcare in the Medieval West: Texts and Contexts* (Burlington, Vt.: Ashgate, 2000).

49. Olivia Remie Constable, *Trade and Traders in Muslim Spain: The Commercial Realignment of the Iberian Peninsula, 900–1500* (Cambridge: Cambridge University Press, 1996), 1. On the role of al-Andalus in the transfer of Arabic advances to medieval Europe, see also Thomas Glick, *Irrigation and Hydraulic Technology: Medieval Spain and Its Legacy* (Brookfield, Vt.: Variorum, 1996).

50. On the role of *muwasshahat* and *zajal* on troubadour poetry, see A. R. Nykl, *Hispano-Arabic Poetry and Its Relation with the Old Provençal Troubadours* (Baltimore: J. H. Furst, 1946), and Maria Rosa Menocal, *Shards of Love: Exile and the Origins of the Lyric* (Durham, N.C.: Duke University Press, 1994) and *The Arabic Role in Medieval Literary History: A Forgotten Heritage* (Philadelphia: University of Pennsylvania Press, 1987). See also Brian A. Catlos, *Victors and the Vanquished* (Cambridge: Cambridge University Press, 2004).

51. Sahar Amer, *Esope au féminin: Marie de France et la politique de l'interculturalité* (Amsterdam: Rodopi, 1999).

52. The resistance of the field of French literature to the implications of cross-cultural contacts between Western Europe and the Arab Islamicate world in the Middle Ages is likely due to the long history of colonialism, the persistence of Orientalist presuppositions, and the contemporary tension with the Maghrebian population in France. Most of the research conducted on cross-cultural relations between East and West in the Middle Ages is still conducted primarily either by scholars of Spanish or by social scientists (historians in particular). Notable exceptions are E. Jane Burns, *Courtly Love Undressed: Reading Through Clothes in Medieval French Culture* (Philadelphia: University of Pennsylvania Press, 2002),

and Sharon Kinoshita, *Medieval Boundaries: Rethinking Difference in Old French Literature* (Philadelphia: University of Pennsylvania Press, 2006).

53. Norman Daniel, *Islam and the West: The Making of an Image* (Edinburgh: Edinburgh University Press, 1960). Nabil Matar has shown the persistence of such metaphors throughout Western colonization of the American Indians. See his *Turks, Moors, and Englishmen in the Age of Discovery* (New York: Columbia University Press, 1999), 109–27; see also John Tolan, *Saracens: Islam in the Medieval European Imagination* (New York: Columbia University Press, 2002); Thomas E. Burman, *Religious Polemic and the Intellectual History of the Mozarabs, c. 1050–1200* (Leiden: E. J. Brill, 1994).

54. On the construction of Islam as a religion that promotes sodomy, see Susan Schibanoff, "Mohammed, Courtly Love, and the Myth of Western Homosexuality," *Medieval Feminist Newsletter* 16 (Fall 1993): 27–32; Boswell, *Christianity, Social Tolerance, and Homosexuality*, 278–82; and David F. Greenberg, *The Construction of Homosexuality* (Chicago: University of Chicago Press, 1988), 172–83.

55. Hrosvit of Gandersheim, *Hrotsvithae Opera*, ed. Helene Homeyer (Munich, 1970), discussed in Jordan, *Invention of Sodomy*, 18–22.

56. This composite view is based on the writings of authors such as Humbert de Romans, Guibert de Nogent, and Thomas Aquinas. These images are summarized in R. W. Southern, *Western Views of Islam in the Middle Ages* (Cambridge, Mass.: Harvard University Press, 1962). Some medieval authors (such as Jacques de Vitry) attempted to explain sexual deviance in the Middle East by the hot climate of the region which promoted bestial behaviors; see Boswell, *Christianity, Social Tolerance, and Homosexuality*, 279 n. 32.

57. William Adam, cited in Boswell, *Christianity, Social Tolerance, and Homosexuality*, 282, and in Norman Daniel, *Islam and the West*, 144.

58. This is described in Michael Uebel, "Re-Orienting Desire: Writing on Gender Trouble in Fourteenth-century Egypt," in *Gender and Difference*, ed. Farmer and Pasternack, 244–47.

59. Mattar, *Turks, Moors, and Englishmen*, 109–27.

60. Sir Richard Burton, "Terminal Essay," in *The Book of the Thousand and One Nights and a Night* (New York, 1886), 10:205–53. On Burton's notion of the "Sotadic Zone," see Stephen O. Murray, "Some Nineteenth-century Reports of Islamic Homosexualities," in *Islamic Homosexualities: Culture, History, and Literature*, ed. Stephen O. Murray and Will Roscoe (New York: New York University Press, 1997), 204–21 and especially 211–17.

61. *Le conte de Floire et Blancheflor*, ed. Jean-Luc Leclanche (Paris: Champion, 1983), vv. 2584–85, translation mine.

62. Like homosexuality in Western scholarship, most of the research on homosexuality in the Arabic tradition focuses on male homosexuality. There have been to my knowledge only two colloquia directly addressing the topic of medieval homosexuality in the Arabic tradition, both resulting in the publication of conference papers: Afaf Lutfi al-Sayyid-Marsot, ed., *Society and the Sexes in Medieval Islam* (Malibu, Calif.: Undena, 1979), and Kathryn Babayan and Afsaneh Najmabadi, eds., *Islamicate Sexualities Studies: Translations Across Temporal and Geographical Zones of Desire* (forthcoming). Only two papers (by Kathryn Babayan and Sahar Amer) in the latter collection address the question of lesbianism.

The most important work conducted on medieval Arab male homosexuality is that of Everett Rowson, Franz Rosenthal, Abdelwahab Bouhdiba, Malek Chebel, Stephen O. Murray, and Will Roscoe. In Murray and Roscoe, eds., *Islamic Homosexualities*, one essay only deals with Arabic lesbianism; see Murray, "Woman-Woman Love in Islamic Societies," 97–104. Unfortunately, Murray collapses medieval representations of lesbian practices with Orientalist and modern perspectives.

63. Galen's view (like al-Kindi's below) is reported in Abul Hasan Ali Ibn Nasr al-Katib, *Encyclopedia of Pleasure*, ed. Salah Addin Khawwam, trans. Adnan Jarkas and Salah Addin Khawwam (Toronto: Aleppo, 1977), 189. One observation regarding the title of this important work: Even though the English translation of this work uses the term "encyclopedia," Ibn Nasr's work is not an encyclopedia in the sense we understand such works to be today. A more accurate, or literal translation of the Arabic title (*Jawami` al-ladhdha*) would be "everything that is known about pleasure." The title might also be a sexual pun since the term *jawami`*, plural form of *jam`*, derives from a root which means to link, to join, to unite, and also to have intercourse. The information cited about Galen and al-Kindi in the *Encyclopedia of Pleasure* cannot be corroborated by the surviving evidence from the medieval medical tradition. In a search for the roots hetairist-, dihetairist-, tribad-, and lesbiain the electronic version of Galen's surviving Greek works held by the Bibliothèque Interuniversitaire de Paris 5, there is no instance of any of those roots being used by him except "lesbia-." As a matter of fact, Galen uses the word "lesbiazonton" only once as an example of a practice he finds repugnant. See Galen's *De simplicibus medicines* X.1 in *Claudi Galeni Opera Omnia*, ed. C. G. Kuhn (Leipzig: Car. Cnoblochii, 1821–33), 12:249, http://194.254.96.21/livanc/?cote=45674x12&p=247&do=page. Al-Kindi's best-known works focus on the physical sciences—mathematics, optics, meteorology—not biology or physiology. According to Baghdadi bookseller al-Nadim's (d. ca. 990–998) *Fihrist* (The Catalogue), al-Kindi wrote 270 items, of which two dozen are medical titles—but none of al-Nadim's titles seem very likely to contain the information we find in the *Encyclopedia of Pleasure*, and most of them are known to be no longer extant; see al-Nadim, *al-Fihrist*, ed. Rida Tajaddud (Tehran: Yutlabu min Maktabat al-Asadi wa-Maktabat al-Ja`fari al-Tabrizi, 1971), 315 and passim. I would like to thank Michael McVaugh for helping me with this information concerning the medical tradition.

64. Ibn Nasr, *Encyclopedia of Pleasure*, 188.

65. Ibn Nasr, *Encyclopedia of Pleasure*, 189. The titles of Yuhanna Ibn Masawayh's (John Mesué) works suggest an interest in women's physiology. Among many others, al-Nadim attributes to him the following works: "Why Physicians Have Abstained from Treating Pregnant Women During Certain Months of Their Pregnancy" and "Treatment of Women Who Do not Become Pregnant," *al-Fihrist*, 354.

66. One finds exactly the same references to the medical origin of lesbianism in Ahmad al-Tifashi's *Nuzhat al-albab fima la yujad fi kitab*, ed. Jamal Juma`a (London: Riad el-Rayyis, 1992), chap. 11, which is devoted to lesbianism. This chapter is available in French translation by René R. Khawam, *Les Délices des coeurs ou ce que l'on ne trouve en aucun livre* (Paris: Phébus, 1981); it has been omitted however from the English translation of this work, *The Delight of Hearts*, trans. Edward A. Lacey (San Francisco: Gay Sunshine

Press, 1988). Other medical views on lesbianism included the size of the vagina. Social constructionist views of lesbianism were also evoked in the Arabic erotic tradition, most notably the desire to avoid adultery and the fear of begetting illegitimate children.

67. Though the *Encyclopedia of Pleasure* is the first extant erotic treatise in Arabic, it is not the first one to exist in the Arabic tradition. In his *Fihrist*, al-Nadim lists thirteen titles of erotic treatises or treatises on copulation (*kutub al-bah*) from Persia, India, and Arabia dating before the tenth century, none of which has survived. Two of the best-known (and most cited) titles that predate Ibn Nasr's work are (1) *Sihaq al-nisa' zinan baynahunna* ["Women's Tribadism Constitutes Fornication Between Them"], which technically is a legal opinion, rather than an erotic treatise; it is ascribed to Syrian jurisprudent (*faqih*) Makhul (d. ca. 730–36); and (2) Abu al-Anbas al-Saymari, *Kitab al-sahaqat* [Book on Lesbians] (end of ninth century). See al-Nadim, *al-Fihrist*, 376, and *Encyclopedia of Islam*, 2nd edition, CD-ROM, s.v.v. "Liwat" and "Sihak."

68. Ibn Nasr, *Encyclopedia of Pleasure*, 88. This anecdote is reported in an earlier text, namely Abu al-Faraj al-Isfahani's tenth-century *Kitab al-aghani* [The Book of Songs], and is later repeated by others, such as al Raghib al-Isfahani (ca. 1000), cited in Everett Rowson, "The Categorization of Gender and Sexual Irregularity in Medieval Arabic Vice Lists," in *Body Guards: The Cultural Politics of Gender Ambiguity*, ed. Julia Epstein and Kristina Straub (New York: Routledge, 1991), 68. As in the West, the origin of homosexuality in the Arab world seems to be that it was "imported" from elsewhere. In the case of the Arabs, al-Jahiz popularized the idea that it spread to the Muslim world at the time of the Abbasids from the army life of the Khurasanians. According to G. E. von Grunebaum, writings about homosexuality coincided with a shift toward an urban setting and a shift of the political center of Islam towards the East; see "Aspects of Arabic Urban Literature Mostly in the Ninth and Tenth Century," *al-Andalus* 20 (1955): 259–81.

69. Ibn Nasr, *Encyclopedia of Pleasure*, 88.

70. Al-Nadim, *al-Fihrist*, 366.

71. Such pedagogical training recalls the one evoked in the *Kama Sutra*.

72. The title of this work means literally "A Journey of the Hearts into what does not Exist in any Book."

73. Interestingly, in his colorful survey of the sexual customs of the East, Allen Edwardes confirms the survival of such lesbian teachings among harem women: "In the restricted harem, esh-sheykheh-el-bezzreh (one who teaches the art of rubbing clitoris against clitoris) taught every girl in the Sapphic sciences." Allen Edwardes, *The Jewel in the Lotus: A Historical Survey of the Sexual Culture of the East* (New York: Julian Press, 1959), 255. Even though rumors of lesbianism in Oriental harems have been regularly reported by Orientalist writers and travelers, they have never been observed or verified. We cannot thus entirely trust the association between harem and lesbian practices, but the parallel between al-Tifashi's and Edwardes's reports is striking.

74. Natalie Zemon Davis, *Trickster Travels: A Sixteenth-century Muslim Between Worlds* (New York: Hill and Wang, 2006), 201.

75. Mustafa Safwan, trans., *Tafsir al-ahlam* [*The Interpretation of Dreams*], by Sigmund Freud (1958; repr., Cairo: Dar al-Ma'arif, 1969); Jurj Tarabishi, trans., *Thalathat*

mabahith fi nazariyyat al-jins [*Three Essays on the Theory of Sexuality*], by Sigmund Freud (Beirut: Dar al-Tali`ah, 1983); and Muta al-Safadi, trans., *Iradat al ma`rifah, al-juz' al-awwal min tarikh al-jinsaniyya* [*The History of Sexuality*, vol. 1 of *The Will* to Know], by Michel Foucault (Beirut: Markaz al-Inma al Qawmi, 1990). This section on the terminology of sexuality and heterosexuality in the contemporary Middle East is indebted to Joseph Massad's article, "Re-Orienting Desire: The Gay International and the Arab World," *Public Culture* 14, no. 2 (2002): 361–85, especially 371–72.

76. On the connotation of these new terms for homosexuality in Arabic, see Scott Siraj al-Haqq Kugle, "Sexuality, Diversity, and Ethics in the Agenda of Progressive Muslims," in *Progressive Muslims: Justice, Gender and Pluralism*, ed. Omid Safi (Oxford: Oneworld, 2003), 199–201.

77. Kugle, "Sexuality, Diversity, and Ethics," 192.

78. On the positive role that sexuality plays in the Qur'an, see Abdelwahab Bouhdiba, *La Sexualité en Islam* (Paris: Presses Universitaires de France, 1986); Abdelkebir Khatibi, *Maghreb pluriel* (Paris: Denoël, 1983), and his *La Blessure du nom propre* (Paris: Denoël, 1986). On the other hand, Franz Rosenthal warns that the description of Paradise as a sensual erotic Eden in Islam should not be taken to exclusively mean that sexuality was permitted on earth. He gives the example of the Zahirite Ibn Hazm who interprets such verses as pointing rather to "the disruptive potential of sexuality for the smooth functioning of the social order" in his "Fiction and Reality: Sources for the Role of Sex in Medieval Muslim Society," in *Society and the Sexes in Medieval Islam*, ed. al-Sayyid-Marsot, 6.

79. Ahmad Ibn Muhammad Ibn Falita, *Rushd al-labib ila mu`asharat al-habib*, ed. Ahmad ben Mohamed al-Yamani (Talah: al-Mayah al-Jamahiriyah al-`Uzma, 2002), 127. The English translation provided here is from *An Intelligent Man's Guide to the Art of Coition*, ed. Salah Addin Khawwam, trans. Adnan Jarkas and Salah Addin Khawwam (Toronto: Aleppo, 1977), 100.

80. Rowson, "Categorization of Gender," 62. See also Kecia Ali, *Sexual Ethics and Islam: Feminist Reflections on Qur'an, Hadith, and Jurisprudence* (Oxford: Oneworld, 2006), chapter 5.

81. Although there was general agreement among Islamic jurisprudents that homosexuality was a major sin (*kaba'ir*), there was no consensus regarding its punishment which varied according to the school of thought (*madhahib*) followed: the Maliki school (which is the strictest one in this regard) considered *liwat* more serious than *zina*, thus deserving the harshest of *hadd* penalties (those defined in the Qur'an and the Sunnah and not left to the judge's discretion), namely stoning to death for both partners. The Shafi`i school assimilated *zina* and *liwat*, and thus distinguished between married and unmarried homosexuals, between active and passive partners. It condemned partners accordingly to be stoned to death (if married) or lashed (if unmarried). The most "liberal" school, the Hanafi (a view later adopted by the Zahiri Ibn Hazm) prescribed a *ta`zir* punishment, that is a discretionary penalty aimed to punish, reform, and deter others, and amounted to no more than ten lashes and an imprisonment term. The sentence for *sahq* (lesbianism) varied also among different jurisprudents. Some viewed it as the least serious form of *zina*, and thus prescribed one hundred lashes; others did not penalize it at all, while Ibn Hazm prescribed

the *ta`zir* punishment (ten lashes, and it remains unclear whether a prison term was also required or not). It must be noted that these punishments addressed *liwat* understood only as anal intercourse by a man. Kissing, caressing, *tafkhidh*, and the like, while considered reprehensible, were technically not *liwat*, and thus were not subject to these penalties. On the punishment of *liwat* and *sahq* in Islamic jurisprudence, see Camilla Adang, "Ibn Hazm on Homosexuality: A Case-Study of Zahiri Legal Methodology," *al-Qantara* 24 (2003): 5–31; Rowson, "Categorization of Gender," 59–62; Kugle, "Sexuality, Diversity, and Ethics," 216–19; Bouhdiba, *Sexualité en Islam*, 44–45; Khaled el-Rouayheb, *Before Homosexuality in the Arab-Islamic World, 1500–1800* (Chicago: University of Chicago Press, 2005), chapter 3 in particular.

82. This is what a poet (al-Raqashi) from the early Abbasid period wrote in a famous poem, cited in Rosenthal, "Male and Female: Described and Compared," in *Homoeroticism in Classical Arabic Literature*, ed. J. W. Wright, Jr., and Everett K. Rowson (New York: Columbia University Press, 1997), 48 n. 31.

83. The *ghulamiyyat* fashion appears to have been launched by Zubayda, wife of Harun al-Rashid and mother of Caliph al-Amin (patron of Abu Nuwas), in an effort to deter her son from his homosexual inclinations. Rowson points out that these cross-dressed women ought not be interpreted as evidence of lesbianism since their role was to compete with boys for the attention of men ("Categorization of Gender," 68). While this may have been true in the case of Zubayda's efforts, one cannot deny the fact that such cross-dressing must have been perceived as an especially liberating fashion for some medieval Arab lesbians. See Mas`udi, *The Meadows of Gold: The Abbasids*, trans. and ed. Paul Lunde and Caroline Stone (London: Kegan Paul, 1989), 390–91.

84. This is Everett Rowson's conclusion in "Two Homoerotic Narratives from Mamluk Literature: Al-Safadi's *Law`at al-shaki* and Ibn Daniyal's *al-Mutayyam*," in *Homoeroticism in Classical Arabic Literature*, ed. J. W. Wright, Jr., and Everett K. Rowson (New York: Columbia University Press, 1997), 158–91.

85. Al-Mutamid's verse is cited in Boswell, *Christianity, Social Tolerance and Homosexuality*, 196.

86. Boswell, *Christianity, Social Tolerance and Homosexuality*, 200.

87. Boswell gives several examples of Muslims having Christian lovers in al-Andalus: al-Mutamin, eleventh-century Muslim king of Saragossa; al-Ramadi, a famous tenth-century poet (*Christianity, Social Tolerance and Homosexuality*, 200).

88. There is a debate among critics as to whether Wallada indeed may be considered a lesbian. Philip K. Hitti has called Wallada "the Sappho of Spain" in his *History of the Arabs from the Earliest Times to the Present*, 9th ed. (New York: St. Martin's Press, 1968). This view was repeated by Abu Khalil ("A Note on the Study of Homosexuality in the Arab/Islamic Civilization," *Arab Studies Journal* 1–2 [Fall 1993]: 34) and by Murray and Roscoe (*Islamic Homosexualities*, 99). However, Everett Rowson takes the opposite view, stating that there is not sufficient evidence to make an assertion about lesbianism in the case of Wallada. Rowson has summarized the debate in his forthcoming book on male homoeroticism in the medieval Arabic tradition. I would like to thank him for sharing his unpublished material on Wallada with me.

89. This is also Rowson's assessment in "Categorization of Gender," 74 n. 4.

90. Rosenthal, "Male and Female," 30. Yahya Ibn Aktham was a well-known homosexual as evident in the enduring expression in medieval Arab writing of a *luti* (homosexual) as someone who "subscribes to the religion of Yahya Ibn Aktham." See Rowson, "Categorization of Gender," 61–62.

91. The definition of *adab* is a complex one and there is no equivalent genre in the West. In the Arabic Middle Ages, this encyclopedic genre of writings aimed at clarifying the rules of conduct of its own society, at imparting ethical attitudes and courtly manners in an entertaining style. Authors of *adab* draw heavily from prior writings which they reorganize. On the definition of *adab*, see André Miquel, *La Littérature arabe* (Paris: Presses Universitaires de France, 1969), 66–68; Charles Pellat, *Le Milieu basrien et la formation de Yahiz* (Paris: Librairie d'Amérique et d'Orient Adrien-Maisonneuve, 1953); von Grunebaum, "Aspects of Arabic Urban Literature." On the production of *adab* works on love during this period, see Jean-Claude Vadet, *L'Esprit courtois en Orient dans les cinq premiers siècles de l'hégire* (Paris: G.-P. Maisonneuve et Larose, 1968); Lois A. Giffen, *Theory of Profane Love Among the Arabs: The Development of the Genre* (New York: New York University Press, 1971); Lois A. Giffen, "Love Poetry and Love Theory in Medieval Arabic Literature," in *Arabic Poetry: Theory and Development*, ed. G. E. von Grunebaum (Wiesbaden: Otto Harrassowitz, 1973), 107–24. On the linguistic virtuosity of *adab*, see Andras Hamori, *On the Art of Medieval Arabic Literature* (Princeton, N.J.: Princeton University Press, 1975).

92. Rowson, "Categorization of Gender," 52. On *mujun* as a literary genre, rather than a sociological phenomenon whose main features are sexuality and scatology, see Julie Scott Meisami, "Arabic *Mujun* Poetry: The Literary Dimension," in *Verse and the Fair Sex: Studies in Poetry and in the Representation of Women in Arabic Literature: A Collection of Papers Presented at the 15th Congress of the Union Européenne des Arabisants et Islamisants*, ed. Frederick de Jong (Utrecht: M. Th. Houtsma Stichting, 1993), 8–30; Robert Irwin, *The Arabian Nights: A Companion* (New York: Penguin, 1994), 165–67.

93. Abu al-Faraj al-Isfahani, *Kitab al-aghani* [The Book of Songs], ed. Abd al-Sattar Ahmad Farraj, 25 vols. (Beirut: Dar al-Thaqafa, 1990). On *Kitab al-aghani*, see Hilary Kilpatrick, *Making the Great Book of Songs: Compilation and the Author's Craft in Abu l-Faraj al-Isbahani's Kitab al-Aghani* (New York: Routledge, 2003) and Ignazio Guidi, *Tables alphabétiques du Kitab al-Agani* (Leiden: Brill, 1900).

94. Al-Raghib al-Isfahani's and al-Jurjani's works have both been studied by Rowson in his "Categorization of Gender." Al-Raghib al-Isfahani. *Muhadarat al-udaba' wamuhawarat al-shu`ara' wa-al-bulagha'* [Lectures by the Literati and Conversations in Poetry and Eloquent Speech], 4 vols. (Beirut: Dar Maktabat al-Haya, 1961); Abu al-Abbas Ahmad b. Muhammad al-Jurjani, *al-Muntakhab min kinayat al-udaba' wa isharat al-bulagha'* [Anthology of Metonymic Devices Used by the Literati and Allusions in Eloquent Speech], ed. Muhammad Shamsul Haq Shamsi (Hyderabad, India: Osmania Oriental Publications Bureau, 1983).

95. This is the perspective upheld by scholars such as Everett Rowson, Julie Meisami, Franz Rosenthal, and Paula Saunders.

96. On this tradition known as Rangstreit in the critical literature, see Ewald Wagner,

Die Arabische Rangstreitdichtung und ihre Einordnung in die allgemeine Literaturgeshichte, Abhandlungen der Geistes- und Sozialwissenschaftlichen Klasse, Jahrg. 1962, Nr. 8 (Mainz: Akademie der Wissenschaften und der Literatur, 1963). On these debates and the role of the parallel Greek tradition of *syncrisis* on Arabic dispute poems, see the collection *Dispute Poems and Dialogues in the Ancient and Medieval Near East*, ed. G. J. Reinink and H. L. J. Vanstiphout (Leuven: Departement Orientalistiek, 1991).

97. Al-Jahiz's *Kitab moufakharati al-jawari wa al-ghilman* [*Boasting Match over Maids and Youths*] has been translated into English by Jim Colville as "The Pleasures of Girls and Boys Compared," in *Sobriety and Mirth: A Selection of the Shorter Writings of al-Jahiz* (London: Kegan Paul, 2002), 202–30; by William M. Hutchins, *Nine Essays of Al-Jahiz* (New York: P. Lang, 1989), 139–66, and into French by Malek Chebel, *Ephèbes et courtisanes* (Paris: Payot et Rivages, 1997). His *Tafdil al-batn `ala al-zahr* [*Superiority of the Belly to the Back*] is located in British Museum OR. 3138, fol. 220B–227B, and it has been translated into English by William M. Hutchins, *Nine Essays of Al-Jahiz*, 167–73. The translation has come under criticism by A. F. L. Beeston. See A. F. L. Beeston, review of *Nine Essays of Al-Jahiz*, translated by William M. Hutchins, *Journal of Arabic Literature* 20 (1989): 200–209.

98. Ibn Falita, *Rushd al-labib ila mu`asharat al-habib*, chapter 10. The Arabic title differs from its English translation by Adnan Jarkas and Salah Addin Khawwam who give instead the heading of "On pederasty" to that chapter.

99. Surprisingly, there are a large number of popularized self-help books on sexual topics that are easily accessible on the streets of major cities in the Arab world. These books are often sold next to mosques, thus appear to be addressed to the conservative Muslim population.

100. Today, there is one artistic sculpture entitled *The Encyclopedia of Pleasure* and it takes its inspiration from the medieval Arabic text. This sculpture is made by Egyptian artist Ghada Amer and hers is the first and only work (in any media) devoted exclusively to this groundbreaking Arabic text. Her sculpture is the unprecedented gesture by an Arab (and an Arab woman) to save from oblivion this essential text and to resurrect a frank and nonjudgmental discussion around sexuality that until today continues to be absent in the East and oftentimes misguided in the West. Moreover, it is the subversive artistic production of an Arab woman artist to break the silence imposed upon eroticism in the Arab world and even in the West today. See Sahar Amer and Olu Oguibe, eds., *Ghada Amer* (Amsterdam: De Appel, 2002).

101. The English translation by Lacey is made from René Khawam's French translation, and is not based on the Arabic text.

102. Edward A. Lacey, introduction to *The Delight of Hearts*, by Ahmad al-Tifashi, 8.

103. A similar approach characterizes French translations of al-Hawrani's work by René R. Khawam, who omits certain sections of the medieval manuscript that he considers to be of lesser stylistic value (see his introduction to his translation of *Les Ruses des femmes* [Paris: Phébus, 1994], 14). Some recent French translations of medieval Arabic literary anthologies and sexological writings published by renowned French presses contribute to another set of problems. Even though they claim to be based on "original Arab manuscripts," the translator does not provide basic critical information, such as the

manuscript used or the name of the library holding the manuscript. This omission does not permit scholarly work or verification of these possibly important contributions. Such is the case of René Khawam's translation of al-Tifashi's *Les Délices des coeurs*; his translation also of al-Suyuti's *Nuits de Noces ou comment humer le doux breuvage des la magie licite* (Paris: Albin Michel, 1972), or his translation of Ali al-Baghdadi, *Les Fleurs éclatantes dans les baisers et l'accolement* (Paris: Albin Michel, 1973).

104. In its theoretical outlook, my work is parallel to the goals of Glenn Burger and Steven Kruger in *Queering the Middle Ages*; they write in their introduction: "Queering the Middle Ages promises the recovery of cultural meanings that are lost, obscured, or distorted in work that either ignores questions of sexuality or attends only to hegemonic or heteronormative understandings of it" (xvi). Except for Gregory Hutcheson's contribution, their collection of essays does not address the cross-cultural dimension with which *Crossing Borders* is concerned.

CHAPTER 2. CROSSING LINGUISTIC BORDERS

Note to epigraphs: Homi K. Bhabha, "Cultural Diversity and Cultural Differences," in *The Post-Colonial Studies Reader*, ed. Bill Ashcroft, Gareth Griffiths, and Helen Tiffin (New York: Routledge, 1995), 209. Al-Jahiz, "The Pleasures of Girls and Boys Compared," in *Sobriety and Mirth: A Selection of the Shorter Writings of al-Jahiz*, trans. Jim Colville (London: Kegan Paul, 2002), 203.

1. Other texts that belong to the genre of estate literature include *La Bible* by Guiot de Provins (ca. 1205), *La Bible au Seigneur de Berzé* and *Le Besant de Dieu* by Guillaume Le Clerc (ca. 1226), and *Le Roman de Charité* by Re(n)clus de Moilliens (early thirteenth century). For an overview of estate literature as a genre, see Charles-Victor Langlois, *La Vie en France au moyen âge de la fin du XIIe au milieu du XIVe siècle, vol. 2, D'après les moralistes du temps* (Paris: Hachette, 1925).

2. All references to Etienne de Fougères's *Le Livre des manières* will be made to Anthony Lodge's edition of the text (Geneva: Droz, 1979).

3. The role that the Anglo-Norman courts of Henry II have played in the transmission of Arabic material to the West in the Middle Ages has been amply demonstrated by numerous critics, including notably Alice Lasater, *Spain to England: A Comparative Study of Arabic, European and English Literature in the Middle Ages* (Jackson: University of Mississippi Press, 1974); Dorothee Metlitzki, *The Matter of Araby in Medieval England* (New Haven, Conn.: Yale University Press, 1977); Charles Burnett, *The Introduction of Arabic Learning into England* (London: British Library, 1997); John Tolan, *Petrus Alfonsi and His Medieval Readers* (Gainesville: University of Florida Press, 1993); and Sahar Amer, *Esope au féminin: Marie de France et la politique de l'interculturalité* (Amsterdam: Rodopi, 1999).

4. Metlitzki, *Matter of Araby in Medieval England*, 8–9.

5. See Metlitzki, *Matter of Araby in Medieval England*, and Tolan, *Petrus Alfonsi and His Medieval Readers*.

6. Because in the Arabic tradition, lesbianism was considered a medical condition, it

was often discussed in Arabic medical treatises which Western authors are known to have consulted, translated, and studied. Jacquart and Thomasset have traced the transmission of Arabic erotic material (by Qusta Ibn Luqa, Samau'al Ibn Yahya, al-Tifashi, Ibn Falita, among others) in Western medical writings (by authors of the *Secretum Secretorum*, Maimonides, Albert the Great, commentators of Avicenna, Michel Savonarole, and Guy Beaujouan, among others); see their *Sexualité et savoir médical au Moyen Age* (Paris: Presses Universitaires de France, 1985), 121–92.

7. Etienne deals with bourgeois women in the preceding section of his poem depicting burghers. Bourgeois women are characterized by their debauchery and adulterous behavior (vv. 841–44). Etienne does not depict peasant women at all.

8. Robert Clark has observed that the placement of the lesbian in this intermediary position reverses the pattern Etienne had established earlier in his poem—from high to low—making this a "liminal moment" in the economy of the *Livre des manières*, "a turning point that marks the threshold between the lowest and the highest, the abject and the holy." Robert L. A. Clark in his "Jousting Without a Lance: The Condemnation of Female Homoeroticism in the *Livre des manières*," in *Same Sex Love and Desire Among Women in the Middle Ages*, ed. Francesca Sautman and Pamela Sheingorn (New York: Palgrave, 2001), 159.

9. I have borrowed the English translation of these stanzas from Robert L. A. Clark in his "Jousting Without a Lance," 166–67.

10. Clark, "Jousting Without a Lance," 164.

11. I will examine the phallocentrism of the *Yde and Olive* texts in Chapter 3.

12. The originality of Etienne's depiction of lesbianism has been pointed out by Robert Clark ("Jousting Without a Lance"). It has been echoed by Jacqueline Murray who writes: "The uniqueness of the discussion and the literary devices de Fougères employed to describe female sexuality make this one of the most important medieval descriptions of lesbianism" (Jacqueline Murray, "Twice Marginal and Twice Invisible," in *The Handbook of Medieval Sexuality*, ed. Vern L. Bullough and James Brundage [New York: Garland, 1996], 204). Similarly, Anthony Lodge, in his 1979 edition of this text, asserted: "This is the only allusion to sapphism in medieval French literature" (35 n. 12; translation mine). And yet, despite the rarity and obvious importance of this section, Lodge ends up undermining the value of these stanzas, as he does not bring up the question of lesbianism in his outline of the text, writing only that in the text "some women go so far as to commit acts against nature" (27; translation mine).

13. Langlois, *La Vie en France*, 25 n. 2; translation mine.

14. Langlois, *La Vie en France*, 6.

15. Lodge, introduction, 34.

16. Etienne's text has been preserved in a single manuscript, held at the Municipal Library of Angers (Maine-et-Loire), MS 304 (295). For a description of the manuscript, see R. Anthony Lodge's introduction to Etienne de Fougères's *Livre des manières*, 9–12.

17. The two problematic words are "trutennes" and "eu" in stanza 277. I will discuss both below.

18. Lodge, introduction, 15–16.

19. On attempts to identify this author, see Franz Rosenthal who claims he may have

been a tenth-century author who lived from 1036 to 1124 ("Male and Female: Described and Compared," in J. W. Wright, Jr., and Everett K. Rowson, *Homoeroticism in Classical Arabic Literature* [New York: Columbia University Press, 1997], 25). In the same article, Rosenthal cites other possible identifications of Ibn Nasr al-Katib suggested by other critics all of them unverifiable (45 n. 7). The problem of identification is compounded by the fact that this author's last name al-Katib means "the writer," "the scribe," or "the secretary," leaving us at a loss in figuring out whether this is a last name or a professional attribute.

20. On the genre of *mujun* literature and on *kutub al-bah*, see Chapter 1.

21. On the organization of al-Jurjani's work, see Everett Rowson, "The Categorization of Gender and Sexual Irregularity in Medieval Arabic Vice Lists," in *Body Guards: The Cultural Politics of Gender Ambiguity*, ed. Julia Epstein and Kristina Straub (New York: Routledge, 1991), 50–79. For a sense of the type of euphemisms recorded by al-Jurjani, consider the example of adultery, whose common Arabic metaphors are "to let down the curtain," or "riding between the wrist-bracelet and the ankle-bracelet." Chastity is rendered as "turning back the toucher's hand." Homosexual relations are "you took my boy away . . . and deprived my monk of his monastery." These examples are translated into English in Rowson's article (56); additional examples can be gleaned from the same article.

22. On women's jousting and fencing in the thirteenth-Century *Tournoiement des dames*, see Helen Solterer, "Figures of Female Militancy in Medieval France," *Signs* 16, no. 3 (1991): 522–49; on a comparable analysis focusing on the German tradition of *Das Frauenturnier*, or *The Ladies' Tournament* (ca. 1300), see Sarah Westphal-Wihl, "The Ladies' Tournament: Marriage, Sex and Honor in Thirteenth-Century Germany," *Signs* 14, no. 2 (1989): 371–98. On the use of the mortar as a metaphor for the vagina in the early modern period, see Francesca Sautman, " 'Des vessies pour des lanterns': Villon, Molinet and the Riddles of Folklore," *Neophilologus* 69, no. 2 (1985): 161–84, and Malcolm Jones, "Folklore Motifs in Late Medieval Art II: Sexist Satire and Popular Punishments," *Folklore* 101, no. 1 (1990): 69–87.

23. Eroticism as a martial scene was a very common metaphor throughout the Islamicate world. Not only do we encounter it in Ibn Nasr's *Encyclopedia of Pleasure* and al-Jurjani's work, but we also find it in tenth- and eleventh-century Andalusian poetry, such as poem 278 of Ibn Khafajah (1058–139). On this poem, its military metaphors and their prevalence in Arabic literature, see Arie Schippers and John Mattock, "Love and War: A Poem of Ibn Khafajah," *Journal of Arabic Literature* 17 (1986): 50–68.

24. Abul Hasan Ali Ibn Nasr al-Katib, *Encyclopedia of Pleasure*, ed. and annotated Salah Addin Khawwam, trans. Adnan Jarkas and Salah Addin Khawwam (Toronto: Aleppo, 1977), 191. All future references to the *Encyclopedia of Pleasure* will be made to this translation. I have also consulted two Arabic manuscripts of the *Encyclopedia of Pleasure*—Istanbul MS Fatih 3729 and Dublin MS Chester Beatty 4635—I would like to thank Everett Rowson for generously making them available to me.

25. Ibn Nasr, *Encyclopedia of Pleasure*, 193 and 73.

26. Al-Jurjani's Arabic text has survived only in an abridged anonymous form edited by Muhammad Shamsul Haq Shamsi, *al-Muntakhab min kinayat al-udaba' wa isharat al-bulagha'* (An Anthology of Metonymic Devices Used by the Literati and Allusions in Elo-

quent Speech) (Hyderabad, India: Osmania Oriental Publications Bureau, 1983), 108. The English translation of this passage is from Rowson, "Categorization of Gender," 65.

27. Ibn Nasr, *Encyclopedia of Pleasure*, 196.

28. Arabic quotations of Ahmad al-Tifashi's text come from the Arabic edition by Jamal Juma'a, *Nuzhat al-albab fima la yujad fi kitab* (London: Riad el-Rayyes, 1992), 246. All translations are mine. As I mention in Chapter 1, there only exists one complete French translation of this important work by René R. Khawam, *Les Délices des coeurs ou ce que l'on ne trouve en aucun livre* (Paris: Phébus, 1981; earlier incomplete edition, 1977). The passage quoted is on p. 262 of this French translation. An English translation of this work by Winston Leyland and Edward A. Lacey, *The Delight of Hearts, or, What You Will Not Find in Any Book* (San Francisco: Gay Sunshine Press, 1988), was based on the French translation by Khawam, but only those sections dealing with male homosexuality are included. The chapter on the lesbian that is of interest here therefore does not exist in English.

29. Frédéric Godefroy, *Dictionnaire de l'ancienne langue française et de tous ses dialectes du IXe au XVe siècle* (Paris: Vieweg, 1888–1920), s.v. "escoer."

30. Ibn Nasr, *Encyclopedia of Pleasure*, 188.

31. The problems of relying on a dictionary when attempting to understand wordplay, puns, and sexual innuendos in medieval texts has been pointed out by Sheila Delany in her "Anatomy of the Resisting Reader: Some Implications of Resistance to Sexual Wordplay in Medieval Literature," *Exemplaria* 4, no. 1 (1992): 19. Similarly, Laura Kendrick has discussed the editorial decisions and thus censorship that occurs in dictionaries which consequently do not permit the validation of subversive readings. See Laura Kendrick, *Chaucerian Play* (Berkeley: University of California Press, 1988), 200, and Ross G. Arthur, "On Editing Sexually Offensive Old French Texts," in *The Politics of Editing Medieval Texts*, ed. Roberta Frank (New York: MAS Press, 1991), 19–64.

32. Ahmad Ibn Muhammad Ibn Falita, *Rushd al-labib ila mu`asharat al-habib*, ed. Ahmad ben Mohamed al-Yamani (Talah: al-Mayah al-Jamahiriyah al-`Uzma, 2002), 131. An earlier incomplete edition (chs. 9–11 only) of this work had been done by Mohamed Zouher Djabri, and accompanied by a German translation. It was submitted as a Ph.D. dissertation at the School of Medicine, University Friedrich-Alexander, Erlangen-Nuremberg, 1967. This edition was based on three of the many known manuscripts of the work: Gotha 2038; Paris, BN, Arabe Sloane 3051; and Berlin, Ahlwardt 6390. An English translation of this work is available under the title, *An Intelligent Man's Guide to the Art of Coition*, ed. Salah Addin Khawwam, trans. Adnan Jarkas and Salah Addin Khawwam (Toronto: Aleppo, 1977).

33. It is certainly also possible that Etienne de Fougères wrote (or intended to write) "srutennes," not "trutennes." The Arabic word *s/r/t* occurs on numerous occasions in all of the Arabic homoerotic treatises that I consulted. It means "navel," and it has a sexual connotation throughout the Arabic homoerotic tradition. It may well be that there is a scribal error in the *Livre des manières* due to a nonrecognition of a foreign word. Such an error would be consistent with a general tendency toward errors on the part of the scribe, a tendency that all editors of this manuscript have recognized.

34. Al-Tifashi, *Nuzhat al-albab*, 238 (translation mine); *Délices des coeurs*, 252.

35. Al-Tifashi, *Nuzhat al-albab*, 238 (translation mine); *Délices des coeurs*, 252–53.

36. Al-Tifashi, *Nuzhat al-albab*, 243 (translation mine); *Délices des coeurs*, 258.

37. Aside from the knowledge we have about Western translators who went to study in Spain, for instance, and who clearly had adequate knowledge of Arabic, there is some indication in various medieval French romances that perhaps a few individuals in courts may have also learned Arabic. Such is the case of *la Fille* in the romance *La Fille du Comte de Ponthieu* who learned to speak "Sarrasinois" once she found herself sold to a Muslim ruler. We can assume that she remained bilingual even after she returned to France at the conclusion of the romance.

38. Ruth Kennedy and Simon Meecham-Jones, eds., *Writers of the Reign of Henry II: Twelve Essays* (New York: Palgrave, 2006), 6. This important collection of essays sheds important light on the linguistic diversity of Henry II's courts. Interestingly, none of the authors addresses the role of Arabic therein.

39. The term "polyglossia" was coined by Mikhail Bakhtin who defines it as "the simultaneous presence of two or more national languages interacting within a single cultural system," in *The Dialogic Imagination*, ed. Michael Holquist, trans. Caryl Emerson and Michael Holquist (Austin: University of Texas Press, 1981), 431. The citation about the death of myths as a consequence of polyglossia is on p. 68.

40. Anthony Lodge has pointed out that Etienne de Fougères combines humor with a serious tone and that he inserts in his text some episodes that are reminiscent of the fabliaux (introduction, 34–35).

41. The notion of the contact zone and the reading practice it involves come from Mary Louise Pratt, "Arts of the Contact Zone," *Profession* 91 (1991): 37. While Pratt focuses on the relations between European, Andean, and Spanish societies, I believe that her ideas are useful in thinking about the contacts between Arabic and French literatures in the Middle Ages.

42. The question of the language and authority (and lack thereof) of subaltern groups is powerfully argued in Gayatri Spivak's classic article, "Can the Subaltern Speak?" in *Marxism and the Interpretation of Culture*, ed. Cary Nelson and Larry Grossberg (Urbana: University of Illinois Press, 1988), 271–313.

43. Al-Tifashi, *Nuzhat al-albab*, 237–38 (translation mine); *Délices des coeurs*, 251–52.

44. Etienne de Fougères's ambiguous metaphors may thus be likened to the strategic use of ambiguity in the homoerotic writings of mystics in medieval Germany, as Ulrike Wiethaus has pointed out. Such ambiguity/obscurity may have allowed both the expression *and* the masking of lesbian sexual practices. See Ulrike Wiethaus, "Female Homoerotic Discourse and Religion in Medieval Germanic Culture," in *Gender and Difference in the Middle Ages*, ed. Sharon Farmer and Carol Braun Pasternack (Minneapolis: University of Minnesota Press, 2003), 288–321.

45. Jeri Guthrie, "La Femme dans *Le Livre des manières: Surplus économique, surplus érotique,*" *Romanic Review* 79 (1988): 254.

46. Robert Clark distinguishes between marginality and liminality and argues that lesbians in Etienne's text are associated with the latter rather than the former ("Jousting Without a Lance," 163–64).

47. Clark, "Jousting Without a Lance," 165.

48. Obscenity has been defined as "the counter-code to whatever orthodoxy prevails" by Renatus Hartogs and Hans Fantel, *Four Letter Word Games: The Psychology of Obscenity* (New York: Delacorte Press, 1968), 20.

49. On the use of Latin to express obscenity, see Jan Ziolkowski, ed., *Obscenity: Social Control and Artistic Creation in the European Middle Ages* (Leiden: Brill, 1998), 10–11. On the tendency of editors to expunge from medieval French texts all sexual vocabulary deemed obscene, see Ross G. Arthur, "On Editing Sexually Offensive Old French Texts."

CHAPTER 3. CROSSING SARTORIAL LINES

Note to epigraphs: Carolyn Dinshaw, "A Kiss Is Just a Kiss: Heterosexuality and Its Consolations in Sir Gawain and the Green Knight," *Diacritics* 24, no. 2 (1994): 223, emphasis in original. Judith Butler, *Gender Trouble: Feminism and the Subversion of Identity* (New York: Routledge, 1990), 110.

1. I am using the term "explicit" depictions of lesbianism to refer to literary representations such as we find in Etienne de Fougères's *Livre des manières* and in his use of military rhetorical devices and metaphors (Chapter 2).

2. Michèle Perret, "Travesties et transsexuelles: Yde, Silence, Grisandole, Blanchandine," *Romance Notes* 25, no. 3 (1985): 328. See also Christiane Marchello-Nizia and Michèle Perret, "Une Utopie homosexuelle au quatorzième siècle: L'île sans femmes d'Agriano," *Stanford French Review* 14, nos. 1–2 (1990): 233.

3. There is a growing body of evidence that suggests that a number of women chose to cross-dress in the medieval and premodern world both in the East and the West. In the West, the surviving documents point to an interplay of spiritual, political, social, and even medical factors that account for the existence of female transvestism. If women who cross-dressed were viewed positively in the literature depicting the lives of saints, since they were perceived to be attempting to emulate men and hence attain a higher level of being, they were viewed with suspicion in the social and political contexts because their cross-dressing threatened the established social order and questioned social and gender hierarchies. In this regard, Joan of Arc is perhaps the most prominent example of a medieval transvestite whose threat was so great that it could only be resolved by fire. In the medieval Middle East, surviving legal edicts indicate that some women may have cross-dressed in urban settings especially during the Mamluk period in the middle of the thirteenth century. On prohibitions against donning male attire in this context, see Mounira Chapoutot-Remadi, "Femmes dans la ville Mamluke," *Journal of the Economic and Social History of the Orient* 38, no. 2 (1995): 151–52. There is also evidence that suggests that women donned male (warrior) attire when they participated in the Crusades (European sources tending to be more reticent on the subject, however, in contrast to Arabic ones). Nevertheless, it appears that when depicting women dressed as knights and fighting in battles alongside men, most medieval authors (Muslim and Christian alike) condemned their behavior and viewed it as "unnatural." On women's participation in the Crusades, see James A. Brundage, *Medieval*

Canon Law and the Crusader (Madison: University of Wisconsin Press, 1969); Elizabeth Siberry, *Criticism of Crusading, 1095–1274* (Oxford: Oxford University Press, 1985); Susan B. Edgington and Sarah Lambert, eds., *Gendering the Crusades* (Cardiff: University of Wales Press, 2001); Megan McLaughlin, "The Woman Warrior: Gender, Warfare and Society in Medieval Europe," *Women's Studies* 17 (1990): 193–209; Helen Nicholson, "Women on the Third Crusade," *Journal of Medieval History* 23, no. 4 (1997): 335–49. For a useful overview of cross-dressing in the Middle Ages, see Vern L. Bullough's chapter on "Cross Dressing and Gender Role Change in the Middle Ages," in *Handbook of Medieval Sexuality*, ed. Vern L. Bullough and James A. Brundage (New York: Garland, 1996), 223–42.

4. Cross-dressing (both literal and metaphorical) is an important textual strategy in fabliaux, especially notable in *Berengier au long cul*, and *Trubert* by Douin de Lavesne. Marian miracle plays from mid-fourteenth-century France and the Robin Hood plays from fifteenth- and sixteenth-century England have been shown to be sites of cultural negotiations of gender and social roles. Representative examples of miracle plays which stage cross-dressed heroines include: *Miracle de Théodore* and *Miracle de la fille d'un roy* (which we will examine in detail below). Evidence of cross-dressed female monks/saints is abundant beginning with Thecla (first century, contemporaneous to Saint Paul) and especially from the middle of the fifth to the start of the sixth century: Anastasia, Apollonaria, Athanasia, Euphrosyne, Hilaria, Theodora; on these female saints, see John Anson, "The Female Transvestite in Early Monasticism," *Viator* 5, no. 1 (1974): 1–32. For a summary of the life of famous transvestite saints from the second to the fourteenth century, see the "Hagiographic Appendix" in Valerie R. Hotchkiss, *Clothes Make the Man: Female Cross Dressing in Medieval Europe* (New York: Garland, 1996), 131–41.

5. Heldris de Cornuälle, *Le Roman de Silence: A Thirteenth-Century Arthurian Verse-Romance*, ed. Lewis Thorpe (Cambridge: W. Heffer & Sons, 1972); *Tristan de Nanteuil, chanson de geste inédite*, ed. K. V. Sinclair (Assen: Van Gorcum, 1971). The story of Grisandole is part of the *The Vulgate Version of Arthurian Romances Edited from Manuscripts in the British Museum*, III, *L'Estoire de Merlin*, ed. H. Oskar Sommer (Washington, D.C.: Carnegie Institution, 1910), 300–312.

6. The names of these earliest cross-dressed women in the Islamicate tradition are: `Azza al-Mila', Umm Sa`id al-Aslamiya, and the daughter of Yahya ben al-Hakam. They are said to ride and race horses and show their ankle bracelets. On the hadith tradition addressing cross-dressing and early women transvestites, see Habib Zayyat, "Al-Mar'a al-ghulamiyya fi al-Islam" [The *Ghulamiyya* in Islamicate Culture], *al-Machriq* 50 (1956): 153–57. See also Everett K. Rowson, "The Effeminates of Early Medina," *Journal of the American Oriental Society* 111 (1991): 671–93.

7. On Abu Nuwas's *ghulamiyyat* poetry, see Ewald Wagner, *Abu Nuwas: Eine Studie zur arabischen Literatur der frühen `Abbasidenzeit* (Wiesbaden: Franz Steiner Verlag, 1965); Philip F. Kennedy, *Abu Nuwas: A Genius of Poetry* (Oxford: Oneworld, 2005); Vincent Monteil, trans., *Abu Nuwas: Le Vin, le vent, la vie: Poèmes traduits* (Paris: Sindbad, 1979). The Arabic literary tradition of *ghulamiyyat* has its historical counterpart in the documented fashion of dressing young girls as boys (at times with painted mustaches) in ninth-century Baghdad at the court of al-Amin (one of Harun al-Rachid's sons and patron of

mujun poet Abu Nuwas). This tradition, instituted by Queen Zubayda in an attempt to "cure" her son (al-Amin) of his homosexuality, was quickly imitated by all urban women, and became a fashion in Baghdad. See Mas'udi, *The Meadows of Gold: The Abbasids*, trans. and ed. Paul Lunde and Caroline Stone (London: Kegan Paul, 1989), 390–91.

8. These Arabic folk and epic romances likely circulated in some early form in the eighth and ninth centuries, though they were written down between the fourteenth and sixteenth century. There is a great deal of borrowing between the *One Thousand and One Nights* and Arabic folk romances. On their interaction, see Robert Irwin, *The Arabian Nights: A Companion* (London: Penguin, 1994), 88–89; on cross-dressing in the *One Thousand and One Nights*, see Irwin, *Arabian Nights*, 159–77; on Arabic folk and epic romances, see M. C. Lyons, *The Arabic Epic: Heroic and Oral Story-Telling*, 3 vols. (Cambridge: Cambridge University Press, 1995). For an overview of women warriors in the Arabic tradition, see Remke Kruk, "The Bold and the Beautiful: Women and 'fitna' in the *Sirat Dhat al-Himma*: The Story of Nura," in *Women in the Medieval Islamic World*, ed. Gavin R. G. Hambly (New York: St. Martin's Press, 1998), 99–116; "Clipped Wings: Medieval Arabic Adaptations of the Amazon Myth," *Harvard Middle Eastern and Islamic Review* 1, no. 2 (1994): 132–51; "Warrior Women in Arabic Popular Romance: Qannasa Bint Muzahim and Other Valiant Ladies," *Journal of Arabic Literature* 24 (1993): 213–30 (pt. 1), and 25 (1994): 16–33 (pt. 2).

9. To my knowledge, there is only one additional Old French text that associates cross-dressing with female same-sex marriage: the mid-fourteenth-century story of Blanchandine developed in the epic of *Tristan de Nanteuil*. I will not examine this text here.

10. The story of *Yde et Olive* is the third of five texts that make up the entire poem of *Huon de Bordeaux: La Chanson d'Esclarmonde, La Chanson de Clariet et Florent, La Chanson d'Yde et Olive, La Chanson de Croissant,* and *La Chanson de Godin*.

11. This work is part of *Les Miracles de Nostre Dame par personages*, a collection of forty plays, performed on a yearly basis in Paris from 1339 to 1382 (except in the years of the urban insurrections of the 1350s) by the Parisian goldsmiths' guild. They are preserved in only one luxury manuscript (Paris, BN, fr. 819–820).

12. This fifteenth-century French prose text of *Yde et Olive* was written for three nobles at the court of Charles VII in 1454 (interestingly, in the midst of Joan of Arc's rehabilitation) and printed in the early sixteenth century. It was translated into English prose in the first half of the sixteenth century by Sir John Bourchier (Lord Berners) and entitled *The Boke of Duke Huon of Burdeux* (reprinted in 1570 and in 1601); it was reedited by S. L. Lee in 1882–84 (London: N. Trübner), and reissued (New York: Kraus Reprint) in 1975 and 1981.

13. The story of *Iphis and Ianthe* is in Ovid, *Metamorphoses*, trans. Rolfe Humphries (Bloomington: Indiana University Press, 1955), 229–33. On the classical sources of Yde and Olive, and on the relation of this text to Ovid's tale of *Iphis and Ianthe*, see Nancy Vine Durling, "Rewriting Gender: *Yde et Olive* and Ovidian Myth," *Romance Languages Annual* 1 (1989): 256–62.

14. Nabia Abbott, "A Ninth-Century Fragment of the 'Thousand Night': New Light on the Early History of the Arabian Nights," *Journal of Near Eastern Studies* 8 (1949):

129–64. The existence of Alf layla wa layla, considered to be a translation of the Persian *Hazar afsaneh* [One Thousand Tales] is also attested in al-Nadim's *Fihrist* which represents a key source for our knowledge of tenth-century Islamicate culture. See Bayard Dodge, ed. and trans., *The Fihrist of al-Nadim: A Tenth-Century Survey of Muslim Culture* (New York: Columbia University Press, 1970), 2:713–14. The tenth-century chronicler Mas'udi also records the existence of a Persian text of the *Nights*, and an Arabic translation; cited in Nabia Abbott, "Ninth-Century Fragment," 150.

15. Al-Qurti cited in René Khawam, ed. and trans., *Les Mille et une nuits* (Paris: Phébus, 1986), 1:26. On the availability of this collection in Fatimid Egypt, see Nabia Abbott, "Ninth-Century Fragment," 132 and 151–52.

16. See especially Alice E. Lasater, *Spain to England: A Comparative Study of Arabic, European and English Literature in the Middle Ages* (Jackson: University of Mississippi Press, 1974), and Dorothee Metlitzki, *The Matter of Araby in Medieval England* (New Haven, Conn.: Yale University Press, 1977).

17. On the original nucleus of stories, see Muhsin Mahdi, *The Thousand and One Nights* (Leiden: Brill, 1984), 1:532–54.

18. I have used the following editions of the Yde and Olive texts. All citations to the thirteenth-century verse epic *La Chanson d'Yde et Olive* are from the latest edition of the text, namely, Barbara Anne Brewska's unpublished doctoral dissertation, "*Esclarmonde, Clarisse et Florent, Yde et Olive I, Croissant, Yde et Olive II, Huon et les Géants*, Sequels to *Huon de Bordeaux*, as Contained in Turin MS L.II.14, an Edition" (Vanderbilt University, 1977), 406–48. There exists an earlier edition of this epic by Max Schweigel, *Esclarmonde, Clarisse et Florent, Yde et Olive: Dreifortsetzungen der Chansun von Huon de Bordeaux, nach der einzigen Turiner Handschrift* (Marburg: N. G. Elwert, 1889). The play *Miracle de la fille d'un roy* is part of *Les Miracles de Nostre Dame par personnages*, ed. Gaston Paris and Ulysse Robert (Paris: Firmin et Didot, 1876), 7:2–117. The French prose text of *Yde et Olive* is part of *Les Prouesses et faictz du trespreux noble et vaillant Huon de Bordeaux, pair de France et Duc de Guyenne*, ed. Benoist Rigaud (Lyon, 1587), fols. 166v–178r. I accessed it electronically at the Bibliothèque Nationale in Paris (www.bnf.fr/). All references will be made to these editions and all translations are mine, unless noted otherwise.

19. While this incestuous plan is the king's own idea in the verse and prose epic versions, it is advice given to him by his barons in the play. On the relation between the incest motif and the later lesbian episode, see Diane Watt, "Read My Lips: Clippying and Kyssyng in the Early Sixteenth Century," in *Queerly Phrased: Language, Gender and Sexuality*, ed. Anna Livia and Kira Hall (New York: Oxford University Press, 1997), 167–77.

20. There is no name change in the play or prose versions.

21. In the play, Ysabel arrives in Greece where she fights the Turks and the Saracens on behalf of the emperor of Constantinople.

22. The emperor of Constantinople in the miracle play.

23. Their conversation is witnessed by a monk placed there as an observer of their wedding night by the emperor of Constantinople in the miracle play.

24. Critical attention to the Yde and Olive stories include Diane Watt, "Behaving Like a Man? Incest, Lesbian Desire, and Gender Play in *Yde et Olive*," *Comparative Liter-*

ature 50, no. 4 (1998): 265–85; Watt, "Read My Lips"; Jacqueline de Weever, "The Lady, the Knight, and the Lover: Androgyny and Integration in *La Chanson d'Yde et Olive,*" *Romanic Review* 81, no. 4 (1991): 371–91; Durling, "Rewriting Gender"; Robert Clark, "A Heroine's Sexual Itinerary: Incest, Transvestism, and Same-Sex Marriage in *Yde et Olive,*" in *Gender Transgressions: Crossing the Normative Barrier in Old French Literature,* ed. Karen J. Taylor (New York: Garland, 1998), 889–905.

25. Marjorie Garber, *Vested Interests: Cross-Dressing and Cultural Anxiety* (New York: Routledge, 1992), 11. Some may argue that the "third term" can function as a stabilizing metaphor instead, as is evident in the concept of the Trinity for instance. Given the context of cross-dressing, however, I find Garber's destabilizing notion particularly useful as it permits a discussion of the queering possibilities of the medieval text.

26. This is the main point of Watt's important article "Behaving Like a Man?" My approach, however, differs from hers.

27. Garber, *Vested Interests,* 16.

28. In the miracle play, despite her cross-dressing and her self-presentation as a soldier in search of a master (vv. 1720–21), Ysabel continues to be portrayed as a noble person and is viewed by others around her as someone from a higher social standing.

29. *Yde et Olive,* v. 6629. In the fifteenth-century prose version, we find a parallel statement: "l'Allemant mena Ide en son hostel pour le servir nonobstant que autrefois ait esté servie" ("the German took Ide to his house so that she could serve him as she was served in the past"), *Prouesses et faicts,* 324.

30. *Yde et Olive,* vv. 2054–55. The sudden change in Yde's linguistic register is reminiscent of that of the Lady of Esclavon in Chrétien de Troyes's *Perceval.*

31. *Yde et Olive,* v. 6784 and v. 6777, respectively.

32. *Prouesses et faicts,* 325.

33. The occurrence of the term "putains" in these contexts can be gleaned from the list of usage compiled by Tobler-Lommatsch in his *Altfranzösiches Wörterbuch* (Wiesbaden: Franz Steiner Verlag, 1967), s.v. "putain."

34. Garber, *Vested Interests,* 32.

35. Perhaps not surprisingly considering the genre of miracle plays, the expression of Olive's desire is utterly absent from *Miracle de la fille d'un roy.*

36. *Prouesses et faicts,* 327. This love at first sight has no equivalent in the epic or play.

37. Andreas Capellanus, *The Art of Courtly Love,* trans. John Jay Parry (New York: Norton, 1969); Ibn Dau'ud al-Isfahani, *Kitab al-zahra,* ed. A. R. Nykl and I. Tuqan (Chicago: University of Chicago Press, 1932); Ibn Hazm, *The Ring of the Dove: A Treatise on the Art and Practice of Arab Love,* trans. A. J. Arberry (London: Luzac, 1953).

38. I have translated the Old French "volentiers" by "enjoyed." The word literally also means "voluntarily" which hints at the active role that Olive plays in the gaze, and in the intimacy that will develop between the two women.

39. In the fifteenth-century prose text, this is how this scene is rewritten: "Olive qui aux creneaux estoit avoit bien veu et regardé les tresgrandes prouesses que Ide avoit fait en la bataille, dont elle l'aima tellement en son coeur que tout luy soubrioit de ioye, et dist si bas que nulle personne ne le l'entendit. A cestuy-la donne m'amour, laquelle ne fut

oncques octroyee à home vivant: mais est bien droit et raison qu'à Ide mon amour soit octroyee et donnee, ainsi et par telles paroles se devisoit Olive à par elle." ("Olive who was at the window had seen and observed the great acts of prowess that Ide had done in the battle. This led her to love him so deeply that all was joyous to her. She spoke to herself so low that no one heard it: 'I give my love to him, a love that was never given to any living man. But it is only right that I should give my love to Ide.'") *Prouesses et faicts*, 330.

40. The physical dimension of Olive's desire is missing in the fifteenth-century prose text.

41. For the sexual meaning of the word "joie" in Old French writings, see Pierre Bec, *Burlesque et obscénité chez les troubadours* (Paris: Stock, 1984), 236.

42. The erotic charge of military prowess is a notion that was established in the medieval West with Geoffrey of Monmouth's mid-twelfth-century *Historia Regum Britanniae; The History of the Kings of Britain*, trans. Lewis Thorpe (London: Penguin, 1969), 206. The Ovidian dictum *militat omnes amans* (every lover wages war) has had a great influence on the concept of love in the Middle Ages. On the relation between Ovid and French romance, see Eugene Vance, "Le Combat érotique chez Chrétien de Troyes: De la figure à la forme," *Poétique* 12 (1972): 544–71; see also Nancy Huston and Sam Kinser, *A L'amour comme à la guerre* (Paris: Seuil, 1984).

43. Chrétien de Troyes, *Lancelot ou le Chevalier de la Charrette*, ed. Mario Roques (Paris: Champion, 1983), v. 6036; translation mine.

44. Only Yde and the reader are privy to the ambiguity raised by the cross-dressing and to the threat posed by Olive's growing attachment.

45. Alexandre Leupin, "Ecriture naturelle et écriture hermaphrodite: Le *De planctu Naturae* d'Alain de Lille, un art poétique du XIIe siècle," *Diagraphe* 9 (1976): 119–41.

46. The evolution in the status of marriage in the twelfth century has been well described by Georges Duby, *Le Chevalier, la femme et le prêtre* (Paris: Hachette, 1981). Duby terms the aristocratic form of marriage, "la morale des guerriers" and the church-sanctioned marriage, "la morale des prêtres." See also James A. Brundage, *Law, Sex and Christian Society in Medieval Europe* (Chicago: University of Chicago Press, 1987).

47. *Prouesses et faicts*, 333; the thirteenth-century verse text of *Yde et Olive* remains more implicit in its depiction of the marriage festivities (vv. 7144–46), while the dramatic rendition gives no information on the subject.

48. Interestingly, none of the critics who have analyzed the Yde and Olive stories address the religious emphasis in the texts.

49. Watt's reading is more resolutely on the side of reciprocal erotic feelings between Yde and Olive; see Watt, "Read My Lips," 173.

50. There is a very large bibliography on the use of erotic expression in religious writings both in Islam and in Christianity. In Islam, sufi (mystic) literature has been read as a space where the expression of the love for God fuses with homoerotic sentiments. See Annemarie Schimmel, *Mystical Dimensions of Islam* (Chapel Hill: University of North Carolina Press, 1975) and her "Eros—Heavenly and Not So Heavenly—in Sufi Literature and Life," in *Society and the Sexes in Medieval Islam*, ed. Afaf Lutfi al-Sayyid-Marsot (Malibu: Undena, 1979), 119–41. In Christianity, see Virginia Burrus, *The Sex Lives of Saints: An*

Erotics of Ancient Hagiography (Philadelphia: University of Pennsylvania Press, 2004); Ulrike Wiethaus, "Female Homoerotic Discourse and Religion in Medieval Germanic Culture," in *Gender and Difference in the Middle Ages*, ed. Sharon Farmer and Carol Braun Pasternack (Minneapolis: University of Minnesota Press, 2003), 288–321; Ann Matter, "My Sister, My Spouse: Woman-Identified Women in Medieval Christianity," *Journal of Feminist Studies in Religion* 2, no. 2 (1986): 81–93; Karma Lochrie, "Mystical Acts, Queer Tendencies," in *Constructing Medieval Sexuality*, ed. Karma Lochrie, Peggy McCracken, and James Schultz (Minneapolis: University of Minnesota Press, 1997), 180–200; Kathy Lavezzo, "Sobs and Sighs Between Women: The Homoerotics of Compassion in the Book of Margery Kempe," in *Premodern Sexualities*, ed. Louise O. Fradenburg and Carla Freccero (New York: Routledge, 1995), 175–98.

51. This is Robert Clark and Claire Sponsler's conclusion in "Queer Play: The Cultural Work of Crossdressing in Medieval Drama," *New Literary History* 28, no. 2 (1997): 341. It is also Watt's overall conclusion in both articles cited above.

52. The deceptive nature of sight has become a topos in medieval literature by the thirteenth century. This topos was a logical development from the famous opposition between *historia* (sight, truth) and *fabula* (language, lie) developed by Cicero and popularized by Macrobius, Isidore of Seville, William of Conches, Bernardus Silvestris, Peter Abelard, and Alain of Lille among many others.

53. I am using the translation provided by Robert Clark (Clark and Sponsler, "Queer Play," 325).

54. Clark and Sponsler, "Queer Play," 326.

55. *Yde et Olive*, v. 7164; *Prouesses et faicts*, 334.

56. *Yde et Olive*, v. 7171; *Prouesses et faicts*, 334.

57. *Yde et Olive*, v. 7190; *Prouesses et faicts*, 334.

58. Yannick Carré, *Le Baiser sur la bouche au Moyen Age: Rites, symboles, mentalités à travers les textes et les images, 11e–15e siècles* (Paris: Le Léopard d'Or, 1992).

59. *Yde et Olive*, v. 6368. The same terms are repeated lines later at vv. 6409–10, v. 6423, and v. 6523. These words are also used in *Prouesses et faicts*, 319. No kissing or hugging is invoked in the *Miracle de la fille d'un roy*, either between father and daughter (the incest motif is absent from the miracle play) or between the two women.

60. The overtly sexual meaning of these words is also explicitly stated by the narrator of the prose text; see *Prouesses et faicts*, 320.

61. Watt, "Read My Lips," 169.

62. Our reading of Yde and Olive thus lends support to Sautman and Sheingorn who invite critics to scrutinize anew the vocabulary of sexual practice in order to recover alternative meanings in the glossary of emotional attachment. See Francesca Sautman and Pamela Sheingorn, eds., *Same Sex Desire Among Women in the Middle Ages* (New York: Palgrave, 2001), 27. See also Judith Butler, "Gender Is Burning: Questions of Appropriation and Subversion," in *Bodies That Matter: On the Discursive Limits of "Sex"* (New York: Routledge, 1993), 122.

63. These lines are absent from both the miracle play and the prose text.

64. The ambiguity of "the way it pleases me" is highlighted by the fact that the barons laugh at Olive's response (v. 7200). The same scene is depicted in *Prouesses et faicts*, 324.

65. Contrary to Ysabel, Yde/Ide does not reveal her social class, however.

66. *Prouesses et faicts*, 334

67. It is indeed worth noting with Jacqueline de Weever that the grammatical gender instability that had been prevalent thus far in the epic ceases at this point. See de Weever, "The Lady, the Knight, and the Lover," 388. It is also important to remember that from the church fathers' point of view, transvestism was tolerated only as long as the woman remained cross-dressed and no one knew about the cross-dressing. On this subject, see Vern Bullough's chapter on cross-dressing in *Handbook of Medieval Sexuality*, ed. Vern Bullough and James A. Brundage, 227–31 in particular.

68. The term appears indeed in *Prouesses et faicts*, 335. Not surprisingly, the word is used by the king himself, although it is reported in indirect discourse.

69. The Buggery Act will establish it as such in England in 1533.

70. The threat of capital punishment is voiced in the thirteenth-century verse epic, vv. 7251–52; *Prouesses et faicts*, 335. On the capital punishment of lesbians in the Middle Ages, see Louis Crompton, "The Myth of Lesbian Impunity: Capital Laws from 1270 to 1791," *Journal of Homosexuality* 6 nos. 1–2 (Winter 1980–81): 11–25.

71. *Yde et Olive*, vv. 7261–72; *Prouesses et faicts*, 335.

72. "Ide et Olive s'allerent coucher ensemble et firent leur deduit, tellement qu'en icelle propre nuict ils engendrerent le beau Croissant." ("Ide and Olive went to bed together and they made love, so much so that in that very night they conceived the beautiful Croissant"), *Prouesses et faicts*, 336.

73. This has been particularly well articulated in Thomas Laqueur's *Making Sex: Body and Gender from the Greeks to Freud* (Cambridge, Mass.: Harvard University Press, 1990).

74. Ovid's tale of "Iphis and Ianthe" describes in detail the growth of the penis on Iphis's body. For a different reading, see Watt, "Behaving Like a Man?" 281.

75. *Yde et Olive*, vv. 6503–21.

76. Only in the miracle play does Ysabel state that she rejoices at the miracle. This is what she replies to Saint Michael who announced to her that God will intervene: "Le cuer m'avez, sire, esjouy" ("Sire, you have rejoiced my heart"), v. 2933. In this case, however, it seems that Ysabel's happiness and relief are due to Saint Michael's announcement that God will not let her down and will reward her for her infinite faith in him. Her happiness appears thus to be due to the news that God will help her, rather than to the sexual transformation that has not yet occurred, and that she still does not know about.

77. Watt, "Behaving Like a Man?" 274. This interpretation applies equally to the prose text. The question of lineage and genealogy in *Yde and Olive* is especially important because it appears to respond to the most pressing issue invoked in condemnations of sodomy in the Middle Ages, namely, its nonreproduction, and its role in bringing about the end of life (and of the world). That sodomy is a crime against humanity is precisely what Lavinie accuses Enéas of in *Enéas, roman du XIIe siècle*, ed. J. J. Salvedra de Grave (Paris: Champion, 1925–31), vv. 8596–98.

78. Garber, *Vested Interests*, 223; emphasis in original.

79. *Yde et Olive*, v. 7309.

80. It is interesting to note that although the end of the Yde and Olive II section in-

forms the reader of this large family engendered by the now successfully transgendered Yde, the end of the Yde and Olive I section had pointed out that Yde and Olive will not have any other children, besides Croissant ("Ydé n'Olive n'orent nul enfant plus" ["Yde and Olive did not have any other children"], v. 7297).

81. The double marriage at the end of the play could, theoretically at least, be considered incestuous. On the relation between incest and female homoeroticism, see Watt, "Behaving Like a Man?" On incest in the Middle Ages, see Elizabeth Archibald, *Incest and the Medieval Imagination* (London: Oxford University Press, 2001).

82. Michelle Szkilnik, "The Grammar of the Sexes in Medieval French Romance," in *Gender Transgressions: Crossing the Normative Barrier in Old French Literature*, ed. Karen J. Taylor (New York: Garland, 1998), 61–88.

83. The entire *Huon de Bordeaux* cycle seems heavily indebted to the Arabic storytelling tradition of the *One Thousand and One Nights*, and this topic merits a separate study in the future.

84. Francesca Sautman, "What Can They Possibly Do Together? Queer Epic Performances in *Tristan de Nanteuil*," in Sautman and Sheingorn, *Same Sex Love and Desire*, 209. However, she does not compare specific echoes between the French text and the Arabic tale from the *Arabian Nights* as I do here. The subject of naming, while important in French romance, has only been examined in relation to Latin sources. On the role of naming, see Michèle Perret's remarks in her "Travesties et transsexuelles," 336–40 and her note 10 especially.

85. One might argue that because the verse epic *Yde and Olive* is written in a Picard dialect (with some East Frankish and Walloon forms), it is associated with Northern Europe and is thus unlikely to have come into contact with the *Arabian Nights*. However, there is a growing body of evidence that documents commercial and religious links between Northern France and the Mediterranean since at least 1087. Michel Rouche, "L'Age des pirates et des saints (Ve–Xie siècles)," in *Histoire de Boulogne-sur-mer*, ed. Alain Lottin (Lille: Presses Universitaires de Lille, 1983), 48.

86. In the fifteenth-century prose rendition of the text, the narrator explains the name of Croissant thus: "on le nomma Croissant pource qu'en celuy iour la lune fut veüe en croissant" ("he was named Croissant because that day the moon was seen waxing"), *Prouesses et faicts*, 336. Sautman points out that the name of Croissant appears "under another guise" in the contemporary *Baudoin de Sebourc*, though she does not specify which ("What Can They Possibly Do Together?" 226 n. 43).

87. Literally, the name "Croissant" would have been rendered in Arabic as "Hilal," not "Qamar" (full moon); it is associated, however, with the general semantic field of "moon."

88. Ibn Nasr al-Katib, *Encyclopedia of Pleasure*, ed. Salah Addin Khawwam, trans. Adnan Jarkas and Salah Addin Khawwam (Toronto: Aleppo, 1977), 192.

89. It is indeed through Qamar al-Zaman's work as a gardener during his separation from Boudour, and his sale of vats full of olives that he will come to be recognized by the cross-dressed Boudour. In the tale from *Arabian Nights*, olives thus play a very crucial role in ensuring the recognition and reunification of the heterosexual couple.

90. Marjorie Garber, "The Chic of Araby: Transvestism, Transsexualism and the Erotics of Cultural Appropriation," in *Body Guards: The Cultural Politics of Gender Ambiguity*, ed. Julia Epstein and Kristina Straub (New York: Routledge, 1991), 237.

91. This character was nicknamed al-Zarqaʾ and would have lived in the pre-Islamic era (Ibn Nasr al-Katib, *Encyclopedia of Pleasure*, 86 n. 100).

92. This is recounted in the epic text vv. 6935–39; *Prouesses et faictz*, 328.

93. The comparison drawn here between Yde and Scheherazade invites the provocative question as to whether the Arabic storyteller can herself also be considered a lesbian. This question merits further investigation.

94. References to *The Story of Qamar al-Zaman and the Princess Boudour* come from Muhsin Mahdi's Arabic edition entitled *Kitab alf layla wa layla* (The Book of alf layla wa layla), 4 vols. (Leiden: Brill, 1984), 1:591. Mahdi's edition has been translated by Husain Haddawy, *The Arabian Nights*, 2 vols. (New York: Norton, 1995). However, Haddawy did not translate *The Story of Qamar al-Zaman and the Princess Boudour* as it appeared in Mahdi, but combined it with material from two key nineteenth-century printed editions, Calcutta II (1839–42) and Bulaq (1835). For this reason, I am providing my own translations of Mahdi's Arabic text.

95. Mahdi, *Kitab alf layla wa layla*, 592.

96. I am using the term "redactor" when speaking about the "authorship" of the *Arabian Nights* for reasons of convenience, as outlined by Andras Hamori, "A Comic Romance from the Thousand and One Nights: The Tale of Two Viziers," *Arabica* 30, no. 1 (1983): 38 n. 1. The term "redactor" has been further developed by David Pinault who writes: "Each redactor will doubtless have benefited from the creativity of oral reciters who transmitted and embellished the given tale before it was committed to writing. . . . The term redactor indicates that person who stands at the end of this chain of oral and textual transmission, that person responsible for the shape in which the story reaches us in its final written form in a given manuscript or printed text." See his *Story-Telling Techniques in the Arabian Nights* (Leiden: Brill, 1992), 16.

97. Garber, "Chic of Araby," 229.

98. On oral performance as a privileged moment of creation, see Albert B. Lord, *The Singer of Tales* (Cambridge, Mass.: Harvard University Press, 2000). While Lord focuses on Homer, his theoretical framework is helpful in understanding the complexity of the *Arabian Nights*, its oral existence in the Middle Ages, about which we have limited knowledge, and its written record.

99. Although Mardrus claims to have translated the Bulaq (1835) and Calcutta II (1839–42) editions of *Alf layla wa layla*, a close reading of his text and a comparison of his translation with both the Bulaq and the Calcutta II editions reveals that he added many details and scenes absent from these earlier renditions.

100. Ibn Nasr, *Encyclopedia of Pleasure*, 261–62.

101. Ibn Nasr, *Encyclopedia of Pleasure*, 235.

102. Ibn Nasr, *Encyclopedia of Pleasure*, 236.

103. We will recall that the same association between heterosexual wedding night and violence had also been made in the French verse epic, as we saw earlier (v. 7191).

104. Judith Butler, *Gender Trouble*, 31.

105. *One Thousand and One Nights*, ed. and trans. into French by Joseph Charles Mardrus; trans. into English by Pomys Mathers (Yugoslovia: Dorset Press, 1964), 2:67.

106. There is a tendency in contemporary scholarship (both in the East and the West) to consider Mahdi's Arabic edition of *Alf layla wa layla* as the most "authentic" version. However, we must not forget the fact that the manuscript he used is simply the sole surviving one in the Middle Ages and that other renditions of *Alf layla wa layla* most certainly existed, though they left no written trace. We must also keep in mind the oral nature of this work which prohibits us from considering any of the surviving texts of the *Arabian Nights* as "definitive." On the relation between oral performance and the written text, see Lord, *The Singer of Tales*, chapter 6 especially.

107. Some may argue that lesbianism is permitted in the Arabic tale precisely because of the cultural practice of the harem. Until today, however, the Western-held association between lesbianism and harem culture, though certainly possible because the harem is an all-female community, has still not been established definitively.

CHAPTER 4. CROSSING THE LINES OF FRIENDSHIP

Note to epigraph: Saint Augustine, cited in Judith C. Brown, *Immodest Acts: The Life of a Lesbian Nun in Renaissance Italy* (New York: Oxford University Press, 1986), 8.

1. Jean Renart, *Escoufle*, ed. Franklin Sweetser (Geneva: Droz, 1974), v. 9073. All references will be made to this edition and all translations are mine. The *Escoufle* is one of three texts attributed to the same author (Jean Renart), including the *Lai de L'ombre* (ca. 1217) and the *Roman de la Rose ou de Guillaume de Dole* (ca. 1228). Presumed to have been composed first, the *Escoufle* is still considered by critics to be the least complex of Jean Renart's literary productions and has thus perhaps consequently been the most neglected of his works.

2. On the symbolism of the kite, see the very useful article by Baudouin van den Abeele, "*L'Escoufle*: Portrait littéraire d'un oiseau," in special issue, ed. Brian Levy and Paul Wachers, *Reinardus: Yearbook of the International Reynard Society* 1 (1988): 5–15.

3. In the *Escoufle*, the lovers' separation leads exactly to 3,105 lines of adventures (from v. 4602 to v. 7707).

4. On the importance of the paratext, see Gérard Genette, *Seuils* (Paris: Seuil, 1987), and Emmanuèle Baumgartner and Laurence Harf-Lancner, *Seuils de l'oeuvre dans le texte médiéval* (Paris: Presses de la Sorbonne Nouvelle, 2002). Critics who have given a prime role to prologues and epilogues in the works of Jean Renart include Jean-Charles Payen, "Structure et sens de *Guillaume de Dole*," in *Etudes de langue et de littérature du Moyen Age offerts à Félix Lecoy* (Paris: Champion, 1973), 483–98.

5. Roberta Krueger, "Transforming Maidens: Singlewomen's Stories in Marie de France's *Lais* and Later French Courtly Narratives," in *Singlewomen in the European Past, 1250–1800*, ed. Judith M. Bennett and Amy M. Froide (Philadelphia: University of Pennsylvania Press, 1999), 148.

6. Although the exact definition of the genre of the "realistic romance" has generated much controversy, most critics agree that it is one that portrays "real" social spaces and incorporates a number of characters who (according to some) could be historically identified. Texts belonging to this genre give an especially prominent role to women, to female close relations, and to the heroines' move across domestic, urban, and courtly settings in order to surmount various types of obstacles (social, familial, psychological). For this reason, realistic romances have also been dubbed "feminocentric." For a definition of the genre of the realistic romance, see Rita Lejeune, "Jean Renart et le roman réaliste au XIIIème siècle," in *Grundriss der Romanischen Literaturen des Mittelalters*, ed. Jean Frappier and Reinhold Grimm, vol. 4, *Le Roman jusqu'à la fin du 13e siècle* (Heidelberg: Carl Winter, 1978), 400–453, and John W. Baldwin, " 'Once There Was an Emperor . . . ': A Political Reading of the Romances of Jean Renart," in *Jean Renart and the Art of Romance: Essays on Guillaume de Dole*, ed. Nancy Vine Durling (Gainesville: University of Florida Press, 1997), 45–82. G. Charlier, speaking of the "realistic" nature of Jean Renart's romances, writes: "Feudal life is described as is, not only by its most glittering features, but also by its most modest facets, in its daily routine." "L'*Escoufle* et *Guillaume de Dole*," in *Mélanges de philologie romane . . . offerts à Maurice Wilmotte* (Paris: Champion, 1910), 1:93, translation mine. The term "feminocentric" romance was coined by Nancy K. Miller in *The Heroine's Text: Readings in the French and English Novel* (New York: Columbia University Press, 1980), and used by Nancy Jones with reference to Jean Renart's romances in "The Uses of Embroidery in Jean Renart: Gender, History, Textuality," in *Jean Renart and the Art of Romance*, ed. Nancy Vine Durling, 13–44.

7. The key role that the kite plays in the *Escoufle* has long puzzled critics in their quest for antecedents. In the introduction to his nineteenth-century edition of the romance, Paul Meyer, first editor of the *Escoufle*, noted the thematic parallel in the use of the thief-kite between this text and other earlier medieval romances, such as *Guillaume d'Angleterre*, attributed to Chrétien de Troyes. In addition, Meyer pointed to the multiple similarities between Jean Renart's *Escoufle* and an Old German tale, *der Busant*, including the theme of the kite that is caught and destroyed by the hero. He concluded however that both the *Escoufle* and *der Busant* (today believed to have been composed slightly later) were likely written independently, presumably with a common source, one that has so far not been identified. See Paul Meyer's introduction to the *Escoufle* (Paris: SATF, 1894). Others, while recognizing the fact that the *Escoufle* is part of an alternative tradition to the matters of Rome, Brittany, France, and even Byzantium, have not examined the relation of this romance to the matter of Araby, as I propose to do here; See Nancy Jones, "Uses of Embroidery," 15.

8. On the intimate relation that develops between Boudour and Hayat al-Nefous, see Chapter 3.

9. I am using this term here as an extension of the meaning given to it by Alison Adams to speak about the less obvious allusions to the Tristan and Ysolde legend in the *Escoufle*. See her "Jean Renart's l'*Escoufle* and the Tristan Legend: Moderation Rewarded," in *Rewards and Punishments in the Arthurian Romances and Lyric Poetry of Mediaeval France: Essays Presented to Kenneth Varty on the Occasion of His Sixtieth Birthday*, ed. Peter V. Davies and Angus J. Kennedy (Cambridge: D. S. Brewer, 1987), 3. Several other critics have ex-

amined the intertextual references between the *Escoufle* and *Tristan and Yseut*, including L. Sudre, "Les Allusions à la légende de Tristan dans la littérature du Moyen Age," *Romania* 15 (1886): 534–57, and Rita Lejeune, "La Coupe de Tristan dans l'*Escoufle* de Jean Renart," in *The Medieval Alexander Legend and Romance Epic, Essays . . . David J. A. Ross*, ed. P. Noble, L. Polak, and C. Isoz (New York: Kraus International, 1982), 119–24.

10. E. Jane Burns, *Courtly Love Undressed: Reading Through Clothes in Medieval French Culture* (Philadelphia: University of Pennsylvania Press, 2002).

11. Ingrid Perbal, "L'Orient dans les soieries du musée de Cluny," *Qantara* (Fall 2004): 19.

12. Olivia Remie Constable, *Trade and Traders in Muslim Spain: The Commercial Realignment of the Iberian Peninsula, 900–1500* (Cambridge: Cambridge University Press, 1996), 173–81 and 199–203 especially.

13. See Kathryn L. Reyerson, "Medieval Silks in Montpellier: The Silk Market ca. 1250–ca. 1350," *Journal of European Economic History* 11 (1982): 117–40; Alexandre André Germain, *Histoire du commerce de Montpellier antérieurement à l'ouverture du port de Cette*, 2 vols. (Montpellier: Imprimerie de Jean Martel, ainé, 1861); Louis Thomas, *Montpellier, ville marchande: Histoire économique et sociale de Montpellier des origines* à 1870 (Montpellier: Librairie Vallat, Librairie Coulet, 1936); Wilhelm Heyd, *Histoire du commerce du Levant au Moyen-Age*, 2 vols. (Amsterdam: Adolf M. Hakkert, 1959); and Louis de Mas Latrie, *Traités de paix et de commerce et documents divers concernant les relations des chrétiens avec les Arabes de l'Afrique septentrionale au Moyen-Age*, 2 vols. (New York: B. Franklin, 1963).

14. While still in the meadow, Aelis has a brief encounter with a young man who stumbles upon her as she is waking up and discovering Guillaume's disappearance. This occurs before she leaves the meadow and enters the city.

15. Heldris de Cornuälle, *Le Roman de Silence: A Thirteenth-Century Arthurian Verse-Romance*, ed. Lewis Thorpe (Cambridge: W. Heffer & Sons, 1972), vv. 2496–688.

16. The threat Aelis feels as a single woman in an urban setting recalls indeed that which many maidens experience in courtly romances, as depicted for example in the customs of Logres. These traditions, portrayed in Chrétien de Troyes's *Lancelot ou le Chevalier de la Charrette*, ed. Mario Roques (Paris: Champion, 1983, vv. 1295–316), indicate that while a maiden traveling alone would bring shame upon a knight who dishonors her, she instantly becomes the property of the man who can defeat the knight who accompanies her without incurring any blame. On the customs of Logres and the precarious status of women in Chrétien de Troyes's romances, see Roberta Krueger, *Women Readers and the Ideology of Gender in Old French Verse Romance* (Cambridge: Cambridge University Press, 1993), 39–41.

17. Frédéric Godefroy, *Dictionnaire de l'ancienne langue française et de tous ses dialectes du IXe au XVe siècle* (Paris: Vieweg, 1888–1920), s.v. "jesir," and "lis."

18. This rule (tentatively attributed to Waldebert of Luxeuil) is translated by Jo Ann McNamara and John Halborg in *The Ordeal of Community* (Toronto: Peregrina, 1993), rule 14, "How they should always sleep in the schola," 92–93.

19. Brown, *Immodest Acts*, 8. The same rule had been already dictated by Donatus of Besançon in the seventh century under rule 65, "How they ought to sleep." See McNamara and Halborg, trans., *The Ordeal of Community*, 67.

20. Brown, *Immodest Acts*, 8.

21. The best known example of a woman who conflates these categories is the maiden in the *Chevalier de la Charrette* who explains to Lancelot the customs of Logres, who helps the knight, all the while staging her own rape (vv. 1195–280).

22. On such damsels in medieval romance, see Krueger, "Transforming Maidens," 164–65.

23. On the term "feminocentric," see n. 6 above. On female heroines in Jean Renart's corpus, see Frédérique Le Nan, "De Quelques 'pérégrines' ou la mobilité des dames dans l'oeuvre présumée de Jean Renart," *Revue des langues romanes* 104, no. 1 (2000): 47–70.

24. G. T. Diller, "L'*Escoufle*: Une Aventurière dans le roman courtois," *Le Moyen Age* 85, no. 1 (1979): 34–43. Critics who have read the romance in nonsexual terms include Linda Clemente, who has noted that in the world that Aelis builds for herself after her separation from Guillaume, she "matures without love," adding that Aelis relinquishes "her old identity, moves into a new world, an unknown city. Her entrance into this world is also her entrance into a world *unadorned by love.* . . . *Love no longer inhabits or forms the guiding principle of her life.*" See her "Aelis' Introspective Silence in the Feminist World of Jean Renart's *Escoufle*," *Cincinnati Romance Review* 10 (1991): 31 (emphasis mine). She also writes that the entire romance may be read as "a manual for how to succeed without love" (32). Even though she recognizes the ambiguous intimacy that Aelis develops with Ysabel and the fact that this same-sex relation satisfies Aelis's need for affection, Clemente never uses the word "love" to describe this intimacy. Similarly, while Nancy Vine Durling points to Aelis's self-reliance and her "ingenuity," and while she observes how "the energetic sensuality of the young lovers [Aelis and Guillaume] is described with refreshing clarity and candor," she remains silent on the entire middle episode of the romance recounting Aelis's intimate friendships (*Jean Renart and the Art of Romance*, 2). Roberta Krueger reads Aelis and Ysabel's bond as a "deep intimate friendship," though not necessarily a same-sex one ("Transforming Maidens," 172–73).

25. Diller, "L'*Escoufle*: Une Aventurière dans le roman courtois," 37.

26. The question as to whether Aelis's decision to form relationships with women after Guillaume's disappearance is due to a defense mechanism (as Diller maintains) or reflects an independent will is difficult to resolve. The fact that she forms multiple intimate bonds with women complicates the picture further. The multiple theories on the "causes" of homosexuality pertain to the discussion at hand: Are Aelis's same-sex relations socially induced, or are they innate?

27. My work on the *Escoufle* thus supports Judith Bennett who states a similar conclusion in her "'Lesbian-Like' and the Social History of Lesbianisms," *Journal of the History of Sexuality* 9, nos. 1–2 (2000): 1–24.

28. The wide definition of aberrant sexualities in the Middle Ages will be expanded in Saint Thomas Aquinas's *Summa Theologiae*. See Pierre J. Payer, *Sex and the Penitentials: The Development of a Sexual Code, 550–1150* (Toronto: University of Toronto Press, 1984), and James A. Brundage, "Sex and Canon Law," in *Handbook of Medieval Sexuality*, ed. Vern L. Bullough and James Brundage (New York: Garland, 1996), 33–50.

29. A. Grisay, G. Lavis, and M. Dubois-Stasse, "La Jeune fille," in *Les Dénominations de la femme dans les anciens textes littéraires français* (Gembloux: J. Duculot, 1969), 157–87.

30. Susan Mosher Stuard, "Single by Law and Custom," in Bennett and Froide, *Singlewomen*, 106. On the status of *ancillae*, see also Charles Verlinden, "Le Mariage des esclaves," in *Il matrimonio nella società altro medievale* (Spoleto: Centro Italiano di Studi sull'Altro Medioevo, 1977), 2:569–601.

31. The conventional medieval system of classification was made up of three sexual orders: virgins, wives, and widows. In addition, both Jacques de Vitry and Gilbert de Tournai composed sermons for male and female servants who stood outside the three commonly accepted social categories in the Middle Ages. See Jean Longère, "Deux sermons de Jacques de Vitry *Ad Servos et Ancillas*," in *La femme au Moyen Age*, ed. Michel Rouche and Jean Heuclin (Maubeuge: Publications de la Ville de Maubeuge, 1990), 261–97, and Sharon Farmer's discussion in "'It Is Not Good That [Wo]man Should Be Alone': Elite Responses to Singlewomen in High Medieval Paris," in Bennett and Froide, Singlewomen, 86–95 and especially her n. 41 on p. 101.

32. The use of the word *ancele* to refer to Ysabel goes hand in hand with the word *meschine* employed several times with reference to her. According to Godefroy, one of the meanings of *meschine* is precisely a servant. Interestingly, this term can also at times mean concubine (Godefroy, *Dictionnaire de l'ancienne langue française*, s.v. "meschine").

33. Jacques de Vitry and Humbert of Romans believed firmly in the threat posed by female servants and hence collapsed the categories of female servants and prostitutes. See Farmer, "Elite Responses," 88–90. We will return to this question in Chapter 5.

34. Medieval church legislation believed that "if the free party—that is, the husband—understood and consented to marriage with an unfree woman, the marriage was valid." See Stuart, "Single by Law and Custom," 119. The question of the rights of slaves to marry was discussed in canon law under the heading of "error of condition."

35. This is parallel to Yde's condition to obtain Olive's consent to marry prior to concluding their marriage in the verse epic of *Yde et Olive*, as we saw in the last chapter.

36. Stuard points specifically to the laws of Walter of Mortagne that gave the right to unfree women to marry regardless of the master's consent and that permitted an *ancilla* to escape if she was prevented from cohabiting with her husband. These ideas found their way into the text *Dignum est* of Pope Hadrian IV, later compilations of papal letters, Bernard of Pavia's *Breviarium extravagantium*, and Gregory IX's 1234 *Decretales* (Stuard, "Single by Law and Custom," 118).

37. Without developing the social argument or lesbian possibilities that I propose here, Krueger reaches a similar conclusion and points to the "benefits of female friendship" in the *Escoufle* and the way "poor women can elevate themselves by association with wealthy women or noble households" ("Transforming Maidens," 174–75).

38. For a different reading, see Jones, "Uses of Embroidery," 32.

39. This is an actual legal category in the Middle Ages, as Stuard demonstrates in "Single by Law and Custom."

40. My reading of the *Escoufle* supports Wiethaus's observation that the medieval discourse on same-sex attraction focuses on kissing and caressing, rather than on genital activity. See Ulrike Wiethaus, "Female Homoerotic Discourse and Religion in Medieval Germanic Culture," in *Gender and Difference in the Middle Ages*, ed. Sharon

Farmer and Carol Braun Pasternack (Minneapolis: University of Minnesota Press, 2003), 295.

41. The same strategy is used in women's devotional writings (such as Hadewijch's) as analyzed by Wiethaus in "Female Homoerotic Discourse," 291.

42. On homosexuality mimicking and undermining heterosexuality, see Judith Butler, *Gender Trouble: Feminism and the Subversion of Identity* (New York: Routledge, 1990), 31.

43. On the notion of "exclusivity in affection" in monastic contexts, see Wiethaus, "Female Homoerotic Discourse," 298–306.

44. The sexual connotations of the relationship between Aelis and Ysabel becomes even more pronounced when contrasted to the development of the friendship between Fresne and Rose in Renaut's *Galeran de Bretagne* (ca. 1216). If Renaut is rewriting the *Escoufle* (as some critics have claimed), I would argue that he is doing so by downplaying all sexual ambiguity and by obscuring evidence of same-sex eroticism between women from his text.

45. Aelis's visit to the lady of Montpellier is not entirely devoid of business interests, of course. In fact, it may also be viewed part of a well thought-out marketing strategy by a skilled businesswoman in her attempt to draw valuable prospective new customers. It could be read as a calculated bribery whose veritable aim is to entice the lady of Montpellier into speaking to her, in fact to *force* her to get acquainted with her (the word "devra" is used, vv. 5564–65). For Aelis, becoming acquainted with the lady of Montpellier is vital to the success of her business, for thanks to the lady's social status and purchasing power, Aelis is faced with the very real potential of increasing her own economic wealth and her social status. The lady of Montpellier can also bestow upon Aelis much needed social recognition if she were to speak to her in church as other ladies do.

46. Although she does not discuss the *Escoufle*, or mention the "friendship gift," Judith Kellogg's work on the gift has been very helpful and my reading throughout this section owes much to her analysis. See her *Medieval Artistry and Exchange: Economic Institutions, Society and Literary Form in Old French Narrative* (New York: Peter Lang), 1989.

47. This is what E. Jane Burns has shown in her *Courtly Love Undressed*, 40.

48. The notion that friendship entails the equality of the partners is a leitmotiv well attested since Cicero. It referred regularly, however, to friendship between men, rather than between women. The question of female friendships has been studied by scholars of the Renaissance, moreso than by medievalists. See, for instance, Laurie Shannon, *Sovereign Amity: Figures of Friendship in Shakespearean Contexts* (Chicago: University of Chicago Press, 2002); Lillian Faderman, *Surpassing the Love of Men: Romantic Friendship and Love Between Women from the Renaissance to the Present* (New York: Morrow, 1981); Reginald Hyatte, *The Arts of Friendships: The Idealization of Friendship in Medieval and Early Renaissance Literature* (Leiden: E. J. Brill, 1994); and Valerie Traub, *The Renaissance of Lesbianism in Early Modern England* (Cambridge: Cambridge University Press, 2002).

49. The same automatic transfer had occurred earlier in the romance when Aelis received the ring from her mother. As soon as she accepted it, she mentally intended to give it to Guillaume as a token of her love (v. 3838). And we will recall that as soon as Guillaume received the ring, he lost it to the kite.

50. The key here is the fact that the liaison is heterosexual. Friendship between women is allowed as long as it is overshadowed (and thus protected by) a heterosexual relation, be it legitimate (marriage) or not (adultery). This invites a comparison. Which one was considered more dangerous or threatening in the Middle Ages: adultery or lesbianism? It appears that in both the West and in the Islamicate world, it was adultery.

51. Although church literature often reiterated the notion that marriage included companionship—arguing that since Eve was created from Adam's rib, she was neither his servant nor his master, but should stand by his side as his companion—there remained a heavy emphasis on the fact that the husband was the lord and master of his house. As a man, he was considered the "head" and woman the "body." See Shulamith Shahar, *The Fourth Estate: A History of Women in the Middle Ages*, trans. Chaya Galai (New York: Routledge, 1983), 65–68; R. H. Bloch, *Medieval Misogyny and the Invention of Western Romantic Love* (Chicago: University of Chicago Press, 1991); and E. Jane Burns, *Bodytalk: When Women Talk Back* (Philadelphia: University of Pennsylvania Press, 1993).

52. Godefroy, *Dictionnaire*, s.v. "per."

53. The timely exit of the servants reminds one of the discreet departure of the servants during Aelis and Guillaume's last private meeting in the emperor's palace (vv. 3373–81). Such parallels between the description of intimacy in heterosexual contexts and in same-sex contexts reveal the extent to which, in the *Escoufle*, same-sex relations are developed along the model of heterosexuality.

54. Diller does not discuss the eroticism of this scene; he explains Aelis's refusal to stay longer with the lady of Montpellier as her desire to remain faithful to her love for Ysabel ("L'*Escoufle*: Une Aventurière dans le roman courtois," 40).

55. Ahmed Ibn Souleiman, *Le Bréviaire arabe de l'amour*, trans. Mohamed Lasly (Arles: Editions Philippe Picquier, 1998), chap. 21, p. 121. On the questionable authorship of this text, see Lasly's introduction. *The Return of the Sheikh to His Youth* is now considered not to have been an original work, but rather a translation and compilation of earlier Arabic sexological treatises.

56. On Arabic as the language of the obscene, see my discussion in Chapter 2.

57. If at this point in the romance, the count of Saint-Gilles is wearing the belt embroidered with the coat of arms of the count of Montpellier, at the end of the romance, he will exchange this coat of arms with that of Guillaume.

58. The important association between sewing and loving in the *chansons de toile* has a vast bibliography. For a recent overview as well as a striking new interpretation, see Burns's *Courtly Love Undressed*, chapter 3.

59. It is interesting to ponder the use of the term *lait* in Old French texts. The same term is used by Jean Renart in his defense of the romance title in the epilogue (*Escoufle*, v. 9073), as we discussed at the beginning of this chapter. It is also the same term that Etienne de Fougères uses to describe lesbians in his *Livre des manières* (v. 1097; see Chapter 2). Could the adjective *lait* have been used to refer to alternative sexual practices?

60. These code words function similarly to the use of Arabic in Old French texts as we saw earlier in this chapter and in Chapter 2.

61. It is important to draw a parallel here with the character of Enide, who is also

depicted as a friend and lover in Chrétien de Troyes's *Erec et Enide* (ed. Mario Roques [Paris: Champion, 1973]). While such a double function was innovative in the context of the depiction of medieval marriage, the establishment of female relations as friends and lovers is equally novel in the context of representations of female friendships in medieval secular literature.

62. The difference between Jaufre Rudel and the princess of Tripoli (or Conrad and Lienor) is social too, though this dimension is never discussed by critics who only take into account the geographical separation.

63. It is unclear who *toutes* refers to exactly. Does it refer only to Aelis and the countess, or does it also include Ysabel? whichever it may be, our proposed interpretation remains unchanged.

64. The associations man-spirit and woman-body have been discussed extensively in scholarship. See among many others Shahar, *Fourth Estate*, 66.

65. On courtliness being depicted as the joining of the hands of a man and a woman, see E. Jane Burns, "Refashioning Courtly Love," in *Constructing Medieval Sexuality*, ed. Karma Lochrie, Peggy McCracken, and James A. Schultz (Minneapolis: University of Minnesota Press, 1997), 125. The notion of joining the hands of two women is especially transgressive when one remembers that it is precisely one of the prohibitions made in the rules and regulations of female communities, such as the seventh-century rule of Donatus of Besançon. See rule 32 in McNamara and Halborg, trans., *The Ordeal of Community*, 51.

66. The erotic connotations of the women's kisses recall the scene in Robert de Blois's thirteenth-century romance, *Floris and Lyriopé*, in which Floris, cross-dressed as his twin sister Florie, kisses the unsuspecting Lyriopé. The latter, believing she is being kissed by her female friend, comments on the fact that she has never heard of two women kissing and loving each other in this way: "Onques mais n'an oï novales / Que s'entremassent dous puceles" (vv. 1010–11); in Robert de Blois, *Floris et Lyriopé*, ed. Paul Barrette (Berkeley: University of California Press, 1968). Roberta Krueger points to the literary gaming present in this scene of *Floris and Lyriopé*, writing that it "is surely to titillate more than it is to instruct." See her "Constructing Sexual Identities in the High Middle Ages: The Didactic Poetry of Robert de Blois," *Paragraph* 13 (1990): 121. It is the same arousing kiss that we encounter in the *Escoufle* between Aelis and the countess; kissing is a highly satisfying experience for the two women.

67. Kathryn Gravdal, *Ravishing Maidens: Writing Rape in Medieval French Literature and Law* (Philadelphia: University of Pennsylvania Press, 1991).

68. The strategy that consists of rendering something unacceptable into something acceptable is also at work in the *pastourelle* where rape becomes authorized. See Gravdal, *Ravishing Maidens*, 104–21.

CHAPTER 5. CROSSING SOCIAL AND CULTURAL BORDERS

Note to epigraph: Terry Castle, *The Apparitional Lesbian: Female Homosexuality and Modern Culture* (New York: Columbia University Press, 1993), 17.

1. All references to Jean Renart's *Escoufle* are made to Franklin Sweetser's edition (Geneva: Droz, 1974), and all translations are mine.

2. On Aelis's intimate relation with Ysabel, and other women, see Chapter 4.

3. Roberta Krueger, "Transforming Maidens: Singlewomen's Stories in Marie de France's *Lais* and Later French Courtly Narratives," in *Singlewomen in the European Past, 1250–1800*, ed. Judith M. Bennett and Amy M Froide (Philadelphia: University of Pennsylvania Press, 1999), 173.

4. Roberta Krueger, "Constructing Sexual Identities in the High Middle Ages: The Didactic Poetry of Pierre de Blois," *Paragraph* 13 (1990): 105–31.

5. Ysabel's transgression of social lines is one manifestation of two other similar social transgressions in the romance: (1) the threat posed by the serfs who had been elevated to the level of advisors by the emperor of Rome and who end up betraying him; and (2) the debate surrounding the appropriateness of a marriage between Guillaume, son of a count, and Aelis, daughter of an emperor. Only in the case of Ysabel do clothes play a role in the confusion of social rank. This may be attributed to the fact that social promotion may have been considered a more significant threat to medieval society when it was the promotion of a woman rather than a man.

6. E. Jane Burns, *Courtly Love Undressed: Reading Through Clothes in Medieval French Culture* (Philadelphia: University of Pennsylvania Press, 2002), 37.

7. James A. Brundage, "Sumptuary Laws and Prostitution in Medieval Italy," *Journal of Medieval History* 13 (1987): 343–55.

8. This double transgression of the personal and the social is another one of the destabilizing elements introduced by the kite in the romance that I discussed in the previous chapter. The kite often had a social meaning in the Middle Ages and was associated with those who attempted to change their social state and to trick others into believing they were part of a social class to which they did not belong. In this sense, Ysabel might be considered to be a representative of the social function of the kite in the romance. See Baudoin van den Abeele, "*L'Escoufle*, portrait littéraire d'un oiseau," in special issue, ed. Brian Levy and Paul Wachers, *Reinardus: Yearbook of the International Reynard Society* 1 (1998): 5–15.

9. Emmanuèle Baumgartner, "Les Brodeuses et la ville," *50 rue de Varenne. Supplemento italo-francese di nuovi argomenti*, 3rd ser., supl. no. 43 (1992): 94. See also A. Adams, "Jean Renart's *L'Escoufle* and the Tristan Legend: Moderation Rewarded," in *Rewards and Punishments . . . Essays Presented to Kenneth Varty*, ed. Peter V. Davies and Angus J. Kennedy (Suffolk: D. S. Brewer, 1987), 1–7.

10. Shulamith Shahar, *The Fourth Estate: A History of Women in the Middle Ages*, translated by Chaya Galai (London: Routledge, 1983), 200; see also Baumgartner, "Les Brodeuses et la ville," 90.

11. This is precisely what Fresne tells the abbess of Beauséjour in *Galeran de Bretagne* moments before her departure from the convent (Renaut, *Galeran de Bretagne*, ed. Lucien Foulet [Paris: Champion, 1925], v. 3881). For other literary examples of women and embroidery, see Baumgartner, "Les Brodeuses et la ville," 90, Nancy Jones, "Uses of Embroidery in the Romances of Jean Renart: Gender, History, Textuality," in *Jean Renart and the*

Art of Romance: Essays on Guillaume de Dole, ed. Nancy Vine Durling (Gainesville: University of Florida Press, 1997), 21–22, and Burns, *Courtly Love Undressed*, 86–87.

12. The most compelling example of the use of embroidery to empower women is that of Lienor in *Guillaume de Dole* who embroiders a belt that will prove both her innocence and the lies of the seneschal who accused her of illicit sexual relations; it is this very belt that will ultimately permit her social ascent and marriage to the emperor. See Helen Solterer, "At the Bottom of the Mirage, a Woman's Body: *Le Roman de la Rose* of Jean Renart," in *Feminist Approaches to the Body*, ed. Linda Lomperis and Sarah Stanbury (Philadelphia: University of Pennsylvania Press, 1993), 213–33. See also Burns, *Courtly Love Undressed*, 87.

13. Krueger "Transforming Maidens." Aelis thus also prefigures the character of Oiseuse in Guillaume de Lorris's *Romance of the Rose* as discussed by Burns, *Courtly Love Undressed*, 77–80.

14. Sharon Farmer, *Surviving Poverty in Medieval Paris: Gender, Ideology, and the Daily Lives of the Poor* (Ithaca, N.Y.: Cornell University Press, 2002), 29.

15. Farmer, *Surviving Poverty*, 23; see also Kathryn L. Reyerson, "Women in Business in Medieval Montpellier," in *Women and Work in Pre-Industrial Europe*, ed. Barbara A. Hanawalt (Bloomington: Indiana University Press, 1986), 117.

16. Maryanne Kowaleski and Judith M. Bennett, "Crafts, Gilds and Women in the Middle Ages: Fifty Years After Marian Dale," in *Sisters and Workers in the Middle Ages*, ed. Judith M. Bennett et al. (Chicago: University of Chicago Press, 1976), 12. Judith Bennett and Maryanne Kowaleski also point out that "in most medieval towns and cities, even the most skilled female trades and crafts never formed gilds" (18).

17. Aelis's remarkable achievements are evident when compared to Marian Dale's finding that most skilled townswomen were married to gild members (Dale, "The London Silkwomen of the Fifteenth Century," *Economic Historical Review* 4 [1933]: 324–35). Similarly, Shahar has pointed out that independent female merchants who engaged in trade (both foreign and domestic) in the Middle Ages were spinsters, married women, or widows (*Fourth Estate*, 195). Aelis of course is none of these. As far as the town of Montpellier is concerned, André Gouron has noted that of all guilds, only the *caritat des fourniers* (a type of baker guild) seems to have included women. See André Gouron, *La Réglementation des métiers en Languedoc au Moyen Age* (Geneva: Droz, 1958), 245–46; Reyerson, "Women in Business," 117–44; and Jones, "Uses of Embroidery." While Jones argues that Renart downplays the economic value of Aelis and Ysabel's embroidery (31), I will demonstrate the opposite.

18. Aelis's business stands in marked contrast to Fresne's embroidery in *Galeran de Bretagne*, a romance to which the *Escoufle* (composed some twenty years earlier) has often been compared.

19. Frédéric Godefroy, *Dictionnaire de l'ancienne langue française et de tous ses dialectes du IXe au XVe siècle* (Paris: Vieweg, 1888–1920), s.vv. "joiaux," "ouvraigne."

20. Judith Bennett has observed that despite the semantic association of *hetaira* (Greek for "courtesan") with *hetairistria* (term used by Plato and others for same-sex female love), the relation between lesbianism and prostitution has not been discussed by medievalists, in contrast to the work done on this association for the modern period. See her

"'Lesbian-Like' and the Social History of Lesbianisms," *Journal of the History of Sexuality* 9, nos. 1–2 (2000): 11–12. On embroidery workshops serving as undercover prostitution houses, see Shahar, *Fourth Estate*, 206–9. The association between Aelis and prostitution is only hinted at by G. T. Diller who calls Aelis a "courtisane aventurière" (adventurous courtesan) in his "*L'Escoufle*: Une Aventurière dans le roman courtois," *Le Moyen Age* 85, no. 1 (1979): 39 and 43. The association between embroidery and prostitution in this romance is all the more striking because it sharply contrasts with the teachings of Western Christianity which have traditionally linked embroidery to the Virgin Mary, virtue, chastity, and industry, see Jones, "Uses of Embroidery," 18–21, 27.

21. Farmer, *Surviving Poverty*, 23. Leah Lydia Otis, *Prostitution in Medieval Society: The History of an Urban Institution in Languedoc* (Chicago: University of Chicago Press, 1985), 65–66, 103; Ruth Mazo Karras, *Common Women: Prostitution and Sexuality in Medieval England* (New York: Oxford University Press, 1996); James A. Brundage, "Prostitution in the Medieval Canon Law," in Bennett et al., *Sisters and Workers*, 79–99.

22. Shahar, *Fourth Estate*, 206–9. Nancy Jones points out a similar association between embroidery and sexuality (though not necessarily prostitution) in Jean Renart's *Guillaume de Dole*. She writes that Lienor's claim to have been raped by the seneschal while embroidering is based upon the idea that in the Middle Ages the embroideress is "inherently tempting to male eyes because of her apparent passivity and self preoccupation." "Uses of Embroidery," 26.

23. On the meaning of "feme" in the Middle Ages and all the various terms that are used to speak about women, see A. Grisay, G. Lavis, and M. Dubois-Stasse, *Les Dénominations de la femme dans les anciens textes littéraires français* (Gembloux: J. Duculot, 1969), 56–68.

24. Grisay et al., *Les Dénominations de la femme*, 63.

25. I am using the word "initiated" with qualification since despite the use of the word "pucele" in the earlier part of the romance, it is questionable whether Aelis's relationship with Guillaume is entirely asexual. But this question falls outside the limits of the present study.

26. Tertullian, "The Apparel of Women," in *Disciplinary, Moral and Ascetical Works*, trans. Rudolph Arbesmann, Emily Joseph Daly, and Edwin A. Quain (New York: Fathers of the Church, 1959), 148. On the influence of Tertullian on twelfth- and thirteenth-century clerics and theologians, see Michel Zink, *La Prédication en langue romane avant 1300* (Paris: Champion, 1982).

27. Zink, *La Prédication en langue romane*, 373; translation mine.

28. Burns, *Courtly Love Undressed*, 40.

29. Their ostentatiousness contrasts with Frene's attempt to go unnoticed in *Galeran de Bretagne* (vv. 4162–65).

30. Shahar notes that a 1364 royal decree in England recognized women's right to engage simultaneously in several crafts to finance their households, in contrast to men (*Fourth Estate*, 197). Even though the *Escoufle* was composed some 150 years earlier and in a different sociopolitical milieu, what we know about medieval Montpellier seems to suggest that the situation was no different on the Continent in the early thirteenth century and that women had to work at several jobs in order to provide for their families.

31. Etienne Boileau, *Le Livre des métiers et corporations de la ville de Paris, xiiie siècle*, ed. René de Lespinasse and François Bonnardot (Paris: Imprimerie Nationale, 1879), 208–9. The information about barbers is included with the category "Surgeons" ("Des Cirurgiens").

32. Monica Green, "Women's Medical Practice and Health Care in Medieval Europe," in Bennett et al., *Sisters and Workers*, 44 and n. 9 especially. See also Stephen R. Ell's article "Barber" in the *Dictionary of the Middle Ages*, ed. Joseph Strayer (New York: Scribner, 1982–89). I would like to express my gratitude to Michael McVaugh for many valuable conversations on medieval medicine.

33. Jacqueline Liault, *Montpellier la médiévale* (Nîmes: C. Lacour, 1990), 218–19; Jean Baumel, *Histoire d'une seigneurie du Midi: Naissance de Montpellier (985–1213)* (Montpellier: Editions Causse et Cie, 1969), 64.

34. Otis, *Prostitution in Medieval Society*, 98–99. Brundage discusses how canon law (and Gratian's *Decretum* in particular) warned Christians against frequenting bathhouses because of the moral threat they posed, in his "Prostitution in the Medieval Canon Law," 95.

35. While Fresne in *Galeran de Bretagne*, like Aelis, excels in embroidery, singing, and game playing, it is important to note that her singing and game playing are situated outside the embroidery business, not part of it: Fresne works during the day; she plays the harp and sings in the mornings and at night, and she plays chess during the holidays. The segmentation of Fresne's life and activities aims at highlighting the nonsexual nature of her actions and at removing any ambiguity at the level of vocabulary or skills depicted. In *Galeran de Bretagne*, written some twenty years after the *Escoufle*, the activities of embroidery, singing, and game playing become associated with the private sphere, and disconnected from the sexual meaning they hold in Jean Renart's romance.

36. I would argue that singing in the *chansons de toile* is equivalent to Aelis's storytelling. On the *chansons de toile*, see Michel Zink, ed., *Les Chansons de toile* (Paris: Champion, 1977), and Burns, *Courtly Love Undressed*, chap. 3. On the relation between poetic skills and cloth work, see Jones, "Uses of Embroidery."

37. Baumgartner, "Les Brodeuses et la ville," 94; translation mine.

38. If anyone in the *Escoufle* fits the description of medieval prostitutes given by critics (Brundage, Karras, Otis, Kettle), it is Ysabel, Aelis's companion: she is young, unmarried, lives in the home of her employer (Aelis); she is an immigrant to the city; she is an unskilled worker who sews towels and wimples (v. 5454) rather than embroidering lavish silks.

39. Godefroy, *Dictionnaire de l'ancienne langue française*, s.v. "plaire."

40. The danger of the association of tales with sexuality was already noticed by canonists who threatened men with excommunication if they were found conversing with women of suspect morals, since these talks could lead to greater intimacy. In the thirteenth century, Jacques de Vitry had even spoken against brothels sharing premises with scholars' halls and thus competing for the clerics' attention. See Brundage, "Prostitution in the Medieval Canon Law," 88–89, 95.

41. Godefroy, *Dictionnaire de l'ancienne langue française*, s.v. "hante."

42. Ruth Mazo Karras, "Sex and the Singlewoman," in *Singlewomen in the European Past, 1250–1800*, ed. Judith M. Bennett and Amy M. Froide (Philadelphia: University of Pennsylvania Press, 1999), 129.

43. This ambiguity might be due to the fact that medieval canonists themselves since Saint Augustine (ca. 354–430) had a very ambiguous attitude toward prostitution, which was considered to be preferable to the general spread of licentiousness; see Brundage, "Prostitution in the Medieval Canon Law," 84.

44. Godefroy, *Dictionnaire de l'ancienne langue française*, s.v. "menestrel."

45. On the association between single women and prostitution, see Barbara A. Hanawalt, "At the Margin of Women's Space in Medieval Europe," in *Matrons and Marginal Women in Medieval Society*, ed. Robert R. Edwards and Vickie L. Ziegler (Rochester, N.Y.: Boydell, 1995), 1–17; Mary Douglas, *Purity and Danger* (London: Routledge and Kegan Paul, 1966), 140–58; Sharon Farmer, "'It Is Not Good That [Wo]man Should Be Alone': Elite Responses to Singlewomen in High Medieval Paris," in *Singlewomen in the European Past, 1250–1800*, ed. Judith M. Bennett and Amy M. Froide (Philadelphia: University of Pennsylvania Press, 1999), 87; see also her *Surviving Poverty*; Karras, "Sex and the Singlewoman," 129.

46. Karras, "Sex and the Singlewoman," 132.

47. Brundage explains that the basic criteria for the legal and theological definition of prostitution is "promiscuity and gain" in his "Prostitution in the Medieval Canon Law," 81. Shahar has argued that medieval society only had very scattered cases of women who worked without being in financial need; Margery Kempe is one of them. See *Fourth Estate*, 195.

48. Karras, "Sex and the Singlewoman," 133.

49. Aelis's religious attitudes stands in contrast to that of Fresne in *Galeran de Bretagne*.

50. My reading contrasts with Linda Clemente's view that after her separation from Guillaume and within the Saint-Gilles household specifically, Aelis's life is marked by an all-feminine space in which "men play very minor roles." See her "Aelis's Introspective Silence in the Feminist World of Jean Renart's *Escoufle*," *Cincinnati Romance Review* 10 (1991): 29.

51. Tibaut, *Le Roman de la poire*, ed. Christiane Marchello-Nizia (Paris: SATF, 1985), vv. 453–54; translation mine.

52. Diller calls the count "le vigoureux libertin" (the vigorous libertine) in his "L'*Escoufle*: Une Aventurière dans le roman courtois," 36. Aelis herself seems to be acutely aware of the compromising relationship she has developed with the count, vv. 7600–601.

53. The nakedness of both Aelis and the count are clear in this scene, despite the fact that the count continues to wear his "braies" and Aelis continues to wear her "chemise." On the naked connotations of this attire in the Middle Ages, see E. Jane Burns's analysis of clothing in "Ladies Don't Wear Braies: Underwear and Outerwear in the French *Prose Lancelot*," in *The Lancelot-Grail Cycle: Text and Transformations*, ed. William W. Kibler (Austin: University of Texas Press, 1994), 152–74.

54. The notion of "lesbian ghosting," like that of the "spectral" used in this section, have been coined and analyzed by Terry Castle, *The Apparitional Lesbian*.

55. Castle, *Apparitional Lesbian*, 2.

56. Contrary to medieval fabliaux and farces, French romance is rarely explicit in its depiction of sexual relations, even heterosexual ones, euphemistically referring to them under the rather polysemic umbrella "surplus."

57. "Intollerabilis malicia . . . Hoc crimine ualde infecti quidame miseri qui ancillas

suas licet turpiores uxoribus preponunt, quamuis sint pulchriores." Jacques de Vitry, cited in Jean Longère, "Deux sermons de Jacques de Vitry *Ad Servos et Ancillas*," in *La femme au Moyen Age*, ed. Michel Rouche and Jean Heuclin (Maubeuge: Publications de la Ville de Maubeuge, 1990), 294.

58. Danielle Régnier-Bohler, "Geste, parole et clôture: Les Représentations du gynécée dans la littérature médiévale du XIIIe au XVe siècle," in *Mélanges . . . Alice Planche* (Nice: Belles Lettres, 1984), 399.

59. Karras, "Sex and the Singlewoman," 129.

60. It must be noted that these manly traits do not include masculine roles such as riding horses or hunting in which cross-dressed heroines typically engage (Silence, Yde).

61. These two activities (sewing and loving) specifically define the female role of famous heroines such as Silence in the thirteenth-century *Roman de Silence*, vv. 2496–688. Heldris de Cornuälle, *Le Roman de Silence: A Thirteenth-Century Arthurian Verse-Romance*, ed. Lewis Thorpe (Cambridge: W. Heffer & Sons, 1972).

62. Krueger, "Transforming Maidens," 161.

63. The important role that some women played at times in the public sphere in the medieval Islamicate world has often not been sufficiently taken into consideration because of the long-standing assumption that they were veiled and hence hidden from the public. This has not always been the case in Islamic history, as Mounira Chapoutot-Remadi, for instance, pointed out in her "Femmes dans la ville Mamluke," *Journal of the Economic and Social History of the Orient* 38, no. 2 (1995): 145–64. On Muslim women's economic contributions, see Maya Shatzmiller, "Women and Wage Labour in the Medieval Ialamic West: Legal Issues in an Economic Context," *Journal of the Economic and Social History of the Orient* 40, no. 2 (1997): 174–206, and Huda Lutfi, "Al-Sakhawi's *Kitab al-Nisa'* as a Source for the Social and Economic History of Muslim Women During the Fifteenth Century A.D.," *Muslim World* 7, no. 2 (1981): 104–24.

64. More has indeed been preserved about the contributions of slave-girls, rather than of aristocratic, freeborn women in the Islamicate Middle Ages because they were at greater liberty to express themselves. Freeborn women, on the other hand, were often veiled and kept outside the public sphere.

65. Ibn al-Washsha', *Kitab al-muwashsha'*, ed. R. E. Brünnow (Leiden: Brill, 1886). This work has been translated into French by Siham Bouhlal, under the title *Le Livre du brocart* (Paris: Gallimard, Connaissance de l'Orient, 2004). Siham Bouhlal explains the title al-Washsha' chose for his book thus: Because the *washi* is the person who weaves and designs silk cloth and embroiders it with gold, the title of the treatise, *Kitab al-muwashsha'*, is a metaphor that consists in showing the reader beautifully composed motifs (as those displayed on a cloth) that can be appreciated on either side (introduction, 10; translation mine). Another important medieval source on *zarf* is Jalal al-Din al-Suyuti's *al-Mustazraf min akhbar al-jawari* [Courtly Tales of Slave-Girl Stories], ed. Ahmad Abd al-Fattah Tammam (Cairo: Maktabat al-Turath al-Islami, 1989). On *zarf*, see Malek Chebel, *Traité du raffinement* (Paris: Payot, 1995), and Mhammed Ferid Ghazi, "Un Groupe social: 'Les Raffinés' (*Zurafa'*)," *Studia Islamica* 11 (1959–60): 39–71; Lois A. Giffen, *Theory of Profane Love Among the Arabs: The Development of the Genre* (New York: New York University Press,

1971); Jean-Claude Vadet, *L'Esprit courtois en Orient dans les cinq premiers siècles de l'hégire* (Paris: G.-P. Maisonneuve et Larose, 1968), 317–51; al-Bashir Majdub, *Al-zarf bi-al-`Iraq fi al-`asr al-`Abbasi* [Courtliness in Iraq During the Abbasid Period] (Tunis: Nashr wa-Tawzi` Mu'assasat `Abd al-Karim Bin `Abd Allah, 1992).

66. These decorations provide us with early examples of body art.

67. Al-Washsha', *Le Livre du brocart*, 244; translation mine.

68. On Princess Wallada, see Devin Stewart's entry "Ibn Zaydun," in *Cambridge History of Arabic Literature: Al-Andalus*, ed. Maria Rosa Menocal and Michael Sells (Cambridge: Cambridge University Press, 2000), 308. See also David Wasserstein, *The Rise and Fall of the Party-Kings: Politics and Society in Islamic Spain, 1002–1086* (Princeton, N.J.: Princeton University Press, 1985); Antonio Arjona Castro, *La Sexualidad en la España musulmana* (Córdoba: Universidad de Córdoba, 1985), 25. Arabic sources on Wallada include Ali Ibn Bassam al-Shantarini (d. 1147), *al-Dhakhira fi mahasin ahl al-jazira* [Positive Attributes of the Andalusians], ed. Ihsan Abbas (Beirut: Dar al-Thaqafa, 1979), vol. 1, pt. 1, pp. 429–33; Shihab al-Din Abu al-Abbas al-Maqqari (d. 1632), *Nafh al-tib min ghusn al-Andalus al-ratib* [The Wafting Scent of the Dewy Andalusian Branch] [*Analectes sur l'histoire et la littérature des Arabes d'Espagne*], ed. R. Dozy et al. (Amsterdam: Oriental Press, 1967), 2:536–68; Jalal al-Din al-Suyuti, *Nuzhat al-julasa' fi ash`ar al-nisa'* [Salon Members' Journey into Women's Poetry], ed. Salah al-Din al-Munajjid (Tunis: Dar al-Ma`arif lel Teba`a wa al-Nashr, 2004), 83–94 (on Mohja) and 101–6 (Wallada); Umar Rida Kahhalah, *A`lam al-nisa' fi `alamay al-`Arab wa-al-Islam* [The History of Women in the Arab and Islamic Worlds] (Beirut: Mu'assasat al-Risala, 1977), 5:287–90. On the role of Andalusian women poets in Islamic Spain, see Wiebke Walther, *Women in Islam* (Princeton, N.J.: Marcus Wiener, 1993), 144–48; Mahmud Sobh, *Poetisas arabigoandaluzas* (Granada: Disputación Provincial, n.d.); Teresa Garulo, *Diwan de las poetisas de al-Andalus* (Madrid: Hyperion, 1985); María Jesús Rubiera Máta, *Poesía feminina hispanoárabe* (Madrid: Castalia, 1989).

69. On these women and others like them (Hafsa of Granada, Hamda Bint Ziyad), see Aisha Bewley, *Muslim Women: A Biographical Dictionary* (London: Ta-Ha, 2004), Abu al-Faraj al-Isfahani, *Kitab al-aghani* [Book of Songs], ed. Abd al-Sattar Ahmad Farraj, 25 vols. (Beirut: Dar al-Thaqafa, 1990); on Sukayna, see *Kitab al-aghani*, 16:93–118; on Aisha Bint Talha, see *Kitab al-aghani*, 11:165–85. See also al-Maqqari, *Nafh al-tib min ghusn al-Andalus al-ratib*, 2:536–76. Also useful is Arie Schippers, "The Role of Medieval Andalusian Arabic Story-Telling," in *Verse and the Fair Sex: Studies in Poetry and in the Representation of Women in Arabic Literature: A Collection of Papers Presented at the 15th Congress of the Union Européenne des Arabisants et Islamisants*, ed. Frederick de Jong (Utrecht: M. Th. Houtsma Stichting, 1993), 139–52; J. M. Nichols, "Arabic Women Poets in al-Andalus," *Maghrib Review* 4 (1979): 114–17.

70. Ghazi, "Un Groupe social," 43. That these Muslim women pronounced judgments in their literary salons is revealed in *Kitab al-aghani*, in the sections devoted to Sukayna and Aisha Bint Talha; it is also mentioned (and additional examples are given) in biographical dictionaries of Muslim women written in the Middle Ages, such as *Nisa' al-khulafa'* [Women of the Caliphs] by Ibn al-Sa`i (1196–1275), ed. Mustafa Jawad (Cairo: Dar al-Ma`arif, 1968). An overview of the biographies of such women is gleaned from Hilary

Kilpatrick, "Some Late `Abbasid and Mamluk Books about Women: A Literary Historical Approach," *Arabica* 42 (1995): 56–78.

71. Al-Jahiz is one of the most important prose writers of the ninth century, during the Abbasid period. He was born in Basra (Iraq), which was at the time one of the greatest cultural centers of the Islamic world. Al-Jahiz represents one of our most valuable sources for our knowledge of the history of Islamic culture.

72. Al-Jahiz's *Risalat al-qiyan* survives only in one manuscript, Istanbul MS Damad 949, folios 177v.–188v. The Arabic text has been edited and translated into English by A. F. L. Beeston, *The Epistle on Singing-Girls of Jahiz* (Warminster, Wilts.: Aris & Phillips, 1980), and into French by Charles Pellat under the title "Les Esclaves-Chanteuses de Gahiz," *Arabica* 10 (1963): 121–47 (quotation on p. 126; translation mine).

73. Al-Jahiz, *Risalat al-qiyan*, trans. Pellat, "Les Esclaves-Chanteuses," 126; translation mine.

74. Suzanne Meyers Sawa, "The Role of Women in Musical Life: The Medieval Arabo-Islamic Courts," *Canadian Women's Studies: Les Cahiers de la Femme* 8 (1987): 94.

75. On *Kitab al-aghani*, see Hilary Kilpatrick, *Making the Great Book of Songs: Compilation and the Author's Craft in Abu al-Faraj al-Isbahani's "Kitab al-Aghani"* (New York: Routledge, 2003), and Ignazio Guidi, *Tables alphabétiques du "Kitab al-Agani"* (Leiden: Brill, 1900). Information about *qayna*s is also found in biographical dictionaries of Muslim women written in the Middle Ages, such as Ibn al-Sa`i's *Nisa' al-khulafa'*, for instance. While al-Sa`i discusses primarily aristocratic women, al-Suyuti (1445–1505) treats slave girls from all sections of society as he focuses specifically on *zarf* in his al-*Mustazraf min akhbar al-jawari*.

76. On `Inan, see Abu al-Faraj al-Isfahani, *Kitab al-aghani*, 22:521; translation mine. See also Ibn al-Sa`i's *Nisa' al-khulafa'*, 47–53, and al-Suyuti, al-*Mustazraf min akhbar al-jawari*, 38–46.

77. Fadl as described in Fatima Mernissi, *Scheherazade Goes West: Different Cultures, Different Harems* (New York: Washington Square Press, 2001), 123.

78. Abu al-Faraj al-Isfahani, *Kitab al-aghani*, 19:257; translation mine. The life of Fadl is also related in Ibn al-Sa`i's *Nisa' al-khulafa'*, 84, al-Suyuti, al-*Mustazraf min akhbar al-jawari*, 50–55, and Ghazi, "Un Groupe social," 48. On the role of *qayna*s in the Islamicate tradition, see Walther, *Women in Islam*, 151–53; Lutfi, "Al-Sakhawi's *Kitab al-Nisa*"; and Ahmad Abd ar-Raziq, *La Femme au temps des Mamlouks en Egypte* (Cairo: Institut Français d'Archéologie Orientale, 1973).

79. On `Arib, see Abu al-Faraj al-Isfahani, *Kitab al-aghani*, 21:58, translated in Suzanne Sawa, "Role of Women in Musical Life," 94. See also Ibn al-Sa`i's *Nisa' al-khulafa'*, 55–63, al-Suyuti, al-*Mustazraf min akhbar al-jawari*, 36–37, and Matthew S. Gordon, "`Arib al-Ma'muniyah (797–890)," in *Dictionary of Literary Biography*, vol. 311, *Arabic Literary Culture, 500–925*, ed. Michael Cooperson and Shawkat Toorawa (New York: Bruccoli Clark Layman Book, 2005), 85–90.

80. The *ghulamiyyat* are those slave girls dressed as boys (at times with painted mustaches) in al-Amin's court whom his mother had introduced in order to turn her son away from homosexuality and toward heterosexuality. This tradition of dressing girls as boys became a veritable cultural fashion in Baghdad and was imitated by aristocratic and bour-

geois women under the Abbasids in the ninth century. See Habib Zayyat, "Al-mar'a al-ghulamiyya fi al-Islam" (The *Ghulamiyya* in Islamicate Culture), *al-Machriq* 50 (1956): 153–92, and Philip F. Kennedy, *Abu Nuwas: A Genius of Poetry* (Oxford: Oneworld, 2005).

81. Al-Jahiz, *Risalat al-qiyan*, trans. Pellat, "Les Esclaves-Chanteuses," 141; translation mine.

82. Al-Jahiz, *Risalat al-qiyan*, trans. Pellat, "Les Esclaves-Chanteuses," 145; translation mine.

83. The tale of Tawaddud or of Sympathy the Learned begins on the 270th night, in Mardrus's translation of the *Arabian Nights*; see *One Thousand and One Nights*, ed. and trans. into French by Joseph Charles Mardrus; trans. into English by Pomys Mather (n.p., Yugoslovia: Dorset Press, 1964), 2:142–69.

84. Mernissi, *Scheherazade Goes West*, 130–31.

85. George Dimitri Sawa, *Music Performance and Practice in the Early Abbasid Era* (Toronto: Pontifical Institute of Medieval Studies, 1989), 20.

86. Al-Jahiz gives a long list of such women; see Pellat, "Les Esclaves-Chanteuses," 132.

87. See Lutfi, "Al-Sakhawi's *Kitab al-Nisa*,'" 115–24, and Chapoutot-Remadi, "Femmes dans la ville Mamluke." It must be noted that the harem is not an Islamic invention, as Orientalist thought might suggest; rather it is a social custom of the upper class that was inherited from the Greco-Roman tradition, after the spread of Islam. For a critique of Eurocentric representations of the harem, see Leila Ahmed, "Western Ethnocentrism and Perceptions of the Harem," *Feminist Studies* 8, no. 3 (1982): 521–34; Emily Apter, "Female Trouble in the Colonial Harem," *Differences* 4, no. 1 (1992): 203–24; Leslie Peirce, *The Imperial Harem: Women and Sovereignty in the Ottoman Empire* (New York: Oxford University Press, 1993); and Inderpal Grewal, *Home and Harem: Imperialism, Nationalism and the Culture of Travel* (Durham, N.C.: Duke University Press, 1995). This reevaluation of the harem must also include scholarship on the solitary confinement of upper-class Western women; see Bram Dijkstra, *Idols of Perversity* (New York: Oxford University Press, 1986).

88. On Shajarrat al-Durr, see Fatima Mernissi, *Forgotten Queens of Islam*, trans. Mary Jo Lakeland (Minneapolis: University of Minnesota Press, 1997), 98; John Glubb, *A Short History of the Arab Peoples* (New York: Dorset, 1969), 202–10; Umar Rida Kahhalah, *A`lam al-nisa' fi `alamay al-`Arab wa-al-Islam*, 2:286–90; al-Suyuti, *al-Mustazraf min akhbar al-jawari*, 33; Ahmad Abd ar-Raziq, *La Femme au temps des Mamlouks en Egypte*, 292–93. Another example is that of Mongol Princess Tandu in the ninth century. See Lutfi, "Al-Sakhawi's *Kitab al-Nisa*,'" 122–23.

89. Mernissi, *Forgotten Queens of Islam*, 90.

90. Similarly, Byzantine women played important, yet often occulted, political roles especially during the crusader period. One example is that of Zoe, Empress of Constantinople, whose exile in 1042 at the hands of her lover, Michel V, resulted in a revolution in the harem, led entirely by women. This story is likely to have been known in the West since a portrait of Zoe appears in the Church of Saint Sophia which was regularly visited by European pilgrims and travelers. Krijnie Ciggaar has argued that the political role played by women at the time of Zoe's exile in the eleventh century represents the intertext for the scene in Chrétien de Troyes's *Cligès* when one thousand noble women intervened against Western doctors who

were attempting to find out whether Fénice was truly dead or feigning it. See Krijnie Cig-gaar, "Encore une fois Chrétien de Troyes et la 'matière Byzantine': La Révolution des femmes au palais de Constantinople," *Cahiers de civilisation médiévale* 38 (1995): 267–74.

91. Mernissi, *Forgotten Queens of Islam*, 134.

92. Gordon, "'Arib al-Ma'muniyah," 87.

93. "L'Exigence d'aimer," interview of Jamal Eddine Bencheikh by Fethi Benslama and Thierry Fabre, in "De l'Amour et des Arabes," special issue, *Qantara: Magazine de l'Institut du Monde Arabe* 18 (January–February 1996): 23.

94. This information regarding the price of *qayna*s is cited in Pellat, "Les Esclaves-Chanteuses," 145. Neither the slave nor her owner has been identified. Similarly, Suzanne Sawa gives the example of 'Ulayyah Bint al-Mahdi's mother who was purchased for 100,000 dirhams; see her "Role of Women in Musical Life," 94.

95. Mernissi, *Scheherazade Goes West*, 125.

96. Ghazi, "Un Groupe social," 50.

97. The Umayyad state of Spain has been described by Lévi-Provençal as an "exact, if smaller copy" of the Abbasid system from the early ninth century onward. Evariste Lévi-Provençal's work on Muslim Spain remains an unparalleled resource, *La Civilisation arabe en Espagne* (Paris: Maisonneuve, 1948). See also Maria Rosa Menocal, *The Arabic Role in Medieval Literary History: A Forgotten Heritage* (Philadelphia, University of Pennsylvania Press, 1987), and Cynthia Robinson, *In Praise of Song: The Making of Courtly Culture in al-Andalus and Provence, 1065–1135 A.D.* (Leiden: Brill, 2002).

98. On Ziryab, see Jésus Greus, *Ziryab: La Prodigiosa historia del sultan andaluz y el cantor de Bagdad* (San Lorenzo de El Escorial: Editoria Swan, 1987); Jamal al-Din Muhsin, *Udaba' baghdadiyun fi al-Andalus* (Baghdadi Authors of al-Andalus) (Baghdad: Maktabat al-Nahda, 1962).

99. Richard Fletcher, *Moorish Spain* (Berkeley: University of California Press, 1992), 44.

100. Ahmad Ibn Yusuf al-Tifashi, *Nuzhat al-albab fima la yujad fi kitab*, edited by Jamal Juma'a (London: Riad el-Rayyes, 1992), 141; *Les Délices des coeurs ou ce que l'on ne trouve en aucun livre*, trans. René R. Khawam (Paris: Phébus, 1981), 130 (translation mine).

101. Zayyat demonstrates this indeed to be the case of the *ghulamiyyat* in his "al-Mar'a al-ghulamiyya."

102. Zayyat, "al-Mar'a al-ghulamiyya," 166.

103. On the history of chess, see Harold J. R. Murray, *A History of Chess* (London: Oxford University Press, 1978), and Jenny Adams, *Power Play: The Literature and Politics of Chess in the Late Middle Ages* (Philadelphia: University of Pennsylvania Press, 2006). Recent scholarship suggests that chess may have originated in China in the second century B.C.E. (rather than in India as was traditionally believed), and reached India only thereafter; see Sam Sloan, "A History of Chess," www.samsloan.com/origin.htm.

104. Storytelling and sexual pleasure are intimately linked throughout the *Arabian Nights*. One of the most famous examples may be the tale of the "Three Women of Baghdad" which is attested in the earliest recension of the *Nights*. This is the tale of seemingly respectable businesswomen who combine merrymaking and storytelling with sexual gratification.

105. My interpretation of the Saint-Gilles household as an Eastern harem is in contrast to Danielle Régnier-Bohler's reading of it as a *gynaceum*.

106. Sharon Kinoshita, "The Politics of Courtly Love: *La Prise d'Orange* and the Conversion of the Saracen Queen," *Romanic Review* 86, no. 2 (1995): 279; see also her *Medieval Boundaries: Rethinking Difference in Old French Literature* (Philadelphia: University of Pennsylvania Press, 2006).

107. If this particular episode does not support a crusader ideology, some critics have argued that the *Escoufle* as a whole might in fact do precisely that. They have submitted that because of its dedication to Baudoin, count of Hainaut, the *Escoufle* may have been composed to encourage the count to go on crusade; and indeed Baudoin VI will participate in the fourth crusade. See John Baldwin, "'Once There Was an Emperor. . . .': A Political Reading of the Romances of Jean Renart," in Durling, *Jean Renart and the Art of Romance*, 51–64.

108. It is important to note that the word "soignentage" (concubinage) is never used to refer to the relation between Aelis and the count, even though it is used once before in the romance to describe Aelis's relation with Guillaume at the moment when she is eloping, v. 3912.

109. In the *Escoufle*, we find other instances of eating (fruit), such as when the narrator describes Aelis and Guillaume's attempt to hide their love for each other by pretending to eat fruit (vv. 4324–29; 4450–57), or when the emperor and his wife eat fruit prior to the wife's manipulation of her husband to put a stop to their daughter's marriage with Guillaume (vv. 2863–75).

110. See David Waines, "Food and Drink," in *Encyclopedia of the Quran*, ed. Jane Dammen McAuliffe (Leiden: Brill, 2002), 2:216–23. See also Arie Schippers, "Hebrew Andalusian and Arabic Poetry: Descriptions of Fruit in the Tradition of the 'Elegant' or *Zurafa*," *Journal of Semitic Studies* 33, no. 2 (1988): 219–32.

111. Cited in Pellat, "Les Esclaves-Chanteuses," 125; translation mine.

112. "Tale of Nour," in *One Thousand and One Nights*, ed. and trans. into French by Joseph Charles Mardrus; trans. into English by Pomys Mathers, 3:299; cited in Malek Chebel, *Encyclopédie de l'amour en Islam: Erotisme, beauté et sexualité dans le monde arabe, en Perse, et en Turquie* (Paris: Payot, 1995), 271. I would like to thank Kenny Levine for help in translating these lines.

113. The refinement in eating manners is described in al-Washsha' 's *Kitab al-muwashsha'*, chaps. 29–30 and 33.

114. The count's gesture is in opposition to Aelis's promise to Ysabel to provide for her needs and to give her some of her fortune (vv. 5279–83). Aelis never promises to share her fortune with Ysabel.

115. Andrew W. Lewis, *Royal Succession in Capetian France: Studies on Familial Order and the State* (Cambridge, Mass.: Harvard University Press, 1981).

116. Diller situates the return to heterosexuality a bit later in the text, namely at the moment when the count realizes that he is in fact the cousin of Guillaume's father (v. 7748); see his "*L'Escoufle*: Une Aventurière dans le roman courtois," 36.

117. Castration was considered to be the legitimate punishment for repeat offenders of adultery and illegitimate sexual encounters. The most famous medieval man who suf-

fered this very punishment is undoubtedly Peter Abelard after his relationship with Heloise.

118. This is only a temporary stop to alternative sexual relations in the *Escoufle*, however, since Ysabel accompanies Aelis in her new heterosexual household. She is not married off at the end of the romance as Rose, for instance, is by Fresne in *Galeran de Bretagne*.

CONCLUSION

Note to epigraph: Homi Bhabha, *The Location of Culture* (London: Routledge, 1994), 36.

1. This is the way Julia Kristeva describes Bakhtin's contribution to structuralism with regard to his work both on Dostoevsky and on medieval carnival and farce. See Julia Kristeva, *Semiotica: Recherches pour une sémanalyse* (Paris: Seuil, 1969), 144; translation mine.

2. Shulamith Shahar has shown how the economic role played by women in medieval towns was silenced by the didactic literature of the period which was interested primarily in the sexual chastity of women and their duties towards their husbands. *The Fourth Estate: A History of Women in the Middle Ages*, trans. Chaya Galai (New York: Routledge, 1983), 196–97.

3. The notion of hybrid textuality has been used by critics with reference to Jean Renart, but with a completely different meaning. By it, they have meant the lyric insertions in the romance of *Guillaume de Dole*. See the collection of articles in Nancy Vine Durling, ed., *Jean Renart and the Art of Romance: Essays on Guillaume de Dole* (Gainesville: University of Florida Press, 1997).

4. This is the main point developed by Edward Said in his *Orientalism* (New York: Pantheon, 1978) and which contributed to the development of the field of postcolonial studies.

5. Chandra Mohanty, "Under Western Eyes: Feminist Scholarship and Colonial Discourses," *Feminist Review* 30 (Autumn 1988): 65.

6. Mohanty, "Under Western Eyes," 70.

7. Mohanty, "Under Western Eyes," 81. She adds a few lines later: "In the context of the hegemony of the Western scholarly establishment in the production and dissemination of texts, and in the context of the legitimating imperative of humanistic and scientific discourse, the definition of 'the third-world woman' as a monolith might well tie into the larger economic and ideological praxis of 'disinterested' scientific inquiry and pluralism which are the surface manifestations of a latent economic and cultural colonization of the 'non-Western' world" (82).

8. Mohanty points out: "Without the overdetermined discourse that creates the *third* world, there would be no (singular and privileged) first world. . . . I am suggesting, in effect, that the one enables and sustains the other." "Under Western Eyes," 82; emphasis in original.

BIBLIOGRAPHY

PRIMARY SOURCES

Abelard, Peter. *Expositio in Epistolam Pauli ad Romanos I.* Vol. 178 of *Patrologia cursus completus: Series Latina.* Edited by J.-P. Migne. Paris, 1841–66.

Abu al-Faraj al-Isfahani. *Kitab al-aghani* [*The Book of Songs*]. Edited by Abd al-Sattar Ahmad Farraj. 25 vols. Beirut: Dar al-Thaqafa, 1990.

Abu Nuwas. *Abu Nuwas: Le Vin, le vent, la vie: Poèmes traduits.* Translated by Vincent Monteil. Paris: Sindbad, 1979.

———. *Der Diwan des Abu Nuwas.* Edited by Ewald Wagner. 5 vols. Wiesbaden: Franz Steiner Verlag, 1958.

Alf layla wa layla [*One Thousand and One Nights*]. Edited by Muhsin Mahdi. 4 vols. Leiden: Brill, 1984.

Arabian Nights, The. Translated by Husain Haddawy. 2 vols. New York: Norton, 1995.

al-Baghdadi, Ali. *Les Fleurs éclatantes dans les baisers et l'accolement.* Translated by René Khawam. Paris: Albin Michel, 1973.

Brantôme, Pierre de Bourdeille. *Vies des dames galantes.* Paris: Garnier Frères, 1841.

Capellanus, Andreas. *The Art of Courtly Love.* Translated by John Jay Parry. New York: Norton, 1969.

Chrétien de Troyes. *Erec et Enide.* Edited by Mario Roques. Paris: Champion, 1973.

———. *Lancelot ou le Chevalier de la Charrette.* Edited by Mario Roques. Paris: Champion, 1983.

Christine de Pizan. *A Medieval Woman's Mirror of Honor.* Translated by Charity Cannon Willard. New York: Persea Books, 1989.

Conte de Floire et Blanchefleur, Le. Translated by Jean-Luc Leclanche. Paris: Champion, 1986.

Conte de Floire et Blancheflor, Le. Edited by Jean-Luc Leclanche. Paris: Champion, 1983.

Enéas, roman du XIIe siècle. Edited by J. J. Salvedra de Grave. Paris: Champion, 1925–31.

Etienne Boileau. *Le Livre des métiers et corporations de la ville de Paris, xiiie siècle.* Edited by René de Lespinasse and François Bonnardot. Paris: Imprimerie Nationale, 1879.

Etienne de Fougères. *Le Livre des manières.* Edited by R. Anthony Lodge. Geneva: Droz, 1979.

Galen. *De simplicibus medicines.* In *Claudi Galeni Opera Omnia*, edited by C. G. Kuhn. 20

vols. Leipzig: Car. Cnoblochii, 1821–33. http://194.254.96.21/livancl/?cote=45674x
12&p=247&do=page.

Geoffrey of Monmouth. *The History of the Kings of Britain*. Translated by Lewis Thorpe.
London: Penguin, 1969.

Gerson, Jean. *Confessional ou Directoire des confesseurs*. Vol. 1 of *Oeuvres complètes de Jean
Gerson*, edited by Palémon Glorieux. Paris: Desclée, 1960.

Al-Hawrani, Abd al-Rahim. *Les Ruses des femmes*. Translated by René Khawam. Paris:
Phébus, 1994.

Heldris de Cornuälle. *Le Roman de Silence: A Thirteenth-Century Arthurian Verse-Romance*.
Edited by Lewis Thorpe. Cambridge: W. Heffer & Sons, 1972.

Hrosvit of Gandersheim. *Hrotsvithae Opera*. Edited by Helene Homeyer. Munich: n.p., 1970.

Ibn Bassam al-Shantarini, Ali. *Al-Dhakhira fi mahasin ahl al-jazira* [Positive Attributes of
the Andalusians]. Edited by Ihsan Abbas. 4 vols. Beirut: Dar al-Thaqafa, 1979.

Ibn Dau'ud al-Isfahani. *Kitab al-zahra* [The Book of the Flower]. Edited by A. R. Nykl
and I. Tuqan. Chicago: University of Chicago Press, 1932.

Ibn Falita, Ahmad Ibn Mohammad. *An Intelligent Man's Guide to the Art of Coition*. Edited
by Salah Addin Khawwam. Translated by Adnan Jarkas and Salah Addin Khawwam.
Toronto: Aleppo, 1977.

———. *Rushd al-labib ila mu`asharat al-habib*. Talah: al-Mayah al-Jamahiriyah al-`Uzma,
2002.

———. *Rushd al-labib ila mu`asharat al-habib*. Chapters 9–11 edited and translated into
German by Mohamed Zouher Djabri. Ph.D. diss., School of Medicine, University
Friedrich-Alexander, Erlangen-Nuremberg, 1967.

Ibn Hazm. *The Ring of the Dove: A Treatise on the Art and Practice of Arab Love*. Translated
by A. J. Arberry. London: Luzac, 1953.

Ibn Nasr al-Katib, Abul Hasan Ali. *Encyclopedia of Pleasure*. Edited by Salah Addin
Khawwam. Translated by Adnan Jarkas and Salah Addin Khawwam. Toronto:
Aleppo, 1977.

Ibn al-Sa`i. *Nisa' al-khulafa'* [Spouses of the Caliphs]. Edited by Mustafa Jawad. Cairo: Dar
al-Ma`arif, 1968.

Ibn Souleiman, Ahmed. *Le Bréviaire arabe de l'amour*. Translated by Mohamed Lasly. Arles:
Editions Philippe Picquier, 1998.

Ibn al-Washsha'. *Kitab al-muwashsha'*. Edited by R. E. Brünnow. Leiden: Brill, 1886.

Ibn al-Washsha'. *Le Livre du brocart*. Translated by Siham Bouhlal. Paris: Gallimard, Connaissance de l'Orient, 2004.

Al-Jahiz. "Les Esclaves-Chanteuses de Gahiz." Translated by Charles Pellat. *Arabica* 10
(1963): 121–47.

———. *Kitab moufakharati al-jawari wa al-ghilman* [*Boasting Match over Maids and
Youths*]. Translated by William N. Hutchins, *Nine Essays of al-Jahiz*. 139–66.

———. *Kitab moufakharati al-jawari wa al-ghilman* [*The Pleasures of Girls and Boys Compared*]. Translated by Jim Colville, *Sobriety and Mirth: A Selection of the Shorter Writings of al-Jahiz*. London: Kegan Paul, 2002. 202–30.

———. *Kitab moufakharati al-jawari wa al-ghilman* [*Boasting Match over Maids and

Youths]. Translated into French by Malek Chebel, *Ephèbes et Courtisanes*. Paris: Payot et Rivages, 1997.

———. *Nine Essays of al-Jahiz*. Translated by William N. Hutchins. New York: Peter Lang, 1989.

———. *Risalat al-qiyan* [*The Epistle on Singing-Girls of Jahiz*]. Edited and translated by A. F. L. Beeston. Warminster, Wilts.: Aris & Phillips, 1980.

———. *Tafdil al-batn `ala al-zahr* [*Superiority of the Belly to the Back*]. Translated by William N. Hutchins, *Nine Essays of al-Jahiz*. 167–73.

Al-Jurjani, Abu al-`Abbas Ahmad b. Muhammad. *Al-Muntakhab min kinayat al-udaba' wa isharat al-bulagha'* [An Anthology of Metonymic Devices Used by the Literati and Allusions in Eloquent Speech]. Edited by Muhammad Shamsul Haq Shamsi. Hyderabad, India: Osmania Oriental Publications Bureau, 1983.

Kahhalah, `Umar Rida. *A`lam al-nisa' fi `alamay al-`Arab wa-al-Islam* [The History of Women in the Arab and Islamic Worlds]. 5 vols. Beirut: Mu'assasat al-Risala, 1977.

Lopez, Gregorio. *Las Siete partidas del sabio rey Don Alonso el Nono, nuevamente glosadas por el licenciado Gregorio Lopez*. Vol. 3. 1565. Reprint, Salamanca, 1829–31.

Maalouf, Amin. *Leo Africanus*. Translated by Peter Slugett. New York: Norton, 1986.

Maillart, Jean. *Roman du Comte d'Anjou*. Edited by Mario Roques. Paris: Champion, 1974.

Al-Maqqari, Shihab al-Din Abu al-Abbas. *Nafh al-tib min ghusn al-Andalus al-ratib* [The Wafting Scent of the Dewy Andalusian Branch], [*Analectes sur l'histoire et la littérature des Arabes d'Espagne*]. Edited by R. Dozy et al. 2 vols. Amsterdam: Oriental Press, 1967.

Mas`udi. *The Meadows of Gold: The Abbasids*. Translated and edited by Paul Lunde and Caroline Stone. London: Kegan Paul, 1989.

Mille et une nuits, Les. Edited and translated by René Khawam. Vol. 1. Paris: Phébus, 1986.

Miracle de la fille d'un roy. In *Les Miracles de Nostre Dame par personnages*, edited by Gaston Paris and Ulysse Robert, 7:2–117. Paris: Firmin et Didot, 1876.

Al-Nadim, Abu al-Faraj. *Al-Fihrist* [The Catalogue]. Edited by Rida Tajaddud. Tehran: Yutlabu min Maktabat al-Asadi wa-Maktabat al-Ja`fari al-Tabrizi, 1971.

———. *The Fihrist of al-Nadim: A Tenth-Century Survey of Muslim Culture*. Edited and translated by Bayard Dodge. 2 vols. New York: Columbia University Press, 1970.

One Thousand and One Nights. Edited and translated into French by Joseph Charles Mardrus. Paris: Laffont, 1999.

One Thousand and One Nights. Translated into English by Pomys Mathers. 4 vols. N.p., Yugoslavia: Dorset Press, 1964.

Ovid. *Iphis and Ianthe*. In *Metamorphoses*, translated by Rolfe Humphries, 229–33. Bloomington: Indiana University Press, 1955.

Plato. *Symposium*. Translated by W. R. M. Lamb. Loeb Classical Library, vol. 3. Cambridge, Mass.: Harvard University Press, 1925.

Al-Raghib al-Isfahani, Abu al-Qasim al-Husayn Ibn Muhammad. *Muhadarat al-udaba' wa-muhawarat al-shu`ara' wa-al-bulagha'* [Lectures by the Literati and Conversations in Poetry and Eloquent Speech]. 4 vols. Beirut: Dar Maktabat al-Haya, 1961.

Renart, Jean. *Escoufle*. Edited by Paul Meyer. Paris: SATF, 1894.

———. *Escoufle*. Edited by Franklin Sweetser. Geneva: Droz, 1974.

————. *Le Roman de la Rose ou de Guillaume de Dole*. Edited and translated by Regina Psaki. New York: Garland, 1995.

Renaut. *Galeran de Bretagne*. Edited by Lucien Foulet. Paris: Champion, 1925.

Robert de Blois. *Floris et Lyriopé*. Edited by Paul Barrette. Berkeley: University of California Press, 1968.

Al-Suyuti, Jalal al-Din. *Al-Mustazraf min akhbar al-jawari* [Courtly Tales of Slave-Girl Stories]. Edited by Ahmad 'Abd al-Fattah Tammam. Cairo: Maktabat al-Turath al-Islami, 1989.

————. *Nuits de noces ou comment humer le doux breuvage de la magie licite*. Translated by René Khawam. Paris: Albin Michel, 1972.

————. *Nuzhat al-julasa' fi ash'ar al-nisa'* [Salon Members' Journey into Women's Poetry]. Edited by Salah al-Din al-Munajjid. Tunis: Dar al-Ma'arif lel Teba'a wa al-Nashr, 2004.

Tertullian. "The Apparel of Women." In *Disciplinary, Moral and Ascetical Works*, translated by Rudolph Arbesmann, Emily Joseph Daly, and Edwin A. Quain. New York: Fathers of the Church, 1959.

Tibaut. *Le Roman de la poire*. Edited by Christiane Marchello-Nizia. Paris: SATF, 1985.

Al-Tifashi, Ahmad Ibn Yusuf. *Les Délices des coeurs ou ce que l'on ne trouve en aucun livre*. Translated by René R. Khawam. Paris: Phébus, 1981.

————. *The Delight of Hearts, or, What You Will Not Find in Any Book*. Edited and translated by Winston Leyland and Edward A. Lacey. San Francisco: Gay Sunshine Press, 1988.

————. *Nuzhat al-albab fima la yujad fi kitab*. Edited by Jamal Juma'a. London: Riad el-Rayyis, 1992.

Tristan de Nanteuil, chanson de geste inédite. Edited by K. V. Sinclair. Assen: Van Gorcum, 1971.

Al-Udhari, Abdullah. *Classical Poems by Arab Women*. London: Saqi Books, 1999.

Vulgate Version of Arthurian Romances Edited from Manuscripts in the British Museum, III, *L'Estoire de Merlin*. Edited by H. Oskar Sommer. Washington, D.C.: Carnegie Institution, 1910.

Yde et Olive. In *Esclarmonde, Clarisse et Florent, Yde et Olive: Dreifortsetzungen der Chansun von Huon de Bordeaux, nach der einzigen Turiner Handschrift*, edited by Max Schweigel. Marburg: N. G. Elwert, 1889.

Yde et Olive. In *"Esclarmonde, Clarisse et Florent, Yde et Olive I, Croissant, Yde et Olive II, Huon et les Géants*, Sequels to *Huon de Bordeaux*, as Contained in Turin MS L.II.14, an Edition," edited by Barbara Anne Brewska. Ph.D. diss., Vanderbilt University, 1977.

Yde et Olive. In *Les Prouesses et faictz du trespreux noble et vaillant Huon de Bordeaux, pair de France et Duc de Guyenne*, edited by Benoist Rigaud, fols. 116v–178r. Lyon, 1587. Accessed electronically at the Bibliothèque Nationale in Paris (http://www.bnf.fr).

Zink, Michel, ed. *Les Chansons de toile*. Paris: Champion, 1977.

SECONDARY SOURCES

Abbott, Nabia. "A Ninth-Century Fragment of the 'Thousand Night': New Light on the Early History of the Arabian Nights." *Journal of Near Eastern Studies* 8 (1949): 129–64.

Abd ar-Raziq, Ahmad. *La Femme au temps des Mamlouks en Egypte*. Cairo: Institut Français d'Archéologie Orientale, 1973.

Abu Khalil. "A Note on the Study of Homosexuality in the Arab/Islamic Civilization." *Arab Studies Journal* 1–2 (Fall 1993): 34.

Adams, Alison. "Jean Renart's l'*Escoufle* and the Tristan Legend: Moderation Rewarded." In *Rewards and Punishments in the Arthurian Romances and Lyric Poetry of Mediaeval France: Essays Presented to Kenneth Varty on the Occasion of His Sixtieth Birthday*, edited by Peter V. Davies and Angus J. Kennedy, 1–7. Cambridge: D. S. Brewer, 1987.

Adams, Jenny. *Power Play: The Literature and Politics of Chess in the Late Middle Ages*. Philadelphia: University of Pennsylvania Press, 2006.

Adams, J. N. *The Latin Sexual Vocabulary*. Baltimore: Johns Hopkins University Press, 1982.

Adang, Camilla. "Ibn Hazm on Homosexuality: A Case-Study of Zahiri Legal Methodology." *al-Qantara* 24 (2003): 5–31

Ahmed, Leila. "Western Ethnocentrism and Perceptions of the Harem." *Feminist Studies* 8, no. 3 (1982): 521–34.

———. *Women and Gender in Islam*. New Haven, Conn.: Yale University Press, 1992.

Ali, Kecia. *Sexual Ethics and Islam: Feminist Reflections on Qur'an, Hadith, and Jurisprudence*. Oxford: Oneworld, 2006.

Amer, Sahar. "Cross-Dressing and Female Same-Sex Marriage in Medieval French and Arabic Literatures," in *Religion, Gender, and Culture in the Pre-Modern World*, edited by Alexandra Cuffel and Brian Britt, 105–35. Religion, Culture, Critique Series. New York: Palgrave, 2007.

———. *Esope au féminin: Marie de France et la politique de l'interculturalité*. Amsterdam: Rodopi, 1999.

———. "Lesbian Sex and the Military: From the Medieval Arabic Tradition to French Literature." In Sautman and Sheingorn, *Same Sex Love and Desire*, 179–98.

Amer, Sahar, and Olu Oguibe, eds. *Ghada Amer*. Amsterdam: De Appel, 2002.

Anson, John. "The Female Transvestite in Early Monasticism." *Viator* 5, no. 1 (1974): 1–32.

Apter, Emily. "Female Trouble in the Colonial Harem." *Differences* 4, no. 1 (1992): 203–24.

Archibald, Elizabeth. *Incest and the Medieval Imagination*. London: Oxford University Press, 2001.

Arthur, Ross G. "On Editing Sexually Offensive Old French Texts." In *The Politics of Editing Medieval Texts*, edited by Roberta Frank, 19–64. New York: MAS Press, 1991.

Babayan, Kathryn, and Afsaneh Najmabadi, eds. *Islamicate Sexualities Studies: Translations Across Temporal and Geographical Zones of Desire*. Forthcoming.

Bailey, Derrick S. *Homosexuality and the Western Christian Tradition*. Hamden, Conn.: Archon, 1975.

Bakhtin, Mikhail. *The Dialogic Imagination*. Edited by Michael Holquist. Translated by Caryl Emerson and Michael Holquist. Austin: University of Texas Press, 1981.

———. *Problems of Dostoevsky's Poetics*. Edited and translated by Caryl Emerson. Minneapolis: University of Minnesota Press, 1984.

Baldwin, John W. *The Language of Sex: Five Voices from Northern France Around 1200*. Chicago: University of Chicago Press, 1994.

———. "'Once There Was an Emperor . . .': A Political Reading of the Romances of Jean Renart." In Durling, *Jean Renart and the Art of Romance*, 45–82.

Baumel, Jean. *Histoire d'une seigneurie du Midi: Naissance de Montpellier (985–1213)*. Montpellier: Editions Causse et Cie, 1969.

Baumgartner, Emmanuèle. "Les Brodeuses et la ville." *50 rue de Varenne. Supplemento italofrancese di nuovi argomenti*, 3a serie, supl. no. 43 (1992): 89–95.

Baumgartner, Emmanuèle, and Laurence Harf-Lancner. *Seuils de l'oeuvre dans le texte médiéval*. Paris: Presses de la Sorbonne Nouvelle, 2002.

Bec, Pierre. *Burlesque et obscénité chez les troubadours*. Paris: Stock, 1984.

Beeston, A. F. L. Review of *Nine Essays of Al-Jahiz*, translated by William M. Hutchins. *Journal of Arabic Literature* 20 (1989): 200–209.

Bell, Laurie, ed. *Good Girls/Bad Girls: Sex Trade Workers and Feminists Face to Face*. Seattle: Seal Press, 1987.

Bencheikh, Jamal Eddine. "L'Exigence d'aimer." Interview by Fethi Benslama and Thierry Fabre. "De l'Amour et des Arabes." Special issue, *Qantara: Magazine de l'Institut du Monde Arabe* 18 (January–February 1996): 23.

Benkov, Edith. "The Erased Lesbian: Sodomy and the Legal Tradition in Medieval Europe." In Sautman and Sheingorn, *Same Sex Love and Desire*, 101–22.

Bennett, Judith M. "Confronting Continuity." *Journal of Women's History* 9, no. 3 (1997): 73–94.

———. "'Lesbian-Like' and the Social History of Lesbianisms." *Journal of the History of Sexuality* 9, nos. 1–2 (2000): 1–24.

———. "Medieval Women, Modern Women: Across the Great Divide." In *Culture and History, 1350–1600: Essays on English Communities, Identities and Writing*, edited by David Aers, 147–75. London: Harvester Wheatsheaf, 1992.

Bennett, Judith M., and Amy M. Froide, eds. *Singlewomen in the European Past, 1250–1800*. Philadelphia: University of Pennsylvania Press, 1999.

Bennett, Judith M., et al., eds. *Sisters and Workers in the Middle Ages*. Chicago: University of Chicago Press, 1976.

Bewley, Aisha. *Muslim Women: A Biographical Dictionary*. London: Ta-Ha, 2004.

Bhabha, Homi. *The Location of Culture*. London: Routledge, 1994.

Blackmore, Josiah, and Gregory S. Hutcheson, eds. *Queer Iberia: Sexualities, Cultures and Crossings from the Middle Ages to the Renaissance*. Durham, N.C.: Duke University Press, 1999.

Bloch, R. H. *Medieval Misogyny and the Invention of Western Romantic Love*. Chicago: University of Chicago Press, 1991.

———. *The Scandal of the Fabliaux*. Chicago: University of Chicago Press, 1986.

Blumreich, Kathleen M. "Lesbian Desire in the Old French *Roman de Silence*." *Arthuriana* 7, no. 2 (1997): 47–62.

Bonnet, Marie-Jo. *Les Deux amies: Essai sur le couple de femmes dans l'art*. Paris: Editions Blanche, 2000.

Boone, Marc. "State Power and Illicit Sexuality: The Persecution of Sodomy in Late Medieval Bruges." *Journal of Medieval History* 22, no. 2 (1996): 135–53.

Boswell, John. *Christianity, Social Tolerance, and Homosexuality: Gay People in Western Europe from the Beginning of the Christian Era to the Fourteenth Century.* Chicago: University of Chicago Press, 1980.

———. *Same-Sex Unions in Premodern Europe.* New York: Villard Books, 1994.

———. "Towards the Long View: Revolutions, Universals and Sexual Categories." *Salmagundi* 58–59 (Fall–Winter 1983): 89–113.

Bosworth, C. E. *The Medieval Islamic Underworld.* Leiden: Brill, 1976.

Bouhdiba, Abdelwahab. *La Sexualité en Islam.* Paris: Presses Universitaires de France, 1986.

Bourdieu, Pierre. *Outline of a Theory of Practice.* Translated by Richard Nice. Cambridge: Cambridge University Press, 1977.

Boyarin, Daniel. *Carnal Israel: Reading Sex in Talmudic Culture.* Berkeley: University of California Press, 1993.

Brooten, Bernadette J. *Love Between Women: Early Christian Responses to Female Homoeroticism.* Chicago: University of Chicago Press, 1996.

Brown, Judith C. *Immodest Acts: The Life of a Lesbian Nun in Renaissance Italy.* New York: Oxford University Press, 1986.

Brundage, James A. *Law, Sex and Christian Society in Medieval Europe.* Chicago: University of Chicago Press, 1987.

———. *Medieval Canon Law and the Crusader.* Madison: University of Wisconsin Press, 1969.

———. "Prostitution in the Medieval Canon Law." In Bennett et al., *Sisters and Workers*, 79–99.

———. "Sex and Canon Law." In *Handbook of Medieval Sexuality*, edited by Vern L. Bullough and James Brundage, 33–50. New York: Garland, 1996.

———. "Sumptuary Laws and Prostitution in Medieval Italy." *Journal of Medieval History* 13 (1987): 343–55.

Bullough, Vern L. "Cross Dressing and Gender Role Change in the Middle Ages." In Bullough and Brundage, *Handbook of Medieval Sexuality*, 223–42.

Bullough, Vern L., and James Brundage, eds. *The Handbook of Medieval Sexuality.* New York: Garland, 1996.

Burger, Glenn, and Steven F. Kruger, eds. *Queering the Middle Ages.* Minneapolis: University of Minnesota Press, 2001.

Burman, Thomas E. *Religious Polemic and the Intellectual History of the Mozarabs, c. 1050–1200.* Leiden: E. J. Brill, 1994.

Burnett, Charles. *The Introduction of Arabic Learning into England.* London: British Library, 1997.

———, ed. *La Transmission des textes philosophiques et scientifiques au moyen âge—Marie-Thérèse d'Alverny.* Aldershot, Hampshire, U.K.: Variorum, 1994.

Burns, E. Jane. *Bodytalk: When Women Talk Back.* Philadelphia: University of Pennsylvania Press, 1993.

———. *Courtly Love Undressed: Reading Through Clothes in Medieval French Culture.* Philadelphia: University of Pennsylvania Press, 2002.

———. "Ladies Don't Wear *Braies*: Underwear and Outerwear in the French *Prose*

Lancelot." In *The Lancelot-Grail Cycle: Text and Transformations*, edited by William W. Kibler, 152–74. Austin: University of Texas Press, 1994.

———. "Refashioning Courtly Love." In *Constructing Medieval Sexuality*, edited by Lochrie, McCracken, and Schultz, 111–34.

Burrus, Virginia. *The Sex Lives of Saints: An Erotics of Ancient Hagiography*. Philadelphia: University of Pennsylvania Press, 2004.

Burton, Sir Richard. "Terminal Essay." In *The Book of the Thousand and One Nights and a Night*, 10:205–53. New York, 1886.

Butler, Judith. "Against Proper Objects." *Differences* 6, nos. 2–3 (1994): 1–26.

———. "Gender Is Burning: Questions of Appropriation and Subversion." In *Bodies That Matter: On the Discursive Limits of "Sex,"* 121–40. New York: Routledge, 1993.

———. *Gender Trouble: Feminism and the Subversion of Identity*. New York: Routledge, 1990.

———. "Imitation and Gender Subordination." In *Inside/Out: Lesbian Theories, Gay Theories*, edited by Diana Fuss, 13–31. New York: Routledge, 1991.

Bynum, Caroline Walker. *Jesus as Mother: Studies in the Spirituality of the High Middle Ages*. Berkeley: University of California Press, 1982.

Cadden, Joan. *Meanings of Sex Difference in the Middle Ages: Medicine, Science, and Culture*. Cambridge: Cambridge University Press, 1993.

Calhoun, Cheshire. "The Gender Closet: Lesbian Disappearance Under the Sign 'Women.'" *Feminist Studies* 21, no. 1 (1995): 7–34.

Carré, Yannick. *Le Baiser sur la bouche au Moyen Age: Rites, symboles, mentalités à travers les textes et les images, 11e–15e siècles*. Paris: Le Léopard d'Or, 1992.

Castle, Terry. *The Apparitional Lesbian: Female Homosexuality and Modern Culture*. New York: Columbia University Press, 1993.

Castro, Antonio Arjona. *La Sexualidad en la España Musulmana*. Córdoba: Universidad de Córdoba, 1985.

Catlos, Brian A. *Victors and the Vanquished*. Cambridge: Cambridge University Press, 2004.

Chapoutot-Remadi, Mounira. "Femmes dans la ville Mamluke." *Journal of the Economic and Social History of the Orient* 38, no. 2 (1995): 145–64.

Charlier, Gustave "L'*Escoufle* et *Guillaume de Dole*." In *Mélanges de philologie romane et d'histoire littéraire offerts à M. Maurice Wilmotte*, 1:81–98. Paris: Champion, 1910. Geneva: Slatkine Reprints, 1972, 2 vols.

Chauncey, George, Jr. "From Sexual Inversion to Homosexuality: Medicine and the Changing Conceptualization of Female Deviance." *Salmagundi* 58–59 (Fall 1982–Winter 1983): 114–46.

Chebel, Malek. *Encyclopédie de l'amour en Islam: Erotisme, beauté et sexualité dans le monde arabe, en Perse, et en Turquie*. Paris: Payot, 1995.

———. *L'Esprit de sérail: Mythes et pratiques sexuelles au Maghreb*. Paris: Payot, 1988.

———. *Traité du raffinement*. Paris: Payot, 1995.

Ciggaar, Krijne. "Encore une fois Chrétien de Troyes et la 'matière Byzantine': La Révolution des femmes au palais de Constantinople." *Cahiers de civilisation médiévale* 38 (1995): 267–74.

Clark, Robert L. A. "A Heroine's Sexual Itinerary: Incest, Transvestism, and Same-Sex Marriage in *Yde et Olive*." In *Gender Transgressions: Crossing the Normative Barrier in Old French Literature*, edited by Karen J. Taylor, 889–905. New York: Garland, 1998.

———. "Jousting Without a Lance: The Condemnation of Female Homoeroticism in the *Livre des manières*." In Sautman and Sheingorn, *Same Sex Love and Desire*, 143–77.

Clark, Robert L. A., and Claire Sponsler. "Queer Play: The Cultural Work of Crossdressing in Medieval Drama." *New Literary History* 28, no. 2 (1997): 319–44.

Clemente, Linda. "Aelis' Introspective Silence in the Feminist World of Jean Renart's *Escoufle*." *Cincinnati Romance Review* 10 (1991): 26–34.

Constable, Olivia Remie. *Housing the Stranger in the Mediterranean World: Lodging, Trade and Travel in Late Antiquity and the Middle Ages*. Cambridge: Cambridge University Press, 2004.

———. *Trade and Traders in Muslim Spain: The Commercial Realignment of the Iberian Peninsula, 900–1500*. Cambridge: Cambridge University Press, 1996.

Crane, Susan. "Clothing and Gender Definition: Joan of Arc." *Journal of Medieval and Early Modern Studies* 26, no. 2 (1996): 297–320.

Crompton, Louis. "The Myth of Lesbian Impunity: Capital Laws from 1270 to 1791." *Journal of Homosexuality* 6, nos. 1–2 (Winter 1980–81): 11–25.

Cuffel, Alexandra. *Filthy Words/Filthy Bodies: Gendering Disgust in Medieval Religious Polemic*. Notre Dame, Ind.: Notre Dame University Press, 2007.

Dale, Marian K. "The London Silkwomen of the Fifteenth Century." *Economic Historical Review* 4 (1933): 324–35.

Daniel, Norman. *Islam and the West: The Making of an Image*. Edinburgh: Edinburgh University Press, 1960.

Davis, Natalie Zemon. *Trickster Travels: A Sixteenth-Century Muslim Between Worlds*. New York: Hill and Wang, 2006.

de Jong, Frederick, ed. *Verse and the Fair Sex: Studies in Poetry and in the Representation of Women in Arabic Literature: A Collection of Papers Presented at the 15th Congress of the Union Européenne des Arabisants et Islamisants*. Utrecht: M. Th. Houtsma Stichting, 1993.

Delany, Sheila. "Anatomy of the Resisting Reader: Some Implications of Resistance to Sexual Wordplay in Medieval Literature." *Exemplaria* 4, no. 1 (1992): 7–34.

de Weever, Jacqueline. "The Lady, the Knight, and the Lover: Androgyny and Integration in *La Chanson d'Yde et Olive*." *Romanic Review* 81, no. 4 (1991): 371–91.

Dictionary of Literary Biography, vol. 311, *Arabic Literary Culture, 500–925*. Edited by Michael Cooperson and Shawkat M. Toorawa. New York: Bruccoli Clark Layman Book, 2005.

Dijkstra, Bram. *Idols of Perversity*. New York: Oxford University Press, 1986.

Diller, G. T. "*L'Escoufle*: Une Aventurière dans le roman courtois." *Le Moyen Age* 85, no. 1 (1979): 34–43.

Dinshaw, Carolyn. *Getting Medieval: Sexualities and Communities, Pre- and Post-Modern.* Durham, N.C.: Duke University Press, 1999.

———. "A Kiss Is Just a Kiss: Heterosexuality and Its Consolations in *Sir Gawain and the Green Knight.*" *Diacritics* 24, no. 2 (1994): 205–26.

Donoghue, Emma. *Passions Between Women: British Lesbian Culture, 1668–1801.* London: Scarlet Press, 1993.

Douglas, Mary. *Purity and Danger.* London: Routledge and Kegan Paul, 1966.

Duby, Georges. *Le Chevalier, la femme et le prêtre.* Paris: Hachette, 1981.

Durling, Nancy Vine. "Rewriting Gender: *Yde et Olive* and Ovidian Myth." *Romance Languages Annual* 1 (1989): 256–62.

———, ed. *Jean Renart and the Art of Romance: Essays on Guillaume de Dole.* Gainesville: University of Florida Press, 1997.

Edgington, Susan B., and Sarah Lambert, eds. *Gendering the Crusades.* Cardiff: University of Wales Press, 2001.

Edwardes, Allen. *The Jewel in the Lotus: A Historical Survey of the Sexual Culture of the East.* New York: Julian Press, 1959.

Edwards, Robert R., and Vickie L. Ziegler. *Matrons and Marginal Women in Medieval Society.* Rochester, N.Y.: Boydell, 1995.

Eisenbichler, Konrad. "Laudomia Forteguerri Loves Margaret of Austria." In Sautman and Sheingorn, *Same Sex Love and Desire,* 277–304.

Eriksson, Brigitte. "A Lesbian Execution in Germany, 1721: The Trial Records." *Journal of Homosexuality* 6, nos. 1–2 (1980–81): 27–40.

Faderman, Lillian. *Surpassing the Love of Men: Romantic Friendship and Love Between Women from the Renaissance to the Present.* New York: Morrow, 1981.

Farmer, Sharon. "'It Is Not Good That [Wo]man Should Be Alone': Elite Responses to Singlewomen in High Medieval Paris." In Bennett and Froide, *Singlewomen,* 82–105.

———. *Surviving Poverty in Medieval Paris: Gender, Ideology, and the Daily Lives of the Poor.* Ithaca, N.Y.: Cornell University Press, 2002.

Farmer, Sharon, and Carol Braun Pasternack, eds. *Gender and Difference in the Middle Ages.* Minneapolis: University of Minnesota Press, 2003.

Fletcher, Richard. *Moorish Spain.* Berkeley: University of California Press, 1992.

Foucault, Michel. *The History of Sexuality: An Introduction.* Vol. 1. Translated by Robert Hurley. New York: Vintage, 1980.

———. *Iradat al ma`rifah, al-juz' al-awwal min tarikh al-jinsaniyya [The History of Sexuality,* vol. 1 of *The Will to Know].* Translated by Muta al-Safadi. Beirut: Markaz al-Inma al Qawmi, 1990.

———. "Sexual Choice, Sexual Act: An Interview with Michel Foucault." Translated by James O'Higgins. *Salmagundi* 58–59 (Fall 1982–Winter 1983): 11–12.

Foulet, Lucien. "'Galeran' et Jean Renart." *Romania* 51 (1925): 76–104.

Fradenburg, Louise O., and Carla Freccero. "The Pleasures of History." *GLQ* 1, no. 4 (1995): 371–84.

———, eds. *Premodern Sexualities.* New York: Routledge, 1995.

Freud, Sigmund. *Tafsir al-ahlam* [*The Interpretation of Dreams*]. Translated by Mustafa Safwan. 1958. Reprint, Cairo: Dar al-Ma`arif, 1969.

———. *Thalathat mabahith fi nazariyyat al-jins* [*Three Essays on the Theory of Sexuality*]. Translated by Jurj Tarabishi. Beirut: Dar al-Tali`ah, 1983.

Fuchs, Barbara. *Mimesis and Empire: The New World, Islam, and European Identities*. Cambridge: Cambridge University Press, 2001.

Garber, Marjorie. "The Chic of Araby: Transvestism, Transsexualism and the Erotics of Cultural Appropriation." In *Body Guards: The Cultural Politics of Gender Ambiguity*, edited by Julia Epstein and Kristina Straub, 223–47. New York: Routledge, 1991.

———. *Vested Interests: Cross-Dressing and Cultural Anxiety*. New York: Routledge, 1992.

Garulo, Teresa. *Diwan de las poetisas de al-Andalus*. Madrid: Hyperion, 1985.

Gaunt, Simon. *Gender and Genre in Medieval French Literature*. Cambridge: Cambridge University Press, 1995.

———. "Straight Minds/'Queer' Wishes in Old French Hagiography—La Vie-de-Sainte-Euphrosine." *GLQ* 1, no. 4 (1995): 439–47.

Genette, Gérard. *Seuils*. Paris: Seuil, 1987.

Germain, Alexandre André. *Histoire du commerce de Montpellier antérieurement à l'ouverture du port de Cette*. 2 vols. Montpellier: Imprimerie de Jean Martel, ainé, 1861.

Ghazi, Mhammed Ferid. "Un Groupe social: 'Les Raffinés' (*Zurafa*)." *Studia Islamica* 11 (1959–60): 39–71.

Ghoussoub, Mai, and Emma Sinclair-Webb, eds. *Imagined Masculinities: Male Identity and Culture in the Modern Middle East*. London: Saqi Books, 2000.

Giffen, Lois A. "Love Poetry and Love Theory in Medieval Arabic Literature." In *Arabic Poetry: Theory and Development*, 107–24, edited by G. E. von Grunebaum. Wiesbaden: Otto Harrassowitz, 1973.

———. *Theory of Profane Love Among the Arabs: The Development of the Genre*. New York: New York University Press, 1971.

Glick, Thomas. *Irrigation and Hydraulic Technology: Medieval Spain and Its Legacy*. Brookfield, Vt.: Variorum, 1996.

Glubb, John. *A Short History of the Arab Peoples*. New York: Dorset, 1969.

Godefroy, Frédéric. *Dictionnaire de l'ancienne langue française et de tous ses dialectes du IXe au XVe siècle*. 10 vols. Paris: Vieweg, 1888–1920.

Goldberg, P. J. P. *Women, Work, and Life Cycle in a Medieval Economy: Women in York and Yorkshire, c. 1300–1520*. Oxford: Clarendon Press, 1992.

Gouron, André. *La Réglementation des métiers en Languedoc au Moyen Age*. Geneva: Droz, 1958.

Gravdal, Kathryn. *Ravishing Maidens: Writing Rape in Medieval French Literature and Law*. Philadelphia: University of Pennsylvania Press, 1991.

Green, Monica. *Women's Healthcare in the Medieval West: Texts and Contexts*. Burlington, Vt.: Ashgate, 2000.

———. "Women's Medical Practice and Health Care in Medieval Europe." In Bennett et al., *Sisters and Workers*, 39–78.

———, ed. and trans. *The Trotula: A Medieval Compendium of Women's Medicine.* Philadelphia: University of Pennsylvania Press, 2001.

Greenberg, David F. *The Construction of Homosexuality.* Chicago: University of Chicago Press, 1988.

Greus, Jésus. *Ziryab: La Prodigiosa historia del sultan andaluz y el cantor de Bagdad.* San Lorenzo de El Escorial: Editoria Swan, 1987.

Grewal, Inderpal. *Home and Harem: Imperialism, Nationalism and the Culture of Travel.* Durham, N.C.: Duke University Press, 1995.

Grisay, A., G. Lavis, and M. Dubois-Stasse. *Les Dénominations de la femme dans les anciens textes littéraires français.* Gembloux: J. Duculot, 1969.

Guidi, Ignazio. *Tables alphabétiques du "Kitab al-Agani."* Leiden: Brill, 1900.

Guthrie, Jeri. "La Femme dans *Le Livre des manières*: Surplus économique, surplus érotique." *Romanic Review* 79 (1988): 251–61.

Halperin, David M. *How to Do the History of Homosexuality.* Chicago: University of Chicago Press, 2002.

———. *One Hundred Years of Homosexuality, and Other Essays on Greek Love.* New York: Routledge, 1990.

Halperin, David M., John J. Winkler, and Froma I. Zeitlin, eds. *Before Sexuality: The Construction of Erotic Experience in the Ancient Greek World.* Princeton, N.J.: Princeton University Press, 1990.

Hambly, G. R. G. *Women in the Medieval Islamic World: Power, Patronage, Piety.* New York: Palgrave, 1998.

Hamori, Andras. "A Comic Romance from the *Thousand and One Nights:* The Tale of Two Viziers." *Arabica* 30, no. 1 (1983): 38–56.

———. *On the Art of Medieval Arabic Literature.* Princeton, N.J.: Princeton University Press, 1975.

Hanawalt, Barbara A. "At the Margin of Women's Space in Medieval Europe." In Edwards and Ziegler, *Matrons and Marginal Women*, 1–17.

Hartogs, Renatus, and Hans Fantel. *Four Letter Word Games: The Psychology of Obscenity.* New York: Delacorte Press, 1968.

Herman, Gerald. " 'The Sin Against Nature' and Its Echoes in Medieval French Literature." *Annuale Medievale* 17 (1976): 70–87.

Heyd, Wilhelm. *Histoire du commerce du Levant au Moyen-Age.* 2 vols. Amsterdam: Adolf M. Hakkert, 1959.

Hillenbrand, Carole. *The Crusades: Islamic Perspectives.* London: Routledge, 1999.

Hitti, Philip K. *History of the Arabs from the Earliest Times to the Present.* 9th ed. New York: St. Martin's Press, 1968.

Hodgson, Marshall G. S. *The Venture of Islam: Conscience and History in a World Civilization.* 3 vols. Chicago: University of Chicago Press, 1974.

Hollywood, Amy M. *The Soul as Virgin Wife: Mechtild of Magdeburg, Marguerite Porete, and Meister Eckhart.* Notre Dame, Ind.: University of Notre Dame Press, 1995.

Holsinger, Bruce. "The Flesh of the Voice: Embodiment and the Homoerotics of Devotion in the Music of Hildegarde of Bingen (1098–1179)." *Signs* 19, no. 1 (1993): 92–125.

Hotchkiss, Valerie R. *Clothes Make the Man: Female Cross Dressing in Medieval Europe.* New York: Garland, 1996.

Huntington, Samuel. "The Clash of Civilizations." *Foreign Affairs* 72, no. 3 (1993): 22–49.

Huston, Nancy, and Sam Kinser. *A L'amour comme à la guerre.* Paris: Seuil, 1984.

Hyatte, Reginald. *The Arts of Friendships: The Idealization of Friendship in Medieval and Early Renaissance Literature.* Leiden: E. J. Brill, 1994.

Irwin, Robert. *The Arabian Nights: A Companion.* New York: Penguin, 1994.

Jacquart, Danielle, and Claude Thomasset. *Sexualité et savoir médical au Moyen Age.* Paris: Presses Universitaires de France, 1985.

Jenness, Valerie. *Making It Work: The Prostitutes' Rights Movement in Perspective.* New York: De Gruyter, 1993.

Jones, Malcolm. "Folklore Motifs in Late Medieval Art II: Sexist Satire and Popular Punishments." *Folklore* 101, no. 1 (1990): 69–87.

Jones, Nancy. "The Uses of Embroidery in Jean Renart: Gender, History, Textuality." In Durling, *Jean Renart and the Art of Romance,* 13–44.

Jordan, Mark D. *The Invention of Sodomy in Christian Theology.* Chicago: University of Chicago Press, 1997.

Karras, Ruth Mazo. *Common Women: Prostitution and Sexuality in Medieval England.* New York: Oxford University Press, 1996.

———. "Sex and the Singlewoman." In Bennett and Froide, *Singlewomen,* 127–45.

Kay, Sarah. *The Chansons de Geste in the Age of Romance: Political Fictions.* Oxford: Oxford University Press, 1995.

Keddie, Nikki R., and Beth Baron, eds. *Women in Middle Eastern History.* New Haven, Conn., Yale University Press, 1991.

Kellogg, Judith. *Medieval Artistry and Exchange: Economic Institutions, Society and Literary Form in Old French Narrative.* New York: Peter Lang, 1989.

Kendrick, Laura. *Chaucerian Play.* Berkeley: University of California Press, 1988.

Kennedy, Philip F. *Abu Nuwas: A Genius of Poetry.* Oxford: Oneworld, 2005.

Kennedy, Ruth, and Simon Meecham-Jones, eds. *Writers of the Reign of Henry II: Twelve Essays.* New York: Palgrave, 2006.

Kettle, Ann J. "Ruined Maids: Prostitutes and Servant Girls in Later Medieval England." In Edwards and Ziegler, *Matrons and Marginal Women,* 24–25.

Khatibi, Abdelkebir. *La Blessure du nom propre.* Paris: Denoël, 1986.

———. *Maghreb pluriel.* Paris: Denoël, 1983.

Kilpatrick, Hilary. *Making the Great Book of Songs: Compilation and the Author's Craft in Abu al-Faraj al-Isbahani's "Kitab al-Aghani."* New York: Routledge, 2003.

———. "Some Late Abbasid and Mamluk Books about Women: A Literary Historical Approach." *Arabica* 42 (1995): 56–78.

Kinoshita, Sharon. *Medieval Boundaries: Rethinking Difference in Old French Literature.* Philadelphia: University of Pennsylvania Press, 2006.

———. "The Politics of Courtly Love: *La Prise d'Orange* and the Conversion of the Saracen Queen." *Romanic Review* 86, no. 2 (1995): 265–87.

Klosowska, Anna. *Queer Love in the Middle Ages.* New York: Palgrave, 2005.

Koenig, Vernon Frederic. "Jean Renart and the Authorship of *Galeran de Bretagne.*" *Modern Language Notes* 49, no. 4 (1934): 248–55.

Kowaleski, Maryanne, and Judith M. Bennett. "Crafts, Gilds and Women in the Middle Ages: Fifty Years After Marian Dale." In Bennett et al., *Sisters and Workers*, 11–38.

Kraemer, Ross S. "The Conversion of Women to Ascetic Forms of Christianity." In Bennett et al., *Sisters and Workers*, 198–207.

Kristeva, Julia. *Desire in Language: A Semiotic Approach to Literature and Art.* New York: Columbia University Press, 1980.

———. *Semiotica: Recherches pour une sémanalyse.* Paris: Seuil, 1969.

Krueger, Roberta. "Constructing Sexual Identities in the High Middle Ages: The Didactic Poetry of Robert de Blois." *Paragraph* 13 (1990): 105–31.

———. "Transforming Maidens: Singlewomen's Stories in Marie de France's *Lais* and Later French Courtly Narratives." In Bennett and Froide, *Singlewomen*, 146–91.

———. *Women Readers and the Ideology of Gender in Old French Verse Romance.* Cambridge: Cambridge University Press, 1993.

Kruger, Steven F. "Conversion and Medieval Sexual, Religious, and Racial Categories." In Lochrie, McCracken, and Schultz, *Constructing Medieval Sexuality*, 158–79.

Kruk, Remke. "The Bold and the Beautiful: Women and 'fitna' in the *Sirat Dhat al-Himma*: The Story of Nura." In *Women in the Medieval Islamic World*, edited by Gavin R. G. Hambly, 99–116. New York: St. Martin's Press, 1998.

———. "Clipped Wings: Medieval Arabic Adaptations of the Amazon Myth." *Harvard Middle Eastern and Islamic Review* 1, no. 2 (1994): 132–51.

———. "Warrior Women in Arabic Popular Romance: Qannasa Bint Muzahim and Other Valiant Ladies." *Journal of Arabic Literature* 24 (1993): 213–30 (pt. 1), and 25 (1994): 16–33 (pt. 2).

Kugle, Scott Siraj al-Haqq. "Sexuality, Diversity, and Ethics in the Agenda of Progressive Muslims." In *Progressive Muslims: Justice, Gender and Pluralism*, edited by Omid Safi, 190–234. Oxford: Oneworld, 2003.

Kuster, Harry J., and Raymond J. Cormier. "Old Views and New Trends: Observations on the Problem of Homosexuality in the Middle Ages." *Studi Medievali*, ser. 3, 25 (1984): 587–610.

Langlois, Charles-Victor. *La Vie en France au moyen âge de la fin du XIIe au milieu du XIVe siècle.* Vol. 2, *D'après les moralistes du temps.* Paris: Hachette, 1925.

Laqueur, Thomas. *Making Sex: Body and Gender from the Greeks to Freud.* Cambridge, Mass.: Harvard University Press, 1990.

Lasater, Alice. *Spain to England: A Comparative Study of Arabic, European and English Literature in the Middle Ages.* Jackson: University of Mississippi Press, 1974.

Lavezzo, Kathy. "Sobs and Sighs Between Women: The Homoerotics of Compassion in the Book of Margery Kempe." In Fradenburg and Freccero, *Premodern Sexualities*, 175–98.

Lejeune, Rita. "La Coupe de Tristan dans l'*Escoufle* de Jean Renart." In *The Medieval Alexander Legend and Romance Epic, Essays in Honor of David J. A. Ross*, edited by P. Noble, L. Polak, and C. Isoz, 119–24. New York: Kraus International, 1982.

———. "Jean Renart et le roman réaliste au XIIIème siècle." In *Grundriss der Romanischen Literaturen des Mittelalters*, edited by Jean Frappier and Reinhold Grimm, vol. 4, *Le Roman jusqu'à la fin du 13e siècle*, 400–453. Heidelberg: Carl Winter, 1978.

Lejeune-Dehousse, Rita. *L'Oeuvre de Jean Renart: Contribution à l'étude du genre romanesque au Moyen Age*. Paris: Droz, 1935.

Le Nan, Frédérique. "De Quelques 'pérégrines' ou la mobilité des dames dans l'oeuvre présumée de Jean Renart." *Revue des langues romanes* 104, no. 1 (2000): 47–70.

Leupin, Alexandre. "Ecriture naturelle et écriture hermaphrodite: Le *De planctu Naturae* d'Alain de Lille, un art poétique du XIIe siècle." *Diagraphe* 9 (1976): 119–41.

Lévi-Provençal, Evariste. *La Civilisation arabe en Espagne*. Paris: Maisonneuve, 1948.

Lewis, Andrew W. *Royal Succession in Capetian France: Studies on Familial Order and the State*. Cambridge, Mass.: Harvard University Press, 1981.

Lewis, Archibald R. "Patterns of Economic Development in Southern France, 1050–1271 A.D." *Studies in Medieval and Renaissance History*, n.s., 3 (1980): 57–83.

Liault, Jacqueline. *Montpellier, la médiévale*. Nimes: C. Lacour, 1990.

Lochrie, Karma. *Covert Operations: The Medieval Uses of Secrecy*. Philadelphia: University of Pennsylvania Press, 1999.

———. "Desiring Foucault." *Journal of Medieval and Early Modern Studies* 27, no. 1 (1997): 3–16.

———. "Mystical Acts, Queer Tendencies." In Lochrie, McCracken, and Schultz, *Constructing Medieval Sexuality*, 180–200.

Lochrie, Karma, Peggy McCracken, and James A. Schultz, eds. *Constructing Medieval Sexuality*. Minneapolis: University of Minnesota Press, 1997.

Longère, Jean. "Deux sermons de Jacques de Vitry *Ad Servos et Ancillas*." In *La femme au Moyen Age*, edited by Michel Rouche and Jean Heuclin, 261–97. Maubeuge: Publications de la Ville de Maubeuge, 1990.

Lord, Albert B. *The Singer of Tales*. Cambridge, Mass.: Harvard University Press, 2000.

Lutfi, Huda. "Al-Sakhawi's *Kitab al-Nisa'* as a Source for the Social and Economic History of Muslim Women During the Fifteenth Century A.D." *Muslim World* 7, no. 2 (1981): 104–24.

Lyons, M. C. *The Arabic Epic: Heroic and Oral Story-Telling*. 3 vols. Cambridge: Cambridge University Press, 1995.

MacKinnon, Catharine. "Does Sexuality Have a History?" In *Discourses of Sexuality: From Aristotle to AIDS*, edited by Domna C. Stanton, 117–36. Ann Arbor: University of Michigan Press, 1992.

Majdub, al-Bashir. *Al-Zarf bi-al-`Iraq fi al-`asr al-`Abbasi* [Courtliness in Iraq During the Abbasid Period]. Tunis: Nashr wa-Tawzi` Mu'assasat `Abd al-Karim Bin `Abd Allah, 1992.

Mallette, Karla. *The Kingdom of Sicily, 1100–1250: A Literary History*. Philadelphia: University of Pennsylvania Press, 2005.

Mann, Vivian, Thomas F. Glick, and Jerrilynn D. Dodds, eds. *Convivencia: Jews, Muslims, and Christians in Medieval Spain*. New York: G. Braziller in association with the Jewish Museum, 1992.

Marchello-Nizia, Christiane, and Michèle Perret. "Une Utopie homosexuelle au quatorzième siècle: L'île sans femmes d'Agriano." *Stanford French Review* 14, nos. 1–2 (1990): 231–41.

Mas Latrie, Louis de. *Traités de paix et de commerce et documents divers concernant les relations des chrétiens avec les Arabes de l'Afrique septentrionale au Moyen-Age.* 2 vols. New York: B. Franklin, 1963.

Massad, Joseph. "Re-Orienting Desire: The Gay International and the Arab World." *Public Culture* 14, no. 2 (2002): 361–85.

Máta, María Jesús Rubiera. *Poesía feminine hispanoárabe.* Madrid: Castalia, 1989.

Matar, Nabil. *Turks, Moors, and Englishmen in the Age of Discovery.* New York: Columbia University Press, 1999.

Matter, Ann. "My Sister, My Spouse: Woman-Identified Women in Medieval Christianity." *Journal of Feminist Studies in Religion* 2, no. 2 (1986): 81–93.

McAuliffe, Jane Dammen, ed. *Encyclopedia of the Quran.* 3 vols. Leiden: Brill, 2002.

McClintock, Anne. "Screwing the System: Sexwork, Race and the Law." *Boundary* 2 (1992): 70–95.

McLaughlin, Megan. "The Woman Warrior: Gender, Warfare and Society in Medieval Europe." *Women's Studies* 17 (1990): 193–209.

McNamara, Jo Ann, and John Halborg, trans. *The Ordeal of Community.* Toronto: Peregrina, 1993.

Meisami, Julie Scott. "Arabic *Mujun* Poetry: The Literary Dimension." In de Jong, *Verse and the Fair Sex,* 8–30.

Menocal, Maria Rosa. *The Arabic Role in Medieval Literary History: A Forgotten Heritage.* Philadelphia: University of Pennsylvania Press, 1987.

———. *Shards of Love: Exile and the Origins of the Lyric.* Durham, N.C.: Duke University Press, 1994.

Menocal, Maria Rosa, Raymond P. Scheindlin, and Michael Sells, eds. *Cambridge History of Arabic Literature: Al-Andalus.* Cambridge: Cambridge University Press, 2000.

Mernissi, Fatima. *Forgotten Queens of Islam.* Translated by Mary Jo Lakeland. Minneapolis: University of Minnesota Press, 1997.

———. *Scheherazade Goes West: Different Cultures, Different Harems.* New York: Washington Square Press, 2001.

Metlitzki, Dorothee. *The Matter of Araby in Medieval England.* New Haven, Conn.: Yale University Press, 1977.

Miller, Nancy K. *The Heroine's Text: Readings in the French and English Novel.* New York: Columbia University Press, 1980.

Miquel, André. *La Littérature arabe.* Paris: Presses Universitaires de France, 1969.

Mohanty, Chandra. "Under Western Eyes: Feminist Scholarship and Colonial Discourses." *Feminist Review* 30 (Autumn 1988): 61–88.

Muhsin, Jamal al-Din. *Udaba' baghdadiyun fi al-Andalus* [Baghdadi Authors of al-Andalus]. Baghdad: Maktabat al-Nahda, 1962.

Murray, Harold J. R. *A History of Chess.* London: Oxford University Press, 1978.

Murray, Jacqueline. "Twice Marginal and Twice Invisible." In Bullough and Brundage, *The Handbook of Medieval Sexuality*, 191–222.

Murray, Jacqueline, and Konrad Eisenbichler, eds. *Desire and Discipline: Sex and Sexuality in the Premodern West*. Toronto: University of Toronto Press, 1996.

Murray, Stephen O. "Discourse Creationism." *Journal of Sex Research* 32 (1995): 263–65.

———. *Latin American Male Homosexuality*. Albuquerque: University of New Mexico Press, 1995.

———. "Some Nineteenth-Century Reports of Islamic Homosexualities." In Murray and Roscoe, *Islamic Homosexualities*, 204–21.

———. "Woman-Woman Love in Islamic Societies." In Murray and Roscoe, *Islamic Homosexualities*, 97–104.

Murray, Stephen O., and Kent Gerard. "Renaissance Sodomite Subcultures?" In *Among Men, Among Women: Sociological and Historical Recognition of Homosocial Arrangements*, edited by Mattias Duyves et al., 183–96. Amsterdam: Sociologisch Instituut, 1983.

Murray, Stephen O., and Will Roscoe, eds. *Islamic Homosexualities: Culture, History, and Literature*. New York: New York University Press, 1997.

Musallam, Basim. *Sex and Society in Islam: Birth Control Before the Nineteenth Century*. Cambridge: Cambridge University Press, 1983.

Nichols, J. M. "Arabic Women Poets in al-Andalus." *Maghrib Review* 4 (1979): 114–17.

Nicholson, Helen. "Women on the Third Crusade." *Journal of Medieval History* 23, no. 4 (1997): 335–49.

Nykl, A. R. *Hispano-Arabic Poetry and Its Relation with the Old Provençal Troubadours*. Baltimore: J. H. Furst, 1946.

Otis, Leah Lydia. *Prostitution in Medieval Society: The History of an Urban Institution in Languedoc*. Chicago: University of Chicago Press, 1985.

Pastre, Geneviève. *Athènes et le "Péril saphique": Homosexualité féminine en Grèce ancienne*. Paris: Librairie "Les Mots à la bouche," 1987.

Patterson, Lee. "On the Margin: Postmodernism, Ironic History, and Medieval Studies." *Speculum* 65, no. 1 (1990): 87–108.

Payen, Jean-Charles "Structure et sens de *Guillaume de Dole*." In *Etudes de langue et de littérature du Moyen Age offerts à Félix Lecoy*, 483–98. Paris: Champion, 1973.

Payer, Pierre J. *Sex and the Penitentials: The Development of a Sexual Code, 550–1150*. Toronto: University of Toronto Press, 1984.

Peirce, Leslie. *The Imperial Harem: Women and Sovereignty in the Ottoman Empire*. New York: Oxford University Press, 1993.

Pellat, Charles. *Le Milieu basrien et la formation de Yahiz*. Paris: Librairie d'Amérique et d'Orient Adrien-Maisonneuve, 1953.

Penn, Michael Philip. *Kissing Christians: Ritual and Community in the Late Ancient Church*. Philadelphia: University of Pennsylvania Press, 2005.

Perbal, Ingrid. "L'Orient dans les soieries du musée de Cluny." *Qantara* (Fall 2004): 19.

Perret, Michèle. "Travesties et transsexuelles: Yde, Silence, Grisandole, Blanchandine." *Romance Notes* 25, no. 3 (1985): 328–40.

Pinault, David. *Story-Telling Techniques in the Arabian Nights*. Leiden: Brill, 1992.

Pratt, Mary Louise. "Arts of the Contact Zone." *Profession* 91 (1991): 33–40.

Puff, Helmut. "Localizing Sodomy: The 'Priest and Sodomite' in Pre-Reformation Germany and Switzerland." *Journal of the History of Sexuality* 8, no. 2 (1997): 165–95.

Régnier-Bohler, Danielle. "Geste, parole et clôture: Les Représentations du gynécée dans la littérature médiévale du XIIIe au XVe siècle." In *Mélanges . . . Alice Planche*, 393–404. Nice: Belles Lettres, 1984.

Reinink, G. J., and H. L. J. Vanstiphout, eds. *Dispute Poems and Dialogues in the Ancient and Medieval Near East*. Leuven: Departement Orientalistiek, 1991.

Reyerson, Kathryn L. "Commerce and Society in Montpellier, 1250–1350." 2 vols. Ph.D. diss., Yale University, 1974.

———. "Medieval Silks in Montpellier: The Silk Market ca. 1250–ca. 1350." *Journal of European Economic History* 11 (1982): 117–40.

———. "Women in Business in Medieval Montpellier." In *Women and Work in Pre-Industrial Europe*, edited by Barbara A. Hanawalt, 117–44. Bloomington: Indiana University Press, 1986.

Rich, Adrienne. "Compulsory Heterosexuality and Lesbian Existence." *Signs* 5, no. 4 (1980): 631–60.

Rieger, Angelica. "Was Bieiris de Romans Lesbian? Women's Relations with Each Other in the World of the Troubadours." In *The Voice of the Trobairitz: Perspectives on the Women Troubadours*, edited by William D. Paden, 73–94. Philadelphia: University of Pennsylvania Press, 1989.

Ringrose, Kathryn. *The Perfect Servant: Eunuchs and the Social Construction of Gender in Byzantium*. Chicago: University of Chicago Press, 2003.

Robinson, Cynthia. *In Praise of Song: The Making of Courtly Culture in al-Andalus and Provence, 1065–1135 A.D.*. Leiden: Brill, 2002.

Rosen, Tova. *Unveiling Eve: Reading Gender in Medieval Hebrew Literature*. Philadelphia: University of Pennsylvania Press, 2003.

Rosenthal, Franz. "Fiction and Reality: Sources for the Role of Sex in Medieval Muslim Society." In al-Sayyid-Marsot, *Society and the Sexes in Medieval Islam*, 3–22.

———. "Male and Female: Described and Compared." In Wright and Rowson, *Homoeroticism in Classical Arabic Literature*, 24–54.

el-Rouayheb, Khaled. *Before Homosexuality in the Arab-Islamic World, 1500–1800*. Chicago: University of Chicago Press, 2005.

Rouche, Michel. "L'Age des pirates et des saints (Ve–Xie siècles)." In *Histoire de Boulogne-sur-mer*, edited by Alain Lottin, 33–53. Lille: Presses Universitaires de Lille, 1983.

Rowson, Everett. "The Categorization of Gender and Sexual Irregularity in Medieval Arabic Vice Lists." In *Body Guards: The Cultural Politics of Gender Ambiguity*, edited by Julia Epstein and Kristina Straub, 50–79. New York: Routledge, 1991.

———. "The Effeminates of Early Medina." *Journal of the American Oriental Society* 111 (1991): 671–93.

———. "Two Homoerotic Narratives from Mamluk Literature: Al-Safadi's *Law `at al-*

shaki and Ibn Daniyal's *al-Mutayyam*." In Wright and Rowson, *Homoeroticism in Classical Arabic Literature*, 158–91.

Roy, Bruno. *L'Erotisme au Moyen Age*. Quebec: Editions de l'Aurore, 1977.

Ruggiero, Guido. *The Boundaries of Eros: Sex Crime and Sexuality in Renaissance Venice*. Oxford: Oxford University Press, 1985.

Sahlins, Marshall. *Stone Age Economics*. Chicago: Aldine Atherson, 1972.

Said, Edward. "The Clash of Ignorance." *Nation* 273, no. 12 (October 22, 2001): 11–13.

———. *Orientalism*. New York: Pantheon, 1978.

Salisbury, Joyce E. "Bestiality in the Middle Ages." In *Sex in the Middle Ages: A Book of Essays*, edited by Joyce E. Salisbury, 173–86. New York: Garland, 1991.

Sautman, Francesca. "'Des Vessies pour des Lanternes': Villon, Molinet and the Riddles of Folklore." *Neophilologus* 69, no. 2 (1985): 161–84.

———. "What Can They Possibly Do Together? Queer Epic Performances in *Tristan de Nanteuil*." In Sautman and Sheingorn, *Same Sex Love and Desire*, 199–232.

Sautman, Francesca, and Pamela Sheingorn, eds. *Same Sex Love and Desire Among Women in the Middle Ages*. New York: Palgrave, 2001.

Sawa, George Dimitri. *Music Performance and Practice in the Early Abbasid Era*. Toronto: Pontifical Institute of Medieval Studies, 1989.

Sawa, Suzanne Meyers. "The Role of Women in Musical Life: The Medieval Arabo-Islamic Courts." *Canadian Women's Studies: Les Cahiers de la Femme* 8 (1987): 93–95.

al-Sayyid-Marsot, Afaf Lutfi, ed. *Society and the Sexes in Medieval Islam*. Malibu, Calif.: Undena, 1979.

Schibanoff, Susan. "Hildegarde of Bingen and Richardis of Stade: The Discourse of Desire." In Sautman and Sheingorn, *Same Sex Love and Desire*, 49–84.

———. "Mohammed, Courtly Love, and the Myth of Western Homosexuality." *Medieval Feminist Newsletter* 16 (Fall 1993): 27–32.

Schimmel, Annemarie. "Eros—Heavenly and Not So Heavenly—in Sufi Literature and Life." In al-Sayyid-Marsot, *Society and the Sexes in Medieval Islam*, 119–41.

———. *Mystical Dimensions of Islam*. Chapel Hill: University of North Carolina Press, 1975.

Schippers, Arie. "Hebrew Andalusian and Arabic Poetry: Descriptions of Fruit in the Tradition of the 'Elegant' or *Zurafa*." *Journal of Semitic Studies* 33, no. 2 (1988): 219–32.

———. "The Role of Medieval Andalusian Arabic Story-Telling." In de Jong, *Verse and the Fair Sex*, 139–52.

Schippers, Arie, and John Mattock. "Love and War: A Poem of Ibn Khafajah." *Journal of Arabic Literature* 17 (1986): 50–68.

Sedgwick, Eve Kosofsky. *Between Men: English Literature and Male Homosocial Desire*. New York: Columbia University Press, 1985.

———. *Epistemology of the Closet*. Berkeley: University of California Press, 1990.

Shahar, Shulamith. *The Fourth Estate: A History of Women in the Middle Ages*. Translated by Chaya Galai. London: Routledge, 1983.

Shannon, Laurie. *Sovereign Amity: Figures of Friendship in Shakespearean Contexts*. Chicago: University of Chicago Press, 2002.

Shatzmiller, Maya. "Women and Wage Labour in the Medieval Islamic West: Legal Issues in an Economic Context." *Journal of the Economic and Social History of the Orient* 40, no. 2 (1997): 174–206.

Siberry, Elizabeth. *Criticism of Crusading, 1095–1274.* Oxford: Oxford University Press, 1985.

Simons, Walter. "Reading a Saint's Body: Rapture and Bodily Movement in the Vitae of Thirteenth-Century Beguines." In *Framing Medieval Bodies*, edited by Sarah Kay and Miri Rubin, 10–23. Manchester: Manchester University Press, 1994.

Sloan, Sam. "A History of Chess." http://www.samsloan.com/origin.htm.

Sobh, Mahmud. *Poetisas arabigoandaluzas.* Granada: Disputación Provincial, n.d.

Solterer, Helen. "At the Bottom of the Mirage, a Woman's Body: *Le Roman de la Rose* of Jean Renart." In *Feminist Approaches to the Body*, edited by Linda Lomperis and Sarah Stanbury, 213–33. Philadelphia: University of Pennsylvania Press, 1993.

———. "Figures of Female Militancy in Medieval France." *Signs* 16, no. 3 (1991): 522–49.

Southern, R. W. *Western Views of Islam in the Middle Ages.* Cambridge, Mass.: Harvard University Press, 1962.

Spiegel, Gabrielle M. "Maternity and Monstrosity: Reproductive Biology in the *Roman de Mélusine*." In *Mélusine of Lusignan: Founding Fiction in Late Medieval France*, edited by Donald Maddox and Sara Sturm-Maddox, 100–124. Athens: University of Georgia Press, 1996.

Spivak, Gayatri. "Can the Subaltern Speak?" In *Marxism and the Interpretation of Culture*, edited by Cary Nelson and Larry Grossberg, 271–313. Urbana: University of Illinois Press, 1988.

Strayer, Joseph, ed. *Dictionary of the Middle Ages.* New York: Scribner, 1982–89.

Stuard, Susan Mosher. "Single by Law and Custom." In Bennett and Froide, *Singlewomen*, 106–26.

Sudre, L. "Les Allusions à la légende de Tristan dans la littérature du Moyen Age." *Romania* 15 (1886): 534–57.

Szkilnik, Michelle. "The Grammar of the Sexes in Medieval French Romance." In *Gender Transgressions: Crossing the Normative Barrier in Old French Literature*, edited by Karen J. Taylor, 61–88. New York: Garland, 1998.

Thomas, Louis. *Montpellier, ville marchande: Histoire économique et sociale de Montpellier des origines à 1870.* Montpellier: Librairie Vallat, Librairie Coulet, 1936.

Tolan, John. *Petrus Alfonsi and His Medieval Readers.* Gainesville: University of Florida Press, 1993.

———. *Saracens: Islam in the Medieval European Imagination.* New York: Columbia University Press, 2002.

———, ed. *Medieval Christian Perceptions of Islam: A Book of Essays.* New York: Garland, 1996.

Traub, Valerie. *The Renaissance of Lesbianism in Early Modern England.* Cambridge: Cambridge University Press, 2002.

Uebel, Michael. "Re-Orienting Desire: Writing on Gender Trouble in Fourteenth-Century Egypt." In Farmer and Pasternack, *Gender and Difference*, 230–57.

Vadet, Jean-Claude. *L'Esprit courtois en Orient dans les cinq premiers siècles de l'hégire*. Paris: G.-P. Maisonneuve et Larose, 1968.

Vance, Eugene. "Le Combat érotique chez Chrétien de Troyes: De la figure à la forme." *Poétique* 12 (1972): 544–71.

van den Abeele, Baudoin. "L'*Escoufle*: Portrait littéraire d'un oiseau." Special issue, edited by Brian Levy and Paul Wachers, *Reinardus: Yearbook of the International Reynard Society* 1 (1998): 5–15.

van der Meer, Theo. "Tribades on Trial: Female Same-Sex Offenders in Late Eighteenth-Century Amsterdam." *Journal of the History of Sexuality* 1, no. 3 (1991): 424–45.

Vanita, Ruth, and Saleem Kidwai, eds. *Same-Sex Love in India: Readings from Literature and History*. New York: Palgrave, 2000.

Verlinden, Charles. "Le Mariage des esclaves." In *Il matrimonio nella società altro medievale*, 2:569–601. Spoleto: Centro Italiano di Studi sull'Altro Medioevo, 1977.

von Grunebaum, G. E. "Aspects of Arabic Urban Literature Mostly in the Ninth and Tenth Century." *al-Andalus* 20 (1955): 259–81.

Wagner, Ewald. *Abu Nuwas: Eine Studie zur arabischen Literatur der frühen ʿAbbasidenzeit*. Wiesbaden: Franz Steiner Verlag, 1965.

———. *Die Arabische Rangstreitdichtung und ihre Einordnung in die allgemeine Literaturgeshichte*. Abhandlungen der Geistes und Sozialwissenschaftlichen Klasse, Jahrg. 1962, Nr. 8. Mainz: Akademie der Wissenschaften und der Literatur, 1963.

Walther, Wiebke. *Women in Islam*. Princeton, N.J.: Marcus-Weiner, 1993.

Warren, M. F. M. "Notes on the romans d'aventure." *Modern Language Notes* 13 (1898): 339–51.

Wasserstein, David. *The Rise and Fall of the Party-Kings: Politics and Society in Islamic Spain, 1002–1086*. Princeton, N.J.: Princeton University Press, 1985.

Watt, Diane. "Behaving Like a Man? Incest, Lesbian Desire, and Gender Play in *Yde et Olive*." *Comparative Literature* 50, no. 4 (1998): 265–85.

———. "Read My Lips: Clippying and Kyssyng in the Early Sixteenth Century." In *Queerly Phrased: Language, Gender and Sexuality*, edited by Anna Livia and Kira Hall, 167–77. New York: Oxford University Press, 1997.

Weeks, Jeffrey. *Coming Out: Homosexual Politics in Britain from the Nineteenth Century to the Present*. London: Quartet Books, 1977.

Welch, J. L. "Cross-Dressing and Cross-Purposes: Gender Possibilities in the Acts of Thecla." In *Gender Reversals and Gender Cultures: Anthropological and Historical Perspectives*, edited by Sabrina Petra Ramet, 66–78. London: Routledge, 1996.

Westphal-Wihl, Sarah. "The Ladies' Tournament: Marriage, Sex and Honor in Thirteenth-Century Germany." *Signs* 14, no. 2 (1989): 371–98.

Wiethaus, Ulrike. "Female Homoerotic Discourse and Religion in Medieval Germanic Culture." In Farmer and Pasternack, *Gender and Difference*, 288–321.

Winkler, John J. *The Constraints of Desire*. New York: Routledge, 1990.

Wright, J. W., Jr., and Everett K. Rowson, eds. *Homoeroticism in Classical Arabic Literature*. New York: Columbia University Press, 1997.

Zayyat, Habib. "Al-Mar'a al-ghulamiyya fi al-Islam" [The *Ghulamiyya* in Islamicate Culture]. *al-Machriq* 50 (1956): 153–92.

Zink, Michel. *La Prédication en langue romane avant 1300*. Paris: Champion, 1982.

Ziolkowski, Jan, ed. *Obscenity: Social Control and Artistic Creation in the European Middle Ages*. Leiden: Brill, 1998.

INDEX

Abbott, Nabia, 53
Abd al-Rahman II, 151
Abelard, Peter, 1, 167n.1, 168n.3, 169n.11,
    216n.117
Abu al-Faraj al-Isfahani, 24, 146, 147
Abu Nuwas, 26, 52
accollee, 67–68, 102
adab, 23–24, 180n.91
adab al-jins `inda al-`Arab, 26
Adam, William, 14–15
adultery, 21, 113, 142, 216n.117
Alain de Lille, 61
al-Andalus, 12, 22, 94
Albertus Magnus, 168n.3, 169n.11
Aleppo Publishing, 26–27
*Alf layla wa layla. See One Thousand and
    One Nights; The Story of Qamar al-
    Zaman and the Princess Boudour*
al-Jahiz, 24, 29, 146, 156, 212n.71
al-Jurjani, Abu al-Abbas Ahmad b.
    Muhammad, 24, 34–36, 184n.21
al-Kindi, 17, 176n.63
al-Malik al-Salih Ayyub, 149
al-Ma'mun, 150
*al-Muntakhab min kinayat al-udaba' wa
    isharat al-bulagha'. See An Anthology of
    Metonymic Devices Used by the Literati and
    Allusions in Eloquent Speech (al-Jurjani)*
al-Nadim, Abu al-Faraj, 19, 177n.67
al-Qurti, 53
al-Raghib al-Isfahani, Abu al-Qasim al-
    Husayn Ibn Muhammad, 24
al-shudhudh al-jinsi, 20
al-Suyuti, Jalal al-Din, 111
alternative sexualities, Arabic tolerance of, 22
al-Tifashi, Ahmad Ibn Yusuf: *The Delight of
    Hearts,* 19, 24, 27, 36–37, 44–48, 151,
    176n.66; and Etienne's use of *eu,* 40; *The*

*Return of the Sheikh to His Youth Through
    Vigor and Coition,* 111
al-Zarqa'. *See* Hind Bint al-Khuss al-
    Iyadiyyah
ambiguity in homoerotic writings, 186n.44
Ambrose, Saint, 168n.3
Amer, Ghada, 181n.100
amie, 116, 118
amor de lonh, 117
De amore. See The Art of Courtly Love
Anastasius, bishop of Antioch, 1
ancele, 99–101, 201n.32
Andreas Capellanus, 57, 146
animal spouses, 172n.38
Anselm, Saint, 168n.3
*An Anthology of Metonymic Devices Used by
    the Literati and Allusions in Eloquent
    Speech* (al-Jurjani), 24, 34–36
Antioch, 12
Apparel of Women (Tertullian), 130
Aquinas, Saint Thomas, 168n.3, 169n.11
*Arabian Nights. See One Thousand and One
    Nights*
Arabic, as language of the obscene, 47, 112
Arabic Book Press, 26
Arabic erotic literature, 177n.67; accessing,
    25–27; current suppression of, 25–26;
    explicitness in, 44; first lesbian couple in,
    18; influence of, 14; literary history of,
    23–25; military metaphors in, 35–37;
    multiple genres in, 35; patrons' respect for,
    48; positive valuation of eroticism in, 21
Arabic literature: and cross-cultural exchanges,
    13–14; erotic (*see* Arabic erotic literature);
    female cross-dressers in, 51–52; folk
    romances, 52, 189n.8; *ghulamiyyat*
    tradition in, 188n.7; intertextuality of Old
    French writing and, 162; lesbianism

Arabic literature (*cont.*)
in, 18–21; name "Moon" in, 74; romances,
52, 189n.8; translations of, 181n.103;
transmission of, 162–164. *See also specific
writings*
Arabic sciences, 12, 174n.48
Arab Islamicate world: and Aelis' social
standing, 143–144; cross-dressed women
in, 188n.6, 188n.7 (see also *ghulamiyyat*);
harems, 154–160; homosexual refinement
in, 151–152; interaction with Western
Europe, 11–14; medieval France's ties
with, 93; modes of resistance in, 165;
qaynas, 146–150; reading through
sociocultural traditions, 152–160; respect
for writings on alternative sexuality, 48;
role of women in, 210n.63; same-sex
desire among women in, 16–23; slave girls
vs. freeborn women in, 210n.64; slave-
singers in, 146–150; *zarf*, 144–146, 150–152
Arethas, 7
`Arib, 146, 147, 212n.79
Aristotle, 2
The Art of Courtly Love (Andreas
Capellanus), 57
associations of lesbians, 19
atache, 110–111
Augustine, Saint, 88, 96, 117
aumosniere, 89, 93–95, 106
autel, 113–115
al-Washsha', 144–145

baisie, 67–68, 102, 118–119
Bakhtin, Mikhail, 42, 167n.2, 186n.39
barbers, 131–132
battle metaphors, 68–69
Baumgartner, Emmanuèle, 125, 134
bed. See *lis, couche*
belletristic tradition, 23–24. See also *adab*
Bencheikh, Jamal Eddine, 150
Bennett, Judith M., 8–9, 127
Bernard de Clairvaux, 117
Bhabha, Homi, 29, 161
bidal, 20
Bieris de Romans, 10–11
bigha', 35
bisexuality, lack of Arabic word for, 20
Boasting Match over Maids and Youths (al-
Jahiz), 24
Book of Gomorrah (Peter Damian), 2

Book of Refinement and of Refined People
(al-Washsha'), 144–145
Book of Songs (al-Isfahani), 24, 146–147
Book of the Flower (Ibn Da'ud), 57
Book on Lesbians (al-Saymari), 177n.67
bougrerie, 70
Brooten, Bernadette J., 171n.29
Brown, Judith, 3, 7
Burger, Glenn, 182n.104
Burns, Jane, 93
Burton, Sir Richard, 15
businesses: embroidery, 125–128; hairwashing,
131–132, 153–154; and prostitution,
128–137; social independence and, 125–128
Butler, Judith, 50, 83–84

çainturiere, 114, 115, 134
capital punishment. *See* death penalty
caressing, 79, 201n.40. *See also* touching
Castle, Terry, 121, 141
castration, 216n.117
The Catalog (al-Nadim), 19, 177n.67
censorship, 26–27, 49, 68
chansons de toile, 114, 134
Chauncey, George, Jr., 170n.20
chess, 152–153, 214n.103
Chrétien de Troyes, 59, 124, 143
Christians: seductive power of homosexuality
over, 15; sexuality of Muslims vs., 169n.16
Chrysostom, Saint John, 168n.3
church literature on marriage, 203n.51;
subversion of this literature, 61, 62, 100
clandestine prostitution, 137
Clark, Robert L. A., 31, 47, 66, 183n.8
clash of civilizations, 12, 173n.46
Cligès (Chrétien de Troyes), 126, 213n.90
clothing: to conceal social nakedness, 137; as
marker of social class, 123–124; and
prostitution, 130–131. *See also* cross-
dressing
conquiert, 102–103
consciousness, identity vs., 171n.26
Constable, Olivia Remie, 94
constructionism, 170n.18
contact zone, 4, 41–43, 170n.17
couche, 109
courtliness. See *zarf*
courtly love: in *Escoufle*, 102; heterosexual
model of, 59; joining of hands in,
204n.65; and lesbian ghosting, 141; and
mal-mariée in *Escoufle*, 113; as model for

homosexual desire, 61; and sewing,
    203n.58; in Yde and Olive stories, 57–59
Courtly Love Undressed (Burns), 93
Croissant, 70; as name and Arabic
    intertextuality, 74
cross-cultural interactions/exchanges, 11–14,
    93
cross-cultural research, 27–28; ethics of,
    165–166; implications of, 164–165; value
    of, 3–4
cross-dressing, 50–61; absence of, in *Escoufle,*
    124; as agent of destabilization and
    change, 71; among Saracens, 14–15;
    church's toleration of, 194n.67; evidence
    of, 187n.3; and female homoeroticism,
    56–61; and female same-sex marriage,
    189n.9; in French romances and plays,
    173n.41; and intertextuality of Yde/Olive
    and *Story of Qamar al-Zaman,* 73–74, 77;
    and medieval gender categories, 10; as
    narrative strategy, 77; and questioning of
    gender roles, 98; reasons for, 179n.83; and
    same-sex marriage between women,
    52–54; and second-degree homosexuality,
    51–52; "social," 124; in *Story of Qamar al-
    Zaman,* 73, 77; as textual strategy in
    fabliaux, 188n.4; in Yde and Olive stories,
    54–56. See *ghulamiyyat*
Crusades, 12, 90, 187n.3
cultural traditions, Arabic influences on, 13,
    152–160
cultural transmission, fragmentation of,
    162–164

dakhala, 78, 84
Dale, Marian K., 127
death penalty (capital punishment): for
    bougrerie, 70; for lesbians, 2, 70, 168n.7,
    194n.70
deduit, 103–104, 134, 135, 138–141
*The Delight of Hearts Or, What One Cannot
    Find in Any Book* (al-Tifashi), 24;
    censorship of, 27; differences between
    Livre des manières and, 43–48; on
    homosexual refinement, 151; military
    metaphors in, 36–37; versions of, 176n.66
delit, 103, 133
desmenbré, 159, 160
devotional texts, 10
Dhat al-Himma, 52
Diller, G., 97

Dinshaw, Carolyn, 50
Disciplina Clericalis (Petrus Alfonsi), 53
droiture, 99, 100

Edwardes, Allen, 177n.68
embroidery, 93, 94, 145, 205n.11; as
    empowering women, 205n.12; and
    sexuality, 207n.22
embroidery business, 125–128; condemnation
    of, 126; financial prosperity from, 127;
    and prostitution, 128–131, 207n.20
Encyclopedia of Pleasure (Ibn Nasr al-Katib),
    24, 176n.63; Arabic edition of, 26;
    intertextuality of *Livre des manières* and,
    34, 36, 38–39; *kissing* defined in, 79–80;
    on male homosexuality, 19; name of first
    lesbian, 75; story of first lesbian couple,
    18–19
The Encyclopedia of Pleasure (sculpture),
    181n.100
England, 30
en liu de, 108–109
Epistle on Singing-Girls (al-Jahiz), 146
Erec et Enide (Chrétien de Troyes), 124
eroticism. See Arabic erotic literature;
    homoeroticism
The Erotic Writings of the Arabs series, 26
errors, scribal, 185n.33
escoer, 38
Escoufle (Jean Renart), 88–144; adaptation of
    Arab tales in, 163; Aelis and Countess of
    Saint-Gilles in, 112–120; Aelis and Saint-
    Gilles household in, 137–143; Aelis's
    friendship with Lady of Montpellier in,
    104–112; Aelis's friendship with Ysabel in,
    95–104; Arabic intertextuality of, 143–144,
    152–160; crusader ideology supported by,
    215n.107; and harems, 154–160;
    intertextuality of *Story of Qamar al-
    Zaman* and, 91–92; Montpellier business
    in, 124–128; parallels between Arabic and
    French dwellings, 152–154; prostitution
    in, 128–137; role of silk in, 92–95; social
    identity in, 121–144
estate literature (France), 30, 31, 41, 42, 182n.1
L'Estoire de Merlin, 51
estraint, 102–103
états du monde. See estate literature (France)
ethics of cross-cultural research, 165–166
Etienne Boileau, 132
Etienne de Bourbon, 130

Etienne de Fougères: ambiguous metaphors of, 186n.44; *Livre des manières,* 29–49
eu, 39–41
euphemisms, Arabic, 35
European sciences, influence of Arabic sciences on, 12

fabliaux, 51, 128, 188n.4
Fadl, 146–147
Farmer, Sharon, 128–129
female couples, archaeological figuration of, 6
female empowerment, 75–76
female friendships, 96, 98, 103, 108 202n.48, 203n.50. *See also* friendship
female homoeroticism: cross-dressing and expression of, 56–61; incest and, 195n.81; and religious expression, 61–64, 192n.48; and spirituality, 192n.50
female homosexuality, terms for. *See* terminology for lesbianism
female mystics, 10, 172n.40
female same-sex sexuality activity. *See* lesbian sexual intimacy
feme, 129–130
feminizing Christ's body, 10
feminocentric, 97, 198n.6
Fihrist. See The Catalog
Floire et Blancheflor, 15–16, 155
Floris et Lyriopé (Robert de Blois), 204n.66
Forgotten Queens of Islam (Mernissi), 150
Foucault, Michel, 4–5, 20, 171n.26
fourmie, 58
Frederick II, 12
French law code, 168n.7
French literature. *See* Old French literature
French romances, 209n.56. *See also specific writings*
fricatrices, 7
friendship: equality of partners in, 202n.48; in *Escoufle,* 103, 108–110, 112; female, 202n.48, 203n.50; gifts as tokens of, 105–107; joining hands as indicator of, 118; lesbianism under guise of, 92, 95–101, 104–105, 108, 116–118, 120
fruit metaphors, 138–139, 156–157
funduks (fondoco), 12, 173n.47

Galen, 17, 176n.63
Galeran de Bretagne (Renaut), 125, 126, 202n.44, 205n.11, 207n.29, 208n.35

Garber, Marjorie, 55, 75
Gay Sunshine Press, 27
gender: association with body vs. spirit, 117, 204n.64; linked to social status, 65, 66; medical view of, 70; presumed preference for masculinity, 71
gender identity, social identity vs., 122
gender roles: questioning of, 51, 98; in *Story of Qamar al-Zaman,* 82–83; in Yde and Olive stories, 55, 60–61
genitalizing Christ's wound, 10
Germain Colladon, 2
ghayriyyah, 20
ghosting, lesbian, 141, 209n.54
ghulamiyyat, 22, 52, 152, 179n.83, 188n.6, 188n.7, 212n.80. *See also* cross-dressing
gift exchange: circulation of gifts, 107–108, 110; lesbianism and, 106–112; medieval functions of, 105; and model of feudal relations, 107; as token of friendship, 105–107
Gilles d'Orléans, 130
gold embroidery, 94, 144
grammatical gender instability, 57, 60–61, 62, 194n.67. *See also* linguistic (grammatical) confusion
Gravdal, Kathryn, 119
Gregory Lopez, 2
Guibert de Tournai, 130
Guilhem VIII, 132
Guthrie, Jeri, 47

haba'ib, 20
hagiographic literature, 51
hairwashing business, 131–132, 153–154
hall al-izaar, 111
Halperin, David, 4–5
Hamduna, 151
Hamza al-Bahlawan, 52
Hanafi school (Islam), 178n.82
harems, 154–160, 213n.87; Eurocentric representations of, 213n.87; lesbianism and culture of, 197n.107; Western assumption of homosexuality in, 16
harem (term), 155–156
Henry II Plantagenêt, 30, 42
Hereford, Countess of, 31
Hereford Cathedral, 30, 31
Herman, Gerald, 172n.38
heteronormativity: in *Escoufle,* 90, 92, 158,

159; in *Story of Qamar al-Zaman,* 92; in
    Yde and Olive stories, 69–72
heterosexuality: 97, 102; Arabic term for, 20;
    constraints of, 126; conventional
    paradigms of, 51, 59; *Escoufle* same-sex
    bonds modeled on, 102–103, 108, 119;
    homosexuality within, 84–86; and lesbian
    ghosting, 141; presumed in marital
    unions, 60
heterosexual violence, 119
Hincmar of Reims, 169n.11
Hind Bint al-Khuss al-Iyadiyyah (al-Zarqa'),
    18; parallel with Yde, 75
Hind Bint al-Nu`man, 18
History of Sexuality (Foucault), 4–5, 20
Hodgson, Marshall G. S., 173n.44
homes, Arabic and French, 152–153
homoeroticism: Arabic narratives of, 25; in
    Arabic poetry, 23–25, 52; cross-dressing
    and expression of, 56–61; incest and,
    195n.81; name "Moon" designating, 74;
    and female mystics, 10, 172n.40
homosexuality: Arabic conventions on, 35;
    Arabic terms for, 20, 35; in Arabic
    tradition, 174n.62; in Arabic writings, 48;
    association of Islam and, 14–16; and
    distinction between desire and acts, 5;
    within heterosexuality, 84–86; Islam and
    punishments for, 178n.82; legal Islamic
    view of, 21; as major sin in Islam,
    178n.82; medical view of, 2–3; in Muslim
    societies, 22; origin in Arab world,
    177n.68; positive Arabic valuation of, 21;
    refinement of, 151–152; religious views of,
    2; scientific view of, 2–3; Western ideas
    about, 20. *See also* lesbianism; male
    homosexuality, terminology for
    homosexuality, terminology for
    lesbianism
horizontal reading, 167n.2
Hrostvit of Gandersheim, 14
Hubsiyya, 150
Hue d'Oisy, 35
hugging, 67, 68, 102
hulaq, 20
humanism, 166
Humbert de Romans, 130
Huntington, Samuel, 173n.46
*Huon de Bordeaux (La Chanson d'Yde et
    Olive),* 52–53. *See also* Yde and Olive
    stories

hybrid textuality, x, 4, 29, 31, 42, 43, 48, 91,
    92, 94, 111, 112, 122, 144, 160, 161, 163,
    216n.3

Iberian peninsula, 12
Ibn al-Washsha', Mohammed, 145
Ibn Da'ud al-Isfahani, 57
Ibn Falita, Ahmad Ibn Mohammad, 21, 24,
    25, 40
Ibn Hazm, 57
Ibn Kamal Pasha, 111
Ibn Maawayh, Yuhanna (John Mesué), 17
Ibn Nasr al-Katib, Abul Hasan Ali, 18–19, 24,
    34, 36, 38–39, 75, 79–80, 176n.63
Ibn Zaydun, 150
identity: distinction between consciousness
    and, 171n.26; gender vs. social, 122;
    sexual, 6, 55; social (*see* social identity)
ijara, 35
`Inan, 146
incest, female homoeroticism and, 195n.81
*An Intelligent Man's Guide to the Art of
    Coition* (Ibn Falita), 21, 24, 25, 40
intercultural connections, 93, 122, 124, 140,
    143–144, 152–156, 160
intertextuality: 167n.2; of Arabic and Old
    French literature, 161–162; of *Escoufle* and
    Arabic literature, 111–112, 143–144,
    152–160; linguistic (*see* linguistic
    intertextuality); of *Livre des manières,*
    34–41; multiple manifestations of,
    163–164; of *Story of Qamar al-Zaman* and
    Escoufle, 91–92; of Yde and Olive stories,
    72–86
intimacy between women, 110, 113. *See also*
    lesbian sexual intimacy
Iphis and Ianthe (Ovid): intertextuality with
    Yde and Olive stories, 53, 189n.13, 194n.74
Iran, 94
Islam: adultery in, 21; association of
    homosexuality and, 14–16; description of
    Paradise in, 178n.78; erotic expression
    in writings of, 192n.50; positive view of
    sexuality in, 21; as religion that
    promotes sodomy, 174n.54; social
    and cultural influences of (*see* Arab
    Islamicate world); and transvestites,
    51
Islamicate, 173n.44. *See also* Arab Islamicate
    world
Italy, 94

Jacques de Vitry, 130, 142
Jarkas, Adnan, 26
Jawami` al-ladhdha. See Encyclopedia of
    Pleasure
jawari, 146
Jean de Meun, 115
Jean Gerson, 1
Jean Renart: Escoufle, 88–120, 163; Romance
    of the Rose or of Guillaume de Dole, 116,
    126, 204n.62, 205n.12, 207n.22
Jerome, Saint, 117
jesir, 96, 99, 100
The Jewel in the Lotus (Edwardes), 177n.73
jild, 35
jins, 20
Joan of Arc, 187n.3
John Mesué, 17
joiaus, 128
joie, 58
joining hands, 118, 204n.65
joust metaphor, 35, 36

Karras, Ruth Mazo, 135–137, 142–143
Kennedy, Ruth, 42
Khawwam, Salah Addin, 26
Kinoshita, Sharon, 155
kissing, 201n.40; erotic connotations of,
    204n.66; in Escoufle, 102, 118–120; and
    heterosexual violence, 119; and
    intertextuality of Yde/Olive and Story of
    Qamar al-Zaman, 79–80; as defined in
    Encyclopedia of Pleasure, 79–80; as key
    signifier of lesbian sexuality, 68; in Yde
    and Olive story, 67, 68
Kitab al-aghani. See Book of Songs
Kitab al-muwashsha'. See Book of Refinement
    and of Refined People
Kitab al-sahaqat. See Book on Lesbians
Kitab al-zahra. See Book of the Flower
Kitab al-zarf wa al-zurafa'. See Book of
    Refinement and of Refined People
Kitab moufakharati al-jawari wa al-ghilman.
    See Boasting Match over Maids and Youths
kite, 88, 90, 197n.2, 198n.7, 205n.8. See also
    Escoufle
Klosowska, Anna, 5
Kowaleski, Maryanne, 127
Kristeva, Julia, 167n.2
Krueger, Roberta, 91, 122, 126, 204n.66
Kruger, Steven, 169n.16, 182n.104
kutub al-bah, 23–24, 177n.67. See also mujun

Lacey, Edward A., 27
lait (lei), 31, 115, 203n.59
lance, 35, 36
Lancelot (Chrétien de Troyes), 59, 200n.21
Langlois, Charles-Victor, 33–34
largesse, 110–111
Latin, 47
Latin Kingdoms of the East, founding
    of, 12
law codes: and aberrant sexuality, 99; and
    homosexuality, 21; and lesbianism, 2, 70,
    99, 168n.7; and marriage, 96; Spanish, 2
Lectures by the Literati and Conversations in
    Poetry and Eloquent Speech (al-Raghib al-
    Isfahani), 24
Leo Africanus, 19
lesbian continuum, 8
lesbian ghosting, 141, 209n.54
lesbianism: anachronistic views of, 5; Arabic
    terms for, 16–18; associations of, 19;
    author's use of term lesbian, 9; cross-
    cultural approach to, 27–28; death
    penalty for, 2, 70, 168n.7, 194n.70;
    definitional fluidity of, 5; in early
    Christianity, 171n.29; early terms for, 66;
    European attitudes toward, 168n.7; of
    female mystics, 172n.40; in female
    mystics' writings, 10; first Arab lesbian
    couple, 18–19, 75; ghosting, 141, 209n.54;
    in Greek period, 171n.29; under guise of
    friendship, 104; and harem culture,
    177n.73, 197n.107; and history of
    women's struggles for independence,
    171n.35; as inborn state, 17; Islamic
    penalties for, 178n.82; lack of commonly
    accepted terms for, 116; legal views of, 2,
    70, 99; lesbian-like, 8–9, 17; medical
    views of, 2–3, 17–18, 38–39, 176n.66,
    182n.6; and medieval cultural interaction,
    11; in medieval Islamicate world, 16–23;
    medieval scholarly neglect of, 1–5;
    positive Arabic valuation of, 21;
    punishment, 21, 178n.81; and
    prostitution, 128–137, 206n.20;
    scholarship on, 10–11; scientific view of,
    2–3; silence about, 1–2; as "the silent sin,"
    2; terms for female homosexuality, 6–7;
    theological views of, 1, 96–97, 100, 162;
    as transgression of social lines, 124; use of
    term, 6–7, 9, 171n.31; in writings of

mystics, 172n.40. *See* terminology for lesbianism

lesbian sexual intimacy: in *Escoufle*, 101–103; and intertextuality of Yde/Olive and *Story of Qamar al-Zaman*, 80–86; in *Story of Qamar al-Zaman*, 79–80; in Yde and Olive stories, 67–68

linguistic (grammatical) confusion: due to lack of commonly accepted terms, 116; in *Escoufle*, 96; in *One Thousand and One Nights*, 74; in Yde and Olive stories, 57–58. *See also* grammatical gender instability

linguistic intertextuality, 162; in *Escoufle*, 111–112; of *Livre des manières* and Arabic literature, 37–41; of *Story of Qamar al-Zaman* and Yde/Olive stories, 80

linguistic transformation, in Yde and Olive stories, 56

lis, 96, 109

literary salons, 133–134, 144

literary traditions, Arabic influences on, 13

literary transmission, fragmentation of, 162–164

Livre des manières (Etienne de Fougères), 29–49; Arabic intertexts for, 34–37; example of contact zone between cultures, 41–43; cross-cultural differences between *The Delight of Hearts* and, 43–48; linguistic resonance with Arabic eroticism, 37–41; military metaphors in, 33–34, 36–37; stanzas depicting lesbian in, 31–33

Livre des métiers (Etienne Boileau), 132

liwat, 20, 21, 35, 178n.81. *See also* male homosexuality

Lochrie, Karma, 2, 5

Lodge, Anthony, 34, 183n.12, 186n.40

love poetry and correspondence, 10–11

luti, 20

luxury trade, 126–127

ma'bun, 20

MacKinnon, Catharine, 1

majlis, 148

Makhul, 177n.67

male homosexuality: in European Middle Ages, 169n.13; medical view of, 2; refinement of, 151–152; religious views of, 2; research on, 175n.62; scientific view of, 2; Western Christian view of, 15. *See also liwat*; terminology for homosexuality

Maliki school (Islam), 178n.82

mal-mariée, 113

Mamluk period, 22

Mardrus, 86, 196n.99

Marie de Champagne, 146

Marie de France, 30, 113

marriage: church literature on companionship in, 203n.51; church-sanctioned model of, 61; in *Escoufle*, 90, 113, 142, 156–158; evolution in status of, 192n.46; gendered expectations of, 95; in laws of Walter of Mortagne, 201n.36; legal age of, 96; presumed heterosexuality of, 60; right of slaves to, 100–101; in *Story of Qamar al-Zaman*, 83–86; between women (*see* same-sex marriage between women)

masculinity, presumed preference for, 71

Maurice de Sully, 130

medieval France: developing urban milieus of, 162; same-sex desire among women in, 9–11

Meecham-Jones, Simon, 42

Meixner, Gabriele, 6

men, as spirit, 117, 204n.64

menbré, 117, 159–160

menestrel, 136

meretrix, 136

Mernissi, Fatima, 148, 150

meschine, 201n.32

metaphors, 184n.22, 184n.23; ambiguous, 46; battle, 68–69; erotic, 35; of Etienne de Fougères, 186n.44; fruit, 156–157; military, 33–36; of unfastened robe, 111. *See* terminology for homosexuality; terminology for lesbianism

military metaphors, 33–36. *See also escoer*; *eu*; *lance*; *shields*; *spear*; *sword metaphor*; *thigh-fencing*; *trutennes*; *war metaphor*

Miracle de la fille d'un roy, 52–53, 62, 64, 81. *See also* Yde and Olive stories

miracle plays, cross-dressing in, 51. *See also* Yde and Olive stories

Les Miracles de Nostre Dame par personnages, 189n.11

mithliyyah, 20

Mohanty, Chandra, 164, 216n.1

monstrous spouses, 172n.38

"Moon" (as name), 74

mubadala, 20
Muhadarat al-udaba' wa-muhawarat al-shu'ara' wa-al-bulagha'. See *Lectures by the Literati and Conversations in Poetry and Eloquent Speech*
Muhammad, Prophet, 14
mujun, 23, 24, 144
mukhannath, 20
Murray, Jacqueline, 3, 183n.12
Murray, Stephen, 170n.20
musahaqat al-nisa', 17
musahiqat, 37
Muslims: *See* Arab Islamicate world; Islam
mutazarrifat, 20, 145, 146, 152, 154
muwasshahat, 173n.50
mystics: ambiguity in writings of, 186n.44; female, 10; lesbianism in writings of, 172n.40

naming, 195n.84; of first Arabic lesbian couples, 18–19; and intertextuality of Yde/Olive and *Story of Qamar al-Zaman,* 74–76; of same-sex desire in Middle Ages, 5–6; of same-sex love between women, 69–70, 113–116. *See* terminology for homosexuality; terminology for lesbianism
Natura (Alain de Lille), 61
nisa' mutarajjilat, 20
Nuzhat al-albab fima la yujad fi kitab. See *The Delight of Hearts Or, What One Cannot Find in Any Book*

obscenity, 47, 187n.48, 187n.49
Old French language, 62
Old French literature: Arabic intertextual resonances in, 7–8, 162; cross-cultural influences on, 13–14, 143–144, 152–156; cross-cultural reading of, 11; cross-dressing and same-sex marriage in, 52–53; cross-dressing as "second-degree" homosexuality in, 50, 51; depiction of harems in, 155, 156; Etienne's accounts of lesbianism, 29–30; exclusion of lesbians in, 47; linguistic detours in, 99; military metaphors in, 35–36; multicultural context for, 161; and polyglossia, 41–43; sign system of alternative sexualities in, 7. *See also specific writings*
"Olive," as name and motif, 74–75

One Thousand and One Nights (Arabian Nights): early written versions of, 53; French adaptation of tales from, 163; function of Scheherazade in, 75, 76; intertextuality of *Escoufle* and, 98; lower levels of society in, 25; name of "Moon" in, 74; oral transmission of stories, 53–54; *The Story of Qamar al-Zaman and the Princess Boudour,* 53, 73–86; storytelling and sexual pleasure linked in, 214n.104; tale of Nour, 156; women warriors and Amazons in, 52
orgasm, methods of speeding, 80
Orient, transmission of stories to Europe from, 13, 30, 53–54
Orientalism, 25–27
ouvraigne, 128
Ovid, 189n.13, 194n.74

Paul, Saint, 168n.3
pear, as sinful, 138–139, 156. *See also* fruit metaphors
penis: metaphor for, 36; Yde's miraculous receipt of, 70–71
per, 108–109
Perret, Michèle, 50, 52
Peter Damian, 2
Petrus Alfonsi, 30–31, 53
Pierre Gentien, 35
Pinault, David, 196n.96
plaire, 134–135
Plato, 6
plurilingualism, 42, 112
poetry: Arabic, homoeroticism in, 23–25, 52; love, 10–11
polygamy, 85–86, 108, 157
polyglossia, 41–43, 186n.39
Pratt, Mary Louise, 170n.17
La Prise d'Orange, 155
prostitution: and Aelis's businesses, 128–137; ambiguous attitude toward, 208n.43; clandestine, 137; and clothing (embroidery), 128–131; criteria for definitions of, 209n.47; and hairwashing business, 131–132; lesbianism and, 206n.20; and literary salon, 133–134; single women and, 209n.45
Les Prouesses et faicts du trespreux noble et vaillant Huon de Bordeaux, pair de France et Duc de Guyenne, 52–53. *See also* Yde and Olive stories

pucele, 99, 100, 104, 115, 116, 130, 138
punishments, 21, 178n.81; for adultery and
    illegitimate sexual encounters, 21, 178n.81,
    216n.117; castration, 216n.117. *See also*
    death penalty
putains, 56, 191n.33

Qamar, 150
qatim, 20
qaynas, 146–150, 152, 154
Qissat Firuz Shah, 52
Queering the Middle Ages (Burger and
    Kruger), 182n.104
queer studies: developments in queer theory,
    9–10; distinction between desire and acts
    in, 5; of Old French texts, 11
Qur'an: description of Paradise in, 14, 21;
    zina in, 21

Rangstreit, 180n.96. *See also wasf* tradition
readings of literature: cross-cultural, 11, 161;
    and developments in queer theory, 9–10;
    Escoufle, 90–91, 97, 104; French, through
    Arab sociocultural traditions, 152–160;
    heteronormativity in, 5; horizontal vs.
    vertical, 167n.2; and position in contact
    zone, 43; queer, 11
realistic romances, 91, 198n.6
redactor (use of term), 196n.96
Régnier-Bohler, Danielle, 142
religious sentiments, expression of female
    homoeroticism in, 61–64
residences, Arabic and French, 152–153
*The Return of the Sheikh to His Youth
    Through Vigor and Coition* (al-Tifashi or
    al-Suyuti), 111
Reyerson, Kathryn, 94
Rich, Adrienne, 8
rijal mu' annathin, 20
The Ring of the Dove (Ibn Hazm), 57
Risalat al-qiyan. See *Epistle on Singing-Girls*
Robert de Blois, 204n.66
Roger II, 12
Romance of `Antar, 52
Romance of the Rose (Jean de Meun), 115
Romance of the Rose or of Guillaume de Dole
    (Jean Renart), 116–117, 126, 205n.12
romances: Arabic, 189n.8; folk, 189n.8;
    French romances, 209n.56; realistic, 91,
    198n.6. *See also specific writings*
Roman de la poire (Tibaut), 139

Roman de Silence (Heldris de Cornuälle), 51,
    96
Rosenthal, Franz, 178n.78
Rowson, Everett, 21, 35, 179n.88
rubbing, 17, 19, 36–39, 45–46
*Ruju` al-Shaykh ila sibahi fi al-quwati `ala
    al-bahi*. See *The Return of the Sheikh to
    His Youth Through Vigor and Coition*
Rushd al-labib ila mu`asharat al-habib. See *An
    Intelligent Man's Guide to the Art of Coition*

sacrifice, 75
"saffron massage," 45
sagement, 104
sahhaqat, 37. See also *sahq*; *sahiqa*; *sihaq*
sahiqa, 16–17, 18, 20, 37. See also *sahq*;
    sahhaqat; *sihaq*
sahq, 16–18, 20, 21, 35, 37, 66, 179n.82. See
    also *sihaq*; *musahaqat al-nisa'*; *musahiqat*
saints, transvestite, 188n.4. *See also individual
    saints*
same-sex desire/sexual practices among
    women. *See* lesbianism
same-sex marriage between women: and
    cross-dressing, 52–54, 189n.9; models of,
    60–61; religious sentiments related to,
    62–63; wedding night, 64–69, 78–80
Saracens, 14–15
Sautman, Francesca, 6, 74, 75
Sawa, George Dimitri, 148
Scheherazade, 75–76, 154, 196n.93
science, 12, 173n.48
"second-degree" homosexuality, 50–52
self-help books on sexual topics, 181n.99
sewing, association of loving and, 203n.58.
    See also *chansons de toile*; embroidery
sexual identity, 6, 55
sexuality: aberrant, legal definitions of, 99;
    alternate, Arabic tolerance for, 22; Arabic
    euphemisms for, 35; in Arabic writings, 48;
    association of tales with, 208n.40;
    bisexuality, 20; of Christians vs. Muslims,
    169n.16; embroidery and, 207n.22; at heart
    of Arabic religious piety, 21; medieval
    French sign system of, 7; in Qur'an,
    178n.78; recognition of lesbianism as, 97;
    religious views of, 2; transsexuality, 70. *See
    also* heterosexuality; homosexuality
sexual knowledge, female empowerment
    through, 75–76
sexual minorities, 42

Shafi`i school (Islam), 178n.81

Shahar, Shulamith, 129

Shajarrat al-Durr, 149–150

Sheingorn, Pamela, 6

shields, 35–37

Sicily, 12, 30

sight, 193n.52

sihaq, 17. See also *sahq; sahiqa; sahhaqat; musahaqat al-nisa'; musahiqat*

Sihaq al nisa' zinan baynahunna (Makhul), 177n.67

silent sin, 2, 7

silk, 92–95, 125; silk purse (see *aumosniere*)

"sinful woman," 137

singing slave-girls. See *qaynas*

single women, 121, 126, 128, 136–137, 142–143; prostitution and, 137, 209n.45. *See also* lesbianism, lesbian-like

Sirat Sayf ben Dhi Yazan, 52

social class: among prostitutes, 129; clothing as marker of, 123–124; and kissing, 119; in Yde and Olive stories, 55–56

social-constructionist view, 97

social disruption, 162; in *Escoufle,* 99–101, 122–124, 130–131, 139–142, 158–159; in Yde and Olive stories, 55–56

social identity: and Aelis's business, 124–128; gender identity vs., 122; and prostitution, 128–137; and Saint-Gilles household, 137–144; and sociocultural geographies, 122–124; and *zarf* practice, 144–151

social minorities, 42

social status: and cross-dressing, 77; gender linked to, 65, 66; and relationships in *Escoufle,* 99–101

sociocultural geographies, 122–124

sociocultural traditions, Arab, 152–160; harems, 154–160; homes, 152–153

sodomy: *bougrerie* as, 70; invention of category, 2, 169n.10; and Islam, 14; women in consideration of, 169n.11

Sotadic Zone, 15, 174n.60

soulas, 103, 135, 139

Spain: homoerotic literature in, 22; Islamic caliphate in, 12; *zarf* in, 150–151. *See also* Wallada

spear, 36

spirit, gender association with, 117, 204n.64

Sponsler, Claire, 66

srutennes, 185n.33

The Story of Qamar al-Zaman and the

Princess Boudour, 73–86; cross-dressing in, 73, 77; female empowerment through sexual knowledge in, 75–76; French adaptation of, 53, 76, 79–80, 87, 163; and homosexuality within heterosexuality, 84–86; intertextuality of *Escoufle* and, 91–92; lesbian sexual intimacy in, 80–84; naming similarities with Yde and Olive, 74–76; open depiction of lesbianism in, 82–86, 98; polygamy in, 157; thematic echoes of Yde and Olive and, 73–74; transmission of, 53; versions of, 197n.106; wedding night in, 78–80

storytelling, 76, 133–134, 154, 214n.104

Stuard, Susan Mosher, 99

Sulayman, Ahmad b., 111

Sunnah, 21

Superiority of the Belly to the Back (al-Jahiz), 24

sword metaphor, 35, 36

Symposium (Plato), 6

Szkilnik, Michelle, 72

ta`awwad-tu, 85, 86

tadahaku, 82

Tafdil al-batn `ala al-zahr. See *Superiority of the Belly to the Back*

tafkhidh, 20, 35

Tauq al-hamama fi al-ulfa wa al-ullaf. See *The Ring of the Dove*

Tawaddud, 147–148

ta`zir, 178n.82

"Terminal Essay" (Burton), 15

terminology for homosexuality, 173n.44; Arabic, 16–17, 20, 35, 39–41; in *Escoufle,* 113–117; female homosexuality, 6–7; lesbianism, 6–7, 9, 16–17, 66. See *liwat, luti*

terminology for lesbianism. See *accolle; amie; ancele; atache; baisie; çainturiere; conquiert; couche; deduit; delit; droiture;* embroidery; *estraint; feme;* fruit metaphors; hairwashing; *jesir; joie; joiaus; lis;* military metaphors; *per; plaire; pucele; sahq; soulas;* storytelling

Tertullian, 130

textiles, 94

textual fragmentation, 41, 53–54, 162–164

thigh-fencing, 46

"third term," 55, 69, 86

"third world women," 164

touching: caressing, 79, 201n.40; hugging, 67, 68, 102; monastic rules against, 96–97; rubbing, 17, 19, 36–39, 45–46; in *Story of Qamar al-Zaman*, 79; in Yde and Olive stories, 65–66. See also *accolle*; *baisie*; *couche*; *estraint*; *jesir*; *lis*
Toul, 95
Le Tournoi des dames (Hue d'Oisy), 35
Le Tournoiement as dames de Paris (Pierre Gentien), 35
trade, 12–13, 94, 126–127
transmission of stories, 53–54; controversy over, 13; fragmented, 41, 53–54, 162–164
transsexualism, 70, 72
transvestite saints, 188n.4
transvestism, 51. *See also* cross-dressing
tribades, 7, 37
Tristan de Nanteuil, 51
trutennes, 39–41, 185n.33
"Twice Marginal and Twice Invisible" (Murray), 3

ubnah, 20, 35
Umayyads, 22, 214n.97
"unfastened robe" metaphor (*hall al-izaar*), 111

van der Meer, Theo, 168n.7
vertical reading, 167n.2
vile affection, 168n.3
violence, heterosexual, 119
vocabulary: explicitness of, 44; for homosexuality (*see* terminology for homosexuality); for lesbianism (*see* terminology for lesbianism); polyglossia, 41–43. *See also* interlinguistic resonances; *and specific words or phrases*
vulva, metaphor for, 36, 37

Wallada, Princess, 22–23, 145, 179n.88, 211n.68
war metaphor, 36

wasf tradition, 24–25
Watt, Diane, 68, 71
weaving, 94
wedding night: in *Story of Qamar al-Zaman*, 78–80; in Yde and Olive stories, 64–69
Western Europe: Arab Islamicate interaction with, 11–14; Eastern commodities in, 94; transmission of stories from Orient to, 41, 53–54, 162–164
women: as accidental deviation, 2, 41; Arab and Muslim, 164–165; as body, 117, 204n.64; brothels kept by, 129; in development of *zarf*, 145–146; in Etienne de Fougères's work, 31, 47; joining hands of, 118, 204n.65; and medicine, 132; medieval system of sexual orders in, 99, 201n.31; proper social role of, 126; "sinful," 137; speeding orgasms of, 80; terms used to speak about, 207n.23; "third world," 164; typical work of, 127–129; without family/male protection, 136–137, 142–143, working, 125, 127, 128. *See also* *ancele*; *feme*; *pucele*
"Women's Tribadism Constitutes Fornication Between Them" (Makhul), 177n.67
work, achieving happiness through, 125

Yde and Olive stories: adaptation of Arab tales in, 163; Arabic intertexts of, 53, 72–86; cross-dressing in, 54–61; gender roles and sexual identities in, 55; religious sentiments in, 61–64; renditions of, 54–55; restoration of heteronormativity in, 69–72; wedding night in, 64–69
"Yde" (as name), 75

zajal, 173n.50
zarf, 23, 144–146, 150–152
zina, 21, 35, 178n.82
Ziryab, 151, 153
Zoe, Empress of Constantinople, 213n.90
zurafas, 145, 152

ACKNOWLEDGMENTS

I have benefited from the advice and support of many friends and colleagues who have shared with me over the years their knowledge, provided encouragement, read and reread drafts, invited me to speak at their universities, and inspired me in ways both large and small. I would like to acknowledge first and foremost the tremendous generosity of Everett Rowson from whom I learned a great deal about homoeroticism in the Arabic tradition. He has kindly shared with me copies of two manuscripts of the *Encyclopedia of Pleasure* and some of his own unpublished work. His example of fine scholarship, good advice, invaluable comments, and constant support accompanied this book from its inception. I also would like to thank the following colleagues for their encouragement, enthusiasm for this project, many fine suggestions, and above all their friendship: Kathryn Babayan, Judith Bennett, Howard Bloch, Matilda Bruckner, Kristen Brustad, Jane Burns, Bob Clark, Alexandra Cuffel, Carl Ernst, Adam Knobler, Norris Lacy, Kenny Levine, Michael Mc-Vaugh, Afsaneh Najmabadi, Stephen Nichols, Ruth Nisse, Lynn Ramey, Sarah Shields, Suzanne Toczyski, and Madeleine Zilfi. I am equally indebted to the librarians and archivists at the Library of Congress for their expertise locating key materials during the early stages of researching this book. I thank also the audience at the many universities where I was invited to speak in the United States and abroad for the many perceptive remarks on earlier drafts of chapters included here: Rice, Emory, University of California (Santa Cruz), Virginia Tech, Amherst, the Radcliffe Institute, Smith College, the University of Umea (Sweden), the University of Nebraska–Lincoln, Vanderbilt, Duke, and the University of North Carolina.

While working on this book, I was fortunate to receive much financial support which has afforded me release time from teaching and allowed me to devote myself to research and writing. I acknowledge with gratitude the Florence Gould Foundation for Studies of French History and Culture which has permitted me to spend one year at the National Humanities Center at Research Triangle Park (2005–6). I would like to thank the fellows at the Center for many vibrant and stimulating conversations and the staff for its cheerful assistance (Karen Carroll for copyediting my manuscript, librarians Jean Houston, Betsy Dain, and Eliza Robertson for their persistence in locating any material needed, however obscure, and Marie Brubaker for timely photo copying). I am also indebted to the Center for Arts and Humanities at UNC, to the College of Arts and Sciences, and the Spray-Randleigh Fellowship at UNC for release time from teaching, research leaves, and travel grants. I owe a great debt to the Fulbright commission for supporting two months of research in Cairo, at the Center for Arabic Study Abroad; I would like to thank especially Dr. Ahmed Kishk, Dean of Dar al-Ulum at Cairo University, for his erudition, his helpful advice, and his generosity in sharing with me some important library holdings.

I am indebted to the three anonymous reviewers of the University of Pennsylvania Press for their careful reading and their perceptive suggestions which have helped me articulate many fine points. I also thank Jerome E. Singerman, Humanities Editor at the University of Pennsylvania Press, and Noreen O'Connor-Abel, my project editor, whose support and encouragement were appreciated at every stage of the publication of this book.

Last, but certainly not least, I would like to thank my parents (Mohamed and Hoda) and my sisters (Noha, Ghada, and Nadia) for their unconditional love, encouragement, and belief in me. To Martine, who patiently read and reread the entire manuscript in its numerous and multiple incarnations, who nourished me both literally and metaphorically throughout the entire process, and who provided a constant source of cheerful support, I dedicate this book.

Parts of Chapter 2 appeared in *Same Sex Love and Desire Among Women in the Middle Ages*, edited by Francesca Sautman and Pamela Sheingorn (New York: Palgrave, 2001), and an earlier version of Chapter 3 appeared in *Religion, Gender, and Culture in the Pre-Modern World*, edited by Alexandra Cuffel and Brian Britt (New York: Palgrave Macmillan, 2007). Reproduced with permission of Palgrave Macmillan.